Representing the Rainbow in Young Adult Literature

Representing the Rainbow in Young Adult Literature

LGBTQ+ Content since 1969

Christine A. Jenkins and Michael Cart

ROWMAN & LITTLEFIELD
Lanham • Boulder • New York • London

Published by Rowman & Littlefield
An imprint of The Rowman & Littlefield Publishing Group, Inc.
4501 Forbes Boulevard, Suite 200, Lanham, Maryland 20706
www.rowman.com

Unit A, Whitacre Mews, 26-34 Stannary Street, London SE11 4AB

British Library Cataloguing in Publication Information Available

Library of Congress Cataloging-in-Publication Data

Names: Jenkins, Christine, 1949– author. | Cart, Michael author.
Title: Representing the rainbow in young adult literature : LGBTQ+ content since 1969 / Christine A.
    Jenkins and Michael Cart.
Description: Lanham : Rowman & Littlefield, 2018. | Includes bibliographical references and index.
Identifiers: LCCN 2017055185 (print) | LCCN 2017060085 (ebook) | ISBN 9781442278073 (elec-
    tronic) | ISBN 9781442278066 (pbk. : alk. paper)
Subjects: LCSH: Young adult literature, American—History and criticism. | Homosexuality in litera-
    ture. | Sexual minorities in literature.
Classification: LCC PS374.H63 (ebook) | LCC PS374.H63 J48 2018 (print) | DDC 810.9/353—dc23
LC record available at https://lccn.loc.gov/2017055185

∞ ™ The paper used in this publication meets the minimum requirements of American
National Standard for Information Sciences Permanence of Paper for Printed Library
Materials, ANSI/NISO Z39.48-1992.

Printed in the United States of America

To the courageous authors whose early contributions to young adult literature created and sustained the literature that provided (and continues to provide) invaluable support to LGBTQ+ teens and their allies:

John Donovan for starting the whole thing in 1969; and pioneering novelists Francesca Lia Block, Aidan Chambers, Nancy Garden, M. E. Kerr, David Levithan, and Jacqueline Woodson.

And to the creators of groundbreaking young adult books in other genres:

Frances Hanckel and John Cunningham for their nonfiction milestone *A Way of Love, A Way of Life: A Young Person's Introduction to What It Means to Be Gay* (1979); Marion Dane Bauer, for her trailblazing short story collection *Am I Blue? Coming Out from the Silence* (1994); Judd Winick, for his transformative graphic novel *Pedro and Me: Friendship, Loss and What I Learned* (2000).

All of you made the way easier for others. Thank you!

Contents

Contents

Acknowledgments

When we (Christine and Michael) first met in person at an American Library Association Annual Conference in the mid-1990s, we were already familiar with each other's work, and thus aware of our common interest in young adult literature with queer (aka LGBTQ+) content, and our common belief was that this literature *mattered* in the lives of LGBTQ+ teens and their allies.

After the conference, we returned to our homes in California (MC) and Illinois (CJ), but kept in touch via e-mail, noting, sharing, and critiquing new titles as they appeared. This body of literature continued to grow, but still the books themselves were often dismissively described as "problem novels." Undaunted, we forged ahead in seeking new YA titles with LGBTQ+ content: identifying, acquiring, and reading them, and alerting each other to our finds. The number of books—still confined to the category of "contemporary realism"—continued to expand, and our sustained mutual interest and conversations turned into a series of collaborations, conference presentations, and, finally, books.

So here we are, decades later, having gathered, examined, and analyzed hundreds of young adult titles with LGBTQ+ content in an increasingly broad range of fiction and nonfiction genres and formats. That said, we are well aware that our collection and analysis of young adult books with LGBTQ+ content can never be absolutely comprehensive; with so many titles now appearing, we are bound to miss a few, and our collection and analysis of young adult books with LGBTQ+ content will always lag behind the actual trajectory of the ever-expanding world of YA literature.

Looking over the past decades, so many people, institutions, and publications have contributed to our work on this book. First, we want to recognize the scholars who provided encouragement and a scholarly perspective in the earliest years of this project: Patty Campbell, Eliza Dresang, Patricia Enciso, Lenore Gordon, K. T. Horning, Phyllis Marquart, and Roger Sutton.

We'd like to acknowledge the help and support we've received from the students, staff, and faculty of the School of Information Sciences at the University of Illinois at Urbana-Champaign.

Thank you to Jeanie Austin, Claire Gross, Melissa Hayes Hahn, Cass Mabbott, Alaine Martaus, Micki Smith, April Spisak, and other current and former doctoral students who identified, located, and helped us evaluate books from throughout the prodigious library collections at the University of Illinois at Urbana-Champaign. We couldn't have done this without you!

Thank you to the many scholars, reviewers, and librarians who were so willing to engage with and discuss the many questions that arose from our research. They include (but are not limited to) Robin Brenner, Betty Bush, Chris D'Arpa, Loretta Gaffney, Betsy Hearne, Karla Moller, Nancy O'Brien, Deborah Stevenson, and others who have helped facilitate this work.

At the University of Illinois, we used the resources of the Center for Children's Books; the Social Sciences, Health, and Education Library; and the Main Library. At the University of Wisconsin, Madison, we used the resources of the Cooperative Children's Book Center, the iSchool Library, and the Graduate Library. Two very different special libraries in Minneapolis were also extremely helpful: the Kerlan Collection in the Children's Literature Research Collections at the University of Minnesota's Anderson Library, and the Quatrefoil Library, a member-supported lending library and community center for the Twin Cities LGBTQ+ communities.

Public libraries' services to young adults also help the scholars who study young adult books. For us this has been the Champaign Public Library, the Urbana Free Library, and the Hennepin County Library.

Thank you to Sarah Park Dahlen, scholar and energetic Sacred Writing Time organizer. And, finally, our enduring thanks to Sue Searing, dear friend and wise reader, our editor with a pen of gold.

Introduction

The first young adult novel with LGBTQ+ content, John Donovan's *I'll Get There. It Better Be Worth the Trip*, appeared in 1969,[1] which was also, coincidentally, the year that the Stonewall riots launched the gay rights movement.[2] Some reviewers welcomed the book's publication, while others were skeptical that such a book could ever be appropriate for teen readers. Nevertheless, it inspired the first stirrings of LGBTQ+ literature for young adults. In the ensuing decades the number of fiction titles rose steadily. Ten young adult titles with LGBTQ+ content were published in the 1970s, forty in the 1980s, eighty-two in the 1990s, 292 in 2000–2009, and 513 titles in 2010–2016. On the one hand, the resulting sum of 937 fiction titles is impressive. One the other hand, during that same time period tens of thousands of YA fiction titles were published in which every character was/is presumed to be heterosexual. Although statistics measuring the number of YA titles published each year are fugitive, we estimate the *average* number to be roughly two thousand per year, a number significantly larger than the yearly average of twenty titles with LGBTQ+ content.

In the early years of this literature YA books with LGBTQ+ content were largely novels and short-story collections, so our earlier research on LGBTQ+ content published from 1969 to 2004 focused almost exclusively on YA fiction.[3] However, a great deal has happened in the world of young adult literature with LGBTQ+ content since our earlier investigation.

One change may be seen in the gradual evolution of the term "gay" to "gay/lesbian" to "gay/lesbian/bisexual" to "GLBTQ" to "LGBTQ+", the last being an acronym in common use now to describe the broad and varied ways in which people experience their sexuality and gender identity. L(lesbian), G (gay), B (bisexual), T (transgender/transsexual), and Q (queer/questioning) appear most frequently in the literature, to which we, like others, add a "+" to

include the far broader spectrum of nonbinary sexual and/or gender identities.[4]

That our focus is primarily on fiction does not discount the importance of
nonfiction titles to readers in pursuit of information, affirmation, and community. Biographies, self-help, and advice books; informational texts about
the social and political history of homosexuality; and first-person accounts of
the lives of LGBTQ+ teens and adults are all useful to inquiring teen readers.
As a result, this book includes chapters on nonfiction and on comics/graphic
novels (which may be fiction or nonfiction), plus chapters on young adult
fiction featuring bisexual and transgender/intersex characters.

A number of the early titles—and even some of the more recent ones—
perpetuate stereotypes by characterizing homosexuals as lost souls doomed
to either premature death or the solitary life of exile at the margins of society.
Others—most, though not all, of a more recent vintage—present gay and
lesbian characters in a more realistic light. YA literature, like other media for
teens, still does not represent the full range and diversity of the lived experiences of young adults in the twenty-first century. At the same time, there are
increasing numbers of young adult books that *do* portray LGBTQ+ people of
various ages, cultures, incomes, and perspectives who are present (as friends,
teammates, family members, neighbors, and mentors) in the lives of teens
and are part of the social web of connectedness that teens of all sexual
orientations navigate on a daily basis.

In addition to the growth in the number of titles, we have noted a trend
toward more character-driven, literary fiction and a concurrent decline in the
stereotypical portrayals of LGBTQ+ people once common in young adult
fiction. Happily, there are also more books in which characters just happen to
be gay and do not experience the Sturm und Drang that beset LGBTQ+ teens
in the fiction of earlier decades. There is also a welcome infusion of humor
into what has admittedly been a darkly serious literature.

Many recent books with LGBTQ+ content are well written, well reviewed, and popular with teen readers of all sexual orientations—these are
books that teens *want* to read. In certain quarters, however, their very existence remains controversial. Books for young readers with LGBTQ+ content
remain among the most challenged titles in America's public and school
libraries, and it appears that the pressure will not be abating anytime soon.
Indeed, from one to five books with LGBTQ+ content have appeared on each
year's Top Ten Most Challenged Books, a list that the American Library
Association's Office for Intellectual Freedom has compiled since 2000.[5] In
1994 novelist and essayist Michael Thomas Ford stated that fear of controversy has often discouraged publishers from issuing gay or lesbian titles.[6]
Two decades later we continue to be aware that while controversy can build a
market for a title, it can also open publishers to criticism, boycotts, and
public censure—particularly when a book is aimed at a young audience.

Clearly, teens who identify as LGBTQ+ must negotiate a complicated social and political environment that is mirrored (and sometimes distorted) in YA literature. While teens may find support they need in books, they are increasingly likely to receive support from their peers. Over the past several decades, hundreds of Gay-Straight Alliances (GSAs) have been organized by students in schools across this country and in other countries as well.[7] Nevertheless, not all teens are comfortable exploring this aspect of their lives in a social setting. These teens may prefer the privacy that reading offers and turn instead to the "community on the page" found in books.

And speaking of books, library and information science research on young adult literature with LGBTQ+ content has examined individual books, authors, series, and/or narrative elements within the context of the larger body of this literature. Though too few in number, there are now a handful of book-length analytical studies that look at the range and depth of the genre.[8]

Though the struggle for gay rights was symbolically initiated nearly five decades ago, the fight for the human rights of LGBTQ+ teens is ongoing. Joyce Hunter, a researcher at Columbia University, sums up the plight of too many LGBTQ+ teens: "These are kids who are lonely, who haven't got their coping skills developed. And they need support. They need to know that they are not alone."[9] What better way to give that assurance than to share good books that offer positive portrayals of homosexual characters and deal compassionately and honestly with homosexual themes and issues? As communications scholar Lynn Cockett has eloquently written, "A balanced [library] fiction collection should assuage the fears of gay and lesbian YAs, assuring them that they are not alone."[10] It is with that belief that we have undertaken the collaborative work of writing this book.

Our goal is both to chart the evolution of the field and to identify titles that are remarkable either for their excellence or for their failures. In the process we aim to establish some useful criteria for evaluating books with LGBTQ+ content. Our judgments of the accuracy of character portrayal and the validity of thematic treatment are, inevitably, based on our own life experiences and our understanding of and familiarity with the historical context(s) in which these books have been published and read. They are also based on a broad reading of young adult literature and some forty years' experience in writing about it. If some of our judgments seem harsh or some of our praise lavish, it is due to our continued belief in the imperative importance of good books, in their capacity to save lives and to change the world by informing minds and nourishing spirits. To provide readers—and authors—a critical context in which to evaluate LGBTQ+ literature, we believe that what is stereotypic, wrongheaded, and outdated needs to be exposed and what is accurate, thoughtful, and artful needs to be applauded.

* * *

We chose to collaborate, instead of writing independent works, for two reasons: (1) We felt it was important to bring both a male and female perspective to the work, and (2) we wanted to present different professional perspectives. Because we are, respectively, a university professor emerita (Christine) and a literary journalist and editor (Michael), this volume addresses different—though often overlapping—audiences. By collaborating we hope to expand the readership for this work, the subject of which is so powerfully important. Though often of one mind, we do not always agree on issues, interpretation, or the evaluation of individual titles. Just as individual young readers respond in their own ways to the stories we examine here, so we, too, each view the landscape of YA literature on LGBTQ+ themes somewhat differently.

While striving for a readable style and accessible content, we nevertheless recognize the importance to the credibility of our work of critical apparatus, of framework and structure. The model created by Christine Jenkins for these twin purposes (described in full in appendix D) is built upon Rudine Sims Bishop's foundational study *Shadow & Substance: Afro-American Experience in Contemporary Children's Fiction.*[11] Sims Bishop proposed a three-part model to describe representations of African American characters in children's books published in the years immediately following the American civil rights movement of the 1960s. First to appear, she stated, were "social conscience" books, books in which race was the problem and desegregation the solution. Next came "melting pot" books, in which racial diversity was present but unacknowledged, and integration was a given. Finally, "culturally conscious" books began to be published, books in which African Americans were portrayed in a culturally accurate manner.

We propose a model using category descriptors that reflect the three general types of stories with gay/lesbian characters published for a young adult audience from 1969 through 2016. They are:

1. Homosexual visibility
2. Gay assimilation
3. Queer consciousness/community

Most of the young adult novels with LGBTQ+ content published in the 1970s and 1980s are stories of *homosexual visibility* in which a character who has not previously been considered gay/lesbian comes out either voluntarily or involuntarily. This revelation may occur at any point in the story, with dramatic tension arising from what *might* happen when the invisible is made visible. Consequently, as with *social conscience* stories of racial integration, a previously homogeneous society is interrupted by the appearance of a character who is clearly *not* "one of us." The response to this interruption is the dramatic substance of the story. *Gay assimilation* assumes the existence—at least in the world of the story—of a *melting pot* of sexual and gender identity. These stories include people who "just happen to be gay" in the same way that someone "just happens" to be left-handed or blond. Stories described as possessing *queer consciousness* show LGBTQ+ characters in the context of a community. As with *culturally conscious* stories told from an African American perspective, the audience for these books is not limited to readers from within the culture; rather, these titles are, at least potentially, for readers at all points on the sexual orientation continuum.

Surveys of attitudes toward homosexuals indicate that people who state they know a gay/lesbian person express more tolerant attitudes than those who say they do not. Could these books perhaps play a positive didactic role in acquainting young readers with realistically portrayed gay/lesbian characters? And could those readers' imaginations be pushed a bit further to see such characters from an empathic rather than simply a sympathetic perspective? Could a young reader not simply feel *for* LGBTQ+ people but also *with* them?

Sims Bishop's *Shadow & Substance* opens with a quote from the African American writer James Baldwin: "Literature is indispensable to the world. The world changes according to the way people see it, and if you alter, even by a millimeter, the way a person looks at reality, then you can change it."[12] Here it must be noted that Baldwin was a *gay* African American author and that his words apply, with equal force, to literature with gay/lesbian content. Baldwin's belief in the indispensability of literature and its power to change the world is foundational to our own analysis.

NOTES

1. John Donovan, *I'll Get There. It Better Be Worth the Trip* (New York: Harper & Row, 1969).

2. Lillian Faderman, *The Gay Revolution: The Story of a Struggle* (New York: Simon & Schuster, 2015), 116–22. The 1969 Stonewall riots are commonly viewed as the symbolic beginning of the gay rights movement, but there were, in fact, various acts of resistance to police harassment by gays and lesbians in various cities in the years before 1969. Drag queens and others who were seen as "flaunting" their difference from mainstream society were routinely harassed, but dressing and behaving "appropriately" was no guarantee against the arrest of individuals who happened to be in the wrong place at the wrong time when police conducted their routine raids of gay bars. Such a raid sparked the Stonewall riots in New York City; the several nights' duration of the disturbance and its close proximity to media outlets (and millions of people) made the Stonewall riots significant and newsworthy, but, as noted, the spirit of resistance was already emerging in the years prior to 1969.

3. Michael Cart and Christine A. Jenkins, *The Heart Has Its Reasons: Young Adult Literature with Gay/Lesbian/Queer Content, 1969–2004* (Lanham, MD: Scarecrow, 2006).

4. For details and further information, see Ashley Mardell, *The ABC's of LGBT+* (Coral Gables, FL: Mango Media, 2016).

5. ALA's Office for Intellectual Freedom (OIF) systematically tracks challenged and banned books and other materials in library and classroom settings. The OIF began publishing

an annual list of the Top Ten Most Challenged Books in 2000, and each year from one to five of the top ten titles have been books with LGBTQ+ content. Since 2005, an average of three of the top ten most challenged books have been for reasons of LGBTQ+ content. Four of the ten books listed for 2015 and five for 2016 were challenged for that reason; nearly half of these (two in 2015, two in 2016) were challenged specifically for their transgender content. See http://www.ala.org/bbooks/frequentlychallengedbooks/top10#2016.

6. Michael Thomas Ford, "Gay Books for Young Readers: When Caution Calls the Shots," *Publishers Weekly* 241, no. 24 (February 21, 1994).

7. Online resources include current information on Gay-Straight Alliances, as well as other useful information for LGBTQ+ teens and their allies: http://gsanetwork.org/, https://www.glsen.org/, and https://en.wikipedia.org/wiki/Gay%E2%80%93straight_alliance.

8. Published book-length works on young adult literature with LGBTQ+ content, 1992–2016:

> Michelle Anne Abate and Kenneth B. Kidd, eds., *Over the Rainbow: Queer Children's and Young Adult Literature* (Ann Arbor: University of Michigan Press, 2011).
> Michael Cart and Christine A. Jenkins, *The Heart Has Its Reasons: Young Adult Literature with Gay/Lesbian/Queer Content, 1969–2004* (Lanham, MD: Scarecrow, 2006).
> Michael Cart and Christine A. Jenkins, *Top 250 LGBTQ Books for Teens* (Chicago: Huron Street Press/ALA Publishing, 2011).
> Alan Cuseo, *Homosexual Characters in YA Novels: A Literary Analysis, 1969–1982* (Metuchen, NJ: Scarecrow, 1992).
> Frances Ann Day, *Lesbian and Gay Voices: An Annotated Bibliography and Guide to Literature for Children and Young Adults* (Westport, CT: Greenwood, 2000).
> B. J. Epstein, *Are the Kids All Right? The Representation of LGBTQ Characters in Children's and Young Adult Literature* (Bristol, UK: HammerOn, 2013).
> Darla Linville and David Lee Carlson, eds., *Beyond Borders: Queer Eros and Ethos (Ethics) in LGBTQ Young Adult Literature* (New York: Peter Lang, 2016).
> Marjorie Lobban and Laurel A. Clyde, *Out of the Closet and into the Classroom: Homosexuality in Books for Young People* (Melbourne, Victoria, Australia: Thorpe/ALIA, 1996).
> Carlisle K. Webber, *Gay, Lesbian, Bisexual, Transgender and Questioning Teen Literature: A Guide to Reading Interests* (Santa Barbara, CA: Libraries Unlimited, 2010).

9. Joyce Hunter, quoted in "Gay Teens' Lives Called More Risky" by Martha Irvine, *Sacramento Bee*, May 5, 1998, A10.

10. Lynn Cockett, "Entering the Mainstream: Fiction about Gay and Lesbian Teens," *School Library Journal* 41, no. 2 (February 1995): 32.

11. Rudine Sims [Bishop], *Shadow & Substance: Afro-American Experience in Contemporary Children's Fiction* (Urbana, IL: NCTE, 1982).

12. M. Watkins, "James Baldwin Writing and Talking," *New York Times Book Review* 23, no. 3 (September 1979): 36–37.

Part I

A Survey of LGBTQ+ Literature

Chapter One

Young Adult Literature in the Pre-Stonewall Era

In his *Notes towards the Definition of Culture*, the poet and critic T. S. Eliot offered three "permanent" reasons for reading: (1) the acquisition of wisdom, (2) the enjoyment of art, and (3) the pleasure of entertainment.[1] In the case of young adult (YA) literature (which we define as books that are published for readers age twelve to eighteen, have a young adult protagonist, are told from a young adult perspective, and feature coming-of-age or other issues and concerns of interest to YAs), we would add a fourth reason to Eliot's list. The stories told in young adult literature feature protagonists, voices, and issues too often rendered invisible by society. As a result, young people have a particularly urgent need to see their own faces reflected in the pages of a book and find the corollary comfort that derives from the knowledge that one is not alone in a vast universe, that there are others "like me."

Novelist and essayist James Baldwin made this point more eloquently when he wrote, "You think your pains and heartbreaks are unprecedented in the history of the world, but then you read. It was books that taught me that the things that tormented me were the very things that connected me with all the people who were alive or who have ever been alive."[2]

In the decades since 1967, the year that S. E. Hinton's *The Outsiders*[3] and Robert Lipsyte's *The Contender*[4]—widely regarded as the first modern young adult novels—appeared, young adult literature has expanded enormously in size, numbers, and readership. At the same time, some aspects have changed very little. Fifty years ago Nancy Larrick challenged the "all-white world of children's books" in her influential 1965 article in *Saturday Review*,[5] prompting the children's publishing world to self-examination and the consequent admission that Larrick's conclusions were accurate: the world of books for young readers was—and remains—overwhelmingly white. At

3

the same time, the actual world in which U.S. teens live has changed far more in that half century than has the worlds portrayed in realistic literature for young readers.

Recent campaigns such as #WeNeedDiverseBooks[6] and ongoing research by the University of Wisconsin's Children's Cooperative Book Center on the presence (or absence) of diverse books in the yearly publishing output of books for youth[7] have raised overall awareness of this lack of diversity. Rudine Sims Bishop notes that multicultural books have several roles, serving the reader as both windows and mirrors. "Books are sometimes windows, offering views of worlds that may be real or imagined, familiar or strange. When lighting conditions are just right, however, a window can also be a mirror. Literature transforms human experience and reflects it back to us, and in that reflection we can see our own lives and experiences as part of the larger human experience. Reading then becomes a means of self-affirmation and readers often seek their mirrors in books."[8]

There is indisputably more diversity portrayed in literature for young audiences now than in earlier decades, and the literature has developed in ways that has given faces to teens of all races, ethnicities, cultures, classes, national origins, abilities/disabilities, and religious beliefs. Members of another group of teen outsiders—LGBTQ+ youth—are in fact members of all the groups listed above, but have been nearly invisible in YA fiction. As we will see, the world represented in young adult literature has gradually begun to grow more diverse, but in the context of the full body of twentieth- and twenty-first-century literature, depictions of LGBTQ+ characters (for both young adults *and* adults) have been largely absent.

Why? Perhaps in part because homosexuality has been regarded, in Lord Alfred Douglas's words, as "the Love that dare not speak its name."[9] Despite the fact that historians of LGBTQ+ American history have pointed out that a gay, largely urban culture existed in the United States as early as the 1890s, homosexuality as a public aspect of mainstream American life was largely invisible.[10] This changed in the 1940s. First, the massive enlistments and wartime draft that accompanied America's entrance into World War II brought together in the U.S. Armed Forces "the largest concentration of gay men ever found inside a single American institution. Volunteer women who joined the WAC and the WAVES experienced an even more prevalent lesbian culture."[11] Three years after the war's end, the publication of *Sexual Behavior in the Human Male* by Alfred Kinsey et al.[12] revealed the startling fact that the sexual histories of one-tenth of American males included sexual experience with men. The book quickly became a best seller, and historian Charles Kaiser has argued that this event marked the point in time at which the existence of homosexuality was publicly acknowledged in the United States. The facts reported by what came to be known as "the Kinsey Report" contributed to what Martin Duberman calls a "critical mass of conscious-ness" that slowly began to be reflected in the literature of the time.[13]

EARLY HOMOSEXUAL FICTION FOR ADULTS

The late 1940s also saw the publication of two important adult novels with gay male characters and themes: *Other Voices, Other Rooms* by Truman Capote[14] and *The City and the Pillar* by Gore Vidal.[15] They are significant for two reasons: First, they were serious works of fiction by writers who would become vital forces in American literature. Second, they were issued by mainstream publishers Random House and E. P. Dutton, respectively. Previously, as Joseph Cady notes, "While there was frank and affirmative gay male American writing from the century's start" (most of it now forgotten except by literary historians), "it was either published abroad or issued in this country by marginal publishers."[16] During the 1950s and early 1960s, other noted works of fiction with gay male characters appeared: *Giovanni's Room* by James Baldwin,[17] *City of Night* by John Rechy,[18] and *A Single Man* by Christopher Isherwood.[19]

Literature with lesbian content followed a somewhat different path. Rad-clyffe Hall's *The Well of Loneliness*,[20] one of the first—and certainly the best-known—novel from a mainstream commercial publisher to include spe-cific lesbian content, was published in England in 1928. It is the story of Stephen Gordon, a young woman of the English landed gentry who is a lesbian or, in the words of English psychologist Havelock Ellis, who wrote the book's preface, "a congenital invert."[21] As she matures, her difference is noted by her mother with disgust, by her father with love and pity, and by her governess with maternal warmth. As an adult, she is an intelligent and aloof outsider. When World War I breaks out, Stephen joins a battalion of female ambulance drivers and meets her soul mate, Mary. They live together for a time, but the story ends tragically when Stephen sends Mary away (and into the arms of a man) so that Mary can escape the stigma of lesbianism, while Stephen nobly resigns herself to a life of permanent loneliness. The book was declared obscene in England because of its subject matter. Indeed, newspaper editor/reviewer James Douglas famously declared that he "would [rather] give a healthy boy or a healthy girl a phial of prussic acid than this book. Poison kills the body, but moral poison kills the soul."[22] *The Well of Loneli-ness* was published in the United States in late 1928. In the early months of 1929 it was challenged by the Society for the Suppression of Vice, brought to trial, and judged obscene. By the end of April, however, the ruling had been successfully appealed, after which the book became a best seller. Other titles of that time with lesbian content, such as *Orlando* by Virginia Woolf,[23] *Extraordinary Women* by Compton MacKenzie,[24] *Nightwood* by Djuna

Barnes,[25] and the avant-garde poetry of Gertrude Stein, were considerably more artful and discreet, making them less accessible and interesting to many teen readers.

In the 1950s, however, the appearance and subsequent popularity of adult lesbian pulp paperbacks were a boon to YAs. Beginning in 1952 with the best-selling *Spring Fire* by Vin Packer (a pseudonym for Marijane Meeker, better known to teens as M. E. Kerr),[26] there came a flood of romance novels that featured naïve young women who were seduced by lesbians but were finally won back to heterosexuality by men who could offer them marriage, a home, and children. If the lesbian was actually a good person, she died. If she was evil, she might also die or she might head off to further conquests. There were, however, some books with happy endings—most notably Ann Bannon's five-book series (1957–1962) that begins with *Odd Girl Out*,[27] a sorority house romance, and ends with *Journey to a Woman*,[28] in which two women, Beth and Beebo, find their soul mates in each other, plus *Beebo Brinker*,[29] a prequel about the early life of the eponymous heroine.

Regardless of their often tragic endings, these books—widely available on paperback racks in drugstores and newsstands across the country—are often cited as having introduced isolated young lesbians to a world of possibilities in the lesbian communities that were slowly becoming visible in urban spaces across the country. And in the 1970s with the rise of the second wave of feminism, small and alternative women's presses began publishing fiction with lesbian protagonists. One of the best-known products of the women-in-print movement was Rita Mae Brown's *Rubyfruit Jungle*,[30] a lesbian coming-of-age novel published by alternative press Daughters Inc. in 1973. Although the book was originally published as an adult title, it was taken up by teen readers and has been a staple in the coming-out narratives of adult lesbians ever since. And to bring the story full circle, Naiad Press, one of the most prolific women's publishers, reissued all of Ann Bannon's novels in 1983. This history of fiction with lesbian content as popular mass-market paperbacks in the 1950s is a unique feature in the specific history of lesbian fiction, viewed separately from gay male fiction.

YOUNG ADULT FICTION—FIRST STIRRINGS

The new homosexual consciousness that appeared during and after World War II coincided with the first stirrings of what has come to be called "young adult literature." Two of the literature's best-known early practitioners, Maureen Daly and Madeleine L'Engle, published their first novels in the 1940s. Daly's *Seventeenth Summer* appeared in 1942,[31] while L'Engle's *The Small Rain* was published in 1945.[32] Though both titles were published as adult novels, they were widely and enthusiastically read by YAs and, interestingly, both also included incidental treatments of homosexuality.

In *Seventeenth Summer*, the protagonist, Angie, and her boyfriend, Jack, go to a club in their town of Fond du Lac, Wisconsin, to hear a musician from Chicago who is portrayed as stereotypically gay: "With his eyes still closed, the colored man leaned back on the bench, way back, one hand limp at his side. . . . 'Look, Jack,' I remember saying, 'He has red nail polish on! Isn't that funny—for a man?'" (14). This brief incident underlines Angie's unworldly innocence as a girl from a small town unversed in the big-city sophistication of this talented, but clearly alien, entertainer.

In *The Small Rain*, the teen protagonist, Katherine, is taken to a squalid gay bar where she encounters "a woman, or what perhaps had once been a woman. Now it wore a man's suit, shirt, and tie; its hair was cut short, out of a dead-white face glared a pair of despairing eyes" (13). The horrified pity of Katherine's response marks her as a naïf among her more worldly friends and points up the finer nature of her character in contrast to the callous voyeurism of her companions.

In J. D. Salinger's 1951 novel *Catcher in the Rye*,[33] another brief homosexual encounter is reported. Like Daly's and L'Engle's books, this novel was also published for adults but was claimed by succeeding generations of young adults as their own. Indeed, many would argue that if these books were first being published today, it would be as young adult titles. Salinger's protagonist, Holden Caulfield, has a—to him—disturbing encounter with his favorite teacher, Mr. Antolini, when he stays overnight at Mr. and Mrs. Antolini's New York apartment:

> What he [Mr. Antolini] was doing was, he was sitting on the floor right next to the couch, in the dark and all, and he was sort of petting me or patting me on the goddam head. Boy, I'll bet I jumped about a thousand feet.
> "What the hell ya *do*ing?" I said.
> "Nothing! I'm simply sitting here admiring—"
> "What're ya *do*ing, anyway?" I said over again. I didn't know *what* the hell to say—I mean I was embarrassed as hell.
> "How 'bout keeping your voice down? I'm simply sitting here—"
> "I have to go anyway," I said—boy, was I nervous! I know more damn perverts at schools and all, than anybody you ever met, and they're always being perverty when *I'm* around. (151)

These are small moments that had little direct impact on the evolution of gay and lesbian literature published specifically for young adults. Nevertheless, for some of their many teen readers, the incidents/settings of these three novels may well have been their first exposure to homosexuality in literature.

A more important treatment of this theme, in the context of a coming-of-age novel, was James Baldwin's *Go Tell It on the Mountain*.[34] Published in

1953, it dealt authentically with its fourteen-year-old protagonist's attraction to a seventeen-year-old boy. Then, in 1959, John Knowles's *A Separate Peace*[35] was published. Like the Daly, L'Engle, Salinger, and Baldwin titles, this novel was aimed at an adult readership but quickly became a YA classic. Though Knowles's book did not deal overtly with homosexuality, to some readers it clearly had a gay—though coded—subtext. And in a 1972 interview, Knowles acknowledged that his main characters, the two boys Finny and Gene, "were in love."[36] Whether teens, then or now, perceive this is moot.

I'LL GET THERE. IT BETTER BE WORTH THE TRIP

However, within ten years the subject would be treated more explicitly when, in 1969, the first young adult novel to deal with homosexuality was published: *I'll Get There. It Better Be Worth the Trip* by John Donovan.[37] There is no simple cause-and-effect relationship between the fact that the publication of this book and the Stonewall riots—a landmark in the gay civil rights movement—happened in the same watershed year, 1969, but it is possible that both were products of the same social/cultural climate. The 1960s were years of turbulent social change, of political unrest, and of sexual revolution. The media—often the first to observe changes in popular culture—took note and, according to Martin Duberman, "the years 1962 to 1965 saw a sharp increase in the amount of public discussion and representation of homosexuality" (97). He cites, in particular, the proliferation of lesbian pulp novels and of motion pictures with homosexual content (*The L-Shaped Room*, *Lilith*, *Darling*, etc.). There was a similar increase in the publication, for adult readers, of serious literary novels with gay/lesbian content, including James Baldwin's *Another Country*,[38] Mary McCarthy's *The Group*,[39] John Rechy's *City of Night*[40] and *Numbers*,[41] Christopher Isherwood's *A Single Man*,[42] Sanford Friedman's *Totempole*[43] and Gore Vidal's *Myra Breckinridge*.[44]

Meanwhile, in the field of books for young readers, the 1960s were seeing the emergence of the first modern young adult fiction; that is, novels of social realism with contemporary settings like *The Outsiders*, *The Contender*, and Paul Zindel's *The Pigman*. This decade also saw the first emergence of heterosexual sex as a theme with the anomalous early exception of Henry Gregor Felsen's *Two and the Town*, published in 1952, which dealt with an unmarried teen's pregnancy. In 1966, for example, in Jeanette Eyerly's *A Girl Like Me*, the unwed teenage friend of the protagonist becomes pregnant; in 1967 it's the protagonist herself, the eponymous heroine of Zoa Sherburne's *Too Bad about the Haines Girl*. The same year saw the publication of Ann Head's adult novel *Mr. and Mrs. Bo Jo Jones* (1967), in which two teenagers, July and Bo Jo, are swept away by passion; she becomes pregnant and they elope. This novel appeared in paperback the following year and became a best seller with young adults through teenage book clubs.[45]

Despite the increasing treatment of teenage heterosexuality in fiction and the increasing awareness of homosexuality in American culture, Harper & Row viewed the publication of Donovan's *I'll Get There* with considerable trepidation. William C. Morris, a vice president of Harper, recalled, "Everyone was very frightened. In fact we went to such great lengths to make it 'acceptable' to the general public that the book got more attention for the fuss we made than for anything that was in it."[46]

One of the "lengths" was the solicitation of a statement for the dust jacket from the acclaimed Dr. Frances Ilg, director of the Gesell Institute of Child Development. In a letter to Ilg dated August 8, 1968, Ursula Nordstrom, director of Harper's Department of Books for Boys and Girls, wrote, "I do not need to tell you that the book will meet with considerable resistance with certain influential persons in the children's book field. Yet surely this is an experience many boys have and one that worries and frightens them badly. It seems strange that a curtain has been drawn over this entire subject in fiction for young readers. Our book will be the first."[47] According to the critic Leonard S. Marcus, "FI [Frances Ilg] responded enthusiastically, providing a comment for publication."[48]

Here it is, as it appeared on the book's rear dust jacket flap: "A moment of sex discovery is told simply but poignantly in the life of a thirteen-year-old boy, through his relationship with a friend of his own sex and age. It is how he absorbs this experience that becomes the key to what will happen next. Davy is able to face the experience and to make his choice."

I'll Get There was Donovan's first novel, but he was no stranger either to writing or to books for young readers. A former attorney, Donovan was the executive director of the Children's Book Council, a position he held until his death in 1992. He was also the author of a picture book, *The Little Orange Book*, and an adult play, *Riverside Drive.* In a query letter to Nordstrom, Donovan described his novel as being "about a kid with love problems."[49] In her cordial reply, Nordstrom said she'd be "delighted" to read the manuscript, adding that she had been waiting "a long time" for a novel that included "buddy love problems."[50]

Davy Ross, the thirteen-year-old protagonist of Donovan's novel, has more problems than buddy love, as it turns out. The son of divorced parents, he has been living near Boston for eight years with his beloved grandmother who, as the novel begins, has just died. Davy is devastated and dubious about being sent to live with his mother in New York City. He has good reason.

Their relationship is strained, to say the least. The mother has a problem with alcohol that causes erratic behavior and unpredictable mood swings. "She's either slobbering all over me or ready to boot me out of the house," Davy tells the reader (189). To make matters worse, she is less than overjoyed by the presence of Davy's pet dachshund, Fred ("Can't you keep the little bastard quiet?" [45]). Her animosity is exacerbated, the reader infers, by her jealousy of Davy's almost obsessive love for Fred who, following the grandmother's death, has become the emotional center of the boy's life.

Davy is also reunited with his remarried father on occasional weekend visits. Their relationship, though not without its awkward moments, is far less strained than that of mother and son. Nevertheless, Davy often feels more tolerated than loved and, in this regard, clearly identifies with Fred when he says, "When you make a dog like Fred part of your family, he is a full-time member, not just someone who will be around when you want him to" (47).

Soon enough, however, someone other than his dog will begin to matter to Davy: his new friend, Douglas Altschuler. Davy's mother has enrolled him in an Episcopal boys' school, and Douglas occupies the seat in front of him in geography class. As we will see, private schools provide the setting for many of the homosexual novels in the early years of the genre—perhaps because, like English boarding schools, they offer a ready-made, same-sex atmosphere for boys or girls away from home for the first time. At any rate, it turns out that the boys have a great deal in common. Both are from broken families, both live with their divorced mothers, and both have suffered a recent emotional loss; Davy has lost his grandmother, of course, while Douglas has lost his best friend to cancer. But for Davy perhaps the most important reason for friendship is that Altschuler shares his affection for Fred.

And it is Fred who, ultimately, provides the opportunity or occasion or excuse for the boys' first physical intimacy. It happens one afternoon after school. They are at Davy's apartment. Mrs. Ross, who works in an advertising agency, is not yet home from work. The two boys are lying on the living room floor where they have been playing with Fred. When the dog darts away, the two are left, face-to-face, eye-to-eye. Though Davy knows he should get up, he doesn't move. Neither does Altschuler. Tension begins to build when, suddenly, Fred jumps in between them, excitedly licking their faces. And then it happens: "I guess I kiss Altschuler," Davy reports,

> and he kisses me. It just happens. And when it stops, we sit up and turn away from each other.
> "Boy," I say. "What was that all about?"
> "I don't know," Altschuler answers.

Awkwardly, the two boys get up and, to break the tension, resume playing with Fred. Then Altschuler lunges at Davy with his fists up like a boxer and the two pretend to spar.

"We are two bantamweight tough guys," Davy says. "I mean very tough. I mean a couple of guys like Altschuler and me don't have to worry about being queer or anything like that. Hell, no" (143).

The boys avoid each other the next day and might have gone on avoiding each other forever if Davy's mother hadn't made plans for the weekend and—to Davy's consternation—invited Altschuler to spend the day . . . and the night.

Davy doesn't tell us anything about the day, but the next morning he tells us that he has a new way of looking at Altschuler "because of what we did together last night."

He is no more specific than that. The catalyst for what they did was not Fred, this time, but the time-honored adolescent male discussion of girls "we had made out with." Davy insists to the reader that he feels there was nothing wrong with what the two did, but his words have the ring of false bravado.

In a letter dated August 5, 1968, Nordstrom wrote to Donovan of the work that was then still in progress, "I know you don't want to hit your readers over their heads, but we do think you can make it clearer, more vivid that David does suffer from considerable worry and guilt feelings."[51] There is no way of knowing what changes to the manuscript this may have inspired, but there is no question that Donovan found a way to create a considerable burden of guilt for Davy to shoulder.

After a week of casual friendship the boys finally talk about what has happened, each acknowledging that he had lied to the other about having made out with girls and agreeing there is no reason they shouldn't be friends "like before" (156). They take Fred for a walk and return to the Ross apartment where, Davy tells us, "I give Altschuler a big dumb kiss. He looks surprised. And so do I" (158).

What happens next seems a bit contrived. The boys decide to sample some whiskey from one of Mrs. Ross's many bottles. They drink enough to become dizzy, sit down on the floor with Fred, and fall asleep with their arms stretched across each other's backs.

Mrs. Ross comes home from work, finds them there, and, predictably, has hysterics. Altschuler quickly leaves for home, and after three cocktails and numerous tears, Mrs. Ross calls Davy's father, who comes over immediately. To give them privacy for what promises to be a serious talk, Mrs. Ross leaves the apartment, taking Fred with her. After acknowledging that the two "don't talk about personal things much, but sometimes it can't be avoided," Mr. Ross asks Davy if he has a crush on Altschuler. Davy immediately becomes defensive: "I'm not queer or anything, if that's what you think," he replies. Mr. Ross, though portrayed as being distant, is not insensitive. He moves quickly from the specific to the general, assuring Davy that many boys experiment but urging him not to "get involved in some special way of life, which will close off other ways of life."

"We only made out once," Davy protests (166). Mr. Ross laughs, and the two continue their conversation until Davy becomes nervous about the length of time his mother and Fred have been absent. He goes to the window just in time to see Fred run around the corner with his mother, who has lost her hold on Fred's leash, in hot pursuit.

Davy is alarmed, since, as he tells his father, "Fred is never off his leash on the street."

The boy then runs downstairs, arriving on the street just in time to hear "a big thud. A terrible, unnatural yelping." Fred has been struck by a car and dies in Davy's arms. The boy is devastated and consumed by guilt over the cause-and-effect relationship he infers between his "making out" with Altschuler and Fred's death. "Nothing would have happened to Fred if I hadn't been messing around with Altschuler. My fault. Mine!" (172).

For six weeks Davy tortures himself with these guilty, self-flagellating thoughts. He avoids Altschuler as much as possible and is distantly polite when school brings them together.

Gradually, however, Davy's anger at himself expands to include Altschuler. He rationalizes this by convincing himself that it was Altschuler's lying about having made out with a girl that "got us started . . . Fred died because of some stupid lies about making out." Davy continues his rationalizing by adding, "It certainly isn't in my nature to queer around. I never did it before. If it hadn't been for Altschuler, I would never have done it at all" (174).

Davy's anger continues to build until, following a school baseball game that has been won by Davy's home run, the two boys encounter each other in the locker room shower.

Congratulating Davy on his "great hit," Altschuler pats him on the shoulder. Davy reacts angrily, saying, "I don't like to be touched."

Altschuler's reply is telling: "Since when?"

Davy blows up. "We're going to end up a couple of queers," he tells Altschuler hotly. "You know that, don't you? All that junk back there before Fred died. You know what happens, don't you?" (176–77).

A fight ensues and only stops when Davy's ear is so badly cut he has to be taken to a doctor. The episode is cathartic, and several days later the two talk about what Davy calls "this queer business." Davy is anxious that Altschuler should know that he had never done anything like "that" before. Altschuler acknowledges that it had upset him, but "it didn't feel wrong. Did it to you?"

"Look what happened," is Davy's terse retort. Altschuler wisely states that what happened to Fred had nothing to do with what they did, but Davy continues to insist that maybe it did. "Go ahead and feel guilty if you want to, I don't," the other boy replies. "I guess the important thing is not to do it again," Davy says, to which his friend replies, "I don't care. If you think it's dirty or something like that, I wouldn't do it again if I were you."

"Maybe," Davy concludes, "if we made out with some girls, we wouldn't have to think about, you know, the other" (188).

The book ends a bit anticlimactically with the two boys agreeing that they can "respect" each other. But it seems clear that, for both of these emotionally vulnerable kids from fractured families, getting there—to adulthood, presumably—will still be no easy trip.

Despite Harper & Row's prepublication anxiety, most reviewers received Donovan's book warmly. Indeed, both the *New York Times* and *School Library Journal* named it to their respective best book lists. Paul Heins, editor of *Horn Book*, called the book's impact "shattering" and praised the protagonist's "frankness and intelligence."[52] Zena Sutherland, in *Saturday Review*, called it "as poignant and honest an account of an unhappy child as one could read."[53] And Lavinia Russ, writing in *Publishers Weekly*, praised it as "a perceptive, funny, touching story, a remarkable book."[54]

Surprisingly, while all the reviews note the homosexual encounter, not a single one mentions that this is the first time the subject has been treated in a book for this age group, though Alice Hungerford did acknowledge what she called "the new sophistication in fiction," adding that this is "a very modern book which directs itself to the increasing maturity of younger readers."[55]

Also, for the most part the reviewers interpret Davy's homosexual encounters with Altschuler as being little more than a routine rite of passage, a lonely boy's reaching out for friendship—indeed, the same interpretation Davy's father seems to apply. Heins called it "a slight homosexual incident."[56] *Booklist* magazine described it as "a spontaneous act of sexuality" that is "tastefully handled."[57] *School Library Journal* called the boys' physical encounters "childish caresses."[58] At the outset, John Weston's *New York Times* review appears to promise more insight. He begins by saying, "The contribution this book makes, giving reason why it should be available wherever young people read, is that it touches, with lyricism and simplicity, upon a spontaneous sexual relationship between two adolescent boys." But then he goes on to say that "such desires" are "something beautiful at the moment, but to be replaced in the natural course of life with interest in the other sex."[59] Which is to suggest, of course, that homosexuality is both unnatural and transient.

Only one reviewer, Martha Bacon, writing in the *Atlantic Monthly*, viewed homosexuality as a major theme of the book and was actively hostile to it. She wrote, "The novel celebrates the child's homosexual encounter with a schoolfellow" (a very odd reading of the book!) and goes on to say, "the language of children is inadequate to [the loss of innocence] and the application of grammar school jargon to corruption and passion is neither natural nor comforting. . . . I am also inclined to think that a book focused on a love affair between schoolfellows might have just the opposite effect on this age group from that which the author intended. It would not meet the needs of the initiated and might arouse unnecessary interest or alarm or both."[60]

In fact, it is a gross overstatement to describe the relationship between the boys as "a love affair." Indeed, love seems not to come into it at all. What disturbs Davy are not his affectional feelings for Altschuler but the fleeting physical expression they are given. For Davy, being "queer" begins and ends with making out. And being "queer" is, indisputably, not a way anyone would want to be.

Writing twenty-eight years after its publication, David Rees, the British critic and novelist who was himself the author of gay-themed young adult novels, commented on this aspect of the book. "John Donovan suggests that teenage homosexuality is so totally unacceptable, socially and psychological-ly, that any young homosexual is likely to have his fears and worries in-creased rather than reduced, and the prejudice of the heterosexual reader against homosexuals is reinforced."[61] This judgment may be a bit harsh, but we do agree that it's hard to imagine any LGBTQ+ teen finding much com-fort or support in this novel.

Nevertheless, nearly five decades after its publication, *I'll Get There. It Better Be Worth the Trip* remains a significant book, not only because it was the first book for young readers to deal with homosexuality in a purposeful manner, but also because it established—for good or ill—a model for the treatment of the topic that would be replicated in many of the novels that followed in the 1970s. The characters are male, white, and upper-middle class. The physical nature of what happens between them remains obscure. A cause-and-effect relationship is implied between homosexuality and being the child of divorced parents—more specifically, having an absent father and a disturbed and/or controlling mother. Homosexuality is presented both as a rite of passage experience with no long-term meaning or consequences (Davy's father tells him "a lot of boys play around in a lot of ways when they're growing up" [166]) and as a matter of conscious choice.

Surely Donovan is not to be taxed too severely for this last, however, since he was simply reflecting the prevailing beliefs of the day. Note that Ilg in her dust jacket comment says as much, too: "Davy is able to face the experience and to make his choice."

And in a 1976 document, "What to Do until Utopia Arrives," drawn up by the American Library Association's Gay Task Force "to help librarians eval-uate the treatment of gay themes in children's and YA literature," the follow-ing startling statement appears: "Librarians should be aware of the need for portrayals of growth and development of gay identity as *a valid life choice*" (emphasis added).[62] Choosing to act upon one's attractions to those of either sex is indeed a choice, but sexual orientation or identity—the emotions and attractions that inform that choice—is something more fundamental than a conscious choice. Most distressing, however, is the close—even causal—

connection Donovan's book makes between homosexuality and death. This equation haunted the early history of gay and lesbian literature, as we will see in the next chapter.

NOTES

1. T. S. Eliot, "Notes towards the Definition of Culture," in *Crosscurrents of Criticism: Horn Book Essays 1968–1979*, ed. Paul Heins (Boston: Horn Book, 1977).

2. James Baldwin, "Talk to Teachers," *Saturday Review* 21 (December 1963): 42–44, 60.

3. S. E. Hinton, *The Outsiders* (New York: Viking, 1967).

4. Robert Lipsyte, *The Contender* (New York: Harper & Row, 1967).

5. Nancy Larrick, "The All-White World of Children's Books," *Saturday Review*, September 1965, 63–85.

6. http://weneeddiversebooks.org/.

7. http://ccbc.education.wisc.edu/books/pcstats.asp.

8. Rudine Sims Bishop, "Mirrors, Windows, and Sliding Glass Doors," *Perspectives: Choosing and Using Books for the Classroom* 6, no. 3 (Summer 1990).

9. Lord Alfred Bruce Douglas, *Two Loves*, 1894.

10. George Chauncey, *Gay New York* (New York: Basic Books, 1994); Graham Robb, *Strangers: Homosexual Love in the Nineteenth Century* (New York: Norton, 2004).

11. Charles Kaiser, "Life before Stonewall," *Newsweek*, July 4, 1994.

12. Alfred C. Kinsey, et al. *Sexual Behavior in the Human Male* (Philadelphia: W.B. Saunders, 1948).

13. Martin Duberman, *Stonewall* (New York: Dutton, 1993).

14. Truman Capote, *Other Voices, Other Rooms* (New York: Random House, 1948).

15. Gore Vidal, *The City and the Pillar* (New York: Dutton, 1948).

16. Joseph Cady, "American Literature: Gay Male, 1900–1969," in *The Gay and Lesbian Literary Heritage*, ed. Claude J. Summers (New York: Henry Holt, 1995).

17. James Baldwin, *Giovanni's Room* (New York: Dial, 1956).

18. John Rechy, *City of Night* (New York: Grove, 1963).

19. Charles Isherwood, *A Single Man* (New York: Simon & Schuster, 1964).

20. Radclyffe Hall, *The Well of Loneliness* (London: Jonathan Cape, 1928).

21. George E. Haggerty, ed., *Gay Histories and Cultures: An Encyclopedia* (New York: Garland, 2000).

22. Diana Souhami, *The Trials of Radclyffe Hall* (New York: Doubleday, 1999), quoted in http://www.galha.org/glh/181/souhami.html, accessed March 24, 2005.

23. Virginia Woolf, *Orlando* (London: Hogarth, 1928).

24. Compton MacKenzie, *Extraordinary Women* (London: Martin Secker, 1928).

25. Djuna Barnes, *Nightwood* (San Diego, CA: Harcourt, 1936).

26. Vin Packer, *Spring Fire* (New York: Gold Medal Books, 1952).

27. Ann Bannon, *Odd Girl Out* (New York: Gold Medal Books, 1957).

28. Ann Bannon, *Journey to a Woman* (New York: Gold Medal Books, 1960).

29. Ann Bannon, *Beebo Brinker* (New York: Gold Medal Books, 1962).

30. Rita Mae Brown, *Rubyfruit Jungle* (N.p.: VT Daughters, 1973).

31. Maureen Daly, *Seventeenth Summer* (New York: Dodd, Mead, 1942).

32. Madeleine L'Engle, *The Small Rain* (New York: Vanguard, 1945).

33. J. D. Salinger, *The Catcher in the Rye* (Boston: Little, Brown, 1951).

34. James Baldwin, *Go Tell It on the Mountain* (New York: Knopf, 1953).

35. John Knowles, *A Separate Peace* (London: Secker & Warburg, 1959).

36. Cady, "American Literature," 37.

37. John Donovan, *I'll Get There. It Better Be Worth the Trip* (New York: Harper & Row, 1969).

38. James Baldwin, *Another Country* (New York: Dial, 1962).

39. Mary McCarthy, *The Group* (San Diego, CA: Harcourt, Brace, 1963).

40. Rechy, *City of Night.*

41. John Rechy, *Numbers* (New York: Grove, 1967).

42. Christopher Isherwood, *A Single Man* (New York: Simon & Schuster, 1964).

43. Sanford Friedman, *Totempole* (New York: E. P. Dutton, 1965).

44. Gore Vidal, *Myra Breckinridge* (Boston: Little, Brown, 1968).

45. W. Keith Kraus, "Cinderella in Trouble: Still Dreaming and Losing It." *School Library Journal* 21, no. 18 (January 1975).

46. Michael Thomas Ford, "Gay Books for Young Readers," *Publishers Weekly*, February 21, 1994.

47. Leonard Marcus, ed., *Dear Genius: The Letters of Ursula Nordstrom* (New York: HarperCollins, 1998).

48. Marcus, *Dear Genius*, 261.

49. Marcus, *Dear Genius*, 257.

50. Marcus, *Dear Genius*, 258.

51. Marcus, *Dear Genius*, 258.

52. Paul Heins, review of *I'll Get There. It Better Be Worth the Trip*, by John Donovan, *Horn Book* 45, no. 4 (August 1969).

53. Zena Sutherland, review of *I'll Get There. It Better Be Worth the Trip*, by John Donovan, *Saturday Review* 52, no. 59 (May 10, 1969).

54. Lavinia Russ, review of *I'll Get There. It Better Be Worth the Trip*, by John Donovan, *Publishers Weekly*, March 17, 1969.

55. Alice Hungerford, review of *I'll Get There. It Better Be Worth the Trip*, by John Donovan, *Washington Post*, May 4, 1969.

56. Heins, review, 4.

57. Review of *I'll Get There. It Better Be Worth the Trip*, by John Donovan, *Booklist*, 65, no. 1174 (June 15, 1969).

58. Review of *I'll Get There. It Better Be Worth the Trip*, by John Donovan, *School Library Journal*, May 15, 1969.

59. John Weston, review of *I'll Get There. It Better Be Worth the Trip*, by John Donovan, *New York Times Book Review*, May 4, 1969.

60. Martha Bacon, "Tantrums and Unicorns," *Atlantic Monthly* 224, no. 6 (December 1969).

61. David Rees, "A Plea for Jill Chaney," *Children's Literature in Education* 8, no. 2 (Summer 1997): 85.

62. American Library Association Gay Task Force, "What to Do until Utopia Arrives," in *Young Adult Literature in the Seventies: A Selection of Readings*, ed. Jana Varlejs (Metuchen, NJ: Scarecrow, 1978).

Chapter Two

Young Adult Literature of the 1970s

The pioneering late 1960s work of S. E. Hinton, Robert Lipsyte, and Paul Zindel became the order of the day in the decade that followed, a period when so many of the grandmasters of the genre (Robert Cormier, M. E. Kerr, Walter Dean Myers, Richard Peck, Judy Blume, etc.) launched their innovative writing careers. Indeed, many critics view the seventies as the first golden age of young adult literature, a time of creative prowess and prodigious production.

Unfortunately, the same cannot be said of LGBTQ+ literature for young adults, since the publication of Donovan's book did not exactly open the floodgates to a torrent of gay-themed novels. In fact, it would be three years before the next YA title to include gay content, Isabelle Holland's *The Man without a Face*, appeared in 1972. Only a handful of other novels with similar themes would follow during the entire decade of the seventies. And too many of these were marred by stereotypical characters and predictable plots centered about the inherent misery of gay people's lives.

In fact, these flaws were characteristic of a kind of fiction that began appearing in the larger world of YA literature in the seventies. Quickly dubbed the "problem novel," this type of fiction was driven by its relentless focus on social issues that plagued some contemporary teens: alcohol or drug abuse, teen pregnancy, parental divorce, and so forth. Highly didactic, these novels were notable for one-dimensional characterization, plot contrivance, and near-total lack of art. Perhaps the most enduring example is *Go Ask Alice* (Prentice Hall, 1971). That homosexuality was viewed by many, at the time, as a social problem only exacerbated the tendency to regard the literature about it as belonging in the "problem novel" category, which robbed homosexuals of individuality and perpetuated stereotypes about them.

In an insightful 1983 article titled "Out of the Closet but Paying the Price,"[1] Jan Goodman lists ten such stereotypes:

1. It is still physically dangerous to be gay.
2. Your future is bleak if you are gay.
3. Gay people lead lonely lives, even if they're happy with each other.
4. Gay adults should not be around children because they'll influence them to be homosexual.
5. Something traumatic in a gay person's past makes him/her homosexual.
6. Gay men want to be women and lesbians want to be men.
7. SEX: Don't worry. If you do "it" once, you may not be gay. It may only be a phase.
8. Gay relationships are mysterious.
9. All gays are middle/upper-middle-class and white.
10. As far as young children know, there's no such thing as a gay person. (13–15)

YA NOVELS AND THE (HETERO)SEXUAL REVOLUTION

The treatment of sexual activity in the handful of novels of the seventies that included a same-sex romance was, at best, obscure—indeed, an erotic encounter between two people was usually described simply as "it." In *The Man without a Face*, for example, the protagonist enigmatically explains, "I didn't know what was happening to me until it had happened" (147). Of course, one argument made against including sexual explicitness in YA novels is that it is merely voyeuristic. Real-life voyeurism is inappropriate, no matter how realistic a work of fiction may be, but readers are in a different relationship with a text than they are with the people observed in their immediate surroundings. Teens who pick up a book are often readers with questions, and as instructors know, when potential learners ask their own questions, they listen to the answers. Given the choice between learning about sex via media (text, films, video, etc.) or via lived experience, mediated information is certainly physically and emotionally safer. In considering sexually explicit texts from this perspective, actively preventing teens from reading them seems an at best foolish—and at worst dangerous—enterprise. But the concern remains that sexually explicit texts encourage readers to "try this at home" (or, more likely, in the car). Perhaps this is precisely why many teens *want* to read about sex—not simply because they are looking for titillation but because they are looking for information that they would actually prefer *not* to discover firsthand—or at least, not yet.

It was the sexual and political revolutions of the sixties, including the advent of the gay rights movement, that made it possible for publishers to experiment, however cautiously, with producing fiction that included the topic of homosexuality, while at the same time expanding their previous timid treatment of other aspects of human sexuality. Judy Blume's groundbreaking novel *Forever* (1975), the first to include detailed scenes of explicit sexual activity between two (straight) teens, was published in 1975. At the time many assumed that it portended an avalanche of sexually explicit novels for teen readers. Instead, *Forever* has remained a high-water mark in terms of the inclusion of sexual detail in young adult fiction. With few exceptions, YA books published before, during, and after 1975 have adhered to the conventions of mainstream PG-13 movies, which generally place physical intimacy at the end of scenes where a couple's embrace and kiss are followed by a convenient fade-out, followed by a scene change.

Nevertheless, YA literature of the seventies often focused less on the sexual act per se than on the unintended—but seemingly inevitable—consequences of it: unwanted teenage pregnancies. Once books with sexual content began to appear, young readers seemed to have an insatiable appetite for them. Indeed, as early as 1970 four of the top five books sold to students through the Xerox Educational Publications' teenage book clubs were about sex and pregnancy.[2] Of course the sex remained resolutely of the hetero sort, but the consequences often involved the same social opprobrium or consequential death that the homosexual sort did, though in this case the cause of death was abortion, which had emerged as a subject of the genre in 1969 with the publication of Paul Zindel's *My Darling, My Hamburger.*

HOMOSEXUAL VISIBILITY

With a few notable exceptions (see below), YA novels with LGBTQ+ content published during the 1970s fit into the category of homosexual visibility, coming-out stories in which a character previously presumed to be heterosexual is revealed to be LGBTQ+.

The Man without a Face, by Isabelle Holland (1972)

A number of these stereotypes marred Isabelle Holland's *The Man without a Face.* Like Donovan's *I'll Get There,* Holland's book is told in the first-person voice of a male protagonist, fourteen-year-old Charles (Chuck) Norstadt. Like David Ross, Chuck lives in a home headed by his much-divorced mother. "Mother's hobby is marrying," he says acidly (11). His family also includes two stepsisters: "repulsive" Gloria, who is sixteen, and "okay" Meg, eleven. Chuck's father is long dead, and the boy has only shadowy memories of him. His only friend in the New England village where the well-to-do family is summering is his pet cat, Moxie.

As the only male in the house (aside from Moxie), Chuck feels he is "drowning in women" (15) and longs for the day Gloria will go away to boarding school. He is so counting on this that—an indifferent student himself—he has "more or less deliberately flunked" the entrance exam to what had been his own intended boarding school destination, St. Matthew's. "'And that's that,'" his mother says when she gets the news, "not even trying to sound unhappy" (16). Chuck's explanation for her matter-of-fact attitude reads like foreshadowing: one of her ex-husbands has told her that boarding schools turn out a high percentage of homosexuals, "and Mother has a thing about homos" (16).

Chuck realizes he is in serious trouble when Gloria blithely announces she has changed her mind about boarding school and plans to remain in her New York day school to be closer to her new boyfriend. "I nearly blew my lid," he fumes (8). Hastily, he writes to the headmaster of St. Matthew's and is told, in reply, that he may sit for the exam again at the end of the summer. At first relieved, Chuck is soon desolate, as he recognizes that he doesn't know where to begin a summer of remedial work.

"Good" sister Meg suggests an unlikely solution: that he find a tutor in the person of Justin McLeod, a local recluse known as "The Man without a Face." The sobriquet derives from the fact that half of the man's face is a mass of scars. Because of his resolute aloofness, McLeod is also called "The Grouch." Though rumors are rife about him, at least one—that he was once a teacher—is promising. And so, while it takes every ounce of courage he can muster, Chuck approaches McLeod, who first rebuffs him ("No. Certainly not" [28]) but then relents, on one condition: "You'll have to do it my way, and that means the hard way" (35).

"I had found myself another Hitler," Chuck thinks ruefully, and some readers may agree. Though McLeod is intended to be a romantic, even a gothic figure (think Heathcliff with scars), he is also a bit of a martinet. Despite this—or perhaps because of it (there is a suggestion that Chuck welcomes the rigid structure the man enforces on his life)—the boy soon warms to his new teacher, who is, improbably, a former St. Matthew's faculty member. Chuck thinks, "I'd never had a friend and he was my friend . . . and I trusted him" (128).

Chuck begins to wish the man were his father. But factored into this increasingly complex emotional equation is Chuck's growing awareness of his physical attraction to McLeod. When the man finally reveals the source of his scars—driving drunk, he had lost control of his car, which crashed, burning him and killing the boy who was riding with him—Chuck reaches out in sympathy to grasp his arm and is harshly rebuffed. The boy is incensed that he has been made to feel as if he were making a "pass."

Several weeks later the two go swimming and, afterward, they sun togeth-er on a rock. Chuck once again finds himself attracted to the man. "I reached over and touched his side. The hot skin was tight over his ribs. I knew then that I'd never been close to anyone in my life, not like that. And I wanted to get closer" (120).

Nothing more happens, but later that day, Chuck blurts out the question that has been bothering him: "Do you think I'm queer?" This would be a common question in early LGBTQ+ literature; Davy asks it in *I'll Get There*; Pete will ask it in *What's This about Pete?* as will Tom in *Sticks and Stones*. While the catalyst for this question is often concern over a same-sex attrac-tion, it can also be a manifestation of the pollution myth; that is, if you have any sort of positive connection with a homosexual, you must be homosexual yourself. Regardless of the question's root, the inevitable answer in these early books is no, which is what McLeod tells Chuck, adding rather glibly that everybody wants and needs affection. "Also, you're a boy who badly needs a father" (121).

All of this is prelude to what happens the night Chuck arrives home to discover Gloria and her boyfriend Percy having sex in his bed. Worse, he discovers that Percy has killed Moxie for soiling Gloria's bed (shades of Davy and Fred). Later that night, Chuck discovers a bundle of news clippings Gloria has heartlessly left for him. They reveal the truth about his late father who, it turns out, had died on skid row of chronic alcoholism.

Bereft, Chuck flees to Justin's house and finds him asleep in bed. McLe-od wakes and in comforting the weeping Chuck, takes him into bed and holds him. And then it happens (yes, "it" again). "I didn't know what was happen-ing to me until it happened," Chuck reports. The next morning McLeod has a one-sided conversation with Chuck who doesn't want to talk about "it." The man assures the boy that nothing of lasting significance has happened. "There's nothing about it to worry you. You reacted to a lot of strain—and shock—in a normal fashion" (148).

Chuck, however, refuses to be comforted and challenges McLeod about his own sexuality and, though the word "homosexual" is never used, the man acknowledges, "I've known what I was for a long time." The conversation ends awkwardly as Chuck's new stepfather (yes, his mother has married again) arrives to take him home.

Chuck retakes and passes the entrance exam and goes off to St. Mat-thew's, where he scarcely thinks of McLeod for two months until he has a dream in which his new stepfather—who, coincidentally enough, is also an old friend of McLeod's—explains that the real "man without a face" is not McLeod but, rather, Chuck's late father. For some reason this convinces Chuck he must see McLeod again but, alas, it is too late, for the man has died of a heart attack while traveling abroad, handily removing any possibility that the two will ever have to discuss their feelings. And, P.S., he has left his entire estate to the boy. In death McLeod becomes a martyred saint. The implication, of course, is that the only good homosexual is a dead homosexual.

What is the reader to make of all this? Holland herself said she intended the novel to be a love story, "an unusual love story but, nevertheless, a love story,"[3] and most reviewers, who were lavish with their praise of this flawed novel, agreed. *Horn Book*, for example, said, "The author has delved into the joy and sorrow concomitant with love and growth."[4] But what does the book actually say about love? When events conspire to drive Chuck into McLeod's arms, the boy is horrified by what happens (as we read it, Chuck has a spontaneous ejaculation) and rejects the man—and his feelings for him. For his part, McLeod himself is made by the author to downplay the event ("There's nothing about it to worry you"), reinforcing the implicit message that Elizabeth Minot Graves states in her *Commonweal* review: "One act of overt homosexuality need not imply real homosexuality."[5] And, lest Chuck rethink his feelings, McLeod is now dead.

The symbolic treatment of McLeod's homosexuality—his horribly scarred face—is also unfortunate. Although certainly teens get information about homosexuality from a variety of sources, within the world of this book, the consequences of being gay include (1) being hideously injured in a car wreck; (2) becoming an embittered, tortured recluse; (3) being rejected by a boy whom you have sought only to mentor, comfort, and reassure; (4) exiling oneself to a foreign land; and then (5) dying prematurely of a heart attack no doubt brought on by (1), (2), (3), and (4). Talk about being "scared straight"!

To her credit, these negative consequences were not Holland's intended message. Indeed, in a *Horn Book* essay, she imagines herself writing to readers of the twenty-first century as follows: "You have to realize they had something in those days they called a taboo against any expression of love between members of the same sex. Yes, I know it's hard to believe, but without that there wouldn't even be a story to tell."[6]

And yet, in reflecting the prevailing social attitudes of her time, the author nevertheless equates homosexuality with disfigurement, despair, and death, and her novel, along with Donovan's, reinforced some of the stereotypical thinking about homosexuality that became a fixture of LGBTQ+ literature.

Trying Hard to Hear You, by Sandra Scoppettone (1974)

To say, simply, that (as noted earlier by Goodman) it was physically dangerous to be gay was not only a stereotype but also a bit of an understatement for these early novels, considering how many of the homosexual characters die. To be perfectly fair, death has always figured large in young adult literature of every sort. But, that said, death would again be the fate of one of the gay characters in the third YA novel to deal with homosexuality, Sandra Scoppettone's *Trying Hard to Hear You*, which appeared two years later in 1974. In this novel, however, it is not the protagonist who is wrestling with his sexual identity but, rather, the protagonist's best friend. Scoppettone's novel is a first-person narrative told by sixteen-year-old Camilla (Cam) Crawford as she recalls the events of the summer of 1973, which led to her discovery that her best friend and neighbor, Jeff, is gay.

The two teens are involved with a group of their other friends in staging a summer stock production of *Anything Goes* (an ironic choice, in retrospect). When Jeff is discovered kissing another boy, Phil, the two come in for a great deal of verbal abuse ("They're goddamn queers" [182]) and worse—they're almost tarred and feathered. Ultimately, Phil cracks under the pressure, screaming at his tormentors that "being a fag was a choice—you know, he could be straight if he wanted to" (238). So he invites a girl on a date, they drink some alcohol, and guess what—they both die in a car crash!

Writing some years later, Scoppettone defended this plot choice: "The ending of *THTHY*, in which one of the homosexual boys dies, was misconstrued by many people. Perhaps this was my fault; I should have made the reason for this clearer. My intention was to show that he died trying to be something he wasn't (heterosexual) and *not* because he was a homosexual."[7] Well, yes, but doesn't this invite the reader to conclude that the gay person is doomed either way—through being homosexual or through trying to deny his sexuality? This damned if you do, damned if you don't quandary was all too typical in the early days of this literature.

In her defense, however, Scoppettone does at least make a clear equation between homosexuality and love. Jeff says to Cam, "As long as people love instead of hate, what difference does it make who they love?" (208). And, later, Cam herself says to another character: "If two people love each other, they should be together, no matter what. Jeff and Phil love each other" (230). This statement evidences Cam's emotional growth, because she had originally been heartbroken to learn that Phil was gay since she had a serious crush on him, becoming, thus, the first of what would be many straight girls who learn, to their sorrow, that boys they desire are gay. As another girl, Brie in Ann Rinaldi's *The Good Side of My Heart* wistfully observes, "All that handsomeness, all that masculinity, wasted. I wanted to cry."[8] Happily, though Phil dies, Jeff survives and heads off to college. At the book's end, Cam reports that Jeff is dating another boy "and he's planning to bring him home for Thanksgiving" (264).

Though well received by reviewers (*Booklist* called it "a teenage story of unusual depth for mature readers"),[9] Scoppettone's novel is, in some ways, even more clearly a snapshot in time of prevailing social attitudes toward homosexuality than either the Donovan or Holland books. It includes, for example, a rebuttal to the egregiously fallacious material about homosexuality contained in the then-popular book *Everything You Always Wanted to*

Know about Sex but Were Afraid to Ask by Dr. David Reuben (1969). A sample from his book: "Since ancient times they [homosexuals] found employment as professional torturers and executioners. More recently they filled the ranks of Hitler's Gestapo and SS."[10] As it happens, Cam's mother is a psychiatrist, and when the girl *finally* (on page 252 of a 264-page book) asks her mother about homosexuality, she replies: "Homosexuality—and that includes lesbianism—has been part of life as long as there have been people and it always will be. I don't think anybody quite understands why some people are and some people aren't. There are several schools of thought: some think it's environment, others think it's biological, still others think it's choice. The uninformed and the ignorant think it's evil or even a disease. . . . Homosexuality and alcoholism are the two things that the medical and psychiatric professions know very little about. But I do know this . . . as long as you don't hurt anyone else, you have a right to be what you want to be."

In fact, it wasn't until two years *after* this novel's publication that the American Psychiatric Association (APA) finally removed the classification of homosexuality as a mental illness. As for being "what you want to be," the APA's 1976 statement firmly declared, "Although we can choose whether or not to act on our feelings, psychologists do not consider sexual orientation to be a conscious choice that can be voluntarily changed."[11]

In the final analysis, *Trying Hard to Hear You* represented a cautious step forward in terms of its attitudes toward and treatment of homosexuality, though, as a work of fiction, it comes dangerously close to being a "problem novel" that suffers from the didacticism and melodrama typical of that genre.

What's This about Pete? by Mary Sullivan (1976)

Mary Sullivan's *What's This about Pete?*, published in 1976, suffers from the same flaws. Although protagonist Pete Hanson is fifteen years old, he appears to be far more child than teen due to his extraordinary naïveté and the author's relentlessly prim, old-fashioned style, diction, and presentation of teen life (boys avidly read a magazine called *Ribald Capers*, for example).

A sensitive "little guy," Pete likes "good-looking things" and enjoys doing "girl's work." No wonder his macho, motorcycle-riding father calls him a "pantywaist" and, when he discovers the boy has been helping his seamstress mother by sewing, angrily claims, "You been turning him into a queer behind my back." Pete is worried his father might be right about him. After all, hadn't he felt "a pleasant hum of recognition—a special awareness" the first time he saw the new guy, Mario (7)? "It was crazy, but there was no other way to say it. I love Mario, he thought" (34), and later, in a panic, he wonders, "Am I turning into a—a homosexual . . . ?" (98).

His concern is exacerbated when "a pleasant young man" in a passing car offers him fifty dollars "if you'll come home with me" (104). Pete is so upset that he finally turns to the school's guidance counselor, kindly old Doc Logan, who tells him, "Just forget your worries about homosexuality—incidentally, many boys go through stages when they think they may be gay, only to outgrow it—just forget your worries and be yourself. Love girls, love boys—but love. It's an old cliché, Peter, but love is what makes the world go round" (115). Pete, his heart "positively light," is freed by this wisdom, freed not to love Mario, who is revealed to be "a lying swine" (120), but to love classmate Barbara instead. And so, the book triumphantly concludes, "Tomorrow this gutsy little guy had a date with Barbara" (125).

Ruby, by Rosa Guy (1976)

The same year that *Pete* was published, a more successful novel—in literary terms, at least—also appeared. It was Rosa Guy's *Ruby*, which is historically important as the first YA novel to feature a lesbian relationship. A sequel to Guy's more celebrated *The Friends*, which has appeared on all five "best of the best" book lists prepared periodically by the Young Adult Library Services Association of ALA, this novel turns the focus from Phyllisia, the protagonist of the first of three novels about a West Indian immigrant family, the Cathys, to her older sister, Ruby. Herself born in the West Indies (in Trinidad), novelist and dramatist Guy was founding president of the Harlem Writers Guild and was a pioneer in writing about the real-life circumstances of immigrants of color, as they carve out new lives in an often inhospitable, urban American environment.

Indeed, in *The Friends* both Cathy girls are routinely bullied and rejected because of their "foreignness." It is the younger, Phyllisia, who finds comfort and support in the friendship she forges with a classmate named Edith Jackson, who would become the titular main character of the third novel. In the second novel, though, it is the desperately lonely Ruby who looks for heartsease in a friendship with another girl, the beautiful Daphne, and finds, instead, a love affair. "At last she had found herself, a likeness to herself, a response to her needs, her age, an answer to her loneliness" (46–47).

The answer proves not to be an enduring one, however; though their relationship finds expression in physical intimacy, the strong-willed Daphne ends the relationship as part of her trajectory toward college and a middle-class future. And despite a seemingly full-hearted commitment to the relationship ("people don't leave people they love" [138]), Ruby—after an initial period of emotional turbulence—seems to recover with astonishing ease and, by book's end, is poised to resume a relationship with her ex-boyfriend Orlando. Since Ruby is portrayed as being heterosexual in both the books that precede and follow this novel about her, the reader is left to conclude, once again, that homosexuality is—as earlier novels of the seventies suggest—simply a rite of passage on the way to mature (read: "heterosexual") adulthood. As reviewer Mary Hoffman put it, "Her lesbian experience is an interlude for her, not a major realization about her own sexual orientation."[12]

It is especially difficult to accept Ruby's affectional about-face since—unlike the young characters in the Donovan, Holland, and Sullivan books—she is eighteen years old, although it could be argued that her limited life experience due to her domineering father, Calvin, has left her emotionally younger than her chronological age. For the passive Ruby, her relationship with Daphne is something that happens to her—she is acted upon, but rarely acts on her own behalf, and there is scant evidence of any emotional growth on her part by book's end.

The *Interracial Books for Children Bulletin* criticized this aspect of the novel and also took it to task for reinforcing "sexist stereotypes about heterosexual males, heterosexual females and lesbians by implying that lesbians are 'masculine' types like Daphne, while 'feminine' types like Ruby are destined to 'go straight.'"[13]

Sticks and Stones, by Lynn Hall (1977)

As its title suggests, Lynn Hall's *Sticks and Stones* is about the power of words—pejorative words, that is—and the negative consequences of being "out." When sixteen-year-old Tom Naylor and his divorced mother move from Chicago to tiny Buck Creek, Iowa, to open an antiques store, the boy is lonely, finding no one near his age who shares his interests (he's a gifted pianist with a quick mind). In fact the only persistent overtures of friendship he receives come from his obnoxious neighbor Floyd Schleffe. When Tom rejects those, Floyd retaliates by starting a rumor that Tom is gay. The situation is not helped when Tom finally finds a kindred spirit in an older boy, Ward Alexander, who has recently returned to Buck Creek after having been discharged from the air force. For there are rumors about Ward, too—that he wasn't discharged for "medical reasons" but for being gay.

Improbably, Tom remains entirely ignorant of these rumors as he begins to wonder why "something" is "wrong between him and the others at school" and why he feels "as though he were in parentheses" (107). The situation comes to a head when the school principal summons Tom to his office to tell him that he will not be allowed to attend the state music finals because of parental complaints: "They don't want their sons making a two-day out-of-town trip with a young man who is a homosexual" (138).

Tom is dumbfounded and understandably devastated. In the weeks that follow, he comes down with a lingering illness (not unlike the way that characters in Victorian melodramas came down with "brain fever" or "the vapors" when things went badly). When he does return to school, he is shunned by his classmates and his life quickly becomes a living hell of isolation. But wait! There is worse to come: when he tells his friend Ward what has happened, the older boy eventually responds by confessing that he has lied about the reason for his military discharge. In fact, "I was discharged because of a 'homosexual involvement' with another guy in my barracks" (183). Stunned and understandably devastated, Tom feels he's lost his last friend. "There were no more sanctuaries" (185).

But wait! There's worse still to come: Tom's isolation and accompanying paranoia so preoccupy him that he fails his semester exams. The principal calls Tom into his office again, this time to tell him that he will not have enough credits to graduate with his class. Moments after Tom receives this news, Floyd, who has missed the school bus, asks Tom for a ride home. Once again understandably devastated, Tom complies reluctantly, but in his eagerness to get rid of Floyd, he drives too fast and loses control of the car, and there is an accident. Floyd is killed, and Tom wakes up in the hospital with an epiphany: "There's probably nothing wrong with my masculinity, only with my stupid head, for not being surer of myself" (187).

At just that moment, a visitor arrives: it is Ward, whom Tom has been studiously avoiding. But no longer. Now that he is sure of his "masculinity," he can reach for his friend's hand and utter the last line of the book: "Ward, I'm glad you came" (187).

Sadly, though Hall's intentions are obviously of the best, her book is typical of the issue-driven problem novels that typified much of YA fiction of the late 1970s and more specifically, YA fiction with LGBTQ+ content. Tom is so clueless, Ward is so decent, and Floyd is so villainous in his rumormongering and so pathetic in believing that he can win Tom's friendship by showing him his "dirty pictures, let him know I've never showed them to anyone else in my life. Then he'll know he's my best friend" (25).

Also, it is scarcely conceivable that Tom could remain ignorant of what is happening for so long but so sadly predictable that he will reject Ward when his friend finally comes out to him. The inevitable car crash that gets Floyd permanently out of the picture, plus Tom's sudden mental health epiphany in the hospital, provide a deus ex machina ending that creaks with artifice.

And yet, it could have been much worse. Lynn Hall wrote to librarians Frances Hanckel and John Cunningham, "One editor wanted me to kill Tom in a car accident." Happily, she resisted that but was not able to fully realize her creative intentions. "I wanted Ward and Tom to love each other, to live happily ever after, and that was the way I ended it," she explained. "But the publishers would not let me do it. In their words this was showing a homosexual relationship as a possible happy ending and this might be dangerous to young people teetering on the brink. At least I held out for a friendship at the end, one which might or might not develop into something more, depending on the reader's imagination."[14]

Though the book was, for the most part, sympathetically reviewed, one critic, Lillian Gerhardt, was more frank and insightful when she wrote, "Although peer group gossip about degrees of masculinity or femininity will undoubtedly continue to make high school life hell for some people, these stock characters neither reflect nor illuminate the situation and the low-action plot fails as entertainment."[15]

Happy Endings Are All Alike, by Sandra Scoppettone (1978)

Small-town attitudes and prejudices were also the subject of Sandra Scoppettone's second novel to deal with homosexual issues. *Happy Endings Are All Alike,* published in 1978, is set in the village of Gardner's Point, a hundred miles from New York City. In the very first sentence of the novel Scoppettone establishes the theme: "Even though Jaret Tyler had no guilt or shame about her love affair with Peggy Danziger, she knew there were plenty of people in this world who would put it down" (1). And so, as the omniscient narrator puts it, "The two girls didn't go around wearing banners but there were some people who knew." One of these is Jaret's mother, Kay, who—despite some early reservations about the truth—quickly assures her daughter, "If you're happy, that's all that counts" (9). Others, however, including Peggy's sister Claire, who refers to the girls' relationship as "deviant," are less sympathetic, to put it mildly. Since Claire is said to "represent society" (26), it is small wonder that the two girls "could imagine what would happen if it" (their affair) "were ever made public." "And," the narrator concludes with ominous foreshadowing, "they were right" (11).

Their affair threatens to become a matter of public knowledge when Jaret is raped by a deranged teen stalker who has "accidentally" observed the two girls making love in their "secret place" in the woods. When Jaret decides to press charges, the local police chief urges her parents to drop the case, because "I guarantee you that this sort of deviant stuff doesn't go over too big in a nice little town like Gardner's Point" (168). Moreover, he tells them, Jaret's former boyfriend has told him that they had been intimate and thus she is not a virgin. What does all this mean? "Let me put it to you this way," the chief explains. "See, we have a hearing and the judge learns your girl's not a virgin and on top of that she's a les. Well, he's not gonna think much of her morals. I'm just trying to give you some friendly advice" (169).

Things go from bad to worse. When Jaret resolutely continues to press charges, Peggy, who doesn't want her private life to become public knowledge, ends their relationship. Fortunately, Peggy ultimately decides, "I don't want to spend the rest of my life being what other people want me to be" (201), and the two reconcile. "They held each other tightly, knowing the future held many surprises, that nothing was guaranteed. And what if happy endings didn't exist? Happy moments did" (202).

Despite its tentatively hopeful ending, Scoppettone's second novel is deeply flawed. The linking of the girls' lesbianism with the rape is confusing.

The rapist's inner thoughts are part of the narrative, but his motivation remains inexplicable. The book includes much exposition about the true meaning of rape and the victimization of women; and the principal antagonists, the police chief and Peggy's sister Claire, become almost allegorical in their relentless representations of misogyny and homophobia, respectively. The sanctification of homosexuals and the corollary demonizing of homophobes will be a recurring problem throughout the entire history of LGBTQ+ literature, one that often, as in the case of *Happy Endings*, will undermine the believability of the entire enterprise. Similarly, the cause-and-effect relationship between homosexuality and physical violence—even death—will continue. As late as 1997, for example, Jack Gantos's *Desire Lines* eerily echoes *Happy Endings* with its story of two teenage lesbians who, when discovered by a boy in the act of making love, instantly enter into a murder-suicide pact as if this were an entirely normal and natural response to being outed.

Hey, Dollface, by Deborah Hautzig (1978)

In the second novel to appear in 1978, *Hey, Dollface* by Deborah Hautzig, the reader returns to the urban world of New York City and the corridors of a private school, where two new girls—Chloe and Val, the first-person narrator—meet and quickly become friends. The novel that ensues is an exploration of their deepening relationship, with all its ambiguities, including those involving their emotional intimacy. Though both girls will ultimately acknowledge having had sexual fantasies about each other, they never act on them and, after a period of uneasiness, agree that, though they love each other, they are not lesbians. Neither the girls nor the reader, however, is quite sure precisely what their feelings might mean about their personal identities. But as Val muses at book's end, "I've had time to think about the Chloe I knew then and all that she meant to me, but it's never been something I could define." And, "What we had was part of the truth, but only a part; the rest was a feeling too complicated and too strong to explain" (150). Chloe's take is more straightforward: "We don't have to fit into any slots, so let's stop trying" (150).

Because of this ambiguity, this suggestion that sexual identity is not cut and dried, *Dollface* may be the most sophisticated treatment of homosexuality we have yet encountered. Certainly it is one of the best written. The emotional tone is just right—often funny, sometimes sarcastic, and never cloying. As for the teenage characters, they're likable, multidimensional, and—best of all—believable—perhaps because the author herself was only twenty-two when this book was published.

GAY ASSIMILATION

I'll Love You When You're More Like Me, by M. E. Kerr (1977)

Just when it looked like there would be nothing but Sturm und Drang in YA literature with gay content, M. E. Kerr poked fun at prevailing gay stereotypes in her delightful novel *I'll Love You When You're More Like Me* (1977). This is the first YA novel with LGBTQ+ content that could be viewed as one of gay assimilation because a secondary character, Charlie Gilhooley, is an openly gay teen who is the best friend and confidant of protagonist Wally Witherspoon. It is Charlie who wryly complains that since the movies and television have been showing great big tough gays, to get away from the stereotypical effeminates, he's been worse off than ever before. "Now I'm supposed to live up to some kind of big butch standard, where I can Indian-wrestle anyone in the bar to the floor, or produce sons, or lift five-hundred pound weights over my head without my legs breaking" (41).

Charlie knows about stereotypes; he's been "out" since he was sixteen, when, Wally reports, "he started telling a select group of friends and family that he believed he preferred boys to girls. The news shouldn't have come as a surprise to anyone who knew Charlie even slightly. But honesty has its own rewards: ostracism and disgrace" (38). Apparently, these "rewards" begin at home, since Charlie's parents do not receive the news of their son's sexual preference with any degree of aplomb. His mother rushes to the local priest to try to arrange an exorcism for her boy while the father, "a round-the-clock, large-bellied beer drinker," breaks his son's nose.

But Charlie's homosexuality is not the theme of the novel or even an issue, since Wally remains a loyal and steadfast friend . . . though on one condition: "My own deal with Charlie was don't you unload your emotional problems on me, and I won't unload mine on you. We shook hands on the pact and never paid any attention to it. I went through a lot of Charlie's crushes with him. Charlie, in turn, had to hear and hear and hear about Lauralei Rabinowitz" (with whom Wally is hopelessly in love) (38).

Despite this—or perhaps because of it—Charlie remains well adjusted, cheerful, and self-deprecatingly humorous, and a lively three-dimensional gay character at a time when young adult literature was portraying homosexual characters as guilt-ridden loners who are destroyed by self or society. The closest Charlie comes to death is his (ironic?) decision to work in Wally's father's funeral home business.

In her first YA novel to deal with homosexuality, Kerr—winner of the 1993 Margaret A. Edwards Award for lifetime achievement in YA literature—quickly established herself as an innovator: the first to offer homosexuality in a humorous context; the first to depict a happy, well-adjusted gay character; and the first to integrate homosexuality into the larger context of a novel that explored other issues of establishing personal identity and being true to oneself. It's small wonder that Kerr has become one of the two or three most important YA writers to include significant gay/lesbian content in her fiction and no surprise at all that she also received the Bill Whitehead Award for Lifetime Achievement from the Publishing Triangle (a gay publishing organization) and the Robert Chesley Foundation in 1998.

QUEER CONSCIOUSNESS/COMMUNITY

In the Tent, by David Rees (1979)

Only one of the YA novels with LGBTQ+ content published in the 1970s, David Rees's *In the Tent*, contains any mention of a gay/lesbian community. Though it's not actively denied in the other novels, community simply does not exist. As a book that first appeared in England in 1979 but was not published in the United States until 1985, *In the Tent* straddles the two decades and foreshadows advances that would enhance the quality of American YA fiction in the decade to come. Until then, however, the "good" gay person in American YA had to isolate himself from others: both Justin in Isabelle Holland's *The Man without a Face* and Ward in Lynn Hall's *Sticks and Stones*, for example, are writers who lead deliberately sequestered lives in isolated houses full of books and solitude. There appears to be little if any social reward for coming out—"to thine own self be true" is all very well, but if the price is social isolation, is it worth it? The rewards—if any—are intellectual and moral rather than emotional. The lack of community is also underlined in both of Scoppettone's novels. In *Trying Hard to Hear You*, for example, Phil and Jeff are introduced as part of a close-knit community of peers—a lively summer theater crowd of longtime friends—but when they fall in love, they face instant ostracism, and their former community becomes an actively hostile environment. The two of them cling to each other, but the newfound warmth of each other's company cannot withstand the cold isolation they face. Although they continue to have each other, they have no one else, and the resulting isolation leads, albeit indirectly, to Phil's death in the drunk-driving accident. Thus, the point is made that the closet is the price that the gay/lesbian character must pay in order to belong—and continue to belong—to his or her community of friends and family of origin.

The same fate befalls Jaret and Peggy in *Happy Endings Are All Alike* as the community the two have grown up in turns hostile when their relationship is discovered by Mid, the deranged stalker who rapes Jaret. And the police investigating the rape are confident that *they* know that the townspeople will turn against any lesbian in their midst, even a battered rape victim, regardless of her former insider status as a popular girl and high school achiever.

Thus, in the context of the other books from the 1970s, Rees's *In the Tent* is all the more remarkable. As the story begins, Tim is a lonely teen who copes with his romantic feelings toward a straight friend through daydreams and self-isolation, but Tim's isolation ends when he and another boy, Ray, come out to each other in the course of a camping trip. Ray tells Tim about a gay newspaper he's seen with an ad for a gay pub. Tim asks, "Why do you want to go there?"

> "To meet others like us, of course. You can't live in a vacuum. . . . We can't be the only two nice decent homosexuals in the world."
> "I suppose not." He had a cheering vision of hundreds of happy uncompli-cated people enjoying themselves together, sharing each other's lives. "I sup-pose not." (106)

Following the camping trip, the two actually do visit the pub. "Last night he and Ray had visited the gay pub. They had gone in with beating hearts and nervous shivers. It turned out to be rather an anticlimax: it was so ordinary. Nothing about the people in there, apart from some fragments of conversa-tion they overheard, indicated that they were different from the rest of the world. . . . No one accosted them, though several people eyed them with a certain curiosity. There's nothing, he thought, to prevent him coming in again" (126). Tim is quietly thrilled with his new knowledge of and access to the gay/lesbian community in his own city, a discovery that—beyond his friendship with Ray—is his reward for coming out.

It is interesting to note that author David Rees, an openly gay man, was also a distinguished children's writer whose 1978 novel *The Exeter Blitz* received the Carnegie Medal, Great Britain's equivalent to the Newbery Medal. It is also interesting, though not surprising, to note that an openly gay man was the only writer of young adult fiction in the 1970s whose book is such a solid representation of queer community. But still, the friendly Eng-lish gay pub that Tim and Ray visit is not quite equivalent to a gay bar in the United States, the former being a place where teens could linger, whereas the latter is a forbidden place for minors.

In the Tent was also a significant contribution to the LGBTQ+ literature of homosexual visibility for YAs. In his struggle to come to terms with his sexuality and to come out, Tim's biggest problem is his Roman Catholicism and the attendant guilt he feels about his sexual orientation. Nevertheless, though Tim is only moderately attracted to Ray, he does find comfort in his embrace and the two become friends. And their relationship helps Tim to find self-acceptance. As he muses, "I'm coming to terms with it, slowly. The next few years will be the aftermath of civil war, mending the parts that bleed. Will I be happy? There's a chance even though growing up's so painful. There will be a time when it all slots into place, there must be. Then I shall be free; I've already chosen to be what I am, which is what I always have been" (127). It's important to note that this kind of choice is different from that which had been a fixture of American novels. Tim is not choosing to be gay but, rather, to embrace "what I have always been," that is, homosexual. It's also noteworthy that Tim's friends, unlike many of the friends in American novels of the time, are quite accepting of his homosexuality. His parents are a different story; next to his religion, his biggest problem is coming out to them.

The biggest problem for the American reader, however, may well be Rees's inclusion of a parallel story, told in flashbacks, set during the 1646 siege of Exeter in the English Civil War. This story-within-a-story is designed to expand, metaphorically, Tim's struggle with his sexuality, which he describes as a "civil war." Reinforcing this is the fact that Ray's family comes from Spain, having fled to England to escape the civil war there. This attempt to integrate the two narratively different stories is an ambitious literary device, but one that U.S. readers may find more confusing than illuminating.

* * *

Beyond the reviews of individual titles, there was little critical writing *about* LGBTQ literature published in the 1970s. The single exception we have found is an article by two librarians, Frances Hanckel and John Cunningham, both of whom were active in ALA's Gay Task Force and who later coauthored one of the earliest YA nonfiction books about homosexuality, *A Way of Love, a Way of Life: A Young Person's Guide to What It Means to Be Gay* (see chapter 10: "Young Adult Nonfiction with LGBTQ+ Content"). Their essay "Can Young Gays Find Happiness in YA Books?" appeared in the March 1976 issue of *Wilson Library Bulletin* and celebrated the appearance of four "pioneering efforts on a controversial theme": *I'll Get There, Man without a Face, Trying Hard to Hear You,* and *Sticks and Stones.* In their discussion, Hanckel and Cunningham fault these four titles for two principal reasons. The books suggest that (1) "Being gay has no lasting significance" (i.e., it's a phase) and/or (2) "[being gay] costs someone a terrible price."[16] As for the latter point, the authors reasonably ask, "In an open democratic society, why must minorities be expected to withstand extraordinary pressures?"[17] Sadly that question has yet to be answered, even more than thirty years later. But as for the former point (the "transitory" nature of homosexuality), many may find the words of the authors' argument dated. They write, "This may be fine reassurance for insecure straight youths but it cheats the ones who want to be gay by presenting such experiences as 'phases' instead of the first step toward a valid choice."[18]

However, given the social opprobrium—and worse—that LGBTQ+ youth have been subjected to, it seems unlikely that any teen would "want" to be gay. The authors' words reinforce the notion that being homosexual is a matter of conscious choice. These reservations aside, it is hard to dispute Hanckel and Cunningham's conclusions. "Where is there honesty and realism in approaching the gay experience?" they ask. And, "Where is there a life-affirming hope for a young person who knows or suspects he or she is homosexual?"[19] For answers to these questions, readers would have to wait until the next decade. And, some would claim, they are still waiting.

NOTES

1. Jan Goodman, "Out of the Closet but Paying the Price," *Interracial Books for Children Bulletin* 14, nos. 3 & 4 (1983).

2. Alan A. Cuseo, *Homosexual Characters in YA Novels: A Literary Analysis, 1969–1982* (Lanham, MD: Scarecrow, 1992).

3. Isabelle Holland, "Tilting at Taboos," in *Crosscurrents of Criticism: Horn Book Essays 1968–1977*, ed. Paul Heins (Boston: Horn Book, 1977).

4. Review of *The Man without a Face*, by Isabelle Holland, *Horn Book* 48, no. 375 (August 1972).

5. E. M. Graves, review of *The Man without a Face*, by Isabelle Holland, *Commonweal* 97, no. 157 (November 17, 1972).

6. Holland, "Tilting at Taboos," 143.

7. Sandra Scoppettone, "Some Thoughts on Censorship," in *Writers on Writing for Young Adults*, ed. Patricia E. Feehan and Pamela Petrick Barron (Detroit: Omnigraphics, 1991).

8. Ann Rinaldi, *The Good Side of My Heart* (New York: Holiday House, 1987), 272.

9. Review of *Trying Hard to Hear You*, by Sandra Scoppettone, *Booklist* 71, no. 340 (November 15, 1974).

10. David Reuben, *Everything You Always Wanted to Know about Sex but Were Afraid to Ask* (Philadelphia: David McKay, 1969).

11. Kelly Huegel, *LGBTQ: The Survival Guide for Queer and Questioning Teens* (Minneapolis, MN: Free Spirit, 2003).

12. Mary Hoffman, "Growing Up: A Survey," *Children's Literature in Education* 15, no. 3 (1984).

13. Regina Williams, *"Ruby,"* *Interracial Books for Children Bulletin* 8, no. 2 (1977).

14. Frances Hanckel and John Cunningham, "Can Young Gays Find Happiness in YA Books?" *Wilson Library Bulletin* 50, no. 7 (March 1976): 528–34.

15. Lillian Gerhardt, review of *Sticks and Stones*, by Lynn Hall, *School Library Journal* 97, no. 3813 (November 15, 1972).

16. Hanckel and Cunningham, "Can Young Gays Find Happiness?," 532.

17. Hanckel and Cunningham, "Can Young Gays Find Happiness?," 534.

18. Hanckel and Cunningham, "Can Young Gays Find Happiness?," 533.

19. Hanckel and Cunningham, "Can Young Gays Find Happiness?," 534.

Chapter Three

Young Adult Literature of the 1980s

The decade of the eighties saw an appreciable acceleration in the pace—if not necessarily the quality—of LGBTQ+ publishing. In the first year of the decade alone, a record three fiction titles addressing the subject were published (the previous record had been two), and over the next nine years, thirty-seven others would follow—four times the number in the 1970s. Ironically the increasing visibility of LGBTQ+ characters and issues coincided with a period of reaction in the larger world of young adult literature, as the pendulum swung from an emphasis on realistic—that is, hard-edged—YA fiction to a renascence of forties-style romance. However, with the notable exception of *Annie on My Mind*, romance remained largely absent from LGBTQ+ fiction.

Unfortunately, of the forty titles published in the eighties, only seven would offer notable contributions to the field in terms of thematic innovation or elevation of literary quality: *Annie on My Mind* by Nancy Garden; *Dance on My Grave* by Aidan Chambers; *Night Kites* by M. E. Kerr; *The Arizona Kid* by Ron Koertge; *Weetzie Bat* by Francesca Lia Block; *Jack* by A. M. Homes; and *In the Tent* by David Rees (its first U.S. edition appeared in 1985). Also worth noting is that of the thirty-seven titles published in the 1980s, only ten (27 percent) included lesbian characters, while twenty-seven (73 percent) featured male homosexual characters. One might expect the gender bias in this body of literature to become less pronounced over time, but in this case there was actually a greater imbalance in the 1980s than the 1970s, when three of the nine titles (33 percent) with LGBTQ content featured female characters. Regardless of innovation or gender of the protagonist, homosexual visibility (i.e., coming out and related issues) remained the single most important focus of LGBTQ literature in the eighties. Though the titles of the eighties varied widely in literary quality, many remain historically important for having introduced new themes, types, and approaches that would become characteristic of this developing genre. Indeed, our chief focus in this chapter will be on those books that were—for their time—innovative.

BOOKS FROM BRITAIN

Another 1980s innovation was the appearance of American editions of LGBTQ+ books that had first been published in England. Three British writers—David Rees (whose *In the Tent* is discussed in the previous chapter), Aidan Chambers, and Jean Ure—emerged as significant figures in the 1980s. Of the three, Chambers is the writer of the greatest lasting importance; indeed, his later novel, *Postcards from No Man's Land*, which also explores considerations of sexual identity, was awarded both England's Carnegie Medal and the American Library Association's Michael L. Printz Award as being the book "that best exemplifies literary excellence in young adult literature."

It is Rees, however, who was the first to write fiction for young readers that included homosexuals and homosexuality. Like Chambers, Rees was both a novelist and a literary critic. Before his death in 1993 from AIDS, he published nearly two dozen works of fiction for both adult and young adult readers. This habit of writing for two different readerships has resulted in some confusion over which of his four novels about homosexuality were actually written for adolescents. In our estimation only two, *In the Tent* (discussed in the previous chapter) and *The Milkman's on His Way* (1982), were intended by the author to speak to this readership. The other two—*Out of the Winter Gardens* (1984) and *The Colour of His Hair* (1989)—have, by virtue of their older teen narrative perspective and the details of their sexual content, been considered adult titles by reviewers, but fans of David Rees have certainly included teens. All four titles feature gay males who seek—and find—a visible queer community; *The Milkman's on His Way* is described in the section below on books with QC content.

Aidan Chambers's *Dance on My Grave* was first published in the United States in 1982. The author's intentions to experiment with his narrative strategies and techniques are announced on the title page in the form of the book's extravagant subtitle: "A Life and a Death/in Four Parts/One Hundred and Seventeen Bits/Six Running Reports/and Two Press Clippings/with a few jokes/a puzzle or three/some footnotes/and a fiasco now and then/to help the story along."

Dance on My Grave is the history of the friendship of two boys: Hal, the narrator, and Barry, who will die in a motorcycle accident, but not before they have become lovers. The title is a reference to a pact they make before

Barry's accident: the survivor must dance on the other's grave. This Hal does and, being discovered in the act, which is regarded as grave desecration, he is arrested and brought to court, where the judge orders him to be counseled by a social worker. The worker's findings are presented as the "six running reports" of the subtitle. As for the one hundred and seventeen bits, they refer to Hal's brief, first-person chapters that comprise the bulk of the narrative and are, indeed, divided into four parts. The book is bracketed, front and back, by two newspaper clippings with the respective headlines, "Grave Damage" and "Youth's Pact 'To Dance on Friend's Grave.'" All of these disparate bits, pieces, and occasional oddments come together in a cleverly coherent structure that Chambers describes as "collages of different ways of telling."[1]

Whether assemblage or collage, the technique reveals not only a great deal about the author's cerebral approach to narration but also about his protagonist, Hal. Barry recognizes that Hal is obsessed with understanding: "That's what you always want, isn't it? To understand" (152). Hal's way of achieving understanding is akin to Chambers's: he must translate his experiences into story. (Chambers states, "Until we have re-formed our lives into story-structured words, we cannot find and contemplate the meaning of our lived experiences.")[2] In order to effect that re-formation, Hal conveys a sense of circling events, examining and reexamining them by evoking memories. His life and his words seem to be an exercise in continuous circumambulation, his circles becoming ever tighter until, finally, he arrives at the essential eureka moment of understanding.

In the meantime his style of storytelling remains consciously self-conscious, hence, that long, almost whimsical subtitle. His style extends to his manner of speaking, which his social worker describes thus: "Throughout the conversation he avoided questions he didn't like by giving flippant replies—sometimes genuinely funny" (24). Like many teenagers, Hal uses humor as a distancing device. And this accounts for the jokes, puzzles, footnotes, and self-conscious reference to "a fiasco now and then."

If *Dance on My Grave* is a story of Hal's obsessive need to understand, it is also about his obsessions with friendship and death, both of which are realized in the person of Barry. Barry's death has been criticized as being another example of the "punishment" of homosexuals that was epidemic in the early years of the genre. But this equation is simplistic. Hal's obsession with death predates his friendship with Barry, who, at one point, says to his friend, "You have death on the brain" (86). This obsession begins when Hal is thirteen and is taken to visit a family grave (a scene that is echoed, some years later, in Chambers's novel *Postcards from No Man's Land*). Barry's life and death become an organic, even inevitable part of the evolution of Hal's obsessive interest in death—and, indeed, in friendship, in memory and in the past, a connection that is made when he and Barry go to see a production of *Hamlet*. Barry comments on the sadness of Hamlet's inability to remember his father; Hal, knowing that Barry's own father is dead, realizes his friend is talking about himself. But the reader will understand that this exchange can also be read as a reference to Barry's ultimate death and Hal's reaction to it.

The complexity of the novel extends to its treatment of homosexuality, which seems to be an admixture of love and sex, of power and submission, of obsession and compulsion, of elation and despair, of one thing and another, of certainty . . . and uncertainty. "Maybe I loved him," Hal muses. "How do you ever know?" (155).

In the richness of its content, in its use of ambiguity and symbol, in the maturity of its uncertainty, *Dance on My Grave* was a significant advance in the evolution of LGBTQ+ fiction for young adults. It was the first literary novel about homosexuality that, in its artistic ambitions and achievements, remained unrivaled until Francesca Lia Block's *Weetzie Bat* (1989) and Chambers's own later novel, *Postcards from No Man's Land* (2002).

The third English writer under consideration, Jean Ure, wrote two gay-themed novels that found American publication in the 1980s: *You Win Some, You Lose Some* (1984) and *The Other Side of the Fence* (1986). Her books are two of the few examples of gay assimilation titles published during the 1980s and are described in that context under the "Gay Assimilation" heading below.

THE ADVENT OF AIDS

The decade of the eighties was notable for the appearance of AIDS (acquired immune deficiency syndrome), which emerged—like a demon from the darkness—in 1981. Though in the early years of the disease its chief victims were homosexuals, hemophiliacs, and others who acquired it through being given tainted blood, AIDS quickly spread to the heterosexual population, including both men and women, achieving widespread public recognition with the 1985 announcement that the well-known actor Rock Hudson had been infected.

Though teenagers—gay and straight—were definitely at risk from the beginning, AIDS was not mentioned in young adult fiction until 1986, when M. E. Kerr courageously wrote her haunting novel *Night Kites*. She admitted in her 1993 Margaret Edwards Award speech that she felt she was committing a form of professional suicide by writing the book, since the disease in her novel is sexually transmitted to a young gay man, not to a straight hemophiliac who had received tainted blood or to a heterosexual drug abuser who had used an infected needle. Why her concern? Let Kerr herself answer that question: "It seemed to me that not to have a homosexual be the AIDS sufferer would be a way of saying I'll recognize the illness but not those who have it . . . a sort of don't ask/don't tell proposition, where the reader can know the nature of the plague, without having to deal with those personalities who threaten the status quo."[3]

The AIDS-infected, status-quo-threatening character in the Kerr novel is Pete, the twenty-seven-year-old brother of the teenage protagonist, Erick. Pete discloses both his homosexuality and his HIV-positive status to his family at the same time, a devastating one-two punch that was not an uncommon pattern then . . . and now. Erick is surprised, since his brother is nothing like "poor Charlie Gilhooley" (the novel is set in Seaville, New York, and Charlie, who first appears in Kerr's earlier *I'll Love You When You're More Like Me*, is still the town's "resident gay"). Pete tartly asks, "Do I get extra points for not looking it [gay]?" (94). Surprise aside, Erick accepts his brother's homosexuality with—for a male teen—refreshing equanimity, telling their father, "It's just another way of being. It's not a crime; it's not anything to be ashamed about" (91). The father's reaction is more typical of the time: he insists this be kept a secret from everybody outside the immediate family. Ultimately, of course, the secret will leak out and, as a result, Erick's girlfriend will leave him. To his great credit, Erick doesn't blame Pete; indeed, his illness brings the two brothers closer together. The book ends on a bittersweet note with the two brothers discussing—in the context of something Pete has written—the end of things, a tacit acknowledgment that AIDS, at that time at least, was virtually always fatal.

Following the publication of *Night Kites*, the silence that had surrounded the disease gradually became less pervasive, as AIDS began to be mentioned in passing, almost always in the context of fear or the need to practice safe sex; nevertheless, it would receive major thematic or topical treatment in only three other YA novels in the eighties. In Gloria Miklowitz's *Good-Bye Tomorrow* (Delacorte, 1987), the HIV-positive character is a heterosexual teenage boy who has been infected by a blood transfusion. In Ron Koertge's *The Arizona Kid* (described below) the infected characters are all gay adults. Lastly, in Francesca Lia Block's *Weetzie Bat* (1989), the disease is present but never referred to by name, a device that, in a way, makes it an even darker, more menacing presence. AIDS becomes a factor late in the novel when Duck, Dirk's lover, disappears, leaving a note saying that his friend Bam-Bam is sick, and asking the plaintive question, "Even though we're okay, how can anyone love anyone when you could kill them just by loving them?" (80).

Bereft, Dirk goes on a quest to find his friend, whom he finally locates in San Francisco. Duck asks, "How did you find me?" And Dirk tellingly replies, "I don't know. But you are in my blood" (85). AIDS, of course, is transmitted by the exchange of body fluids, including blood. To invoke the word "blood" in this context is to remind the reader that love, too, is in one's blood and therefore is as essential to life as blood, even though, as Dirk reflects, "Love is a dangerous angel. Especially nowadays" (84).

Although we will return to this topic in the next chapter, the reader will find an even more comprehensive discussion and analysis of AIDS literature in Virginia A. Walter and Melissa Gross's *HIV/AIDS Information for Children: A Guide to Issues and Resources*[4] and in Gross's subsequent journal article "What Do Young Adult Novels Say about HIV/AIDS?"[5]

GAY/LESBIAN PARENTS AND FAMILY MEMBERS

In the first year of the decade, Norma Klein's *Breaking Up* (1980) became the first YA novel to feature a clearly gay parent. It is not surprising that Klein, the author of nearly two dozen novels for young adults, should have been an innovator. Her first book for young readers was the groundbreaking *Mom, the Wolfman and Me* (Knopf, 1972), a story told in the voice of eleven-year-old Brett, a girl who has been raised by her single mother and has never met her biological father—he is, in fact, unaware of her existence. But Brett's "problem" is not her fatherlessness—how can you miss what you've never had?—but rather the possible changes in her hitherto pleasant and predictable life when "the wolfman" (Brett's friendly nickname for her mother's boyfriend, who owns an Irish wolfhound) moves in with them. Forty-five years later, this seems a bit tame, but at the time many adults were shocked to encounter a happy, well-adjusted child of a never-married mother in a book intended for young readers.

In the years before Klein's untimely death in 1989, she became an increasingly vocal advocate for making the sometimes uncomfortable truths of teen lives visible on the page, once writing, "What is shameful in life is concealment and distortion and evasion, not truth."[6] In *Breaking Up*, Alison lives in New York City with her older brother, her mother, and her mother's partner, Peggy. When the children spend the summer in California with their newly remarried father, it becomes evident to Dad that Mom and Peggy are more than "just good friends." Ali muses, "I thought about Mom and Peggy. It did seem strange in a way but not that strange. Maybe it was because Mom is such a regular sort of person, not that far-out or weird in any way, so it seems like anything she would do seems okay. I wonder if Mom loves Peggy more than she used to love Daddy when she loved him" (180–81). In fact, the father's reaction is far less salutary than Ali's. "Everything about this is odd," he says (95) and later tells his daughter, "You're old enough to realize that raising children in a household with two homosexual women isn't exactly some kind of ideal" (102).

"If Mom is gay," Ali asks, "how come you married her?"

"She wasn't when I married her," he replies (142).

Despite his continuing—and often bitter—reservations, the father finally agrees to permit his daughter to return to New York to live with those "two homosexual women." Ali reports, "The odd thing is, nothing seems very different. I thought now that I know about Mom and Peggy, I would notice things I hadn't before, but I don't" (163).

Klein returned to this theme in her 1988 novel *Now That I Know*. Once again a teenage female protagonist learns that a parent is gay, though this time it's the father. But thirteen-year-old Nina does not react as well as Ali. "In a sadistic way I wanted to hurt him. I felt like he'd hurt me" (78). Later, she adds, "I hope he and Greg [his lover] die in their sleep" (83). Ultimately, however, Nina comes around, helped in part by the discovery that her new boyfriend's brother is also gay and by her cathartic confession to her father that she is afraid he will get AIDS. The father's answer—intended by Klein to be reassuring—is actually a dangerous bit of misinformation. "Neens," he says, "the sad, dull fact is that I'm a monogamous guy. I was with Jean [his ex-wife] and now I am with Greg" (162). What isn't mentioned, of course, is Greg's sexual history and the fact that the father is not only having sex with his partner but also in effect with everyone else his partner has ever been intimate with. Aside from this misinformation—and the improbable fact that in both books the straight parent is as startled as the teen protagonist to learn of his or her former spouse's homosexuality—Klein's examination of gay parents is sympathetic, though the situation is treated, perhaps too clinically, as one of several "problems" or "issues" the protagonist must resolve.

Happily, love is much more clearly an integral part of the same-sex relationships that parents launch in the two other novels from the eighties that explore this subject: George Shannon's *Unlived Affections* and A. M. Homes's *Jack*, both published in 1989. In the former, Willie—an eighteen-year-old boy who has been raised by his recently deceased grandmother—discovers a cache of letters from his father, whom he has never known, to his mother, who died when the boy was two. Reading them, Willie, discovers his father was gay. "I can't love you the way you should be loved by a husband," the man writes to his wife, "I love you, you have to believe that, like a friend, my best friend, but not like a lover. I love men" (67). Later, the father will write, "I finally told Evan that I loved him and hoped he had feelings for me. . . . Being with him feels so bright and alive, so safe and warm that making love is the truest thing to do no matter what anybody else says" (108–9). Willie's initial reaction is to mutter, "Damn queers," but he immediately repents and is glad "no one had heard him. . . . Willie had lived too much of his father's life through the letters to dismiss him like that" (108). The boy ultimately comes to terms with his new knowledge, telling his girlfriend, "He loved my mom but he was . . . gay." And there is a suggestion, at book's end, that he plans to seek out and get to know his father.

The latter novel (i.e., *Jack*) is not only the most substantial treatment of having a gay parent in the body of the literature, it is also one of the most engaging. Amazingly, it was written when Homes was only "19 or 20." Finished in 1985, the book didn't see print for four years, however, because "more than one publisher wondered how to position this novel." The author had no doubts, though, telling *Publishers Weekly*, "It's a novel for every-body."[7] Ultimately Macmillan would publish it as a YA title and Vintage would publish it in paperback as an adult title. (The same thing happened seven years later when Simon & Schuster published Michael Cart's gay coming-of-age novel *My Father's Scar* as a YA novel and St. Martin's subsequently reissued it in paperback as an adult book.) In fact, like Frances-ca Lia Block's *Weetzie Bat*, which was published the same year, *Jack* is one of the first "crossover" novels, those books with intrinsic multigenerational appeal that became a fixture of YA literature in the mid- to late nineties.

It is also squarely in the tradition of J. D. Salinger's *The Catcher in the Rye*, for the eponymous protagonist, Jack, who tells the story in his own first-person voice, sounds remarkably like Salinger's Holden Caulfield, only less disturbed and (arguably) nicer. Jack is also a character who evokes different responses from this text's two authors: Michael finds him likable, even charming; Christine sees him as a clueless loudmouth whom Holden would have scorned.

Jack is fifteen when his divorced father rows him out into the middle of a lake to tell him . . . something. "As soon as we were out there in the middle of nothing, he started getting the look fathers get when they're about to say something they know is gonna make you lose your lunch" (18). Jack doesn't receive the news of his father's homosexuality gladly. "It makes me sick, seriously," he tells his mother's live-in boyfriend Michael. "My father's a fucking faggot." Michael, an appealingly laid-back ex-hippie, replies, "Jack, just because your father is gay is no reason for you to be dramatic. It doesn't mean anything."

Jack: "They're queer [his dad and his dad's new lover]. I mean, it's not the normal thing."

Michael wisely replies, "Who's to say what's normal?" (28–29).

Word about Jack's father soon gets out and the boy discovers that some-one has painted the word "faggot" on his locker. Worse, other kids soon start calling him "fag baby." Jack, who finds this maddening but not life threaten-ing, is somewhat mollified when he discovers that his new girlfriend Maggie also has a gay father (this sounds contrived but, as Homes artfully presents it, it's not). The boy's appreciation of his gentle father is also heightened when he discovers that the straight father of his best friend is battering his wife.

What makes this book so memorable is that it tells the truth with welcome humor and without melodrama. With the exception of the brutish wife batter-er, there are no villains here, just human beings who are trying to find out who they are and how to cope with what they find. The characters are complex and sympathetic, and they react in believable, authentically human ways. Moreover, the author shows the impact of the father's being gay not only on Jack but on his whole family. The book is vastly more than a one-issue novel.

Another of the best books of the eighties, Ron Koertge's *The Arizona Kid* (1988) features not a homosexual parent but an uncle. Given the stereotypical place in popular culture of the gay-uncle-about-whom-we're-not-supposed-to-speak, it's surprising that it was not until 1988 that a homosexual uncle should have appeared as a character in a YA novel. Fortunately the uncle in Ron Koertge's *The Arizona Kid* is anything but a stereotype. In this memorable novel, sixteen-year-old Billy heads to Tucson, Arizona, to spend the summer with his uncle Wes, his father's brother, whom he's never met but has long known is gay. Billy—straight and from a small town in the Midwest—has some initial reservations about living with "somebody who was really different from me. Somebody who was homosexual. Believe me, I hadn't told anyone in Bradleyville High School. They just wouldn't have understood" (13). Arriving in Arizona, Billy quickly realizes he's not in Missouri any more. "In Bradleyville, most people thought gay men were diseased Commies and here my uncle got his picture in the paper" (44).

It turns out that Uncle Wes, who, Billy says, "might have been the best-looking guy I'd ever seen outside of the movies," is a prominent local citizen and an AIDS activist. The two hit it off immediately, though Billy still has to get past some stereotypical thinking. When Uncle Wes fixes him breakfast, the boy thinks, "I wanted to ask him if he could cook because he was gay or if he was gay because he could cook. But that seemed stupid, barely a notch above, 'Hey, so how's it feel to be queer, huh?' Dad had said to just be cool about it" (14). And Billy does a good job of that. When an obnoxious fellow employee at the racetrack where Billy works jeers, "You've got a gay uncle—what does that make you?" Billy coolly replies, "His nephew" (39).

As this implies, though Tucson may not be Bradleyville, it is not without prejudice and the threat of homophobic violence. When Uncle Wes attends a public healing service for AIDS patients, for example, a carload of men follow him home, throw a beer can at his house, and taunt him with cries of "You fucking faggots" and "You dirty cocksuckers."

"Another opening, another show," Uncle Wes calmly says to Billy as he closes the door on them (71). AIDS is presented as a fact of life—and death, as one of Uncle Wes's friends dies in the course of the book. And Wes responds to the news of his friend's death by coming home drunk and then vomiting—to Billy's bemusement.

"I hate for you to see me like this," the man groans.

"I'm just surprised you throw up like everybody else," Billy replies. "Knowing you, I thought it'd come out gift-wrapped" (107).

Uncle Wes is himself sexually active—arguably the first time an adult gay character is depicted thus—but is careful to practice safe sex and tells Billy, who is falling in love with Cara Mae, that he must, too. But this is presented as an integral part of the story, nondidactically and with humor. When Uncle Wes comes home from a date, for example, Billy asks, "Will you not get mad if I ask you something?"

Uncle Wes: "Who knows."

Billy: "Do you kiss these guys?"

Uncle Wes: "Sometimes."

Billy: "Yuk."

Uncle Wes: "Do you kiss Cara Mae?"

Billy: "Well, sure."

Uncle Wes: "Yuk." (151)

Compassionate, principled, and funny, Uncle Wes is a memorable character and just like anybody else—only handsomer, smarter, funnier, and more successful. More importantly, though, he is a happy, fulfilled human being, though often heartsick, like all men of compassion and conscience, as he faces the ever-present specter of AIDS. He is, in short, what had been all too absent from LGBTQ+ literature to this point: a viable role model for young homosexuals and, come to think of it, for all young people.

GAY EDUCATORS AND MENTORS

The second year of the decade saw another innovation when Gary Barger introduced the first working gay teacher in YA literature in his novel *What Happened to Mr. Forster?* (Clarion, 1981). Since teachers are typically among the first nonfamilial adults most young people encounter, it's surprising that they did not figure in LGBTQ+ fiction until the 1980s when, in addition to Mr. Forster, four other novels included homosexual educators as characters (*Call Me Margo, Annie on My Mind, Just the Right Amount of Wrong,* and *Big Man and the Burn-Out*).

Set in Kansas City in 1958, Barger's novel is the story of an effeminate sixth-grade boy named Louis, who is called "Billy Lou" by his aunt Zona, with whom he lives, and by everyone at the Louisa May Alcott Elementary School. Well, everyone but his new teacher, Mr. Forster, who calls him Louis and helps him develop his talent as a writer. Unfortunately Mr. Forster, a "high church Anglican," antagonizes a number of parents because of his liberal attitudes, and when people learn that he lives with his "best friend," a whispering campaign ensues and Mr. Forster is "called away." Louis is devastated when a classmate, Veronica, explains, "Mr. Forster wasn't 'called away,' he was fired. And everybody knows why" (152). Even Louis's best friend Paul says with a sigh, "Well, God, Louis. Okay, Mr. Forster is a nice man. He's even a pretty good teacher, as teachers go. But after all, he is a queer" (168).

Reluctant to accept this, Louis visits his ex-teacher, who acknowledges that he is, indeed, homosexual.

"But how can you just quit teaching?" the boy demands.

"Oh, Louis," the teacher replies, "Sometimes we have to do things we don't want to do. Of course, I don't want to quit teaching. But in this situation I have no choice. The decision has been made for me" (162).

Unfortunately but predictably, the homosexual teacher as victim or who quietly accepts his or her fate became somewhat of a fixture of YA literature. Even in Nancy Garden's otherwise exemplary *Annie on My Mind*, two teachers are fired when it is revealed they are lesbian lovers and, instead of contesting their termination, they go gently into that good night of early retirement. This compromises their viability as otherwise sympathetic role models, but it also reflects the very real problems that gay teachers faced in the 1980s—and which many gay teachers continue to face today.

For example, in 1984 David E. Wilson, a teacher at Kirkwood Community College in Cedar Rapids, Iowa, published an article titled "The Open Library: YA Books for Gay Teens" in *English Journal*. The article was a sympathetic but hardly incendiary call for more novels that "gay young adults" can look to, "hoping to find answers and positive role models."[8]

Two years later, Wilson published a second article in *EJ* in which he described the consequences of the first. "My phone rings. It's the principal of the private high school where only two weeks earlier I had accepted a teaching position. I hadn't yet signed a contract. 'I have to inform you that the job is no longer available,' he says. 'I'm sorry but we won't be needing your services.'" Subsequently he pursues two other job offers. "Both schools—which formerly courted me—now refuse to write or take my calls. Finally, an administrator from one confides in a mutual friend, 'We'll never touch him after that article.'"[9]

A year earlier, the editors of the *Interracial Books for Children Bulletin* noted (perhaps wryly?) that Jan Goodman, Boston-area teacher and author of the article cited in chapter 2 on stereotypes of gay/lesbian characters in young adult books had decided "in a sudden burst of lesbian pride and affirmation . . . to sign her actual name to this article instead of her usual pseudonym."[10] New York City high school teacher Carol Bloom, author of another article in the same issue, "Getting Books on Gay Themes into the

Library: An Action Plan," also used her real name to write about her modest efforts to broaden the scope her school's library collection by donating twelve books with LGBTQ+ content to the school's library. A New York tabloid caught wind of her efforts, and she was featured in a sensational article that framed her "action plan" as a blueprint for subverting—even perverting—the educational role of the library by make such books available to high school students. The furor eventually died down, but not before Ms. Bloom faced a real threat of dismissal. Other gay and lesbian educators have wrestled with similar dilemmas regarding openness, as Rita M. Kissen demonstrated in her thoughtful—and sometimes heartbreaking—1996 book, *The Last Closet*, about "the real lives of lesbian and gay teachers."[11]

The danger of being a gay teacher is dramatically illustrated in Alice Childress's 1989 novel *Those Other People,* in which a young and closeted gay teacher is blackmailed and finally resigns his position (see below for a further discussion of this book). Another depiction of gay educators as pathetic losers is found in Judith St. George's *Call Me Margo* (1981), which presents the dismal case of Miss Frye and Miss Durrett, lesbian teachers who are two halves of a former couple and definitely not people one would want teaching children of any age. Miss Frye, a tennis coach, is friendly and attractive but abuses her position of authority to get close to girls; Miss Durrett, an English teacher, is a disagreeable shrew who is described as being "very crippled. In fact, she wore braces on both her thin, misshapen legs and large orthopedic shoes" (33). Not since the man without a face has sexual identity been branded with such an unfortunate symbolic presentation.

In light of this, the presence, in Clayton Bess's 1985 novel *Big Man and the Burn-Out*, of an openly gay male teacher, who not only doesn't lose his job but is presented as a hero, may seem almost like wish fulfillment. However, in this story of a boy named Jess struggling to find his sexual identity, the presence of a positive adult role model, whose homosexuality is not an issue but is simply presented as part of his larger identity, is a refreshing change and a template for the future treatment of such characters. As an early example of gay assimilation literature, it is the first of several LGBTQ YA novels in which the reader is provided with more insight about a character's sexuality than is the protagonist him- or herself.

Seven other homosexual adults appear in novels of the eighties. In Marilyn Levy's *Come Out Smiling* (1981), the gay character is a counselor/riding instructor at a posh girls' summer camp. In Larry Hulse's *Just the Right Amount of Wrong* (1982), not one but two adults are secretly gay: the school principal and the local sheriff (who murders the principal to protect his secret!). In Catherine Brett's *S.P. Likes A.D.* (1989), an adult lesbian couple helps the protagonist create a challenging art project while providing a model for a same-sex adult relationship. In Madeleine L'Engle's *A House Like a Lotus* (1984), Polly, the young protagonist, is shocked by a rumor that dear family friends Maximiliana (Max) and Ursula are a lesbian couple. And in Carolyn Meyer's *Elliott and Win* (1986), a possibly gay man serves as an Amigo (read: Big Brother) to a fatherless boy. Two of these characters— Elliott and Max—are intriguingly memorable.

Fourteen-year-old Win's first meeting with his new Amigo Elliott begins inauspiciously as Elliott serves him a kid-unfriendly lunch of gazpacho followed by a dessert of cheese and walnuts. Win is dismayed to learn that Elliott—a confirmed bachelor, gourmet cook, and opera lover—hates baseball and organized sports and (to Win's horror) doesn't even *own* a television set. But is Elliott really gay? There is no doubt in the mind of Win's cretinous friend Paul, who warns, "You hang around with a faggot, people are going to start thinking you're a faggot, too. What do you think a confirmed bachelor is, anyway?" (27–28).

Of course, in an act of convenient authorial contrivance, it is not Elliott but Paul's divorced father who is revealed as being gay. Elliott's sexual identity is never specified, the point of this well-intentioned but didactic book being that it shouldn't make a difference. And of course it shouldn't, though Michael found Elliott to be the most annoyingly self-important adult figure this side of Justin McLeod. Christine, on the other hand, was impressed by Elliott's warm compassion in helping Win deal with the trauma of witnessing—but being unable to stop—the assault and rape of his friend Heather.

And then there is Madeleine L'Engle's *A House Like a Lotus*. The protagonist narrator is Polly, the sixteen-year-old daughter of Meg and Calvin O'Keefe, who readers may have met as protagonists in L'Engle's Newbery Award–winning *A Wrinkle in Time*. Although intelligent and mature, Polly is suffering the pangs of adolescent gawkiness and feels "out of it" with her high school peers. Then along comes Maximiliana, a world-famous painter friend of the O'Keefes, who lives nearby with Ursula, her companion of thirty years (and a world-famous brain surgeon). Max takes Polly under her wing, and her friendship gives Polly confidence and self-appreciation. But Max appears ill and is in fact dying. She has kept her condition a secret, but Polly guesses the truth. And Max has another secret as well—she and Ursula are lovers. The story then veers into a southern gothic tale of passion and betrayal: Max uses alcohol to dull her physical pain, and one dark and stormy night she makes a drunken pass at Polly, who flees barefoot into the rain and injures her foot. When Polly heads to town to get her foot taken care of, she ends up at the very hospital built by Max's lecherous father and named for Max's delicate sister who died young from the pneumonia she contracted while fleeing (barefoot, no doubt) into the rain to avoid her father's sexual advances . . . and so on. In the end Max makes elaborate amends and Polly is finally able to accept Max as the flawed-but-beautiful person she is. The author advocates tolerance, at least up to a point (as Polly's father Calvin declares, "I thought it was now agreed that consenting adults were not to be persecuted, *particular if they keep their private lives private*" [emphasis added; 111]), but L'Engle's portrayal of gayness is an odd one indeed. Max explains to Polly that she herself is a lesbian because she couldn't forgive her father for her sister's death. And Ursula is a lesbian because she is a brain surgeon (no, really—"Ursula is the way she is. She's competed in a man's world, in a man's field. There are not many women neurosurgeons" [120]). But Max—with her midnight-black hair and silver-gray eyes outlined in kohl—is unquestionably an intriguing character, and readers may well remember this charismatic mentor long after they've forgotten the unlikely plot and Polly's irritating penchant for demonstrating her "amazing innocence" (120)—and her heterosexuality—at every turn.

LGBTQ+ YOUNG ADULTS

The eighties also saw increasing numbers of LGBTQ+ teens as secondary characters. Of the nearly sixty LGBTQ+—more often, questioning—characters in the novels of the eighties, thirty-seven are young adults. However, only ten of the thirty-seven are protagonists, with the balance being the protagonists' friends (twenty-one), boyfriends (four), or older brothers (two). This trend of placing a certain distance between the teen protagonist and the story's LGBTQ+ content serves to both broaden and narrow the scope of LGBTQ+ YA literature. On the one hand, this distance allows a YA novel (which is, after all, a story told from a teen perspective) to include gay/lesbian characters of various ages, backgrounds, and relationships to the protagonist. Thus we have gay/lesbian parents, teachers, older brothers, and mentors. One the other hand, this has meant that most of the teen protagonists in the novels of the 1980s have been heterosexual, so the reader is usually seeing that character at a remove from the protagonist. What these numbers seem to suggest is that it was much easier (safer?) for authors in the eighties to include LGBTQ+ characters as secondary characters. This distancing may also further isolate LGBTQ+ teen readers (though, in this chronological context, one might as well drop the "B" and the "T" altogether, since bisexuality would not be treated until M. E. Kerr's 1997 novel *"Hello," I Lied* and transgender issues would not be addressed until the 2004 publication of Julie Anne Peters's *Luna*). One is tempted to suggest that the "L" could be dropped, too, since after 1984, only three adolescent characters are lesbians (and one of those is secondary). And in the eight novels published between 1980 and 1984 that did, even marginally, deal with female sexuality, only one, *Annie on My Mind*, treated it positively.

Six of the eight that include lesbian characters are so similar they might be carbon copies. All six—*Bouquets for Brimbal* by J. P. Reading (1980),

The Last of Eden by Stephanie Tolan (1980), *Crush* by Jane Futcher (1981), *Come Out Smiling* by Elizabeth Levy (1981), *Call Me Margo* by Judith St. George (1981), and *Flick* by Janice Kesselman (1983)—feature white female upper-middle-class protagonists, most of whom attend posh private schools (or, in the case of Levy's novel, a posh girls' summer camp). And in virtually all, the treatment of sexuality is foggy once it proceeds past the first kiss. While this lack of sexual detail is evident throughout most YA literature, fictional gays and lesbians seem to have exceptionally limited sex lives. Too, the consensus seems to be that homosexuality is a phase, a crush, a passing fancy. As a "wise" teacher tells Michelle ("Mike"), the protagonist of *The Last of Eden*, who has had a crush on another girl, Marty, "The only thing we know for certain is that some kind of homosexual experience, sometimes it's physical, sometimes psychological, is natural—'normal,' Mike—during adolescence. It's a part of figuring out who you are, a first step with someone like yourself, before you take the chance of reaching out to the other sex" (151–52). Like all of the novels of the 1980s featuring gay/lesbian parents, all of the above-named titles exemplify the theme of homosexual visibility, in which a character's homosexuality is revealed, a transformation that invariably shocks the teen protagonist.

HOMOSEXUAL VISIBILITY

Typically the girls who are undergoing these rite-of-passage experiences are deeply conflicted about their feelings. Jenny Mandel in *Come Out Smiling*, for example, is horrified to discover that her camp counselor Peggy, on whom she has a major crush, is a lesbian. "Did this whole thing mean I was a lesbian?" she agonizes. "It might be normal to have crushes, but it was definitely not normal to have a crush on a lesbian. I had to be queer. I could see my whole life ahead of me. I'd never get married. I'd die all alone. Maybe I would kill myself instead" (126). Jinx, in *Crush*, frets, "Maybe everyone was partly queer and just didn't call it that. They called it having a crush" (255).

Jinx's crush is on a girl named Lexie Yves, a manipulative beauty who charms and seduces her, but then slides out of trouble with school authorities by blaming the two girls' escapades on Jinx's "unnatural" affection for her. Unfortunately, Lexie's "pretty poison" temptress persona set the pattern in these books for the worldly and seductive young women who lead their naïve and trusting friends astray. Like Daphne in Rosa Guy's *Ruby*, they are domineering, self-absorbed, and cruelly capricious in dispensing their emotional largesse. Consider the eponymous *Flick* in Wendy Kesselman's novel, who might be Lexie's even more evil twin. She summarily dumps Nana, the one and only protagonist in this suite of novels who actually considers herself a lesbian. Bereft and alone at the novel's end, Nana masochistically muses, "I close my eyes and a longing sweeps over me. And I think of Flick, as I know I shall always think of her, the night we leaped down the dune and dove into the sea, the night she found a long gray stick and wrote our names deep in the sand" (136).

But what does it actually mean to be a lesbian—aside from being left to drown in a sea of loneliness? Jinx, who has been ordered to see a psychiatrist, reports, "It has to do with sexual feelings. If you have *sexual* feelings for a girl, then it's more like being lesbian" (221). This simplistic equation of homosexuality and the physical act of sex is reinforced by the fact that three adult lesbians in these books—Miss Frye and Miss Durrett in *Call Me Margo* and Maximiliana in *A House Like a Lotus*—are depicted as being sexual predators.

And it is neatly summarized in this typical exchange from J. P. Reading's 1980 novel *Bouquets for Brimbal*. Macy and her boyfriend Don are talking about Macy's discovery that her best friend, Annie Brimbal, is a lesbian. Don asks, "You can't feel being gay is 'wrong' or 'bad,' can you?"

"I don't know," Macy replies. "I've never really thought of it in terms of actual people. Or as if it were love, a deep feeling, you know? I just think about sex and being 'queer.' Loose-jointed decorators and big butchy girls with mustaches who wear leather jackets. I've just never thought of 'gay' in terms of caring" (164). So what, in the context of these novels, did it mean to be a lesbian? Apparently it is simply a matter of same-sex physical intimacy, so there is little same-sex emotional intimacy happening anywhere that the protagonist—and by extension the reader—can see it.

Happily, a vastly more balanced and emotionally eloquent definition is offered by Nancy Garden in her 1982 novel—and now acknowledged classic—*Annie on My Mind*. Liza Winthrop and Annie Kenyon are seventeen when they first meet at New York's Metropolitan Museum of Art. Though the girls feel an instant kinship, the evolution of that bond into expressed feelings of love takes place gradually, naturally, and plausibly—even to the uncertainty the first time they kiss. Liza, who is the first-person narrator, describes her feelings: "It was like a war inside me; I couldn't even recognize all the sides. There was one that said, 'No, this is wrong; you know it's wrong and bad and sinful,' and there was another that said it was happening too fast, and another that just wanted to stop thinking altogether and fling my arms around Annie and hold her forever" (93). As it will later and more powerfully, Liza's heart wins this tug-of-war and she stammers, "Annie, I think I love you." And immediately she thinks, "The moment the words were out, I knew more than I'd ever known that they were true" (94).

But does this mean she's homosexual? At first, Liza is uncertain. She's never consciously thought about being gay, though it turns out Annie has. But she senses Liza's confusion and writes her a note saying that it wouldn't be fair to influence her, to try to push her into something she doesn't want, concluding, "Liza, if you don't want us to see each other anymore, it's okay" (104). Happily, this noble self-sacrifice is unnecessary, for Liza does want to see Annie again and the two girls begin a relationship that Liza thinks of as "magical"—"and a big part of that magic was that no matter how much of ourselves we found to give each other, there was always more we wanted to give" (108).

The one thing, however, that is not portrayed at this point is a sexual dimension to the relationship. Gradually this adds a layer of unspoken tension to their interpersonal dynamic, causing the two to become awkward and restrained around each other. Ultimately—and believably—it leads to an emotional explosion and a confrontation in which Annie tells Liza that she's making her afraid "because you seem to think it's wrong or dirty or something" (121).

Liza denies this, but she can't stop thinking about her confusion and her fear of the power of her feelings for Annie. "You're in love with another girl, Liza Winthrop," she tells herself, "and you know that means you're probably gay. But you don't know a thing about what that means" (143). Looking for knowledge, she reads the entry for "Homosexuality" in her father's encyclopedia and is incensed when she realizes that "in that whole long article, the word 'love' wasn't used even once. That made me mad; it was as if whoever wrote the article didn't know that gay people actually love each other" (143). And so when the two finally do become intimate, the experience transcends the purely physical; it is an act not only of consummation but also of bonding that is almost spiritual as Liza describes the "wonder of the closeness": "We can be almost like one" (146).

Seeing these words, the reader will remember what Liza said earlier, recalling the first time they had kissed: "Have you ever felt really close to someone? So close that you can't understand why you and the other person have two separate bodies, two separate skins?" (91).

The book's particularized treatment of falling in love is so effectively drawn that it can easily be generalized or extrapolated to the heterosexual experience of first love. And indeed, with the exception of Maureen Daly's *Seventeenth Summer* (1941), it's hard to recall a more nuanced picture of the gradually deepening intimacy of teens falling in love than *Annie on My Mind*. We've given so much attention to describing the evolution and complex nature of the relationship between Liza and Annie because it is the most enduringly important aspect of the book. Garden agrees with this assessment. In an e-mail to Michael Cart she wrote, "It's the emotional content of *Annie* that still speaks to readers."[12]

In addition to Liza and Annie's first-love relationship, the book also portrays a longtime lesbian relationship in the depiction of Ms. Widmer and Ms. Stevenson, who are presented as three-dimensional characters: first as teachers at Liza's school and then as hosts of a student council fund-raising meeting in the home they share. As Liza notes, "It seemed like they'd probably been living together for quite a long time . . . they seemed so comfortable with each other . . . like a couple of old shoes, each with its own special lumps and bumps and cracks, but nonetheless a pair that fit with ease into the same shoe box" (132).

Other aspects of the book have not endured quite so well. Those who have read the novel will know that, in a scene that now seems a bit contrived, Annie and Liza are discovered in bed together by a teacher from Liza's school. Worse, the discovery takes place in the home of Ms. Widmer and Ms. Stevenson, who are presumed to be the "bad influence" that drove the girls to lesbianism. Liza survives a disciplinary hearing, but the two teachers do not. Like Mr. Forster, they are fired and do not contest their dismissal. Also, the portrayal of the antagonists—the headmistress, Mrs. Poindexter, and her administrative assistant Ms. Baxter—seem one-dimensional, and many of the scenes involving them are tinged with melodrama.

Nevertheless, the characters of Liza and Annie and the wonderful integrity of their relationship have made the book one of the few enduring classics of LGBTQ+ literature. It was the principal reason that, in 2003, Garden received the American Library Association's prestigious Margaret A. Edwards Award for Lifetime Achievement in Young Adult Literature. The award citation noted that "Garden, in writing *Annie on My Mind* also has the distinction of being the first author for young adults to create a lesbian love story with a positive ending."[13]

Just as Annie and Liza discover much about themselves through reading ("I felt as if I were meeting parts of myself in the gay people I read about," Liza notes [144]), so, too, have generations of gay, lesbian, and questioning teenagers discovered themselves and the truth about homosexuality by reading Garden's novel. "Don't let ignorance win," one of the two lesbian teachers tells Liza. "Let love" (232). Garden has made such a victory possible.

Readers would have to wait until the very end of the decade for a book that treated male partners with such largehearted acceptance. Francesca Lia Block's *Weetzie Bat* (1989) was that novel, and the partners were Dirk and Duck. Dirk's coming-out to his best friend Weetzie is beautiful in its simplicity and breathtaking in the sweetness of its spirit of acceptance.

"I'm gay," Dirk said.

"Who, what, when, where, how—well, not how," Weetzie said. "It doesn't matter one bit, honey-honey," she said, giving him a hug.

Dirk took a swig of his drink. "But you know I'll always love you the best and think you are a beautiful, sexy girl," he said.

"Now we can Duck hunt together," Weetzie said, taking his hand. (9)

Duck hunting, in Block's wonderfully inventive argot, is searching for your soul mate. It's just one of the many delights of this punk fairy tale that Dirk's duck should turn out to be a boy whose name is in fact "Duck." In like fashion, the romantic "secret agent lover man" that Weetzie seeks turns out to be a rakish filmmaker with green eyes, a slouchy hat, and a trench coat. His name? What else? "My Secret Agent Lover Man."

Dirk and Duck are featured players in the four cinematic novels that follow about Weetzie and her very nontraditional, extended family of musicians and filmmakers, and Dirk will even have a novel, *Baby Bebop*, all of his own. But that will not happen until the next decade, and our further discussion of Block and her novels will have to wait for the next chapter of this book.

While the eighties, as previously noted, saw the appearance of twenty-seven characters who were male homosexuals, only eight of those were protagonists (and four of those appear in novels first published in England). Of the nineteen gay secondary characters, eight are adults, two are the protagonists' older (but still young adult) brothers, and the nine remaining are friends or boyfriends of the protagonists. As was the case with lesbian characters, this suggests that maintaining a certain distance from the protagonist remained the order of the day, an obligatory comfort factor that didn't necessarily serve either the characters in or the readers of these novels terribly well. However, a case could be made that having a heterosexual protagonist observing a homosexual character does make the book more accessible to straight readers who might balk at identifying with a gay or lesbian protagonist. When the observing is done with insight and affection—as in the case of the several novels by M. E. Kerr that employ this device—such books can be enlightening.

But what of the four gay male protagonists in U.S. novels who were dealing—or attempting to deal—with the immediacy of their own sexual identity? In the case of Neil, the eighteen-year-old protagonist of Frank Mosca's *All-American Boys* (Alyson, 1983), there is no doubt. In the very first sentence of the novel he declares, "I've known I was gay since I was thirteen" (7). How does he react to this? With startling aplomb: "According to one of the lousy books I read back then, I'm supposed to tell you it came as some sort of huge shock that sent me into fits of suicidal depression. Actually, it was the most natural thing in the world. I thought everyone was" (7). Fortunately, for him, he doesn't share this discovery with anyone, since, when he gets to high school the next year, he encounters a group of "queer-bashers" and in the interest of self-preservation dives headlong back into the closet.

The agony of coming out becomes the theme of this book when Neil meets Paul, whose family has just moved to town (where would young adult literature be without the obligatory new kid in town?), and the two fall in love. Paul is more candid about his sexuality than Neil, whom he criticizes for his "closet mentality." Neil's prudence would seem to be justified, however, when the same gang of queer-bashers attacks Paul and nearly beats him to death. At this point the novel turns into a revenge fantasy. Neil has a black belt in kung fu, and when he encounters the gang, the tables are turned. Many homosexual readers will derive some guilty pleasure from seeing bullies get their own back, but one hopes that, on mature reflection, they will reject violence as the sole useful strategy for coping with yet another dispiriting and dehumanizing example of gay-bashing. That aside, it is refreshing to see a protagonist who realizes his sexual identity at such an early age and accepts it without guilt or self-hatred. Both Paul and Neil are sweet and likable characters, but the novel is one of the most didactic of the eighties, an unfortunate characteristic of novels published by Alyson, one of a handful of small, independent publishers specializing in gay and lesbian literature at that time.

A second Alyson novel from the eighties is Don Sakers's *Act Well Your Part* (1986), the story of Keith, the new boy in school (and the protagonist this time) who falls in love with an "older man," Brian, who is a senior (Keith is a junior). Brian returns his feelings, and the two become partners. For the most part, the other students are surprisingly accepting of this but, then, they are members of the school's Drama Club. Keith's mother is also the most amazingly accepting parent thus far encountered in this chronology. "Good heavens, son, you don't think I love you any less? Of course not. I don't care who you're attracted to—you're still the same boy you've always been" (100). While this may seem more wish fulfillment than reality, it is refreshing to see a parent who doesn't respond to a teen's being gay by kicking him or her out of the house or calling an exorcist. Otherwise, this, like Mosca's novel, is a gracelessly written and didactic exercise. Like *All-American Boys*, Sakers's book was marketed as an adult title, though both were reviewed by *School Library Journal* as young adult titles. One doubts that very many libraries would have purchased these two books, however, since they were published as paperback originals and their pulp-novel covers were targeted at an adult trade bookstore market.

A third novel with a gay protagonist, B. A. Ecker's *Independence Day* (1983), was also published as a paperback original. The story of Mike, a high school soccer player, is one of the first gay sports novels. The only other gay sports novel of the 1980s, *Counterplay* by Anne Snyder and Louis Pelletier (Signet/NAL, 1981), was also published as a paperback original. Both of these novels treat homosexuality positively, but neither is an enduring work of literature. Though out of print for years and almost impossible to find today, the books, like many paperbacks of that period, sold briskly and, in fact, *Counterplay* was turned into *The Truth about Alex*, a made-for-television after-school special featuring *Happy Days* television star Scott Baio.

Nevertheless, it wasn't until the 1990s that a gay sports novel, Diana Wieler's *Bad Boy* (1992), was published as a hardcover targeted at the library and school market.

Meanwhile, the fourth novel to feature a gay protagonist was Scott Bunn's problem novel, *Just Hold On* (1982), the melodramatic story of two teens: Charlotte, who is being molested by her doctor father, and Stephen, whose doctor father is a hopeless alcoholic. The over-the-top melodrama is unfortunate, since the treatment of Stephen's emerging homosexuality is fairly positive (if one overlooks the fact that his father does die of a heart attack on the morning after Stephen and his friend Rolf finally consummate their relationship!). And Stephen's antic best friend, Wharton, is remarkably—though convincingly—blasé in his acceptance of his friend's gayness. Discovering that his friend is gay by finding him in bed with Rolf, Wharton, after a moment's consideration, says "'Rolf, I guess you're an okay person, since Stephen obviously likes you. . . .' Wharton sat down on the chair and stared back and forth from Rolf to Stephen. 'Obviously likes you,' he repeated, then looked to the ceiling. 'That's for sure . . .'" (135). Ultimately Stephen and Rolf move to New York City, where they share an apartment with Wharton and his girlfriend, though the precise nature of the relationship between Stephen and Rolf by that time is frustratingly ambiguous.

Equally ambiguous and annoying is the undefined relationship of Eric, the nineteen-year-old protagonist of Emily Hanlon's *The Wing and the Flame* (1980), and his best friend Chris. Told in flashbacks, the story is principally that of Eric's relationship with Owen Cassell, an eccentric, seventy-one-year-old sculptor whom Eric's father suspects of being a pedophile. The man is not, but this plot point does introduce the element of homosexuality, though when Eric and his friend Chris finally have a moment of intimacy (on page 127 of a 147-page novel), it catches the reader and, apparently, Eric by surprise. "Why can't we just be friends?" he asks, sounding remarkably like Val in *Hey, Dollface*. "Just ordinary friends like everyone else has friends?"

Subsequently, the author writes, "He knew his feelings for Chris hadn't changed." (And now he begins to sound like Jinx in *Crush*.) "The difference was those feelings had a name now—a name which caused him to fear what he loved most about their friendship—the joy he felt from their closeness. He was held back by his fear of what loving Chris meant. Gay, queer, fag—the words loomed threateningly before him" (131–32). Sensing Eric's distress, Chris—who, like Davy's friend Altschuler, has no such conflicted feelings about his homosexuality—nobly says, "Don't you see, Eric? It doesn't ever have to happen again" (131). And the two remain friends. There's nothing wrong with that outcome, but it seems fairly likely that Eric, too, is gay but simply doesn't want to confront this fact. And both Chris and the author give him a free pass: the author by changing the subject and Chris, by sacrificing his own feelings to maintain Eric's comfort level.

The temptation to deny oneself, either by discounting one's sexual identity (like Eric or Davy Ross or Tom Naylor), or by denying one's own emotional needs (as Chris or Altschuler or Ward do), is a recurring theme in gay and lesbian literature. It is all part of the larger issue of first, discovering one's sexual identity, then second, struggling to come to terms with it, and third, sharing the truth about oneself with others.

The impact on others of the decision to deny the truth and to choose to live what is, in effect, a lie is demonstrated in the several novels we have examined in which parents belatedly come out of the closet. But it also figures in two novels from the eighties in which girls discover that their boyfriends are gay: Hila Colman's *Happily Ever After* (1986) and Ann Rinaldi's *The Good Side of My Heart* (1987). Both of these not terribly good novels are weakened by the fact that the female characters—Melanie in the former and Brie in the latter—seem almost impossibly naïve in not seeing what a current-day reader readily discerns: the homosexuality of their respective boyfriends. Nevertheless, the pain the girls feel on discovering the truth is real and even poignant, though Brie's initial reaction, at least, is irritating as well: "All that handsomeness, all that masculinity wasted. I wanted to cry" (272). Melanie reacts in a similar manner: "He couldn't be what he had said. He was tall, handsome, manly—he was nothing like anyone who was odd or queer, nothing like the man who had the interior design shop in the village who everyone said was gay" (102). Her erstwhile boyfriend Paul will lecture her, later, about this attitude: "We're people like everyone else—and we're men, too. All kinds of men—weak, strong, big, little, even great athletes" (121). As one might infer from these quotations, both of these books also suffer from didacticism, plus the "sad-eyed loner" trope that is frequently used as an indication of a male character's homosexuality.

The Good Side of My Heart by Ann Rinaldi is, however, interesting for a second reason: it is the first to feature religion as a major theme. Earlier, religion appeared as a minor theme in Barger's *What Happened to Mr. Forster?* in which conservative religious beliefs are a contributory reason for the teacher's firing. In Rinaldi's book, Brie's older brother, Kevin, is a Roman Catholic priest, whose reaction to the news that her boyfriend is gay is to explain the Church's position on homosexuality, noting that if the homosexual isn't practicing his sexuality, there is no sin. Kevin, who is in the midst of a crisis involving his vocation, acknowledges that he doesn't agree with the Church's position, since he has "trouble with denying a person their sexuality if they're made that way" (244). Of course, this is academic, since Josh has already told Brie that he is celibate: "You know, like your brother" (222). Kevin's ultimate advice to his sister is the hoary truism "Hate the sin and love the sinner." Thus, homosexuality is once again defined not as a complex condition of self-identity but, rather, as a physical act, which may or may not be sinful.

The reductive treatment of homosexuality and personal denial reaches its acme—or nadir, depending on one's point of view—in Alice Childress's novel *Those Other People* (1989), a story that is told from multiple points of view, including that of seventeen-year-old Jonathan, who is portrayed as a stereotypically self-hating homosexual. Deeply closeted and proud of it (in and proud?), he decides to delay going to college for a year because "being gay was slowly becoming uncomfortable," and when he does go to check out a college, he is appalled by "signs and posters all over campus" about "sexual stuff. Gay rights discussion! Lesbians united. Bisexual society" (13). So he moves to New York (there's no homosexuality there!), where his gay room-mate, Harp, pressures him to come out. Harp orchestrates a gathering of gays at their apartment and tells Jon beforehand, "You'll meet a pitifully over-fifty swish Nellie" (19). Of course, when Jon, at the meeting, protests that he doesn't want to come out ("Hell, it's my closet, I can live in it if I want to" [19]), "Nellie was the only one who spoke up for me." Later, Jon thinks, "I was not then, and am not now, comfortable with who and what I am" (75). When Harp drunkenly outs him to his parents, Jon's mom thinks, "Our first hope is that we're dealing with a passing phase" (90). At the end, Jon is forced to come out because he is being blackmailed. As a result, he resigns from the temporary teaching position he has taken and moves back home to his parents. Though the ethicality of outing closeted homosexuals, even for political reasons, is dubious, this may be one of the only contemporary YA novels in which being out (as opposed to closeted) is presented as something to be actively deplored. As a result, the novel seems anachronistic; worse, it is replete with one-dimensional characters and some of the most unfortunate homosexual stereotyping in the literature.

Homosexuals are not the only characters in LGBTQ+ literature who are self-hating, as demonstrated in three novels by Barbara Wersba: *Crazy Vanilla* (1986), *Just Be Gorgeous* (1988), and *Whistle Me Home* (1997). Wersba writes very much in the tradition of J. D. Salinger and John Donovan, with a soupçon of Paul Zindel. Five of her sixteen YA novels, including *Whistle Me Home*, have been selected as ALA Best Books for Young Adults.

In *Crazy Vanilla*, the first and definitely the best of these novels, the protagonist is Tyler, a fourteen-year-old boy and aspiring nature photographer who falls in love with Mitzi, a brash, cosmically wise fifteen-year-old girl who shares his interest in photography. Tyler's adored older brother, Cameron, is estranged from their father as a result of one too many argu-ments about Cameron's being not only gay, but a gay interior designer. Tyler and his brother continue to see each other, but when Cameron falls in love and moves in with Vincent, a handsome Italian interior decorator, Tyler distances himself from Cameron. Canny Mitzi sees what's going on:

"You've decided to cut that poor guy right out of your life, simply because of Vincent. You want to pay him back for being in love" (143). At book's end, Mitzi abruptly moves to Santa Fe with her nomadic hippie mother and Tyler finally picks up the phone and calls his brother, presumably to begin a process of reconciliation and healing.

In Wersba's two other novels, the protagonists are—like Melanie in *Happily Ever After* and Brie in *The Good Side of My Heart*—straight girls who fall in love with gay boys, but with far less favorable outcomes. In *Just Be Gorgeous*, the girl is sixteen-year-old Heidi, who loses her heart to Jeffrey, a flamboyantly gay, twenty-year-old street performer who lives in an abandoned building and dreams of getting his big break on Broadway. When this doesn't happen, Jeffrey—to Heidi's dismay—decides to accept an offer from a somewhat older gay couple to move with them to Hollywood. Bleakly, Heidi thinks, "So once again I realized that there was a special club on this earth called 'being gay' and that I was not a member" (145). (This may be one of the few times in YA literature when a straight character expresses a genuine yearning to be gay!)

Wersba returned to this theme nine years later in *Whistle Me Home*, the story of a wealthy girl named Noli who falls in love with the new boy in her English class, only to reject him ("You dirty faggot!") when she learns he is gay. This story is described more fully in chapter 4.

GAY ASSIMILATION

Gay assimilation is rarely found in the novels of the eighties. Jean Ure, a prolific British children's author who is probably best known in England for her books for elementary- and middle-school-age readers, wrote a number of thoughtful YA novels, including two with LGBTQ+ content: *You Win Some, You Lose Some* (1984) and *The Other Side of the Fence* (1986). Her books are two of the few examples of gay assimilation titles published during this decade. Michael judges the first novel to be the more successful of the two, while Christine prefers the second. *You Win Some, You Lose Some* features seventeen-year-old Jamie, who has dropped out of school to pursue his dream of becoming a dancer. Ure examines the stereotypes that surround this calling; most people, for example, presume that Jamie's desire to dance must mean he's gay (or, in the characters' patois, a "gawker"). In fact, he's not but, as it turns out, his roommate, Steven, who is also a dancer, makes no secret of his desire to have sex with Jamie. In fact, this is one of the only YA novels in which a common stereotype—the homosexual who tries to seduce heterosexuals—is depicted, though in an almost casual manner that Jamie clearly finds more humorous than threatening. Ure's light touch in dealing with issues of sexuality in this novel are a welcome relief from the Sturm und Drang of so many other titles from this period.

Ure's *The Other Side of the Fence* includes both homosexual visibility and gay assimilation. The protagonist Richard, eighteen, is kicked out of the house when his odious father discovers his son's homosexuality. On his own and without any means for the first time in his heretofore privileged life, Richard meets a homeless girl, Bonny, and the two find an abandoned house and move in together. Bonny herself has been abandoned by her cretinous boyfriend and gradually falls in love with Richard, who cannot bring himself to tell her he is gay. The reader may infer that the fence that divides the two is the boy's sexual orientation, but there is also the matter of class and circumstance: Richard is a child of privilege, and Bonny is from a working-class background. After what seems to be an implausibly long time, Bonny discovers the truth and the two young people eventually—and amicably—part as friends. Bonny spends most of the book on a quest to find her former foster family, who turn out to be a lesbian couple, a fact that is presented but not commented upon.

Marilyn Singer's *The Course of True Love Never Did Run Smooth* (1983) is another example of gay assimilation in novels of the 1980s. Becky, the protagonist and narrator, is sixteen, as is her best friend Nemi (short for Nehemiah). The setting is a high school production of *A Midsummer Night's Dream* in which the teen actors emulate the characters they play in acknowledging a mutual attraction while encountering a problem that must be overcome before they can be together. For some cast members this barrier is class or race, and one couple, Richie and Craig, must come out to their parents in order to be together. This is a quietly engaging novel of teenage attractions as Becky and Nemi (who finally realize that their relationship is more than "just good friends") and their straight and gay friends successfully overcome their respective obstacles to find their true love all the better for having weathered some rough patches.

Norma Klein's *My Life as a Body* (1987) is another novel of gay assimilation, in which Augie tells the story of her senior year in high school and first year in college. Augie's best friend is Claudia, who "claims she's known since she was five that she was gay" (5). Later, when Augie goes to college, her best friend will be Gordon ("I knew he was gay. But everyone here seemed pretty up-front about the gay thing" [178]). Both Claudia and Gordon are notable for their "directness," their "cut-the-crap kind of honesty" (178), traits they share with their creator. In this book, as in other works by Klein, characters are defined or evaluated in part on the basis of their comfort with sexual activity, their own and others'. Augie, who has a sexual relationship with a physically disabled male classmate in high school and with one of her male professors in college, embodies this attitude when she thinks, "I learned that you can make love with someone you're fond of without 'falling' or being in love. There didn't seem to be any price tag, no talk of future, of promises, of ultimate decisions" (243). In books featuring gay assimilation, same-sex romantic relationships are no big deal.

QUEER CONSCIOUSNESS/COMMUNITY

Where? When? How? Seeking and Finding a Queer Community

Although YA novels with LGBTQ+ content published in the 1980s include significantly more evidence of queer community than those of the 1970s, isolation is still common. Many of the places where readers find hints of a fictional gay community are offstage and often in the past. This is particularly true for YA novels depicting HIV or AIDS. In M. E. Kerr's *Night Kites*, for example, Erick's older brother Pete, who has lived in New York City after college, returns to the family home to die. The reader learns that Pete's life in New York included work as a teacher and writer and much socializing with other gay men in bars and at parties. Pete tells his younger brother about the thrill of moving to New York City after graduating from college: "When I saw all the gay bars and discos here, I just wanted to dance and drink and play" (96). But all of that is in the past and none of it is visible to Erick or the reader.

The gay community is also definitely located in the past in David Rees's *Out of the Winter Gardens* (1984), in which sixteen-year-old Michael gets to know his gay father, whose absence from Michael's childhood was due to his mother's refusal to allow contact between them (also the theme of Sonya Sones's much later novel *One of Those Hideous Books Where the Mother Dies*). But when Michael arrives for his first visit, his father's partner immediately moves out, and the father is certain that he will spend the rest of his life alone. At one point he reminisces wistfully about their years together, full of "parties and mutual friends, holidays in California and the Greek islands, dancing at discos" (54). But again, it's all in the past.

In addition to gay loners, there are also gay/lesbian couples, but most are portrayed as a singular unit with no connections to other gay/lesbian people. In Madeleine L'Engle's *A House Like a Lotus*, for example, Max and her partner Ursula live in an isolated mansion on the unpopulated end of a remote island. The adult lesbian couple in Catherine Brett's *S.P. Likes A.D.* (1989) is another singular unit, though in this case they live openly as a couple in an urban setting among (straight) friends and colleagues. Likewise, Liza and Annie (in Nancy Garden's *Annie on My Mind*) become aware of a larger gay/lesbian community as they read *Patience and Sarah*, a lesbian love story, and hunger for more evidence of kindred spirits. Yet when the lesbian teachers, Ms. Stevenson and Ms. Widmer, are fired because of their relationship, the partners are pictured in an apartment full of cardboard boxes but devoid of other people. How realistic would it be for an intelligent and sociable lesbian couple to have lived in Brooklyn Heights for two decades and to have no friends to help them pack? In this case, the community that Liza and Annie were so heartened to read about in New York's gay newspapers is no longer in evidence when it's time to help the teachers move. Countering this lonely image, there is a hint of better times ahead. And, as Ms. Stevenson says, "I can't lie to you and say that losing our job like this is easy. It isn't. But the point is that it'll be okay; we'll be okay" (230).

Like Liza and Annie, some LGBTQ+ characters see no queer community in their present lives, but staunchly—or wistfully—hope that there will be a queer community in their future. For example, in Hila Colman's *Happily Ever After* (1986), protagonist Melanie believes that she and her childhood sweetheart Paul will eventually become lovers. Thus, when Paul comes out to her, she feels a personal sense of loss as her dream of marriage falls apart. She and Paul talk about the future, and she asks him if he is thinking about college. He says,

> "I want to go to a place that has a gay group on campus." Melanie's heart thumped—"Why?"
> "Why not? I feel so darn alone—I want to be with other guys like myself. It's natural, isn't it?"
> "I thought you wanted to keep it secret. . . ."
> "Around here, yes. But not outside, not forever." (131)

To Paul, his vision of future happiness is closely linked to finding a community. Melanie views Paul's gayness as a tragic disability as she mournfully tells him, "'Paul, I hope you will be happy.' 'Don't cry for me,' he said gently. 'I know it's not going to be easy. But I'm not alone. I'll find someone someday'" (168). Alas, if "someday" happens, it will be well after the close of the book.

Other novels of the 1980s provide the protagonist and the reader with tantalizingly brief glimpses of queer community. In Barbara Wersba's *Crazy Vanilla*, for example, protagonist Tyler Woodruff, a Long Island teenager, reaches out to his gay older brother Cameron, who works at a high-end New York City decorating firm owned by his lover, Vincent. When Tyler phones Cameron to talk, the brother and his lover are in the midst of "having a few friends over for cocktails" (128). This brief telephone conversation is the closest the reader gets to Cameron's world. In fact, to Tyler the distance between his family's Long Island suburb and Manhattan is unbridgeable.

Wersba provides another snippet of gay community in *Just Be Gorgeous*. Heidi, a straight teen, befriends Jeffrey, a gay street kid who supports himself by tap-dancing to show tunes on street corners. Although his day-to-day life in New York City is precarious, Jeffrey's stubborn faith in his own future as a star impresses Heidi, who is deeply skeptical of her own ability to succeed at any endeavor. Their friendship is the mutual attraction of two loners who each find a supportive listener in the other. Heidi is drawn to Jeffrey for his openness to friendship and self-confidence in the face of obstacles. "It doesn't matter what people think of you—it only matters what you think of yourself" (63). Six months into their friendship, Jeffrey makes some other friends, Peter and Eugene, a gay couple whose couch becomes his temporary bed. When invited to their apartment for dinner, Heidi is prepared to dislike them but finds them both articulate and likable. "I could not hate them—but at the same time, something told me that they were replacing me, that they were providing Jeffrey with the one thing I could not give him: a home" (146). The book ends as Jeffrey drives off to Los Angeles and a new life with his gay friends. The reader gets no further glimpse of Jeffrey's new life, but it's clear that he is confidently moving toward a community of his own.

Several novels of the 1980s depict gay bars, but there is little evidence of the friendliness of Tim and Ray's gay pub from *In the Tent*. For example, in Snyder and Pelletier's *Counterplay* (1981), protagonist Alex self-identifies as gay but has never met any other gay people. One night he visits Kelly's Place, a gay bar, steeling himself, telling himself: "This was his future, these people, his kind. . . . Alex looked at the dancers. Men with men. Some in leather jackets, some with tank tops, most virile, very masculine looking. A few tables of obviously straight couples, men and women, ogled the dancers, laughed somewhat furtively behind their hands, whispered, gawked" (94). While not frightening, this image of gay community is hardly inviting.

Mike, the protagonist of B. A. Ecker's *Independence Day* (1983), has known he was gay since he was fifteen but has told no one. When he and his best friend take a weekend trip to New York City, he marvels as they walk down a Greenwich Village street: "There are many men walking these streets holding hands. No one is looking at them. They share secrets and laughter together and it makes me feel good to watch them. I have the feeling of home in this place. This is where I want to live; where I'll be judged on other things besides my sexual preference" (106). Later that evening he walks into a gay bar, sees men standing around a piano singing, and spots the friend who told him about the bar by the piano. "'Just sing along,' Jan says, and I do. I feel better than I have in the past year. I feel like I belong. . . . It's been a strange night. I feel that the old me has died and left everything behind him. Where do I fit into all of this? Will my life be spent in hallways with quick, furtive kisses and hugs? Or will I someday be comfortable enough with the knowledge of who I am to be able to love in the open?" (111). That night he dreams he is knocking at the door of his home, but his family won't let him in. For Mike, finding a community could mean losing his family. This juxtaposition of gay community and family as polar opposites is another common element in YA books with gay/lesbian content.

In David Rees's *The Milkman's on His Way* (1982), a gay teen, Ewan, lives a lonely life as a townie in a resort village, where he waits with waning patience for the end of his schooling and the beginning of adulthood and his future as a gay man. When he encounters a group of men on holiday at the beach, he can see for the first time what a world of out friends would look like. Although the visitors soon return to London, Ewan is reassured by this evidence that he, too, will find kindred spirits when he finally leaves home, which is, indeed, the case.

In Mosca's *All-American Boy*, Neil and Paul socialize with an older gay couple, are invited to the men's anniversary party, and discover an active gay-lesbian center at the college they attend. In two 1988 books, Norma Klein's *Now That I Know* and Ron Koertge's *The Arizona Kid*, straight teen protagonists attend parties hosted by their gay father and uncle, respectively. In both cases, the narrators are the youngest people there—and while they are made welcome, the queer community they visit is adults only.

Lastly, just as *In the Tent* was a 1970s text that was a harbinger of the 1980s, so might Francesca Lia Block's *Weetzie Bat* be viewed as a preview of the more gay community–friendly 1990s, for her characters Dirk and Duck meet, and fall in love in and construct a community of their own in Los Angeles with the help of friends of various backgrounds and sexualities. Though, as previously noted, Duck panics in the face of AIDS and flees to San Francisco, he is followed by Dirk, who finally tracks him down in a gay bar. He spots him across the dance floor:

"Who was that beautiful blonde boy? Love is a dangerous angel, Dirk thought. Especially nowadays. It was Duck. Out of all the bars and all the nights and all the people and all the moments, Dirk had found Duck" (84–85). Tenderly reunited, the two return to Los Angeles where they are embraced by their chosen family and community as they gather around the dinner table, "all of them lit up and golden like a wreath of lights" as Weetzie muses, "I don't know about happily ever after . . . but I know about happily" (88).

NOTES

1. Aidan Chambers, "Ways of Telling," in *Booktalk: Occasional Writing on Literature and Children* (New York: Harper & Row, 1985), 111.
2. Chambers, "Ways of Telling," 112.
3. M. E. Kerr, "1993 Margaret A. Edwards Award Acceptance Speech," *Journal of Youth Services in Libraries* 7, no. 1 (Fall 1993): 9.
4. Virginia A. Walter and Melissa Gross, *HIV/AIDS Information for Children: A Guide to Issues and Resources* (New York: H.W. Wilson, 1996).
5. Melissa Gross, "What Do Young Adult Novels Say about HIV/AIDS?" *Library Quarterly* 68, no. 1 (January 1998).
6. Norma Klein, "Books to Help Kids Deal with Difficult Times, I," *School Media Quarterly* 15, no. 3 (Spring 1987): 163.

7. "Flying Starts," *Publishers Weekly*, December 22, 1989.

8. David E. Wilson, "The Open Library: YA Books for Gay Teens." *English Journal* 73, no. 2 (November 1984): 2.

9. David E. Wilson, "Advocating Young Adult Novels with Gay Themes," reprinted in *Education Digest* 52, no. 2 (October 1986): 46–47.

10. Jan Goodman, "Out of the Closet, but Paying the Price," *Interracial Books for Children Bulletin* 14, nos. 3–4 (1983): 4.

11. Rita M. Kissen, *The Last Closet: The Real Lives of Lesbian and Gay Teachers* (Portsmouth, NH: Heinemann, 1996), 5.

12. Nancy Garden, e-mail message to the coauthor, September 14, 1999.

13. 2003 Margaret A. Edwards Award Winner, Nancy Garden, 7. http://www.ala.org/yalsa/booklistsawards/margaretaedwards/maeprevious/2003nancygarden.htm.

Chapter Four

Young Adult Literature of the 1990s

As we have seen, LGBTQ+ literature for young adults—like the larger body of young adult literature to which it belongs—does not exist in a vacuum. Though there is a tendency to "ghettoize" it, LGBTQ+ literature remains a reflection of trends in the larger world of publishing (for both teens *and* adults) and of prevailing cultural, social, economic, and even political attitudes. Thus, one can read this literature to learn how society views and reacts to homosexuality—or at least to learn what publishers believe, however correctly or incorrectly, will appeal to teen readers.

For example, pivotal scenes in two novels, both published in 1990, illustrate the broad range of coming-out narratives and of attitudes toward LGBTQ+ people and their lives that would be represented in the literature published throughout the nineties. They also reflect the wide spectrum of attitudes toward LGBTQ+ people in the larger society. In the first, Joyce Sweeney's *Face the Dragon*, Paul comes out to his best friend Eric as they walk on a deserted beach:

> "I'm different from you. . . . For a while I wasn't even sure about this, but lately, and especially after last night . . . I'm just not very interested in . . . girls."
>
> It was so sudden, Eric didn't get it. "Well, you probably . . ." Then he did get it. "What do you mean?" he asked warily.
>
> Paul wouldn't look at him now. "You know what I mean."
>
> "You're crazy. I've known you all your life. I'd know if you were like that."
>
> "How would you know? If I never said anything, you wouldn't know. You just said you didn't have a clue how I felt about that stuff. Well, now I'm telling you. When I think about that stuff, I think about . . . the wrong people. . . ."

"Well, if I were you, I'd try to keep my options open. I'm saying it because you're talking about something that's risky and dangerous and makes your whole life a million times harder than it has to be. So if there is a way out, I think you should look for it." (102)

Paul's talk with Eric makes it clear that the isolation he feels is based on an accurate reading of his peers' probable responses to his coming out. No wonder all of his statements are negative and/or coded. He states what he isn't rather than what he is: he's "not very interested in girls," he thinks about "the wrong people." Eric is no more forthright when he says he'd know if Paul were "like that," and follows this up with his own positive images (not favorable, but describing homosexuality by what he thinks it *is* rather than by what it *isn't*). But his images are stereotypes, apparently based on popular images of gay men in the early years of AIDS. Eric, the instant expert, declares that homosexuality is risky, dangerous, and will make Paul's life "a million times harder that it has to be," and urges him to turn himself into a heterosexual. And finally, though this is clearly a coming-out scene, Paul and Eric somehow manage never to utter the "G" word, much less the "F" word, the "H" word, or the "Q" word.

In contrast, Paul Robert Walker's *The Method* features Albie, a fifteen-year-old protagonist, who participates in an intensive summer workshop in the techniques of method acting (yes, this is another gay-themed novel set in the theater), where he meets a new friend, Mitch. Toward the end of the book, Mitch takes Albie to a gay pride parade and from there to a crowded gay restaurant, and Mitch comes out to Albie as they drink their chocolate sodas. Albie reacts with laughter, to which Mitch responds:

"I'm sorry that it makes you nervous, Albie. But I want you to know. I'm gay. I'm queer. I'm a faggot. I'm a homosexual. This is not a joke. This is my life."
Albie . . . turned toward Mitch and asked, "Why are you telling me this?"
"I need to."
"How do you know? I mean, about being . . . you know . . . gay?"
"I know. Believe me. Albie, there's something I want to ask you, and I want you to be completely honest. Will you do that? Are we still friends?"
Albie reached out and covered Mitch's hand with his own. "You know we are." (137–38)

Notice that in contrast to Paul in *Face the Dragon*, Mitch first tells Albie he's gay, and when Albie responds with nervous laughter, Mitch restates, "I'm gay" and follows this with a list of the other words, negative, positive, and neutral, used to describe gay people. Mitch is going to make sure that Albie understands him in whatever language Albie uses. The other clear contrast between these two scenes is in their settings. Paul and Eric walk on a lonely beach, a setting that reinforces the lonely life that Paul has led, and apparently will continue to lead in the future.

Such negative depictions being preferable to invisibility is subject to debate but, happily, some books have included realistic LGBTQ+ characters who are integral to the plot and whose stories even provide the novel's central narrative.

THE NEGATIVE SIDE OF SEXUALITY

When YA literature of the sixties and seventies portrayed heterosexual intimacy between teens, the health consequences were predictable. Even if the sexual act occurred only once, girls who had sex almost inevitably got pregnant. They then had several options: If the pregnant girl was a secondary character, she would usually simply disappear from the story. If she had a steady boyfriend, the two might get married, to the chagrin of all, including themselves. If she had no steady boyfriend, the girl might get an abortion, which was likely to leave her either dead or unable to have future children. There are, of course, exceptions to all these fictional scenarios, but the majority followed the course(s) described above.[1]

As for same-sex sexual activity, the most frequent unintended health consequence of it in YA novels of the 1980s and the 1990s was, of course, HIV/ AIDS. In YA novels, only males contracted AIDS. However, no matter how widespread or unremitting the disease, AIDS-related literature remains a very modest subgenre of LGBTQ+ literature. As previously noted, only three novels from the eighties (*Night Kites*, *The Arizona Kid*, and *Weetzie Bat*) dealt with the subject. Thirteen more that included *any* character who was HIV positive or had AIDS appeared in the nineties. Since then, with few exceptions, the subject has scarcely been treated, despite the fact that AIDS remains an epidemic problem among young people. During the 1990s, the Advocates for Youth website reported that "half of all new HIV infections occur in people under age 25."[2] Yet of these AIDS-related titles from the nineties, only one—*My Brother Has AIDS* by Deborah Davis (1994)—features a young adult as the infected character. And among *all* the AIDS-related titles within this body of YA literature, the character who is HIV positive or has AIDS is never the protagonist. Judging from these novels, readers might presume that AIDS only infects adults—usually uncles or teachers.

Young adult novels published since the 1990s continue to reflect this misperception. Despite the fact that AIDS is rarely in the spotlight among fictional teens, AIDS remains a very real presence in the lives of many young people. The new antiviral drugs and treatment regimens have significantly increased survival rates of people contracting HIV, and people with AIDS can now, with proper treatment, look forward to a life that is impacted, but not cut short, by AIDS. At the same time, recent (2015) health statistics indicate that youth aged thirteen to twenty-four account for more than one in five new HIV diagnoses, with young gay and bisexual males accounting for 80 percent of those diagnoses.[3] However, HIV/AIDS is no longer a significant factor in the lives of teens who populate the world of young adult fiction.

Another negative aspect of the sexual act—as violence or as an abuse of power—was first addressed in 1976 in Richard Peck's influential young adult novel about heterosexual rape, *Are You in the House Alone?* (Viking). Two years later, the rape of a young lesbian occurred in Sandra Scoppettone's *Happy Endings Are All Alike*. The rapist insists that it was watching the young woman, Jaret, and her female partner make love that drove him to rape Jaret. So perhaps this could be seen as another example of a girl's being punished for having sex: if she can't get pregnant, she gets raped instead. It would be another fifteen years before gay rape would first be addressed, in Kathleen Jeffrie Johnson's *Target* (2003), while sexual abuse in the form of forced (i.e., nonconsensual) gay sex had been the subject, four years earlier, of Catherine Atkins's novel *When Jeff Comes Home* (1999).

Yet another form of sexual abuse, incest, was strictly off limits to YA authors for years. It was subtly included in Scott Bunn's *Just Hold On* (Delacorte, 1982) as the probable cause of Charlotte's eventual mental breakdown (see chapter 3), but it was not introduced as the central focus of a YA novel until Hadley Irwin's 1985 *Abby, My Love* (Atheneum). Several other novels on this subject—including Ruth White's *Weeping Willow* (FSG, 1992), Cynthia D. Grant's *Uncle Vampire* (Atheneum, 1993), and Francesca Lia Block's *The Hanged Man* (Harper, 1994)—have centered on a girl and an abusive, older male relative.

When we turn our attention to the world of young adult literature as a whole, it's evident that the decade of the nineties was one of profound change. Though pronounced near death by most observers at the beginning of the decade, the form made a remarkable recovery and by 1995 was entering a period of expansion, creative growth, and literary sophistication that has continued to the present day.[4] Among the indicators of YA literature's artistic maturity was the 1999 establishment of the Michael L. Printz Award by ALA's Young Adult Library Services Association (YALSA). Like the Newbery and Caldecott Awards, the Printz Award is based on literary merit. The award acknowledges, thus, that young adult literature has finally come of age *as literature*. The expansiveness of the book categories eligible for the Printz reflect not only the new maturity of the literature but also the many innovations that are enriching its content. For example, the eligibility of books first published in other countries signals the expansion of the YA field beyond U.S. borders, while the eligibility of poetry, short-story collections, and graphic novels demonstrates the creative reach of young adult literature into forms and genres beyond that of contemporary realism.

LGBTQ+ YA FICTION IN THE 1990S

The decade of the nineties was one of expansion for LGBTQ+ young adult fiction, too, though this expansion was more in volume than in creative or thematic innovation. The number of LGBTQ+ fiction titles published nearly doubled: seventy-four titles (sixty-nine novels and five short-story collections) appeared in the nineties, and seven of these (10 percent) originated in other countries. Thus the books appeared at a rate that went from an average of four titles per year in the eighties to seven titles per year in the nineties.

However, the gender imbalance in the books' content did not shift appreciably from the eighties to the nineties. Generally speaking, most of this body of literature remains rigidly segregated by gender. Books include *either* gay male *or* lesbian content; only rarely do both appear in the same story. And if a book can only include one or the other, it's typically a gay male character. In fact, of the forty books published in the 1980s, twenty-nine (73 percent) included gay male characters and eleven (28 percent) included lesbian characters. Of the sixty-nine LGBTQ+ YA novels of the nineties, forty-seven (68 percent) included gay male characters and eighteen (26 percent) included lesbian characters, and only four titles (6 percent) included both gay males and lesbians.

The proportion of books having a LGBTQ+ protagonist relative to books with LGBTQ+ secondary characters increasingly favored those with secondary characters. During the eighties, sixteen (40 percent) of the titles included LGBTQ+ protagonists and twenty-four (60 percent) included LGBTQ+ secondary characters. During the nineties, nineteen (28 percent) of the titles included LGBTQ+ protagonists, forty-nine (71 percent) included LGBTQ+ secondary characters, and one title (1 percent) had two narrators, one gay and one straight.

In terms of creative or thematic innovation, however, the principal focus remained stuck on homosexual visibility, that is, the voluntary or involuntary coming-out of a character. Who it is who comes out, under what circumstances, and with what consequences remained the substance of the story. And while there is some latitude for variety in this, there is also an inescapable air of sameness, a problem that has dogged LGBTQ+ literature since its beginnings. Of the nearly seventy novels published in the decade of the 1990s, fifty-one (74 percent) were titles of "homosexual visibility" that dealt, in one way or another, with coming-out issues. Twenty-two (32 percent) contained at least some elements of "gay assimilation" (i.e., the stories are about or include people who "just happen to be gay"). Only eleven (16 percent) included elements of "queer consciousness" or "queer community." (Some book fall into more than one category; hence the total is greater than 100 percent.)

As in previous decades, the numbers of titles published varied from year to year, beginning modestly in 1990 with only four titles, a number that steadily increased over time to the decade's high point of thirteen titles in 1999. (See appendix A for a chronological list of titles.) Because there is not sufficient space in this chapter to focus on each of the sixty-nine novels published during the nineties,[5] we will highlight and examine the most significant titles in each of our three framework categories, beginning with homosexual visibility.

HOMOSEXUAL VISIBILITY

During the first half of the 1990s, one of the most common methods of outing—or revealing a character's sexual identity—was the discovery that the (invariably male) character had contracted AIDS from having had unprotected sex with a male partner. As noted above, this happened in thirteen novels but in only one (*My Brother Has AIDS*) is the character a young adult, and in none of these is the infected character the protagonist. Also, in only one—Theresa Nelson's moving novel *Earthshine* (Orchard, 1994)—is the PWA (person with AIDS) openly gay from the novel's outset.

In only sixteen of the sixty-nine LGBTQ+ novels is the character who comes out—to him- or herself and/or to the world—the protagonist. In all of the rest (i.e., fifty-three), the character is a member of the "supporting cast," usually a friend or relative of the protagonist. This removal of the homosexual character from center stage is a feature of titles in our other two framework categories, gay assimilation and queer consciousness, as well. As we have noted, this shift in the book's narrative distance with regard to gay/lesbian content—that is, away from gay/lesbian protagonists and toward gay/lesbian secondary characters—was a trend that continued and actually intensified through the nineties.[6] Did this strengthen or did it weaken the genre? The answer, not to be unduly coy, is yes.

If, as we believe, a purpose of this literature is to give faces to LGBTQ+ youth, increased narrative distance may blur the portrait. Placing an intermediary, heterosexual character between the reader and the gay or lesbian character may also reduce the possibility of emotional involvement by the reader, and it may even diminish the authenticity of the LGBTQ+ experience. On the other hand, the presence of a heterosexual protagonist may well provide an easier point of access to the story for straight readers, who are also an important audience for these stories. And in terms of verisimilitude, the presence of secondary gay characters could seem to positively reflect the growing awareness of the universal presence of gay/lesbian persons in society. The bottom line is that more LGBTQ books than ever appeared in the 1990s, but overall the gay/lesbian characters moved further from center stage.

Coming-out stories featuring gay secondary characters were published throughout the nineties. This chapter began with a descriptive comparison of two of them: Joyce Sweeney's *Face the Dragon*, in which Paul comes out to protagonist Eric on a deserted beach, and Paul Robert Walker's *The Method*, in which Mitch comes out to protagonist Albie in a gay restaurant. Although both were published in 1990, the former is one of the dreariest coming-out scenes in this entire body of literature, while the latter is one of the most affirming.

Indeed, Albie's ready acceptance of Mitch's identity is as reassuring to gay readers as Weetzie's response to the news that *her* friend Dirk is gay. In critical terms, although homosexuality is only a subplot, its inclusion in the context of a coming-of-age novel that involves emerging sexuality is entirely appropriate and unforced. In addition, both *Weetzie Bat* and *Method* present a fairly diverse range of gay/lesbian characters who are depicted with affection, humor, and accuracy. In contrast, *Dragon*'s Paul is one more lonely misfit, a role played by teens of all sexual orientations at various points in their teenage years. But such a consistently one-note portrayal of gay male teens has become a cliché in YA fiction.

Other nineties novels that address the homosexuality of secondary characters who are friends of the protagonists include: Jesse Maguire's *Getting It Right* (1991); Diana Wieler's *Bad Boy* (1992); Chris Lynch's *Dog Eat Dog* (1996); Barbara Wersba's *Whistle Me Home* (1997); Stephen Chbosky's *The Perks of Being a Wallflower* (1999); Phyllis Reynolds Naylor's *Alice on the Outside* (1999); Laura Torres's *November Ever After* (1999); and Lois-Ann Yamanaka's *Name Me Nobody* (1999). They range in treatment from the very good (*Perks*) to the very bad (*Whistle*).

The Perks of Being a Wallflower has become something of a YA cult classic since it was published in 1999 as a paperback adult title. An epistolary novel, it is the haunting story of a deeply troubled but precocious fifteen-year-old boy named Charlie who writes letters about his freshman year in high school to someone who is identified only as "Dear Friend," a recipient who could well be the reader him- or herself. During that eventful year, Charlie is befriended by two seniors, Samantha and Patrick, who are stepsister and stepbrother. In short order, the two become Charlie's best friends. When Charlie discovers Patrick kissing another boy, Brad, at a party, he (accurately) concludes that Patrick is gay, a fact that clearly does not affect Charlie's warm feelings for his friend. Patrick is aware of this, telling him appreciatively, "You see things. You keep quiet about them. And you understand" (37).

Indeed, Charlie is wonderfully understanding. When Patrick is despondent over the imminent breakup of his already shaky relationship with Brad, Charlie continues to be there for him. At one point Patrick says to Charlie, "It's too bad you're not gay." And Charlie's response? "You know, Patrick? If I were gay, I'd want to date you."

"I don't know why I said it," he adds in an aside to the reader, "but it seemed right" (137). Later, when Patrick becomes the object of a gay-bashing (instigated by his closeted former boyfriend), Charlie—who has learned to fight from his older brother, now a football star at Penn—rushes to his friend's defense, heedless of his own physical vulnerability as one against many. And still later, when the traumatized Patrick gets drunk, kisses Charlie, and then immediately apologizes—more than once—Charlie's reply is "No, really. It was ok."

"Then," Charlie writes, "he started crying. Then he started talking about Brad. And I just let him. Because that's what friends are for" (160–61). This attitude of generous and full-hearted acceptance of a friend's difference is, of course, the nonpareil of hoped-for responses.

An entirely different reaction is found in *Whistle Me Home*. This slender, 1997 novel (108 pages) is another title from Barbara Wersba about a troubled girl. Noli, seventeen, has "a little problem with alcohol" and a big problem with her mother, whom she hates. Oh, yes—she also has a problem with shoplifting. These problems pale in insignificance, though, when, on the first day of school, she sees a new boy in town (Sag Harbor, New York) and falls instantly in love with him. His name is TJ and he is described thus: "The boy is beautiful—with the face of an angel and the body of an athlete. His thick curly hair is longer than any boy's in the room. And he is wearing an earring." His physical presence is alluring, but what sends Noli head over heels is his announcement in English class that, over the summer, he has read a biography of Gerard Manley Hopkins, and then, at the teacher's invitation, he shyly (but brilliantly) reads aloud one of Hopkins's poems.

Noli is captivated. As the omniscient narrator describes it, "The idea that *anyone*—and especially somebody new—could get up in class and read the work of a nineteenth-century priest . . . this idea is dizzying to her."

"'He was famous for something called sprung rhythm,' TJ says quietly. 'Hopkins, I mean.'"

By this point (page 11) many readers may wonder if TJ's playing against male gender stereotypes and his stance as high school aesthete signals that he is gay. But naïve Noli doesn't have a clue. Not even when the two become friends, and she discovers that TJ prefers that he and she dress alike "in stonewashed jeans, boots, heavy jackets, and wool caps" (60). When Noli is (understandably) mistaken for a boy, she says, "God! I really must grow my hair longer, TJ. And wear dresses."

"Forget it," he answers. "You're fine."

When the two finally try to have sex, TJ is unable to become aroused. And "at last she says the words that must be said—and her voice breaks a little as she says them. 'You're gay aren't you?'" (72). He bursts into tears and Noli is initially sympathetic, but when the two begin to talk and TJ admits that he has had earlier "experiences" with males, the girl becomes upset.

"What do you do with these people?" she asks.

"That's none of your business. I'm sorry."

And that's when she explodes—all of her goodwill disappearing. "Who am I supposed to be," she demands, "an experiment that will turn you straight? God! What a coward you are . . . you chose me because I look like a boy."

"Not true. I love you."

"*Do not use that word to me!*" she screams. "You dirty faggot" (73–74).

Needless to say, this ends their relationship.

Some months later the two encounter each other on the street and have an awkward conversation. Frustrated by Noli's continuing coldness, TJ demands, "Can't we be *friends*? Do we have to throw the whole thing away?" (104).

"'I'm sorry, TJ Baker,' she replies, 'but I cannot be your friend.' Yes, she says silently, that's it. I need to be free of you so I can find *me*" (105).

And she turns on her heel and walks away. Well, the reader may think, at least she didn't call him a dirty faggot this time, I *guess* that's an improvement. Yet the characters are so uniformly unsympathetic, the reader may not really care whether or not they finally find themselves.

In lieu of this high drama, other readers may instead want to take a page from *Amy's True Love* (Sweet Valley High #75), Francine Pascal's book featuring a school friend of the Wakefield twins. Amy Sutton has set her sights on Tom McKay, a tall, blond, and popular member of the school's tennis team. Amy doesn't really know Tom, but she is determined to snag a date with him—and, hopefully, a steady relationship—which she believes will persuade her parents that she is mature enough to have her own car. (Go figure.) Despite her overtures, he is clearly not interested in a romantic relationship with Amy, which she takes as a personal blow. But not to worry— Tom's rejection isn't a reflection of her undesirability—that fact is, he's gay! Her self-esteem rebounds, which enables her to see that Tom's friend Barry, a straight but shy fellow who has had his eye on her for some time, is in fact the guy for her. Relief all around! As for Tom, well, his friends so appreciate his courageous act of self-disclosure that they vow to stand by him despite his, um, disability.

In the novels discussed so far, the focus is on the impact that coming out can have on friendships. What about the impact on families? To answer that, we return to 1991, when two supporting characters whom the reader already knows to be gay partners—Dirk and Duck, whom we first encountered in 1989's *Weetzie Bat*—reappear in *Witch Baby*, the second of what would ultimately be five novels by Francesca Lia Block about her "slinkster cool" characters. The protagonist of this novel, however, is not Weetzie but rather her young "almost" daughter Witch Baby, who—during the course of the novel—outs Dirk and Duck to Duck's unsuspecting mother, Darlene. Certainly some readers may take exception to Witch Baby's action, but the point should be made that she isn't motivated by malice or spite. On the contrary, she loves both Dirk and Duck and identifies with their outsider status, since she herself feels that she doesn't belong anywhere. "What time are we on and where do I belong?" she plaintively wonders at the novel's outset.

Her rationale for outing the two is complicated. Part of it has to do with her wanting them to know that she understands them better than anybody else; another part is her belief in the purity of their love and her wanting others to share this belief. "They love each other more than anyone else in the world," she tells a startled Darlene (47). Though a period of emotional turbulence follows in the wake of Witch Baby's announcement, rapprochement arrives by the end of the novel. Indeed, Duck's mother, Darlene, thanks her, saying, "You knew more about love than I knew. You helped me get my son back again." Duck agrees: "Without you," he tells Witch Baby, "we [i.e., he and his mother] might never have really known each other" (99). In other words, being honest about one's sexuality is presented as being a good, even necessary thing that brings families together.

A second important novel involving the outing of a secondary character who is also a family member is A. M. Jenkins's *Breaking Boxes* (1997). In this novel, which has strong echoes of S. E. Hinton's *The Outsiders*, two brothers—sixteen-year-old Charlie and twenty-four-year-old Trent—are living on their own, their father having abandoned them years before and their mother having drunk herself to death. Trent, who goes to college part-time and works in a bookstore to support himself and his younger brother, is gay, a fact that Charlie has known since he was "ten or eleven." The younger boy is completely accepting of this, but also acknowledges that his brother keeps this part of his life "compartmentalized" in order to spare Charlie the perceived stigma of living with a gay person (even though that person is his brother, not his lover).

Another kind of compartmentalization—class conflict—is evidenced in Charlie's sometimes violent interactions with boys of privilege at his school. This begins to change, though, when Charlie befriends Brandon, one of the privileged (or, as Hinton would call them, "Socs"). Unfortunately, the boys' friendship is shattered when Charlie tells Brandon that Trent is gay. Brandon, who may be conflicted about his own sexuality, violently overreacts, ending his friendship with Charlie and, worse, outing Trent to Luke, the de facto leader of the privileged boys, who taunts Charlie, making cruel jokes about

Trent and suggesting Charlie may also be gay like his brother ("I hear it's genetic" [162]).

Charlie—thinking, "God. I can take almost anything but I can't take it when people who don't know Trent see him as less than he is. And *laugh*" (178)—physically attacks Luke. Events thereafter conspire plausibly to bring Charlie and Brandon back together and to restore their friendship.

Charlie's acceptance of and devotion to his older brother is touching. More importantly, A. M. (Amanda) Jenkins displays an extraordinary ability to create multidimensional male characters, both straight *and* gay, and to capture the authentic sounds of their conversation. Also, as in *Witch Baby*, the revelation of a member's homosexuality ultimately strengthens the emotional viability of a family.

Unfortunately, the opposite situation—homosexuality driving families apart (at least initially)—is a more common outcome in YA novels of the nineties, such as Marilyn Levy's *Rumors and Whispers* (1990); Christina Salat's *Living in Secret* (1993); Nancy Springer's *Looking for Jamie Bridger* (1995); Margaret Bechard's *If It Doesn't Kill You* (1999); and Han Nolan's *A Face in Every Window* (1999). All of these books feature punishing fathers who seek to expel a gay/lesbian character from the nuclear family.

It is interesting to note, however, that among the books published in the nineties, all but a handful of secondary characters who come out are family members. The exceptions are the novels that include AIDS, in which the PWA might be a father, uncle, or older brother, but is equally likely to be a teacher. The only nonfamily adult to come out in a book that doesn't feature AIDS is also a teacher, the protagonist's social studies teacher Mr. Padovano in Ellen Jaffee McClain's ironically titled *No Big Deal* (1993).

Of far more compelling interest to this study are the sixteen 1990s novels of homosexual visibility in which the gay/lesbian character who is outed or who voluntarily comes out is the protagonist. As with the novels already discussed, these range from the very good (e.g., *Baby Bebop* by Francesca Lia Block, *Deliver Us from Evie* by M. E. Kerr, *Peter* by Kate Walker, *What I Know Now* by Rodger Larson, and *Dare Truth or Promise* by Paula Boock) to the frankly unfortunate (*The Drowning of Stephan Jones* by Bette Green and *Desire Lines* by Jack Gantos).

Three of the best titles—*Peter* by Kate Walker, *The Blue Lawn* by William Taylor, and *Dare Truth or Promise* by Paula Boock—are imports, one (Walker) originally published in Australia and two (Taylor and Boock) in New Zealand. Together, they demonstrate that teens in other Western societies share the exciting but often painful experience of discovering one's homosexuality, coming to terms with the discovery, and sharing it with others.

Peter (1993) is the story of a fifteen-year-old Australian boy whose ambitions are simple: finish school, get a road license for his dirt bike, and find a job with cameras. But things begin to change when he meets David, his college student brother's best friend. David is openly gay, and Peter begins to worry that the strong attraction he feels to the older boy may mean that he, too, is gay. For Peter, whose knowledge of homosexuality is rooted in societal stereotypes, the prospect is not pleasing. Despairingly, the boy at one point thinks, "I didn't want to be a poofter joke, a social outcast, a candidate for AIDS" (144).

Yet, as author Walker dramatically demonstrates, identifying as a straight male can mean subscribing to ignorant and often mean-spirited sexual stereotypes. It can mean repeatedly having to prove your manhood by performing empty-headed and dangerous feats of derring-do on your dirt bike and by having urgent, impersonal, exploitative sex with girls you hardly know. As he contemplates these problematic macho expectations, Peter worries, "You could die of this" (144).

Fortunately, he finds in David a gay young adult who is not a stereotype but a warm, intelligent, caring human being. "David wasn't a creep," Peter muses. "He was nice, ordinary" (42). When David gently rebuffs Peter's awkward advances, the younger boy learns that sexual identity is more than the simple act of sex, but rather one of the most complexly ambiguous aspects of being human. Indeed, when the book ends, Peter is still uncertain about his own sexual identity. At David's suggestion, however, he is more comfortable with giving himself the time to see how his life unfolds. Readers will understand that whatever Peter ultimately discovers, he will turn out to be—like David—nice and ordinary on his own terms. And most importantly, he will be loved and cared about like everyone else.

William Taylor's *The Blue Lawn* (1999) is another international novel that explores young teenagers' uncertainties about their sexuality. Set in New Zealand, where it was first published in 1994, this is the story of fifteen-year-old David, a star rugby player who is strongly attracted to Theo, a new boy in school. Theo, who is slightly older, is living with his wealthy grandmother while his mother is abroad for a year. David soon learns that Theo is similarly drawn to him. Ironically it is a car crash (yes, another one) that provides the evidence. Theo wrecks his car while the two are on a drive in the country. Neither boy is hurt and, giddy with relief, Theo covers David's hand with his. It's an awkward moment; neither boy says anything, but both seem to realize that their friendship might be more complex than they had thought.

While David is comfortable with this, Theo is deeply conflicted about his feelings. "See," he later tells David, "I don't want to live with the idea that I'm a queer and that I'll always feel like this."

"Bloody hell, Theo," David hotly replies. "If you're made this way, you go on being made this way."

Theo is unconvinced. "You could go through your life as a queer? As a poof? As a pansy? And there's worse words than them for what it is." David responds by chiding Theo: "Just let things be as they are for as long as it seems right" (71–72). Though not completely convinced, Theo is willing to continue the friendship, which gradually deepens. However, the two never give physical expression to their feelings except for occasionally holding each other and sleeping entwined in each other's arms.

It is on one of those occasions that Theo's grandmother discovers the boys asleep together. David is unaware of her discovery until his next visit, three days later, when he discovers that Theo, without even a word of fare-well, has gone home to Auckland. Devastated, David understands immediately that the grandmother has sent Theo away.

"We never did no harm," David tells her in a deeply moving scene of confrontation. "We never did anything wrong and it's not wrong. It isn't. You know about him'n'me, eh? And you got rid of him."

"My dear, my dear," she replies, "it is better . . . better . . ."

"Better?" David asks bitterly. "Better for who?" (104).

After a month without hearing from Theo, David finally goes to visit his older sister, who conveniently lives in Auckland, and to find Theo, who remains conflicted about his own feelings toward David. "I don't know how I see you. I don't know whether I see you as a friend. As a brother. As a lover. God knows, maybe we do need a bit of time apart so's we can see what our feelings really are and what it is we really are" (112). David can do little but accept this; the two boys embrace and Theo promises he will visit again, but it seems unlikely that Theo will sort out his feelings anytime soon.

Later David poignantly asks his sister if she has ever been in love. When she acknowledges that she has, he asks, "Can you tell me, does it always hurt? Does it always hurt so really, really bad?" (116). She can offer no answers to her brother's questions, but she proves to be an accepting and sympathetic listener. For readers who prefer unambiguously happy endings, this may seem like cold comfort but the fact is that love, for the young, can be both painful and mysterious. Is the wisdom of the heart deeper than that of the mind? Perhaps David and Theo will find out in their own time.

From a different perspective, this narrative could also be viewed as a more recent version of the story told over and over again in the lesbian pulp romances of the 1950s: two same-sex, star-crossed lovers meet only to be driven apart by social taboos. One partner heads toward a limited but socially acceptable heterosexual future, while the other, remaining homosexual, is left with painful memories and a broken heart.

Another nineties novel from New Zealand (whose plot also includes a car crash) is Paula Boock's *Dare Truth or Promise* (1999), which recounts the story of Louie (short for Luisa) and Willa, who meet and fall in love. For Louie, this is a first experience of love. Willa, however, is slowly mending from the emotionally traumatic breakup of an earlier relationship with a girl named Cathy, whose family—religious fundamentalists—have been instrumental in separating the two girls. Once burned, twice shy, Willa is at first reluctant to open her heart to Louie but, in fairly short order, the two fall mutually and deeply in love. But even then the relationship is a difficult one. Cathy, now deeply disturbed emotionally, reappears. Though the young women are "out" selectively (Willa's loving mother knows and is supportive; Louie comes out to her best friend, Mo, who is also supportive), they are well aware that there is no place in their small, conservative community where they can go to be open about their love. Religion becomes a problem again, since Louie's Roman Catholic family regards homosexuality as sinful.

When Louie's mother discovers the two girls together in bed, she orders Willa out of the house and does all she can to keep the two apart. Finally, Louie gives in and asks Willa for a "time-out" from their relationship, and Willa is heartbroken. Louie's mother pressures her to accept a date with a boy to the school dance. But when Willa, too, appears at the dance with a boy, Louie is devastated and finally drives off. It is not hard to guess what happens next.

Concerned, Willa follows and finds Louie in the wreck of her car, which she has crashed in a suicide attempt. Fortunately, Willa is able to perform impromptu first aid, saving Louie's life, and the two are reconciled in the hospital. Although this melodramatic finale is by now a cliché in LGBTQ+ YA fiction, it is the only off-key note in an otherwise satisfying and realistic romance. And the car crash as catalyst for salvaging a relationship is a neat twist that turns this convention of early LGBTQ+ fiction on its head. (Unfortunately the equation of homosexuality and death by automobile still occasionally continues to appear, most recently in Sharon Dennis Wyeth's 2004 novel *Orphea Proud.*)

A few of the plot elements in Boock's otherwise successful novel do seem a bit too pat; for example, the author is overly fond of parallels that seem—à la a school examination—to compare and contrast. Willa's mother is the direct opposite of Louie's, for example, warm and understanding where the other is cold and rigid. Too, as the relationship between Willa and Louie starts to unravel, it begins to seem eerily like Willa's failed relationship with Cathy. Even Willa has a sense of déjà vu. Any failures of plotting are redeemed, however, by the characterizations that are strong throughout, even those of the minor characters. Another plus factor is that the point of view of the story shifts back and forth between Willa and Louie, a device that helps readers track the characters' respective emotional developments.

Religion is negatively involved in both relationships. Yet the author offers a contrast here as well when Louie has a heart-to-heart talk with her extraordinarily understanding parish priest. "How lucky you are to love and be loved in return," he says. According to him, love is a gift from God; thus, to reject love—any kind of love—is to reject God. He also manages to avoid didacticism as he simply states his beliefs, which Louie is free to take or leave. With its focus on homosexuality as an aspect of love, this novel may be regarded by many readers as an *Annie on My Mind* for the 1990s.

Speaking of *Annie* invites the observation that its author, Nancy Garden, remains one of a small group of American writers for teens who have each produced a number of insightful and emotionally satisfying novels about young people discovering and coming to terms with their sexual identities. Other prolific authors in this group are M. E. Kerr, Jacqueline Woodson, and Francesca Lia Block.

In 1995, for example, Block wrote the fifth and final novel in her Weetzie Bat (Dangerous Angel) cycle. Titled *Baby Bebop*, it is a prequel to *Weetzie Bat* and tells the story of Weetzie's friend, Dirk McDonald, and his life before he met either Weetzie or the love of his life, Duck Drake. Like Witch Baby, Dirk is in search of his place in the world. Raised by his grandmother Fifi, Dirk has known "since he could remember" (3) that he likes boys. Though he dreams of being on trains with "naked fathers . . . taking showers together," Fifi says it's just a phase. "Just a phase. Dirk thought about those words over and over again. Just a phase. Until the train inside of him would crash. Until the thing inside of him that was wrong and bad would change" (6).

When it doesn't, Dirk decides "the main thing was to keep to himself and never to seem afraid."[7] He doesn't want to be like his grandmother's friends, Martin and Merlin, a longtime gay couple who "had been hurt because of who they were. Dirk didn't want to be hurt that way. He wanted to be strong and to love someone who was strong" (6). Unfortunately he falls in love with someone who isn't—his best friend, Pup Lambert. "Dirk's heart sent sparks and flares through his veins like a fast wheel on cement when he was with Pup" (18). But when he attempts to tell Pup about his feelings, the other boy responds, "'I love you, Dirk. But I can't handle it.' And then before Dirk knew it, Pup was gone" (31).

This rejection leaves Dirk afraid and riddled with self-hatred. In an act of borderline self-mutilation he shaves his hair into a Mohawk and begins to dress in black. Concerned, his grandmother gives him a family heirloom, a lamp (perhaps the same magic lamp that Weetzie Bat is given in the first of Block's series of novels) and tells him that when he is ready, he can tell his story into the lamp.

This time, however, it is the lamp that will tell *him* stories. Going to a club to hear a band, symbolically named "Fear," Dirk is set upon by a gang of skinheads and beaten nearly to death. Somehow he manages to get home and collapses onto his bed with the lamp his grandmother has given him. "Help me," he thinks, "tell me a story. Tell me a story that will make me want to live because right now I don't want to live. Help me" (49).

In fact, in an echo of Dickens's *Christmas Carol*, Dirk will receive stories of past, present, and future from the spirits of his dead great-grandmother, his parents, and the genie of the lamp. From them he learns the importance of being true to oneself, of being different, of rejecting fear, of telling one's own story unashamedly. In a beautiful moment he comes out to his father who has told him, "I want you to fight, I want you not to be afraid."

"'But I'm gay,' Dirk said. 'Dad, I'm gay.'"

"'I know you are, buddy,' Dirby said. And his lullaby eyes sang with love" (86).

Perhaps best of all, though, Dirk receives, from the genie, a vision of his future love, Duck Drake, to help him see that love is waiting, that love will come.

Block writes so luminously and openheartedly about the viability of love in whatever form it may come to us that it is almost a disservice to her work to attempt to synopsize it. In a way, all of her work is itself a dream, a vision of the transformative power of love. Indeed, a number of teens and adults have found reading Block's powerfully lyrical texts to be a transformative experience in itself. Certainly the Weetzie Bat Dangerous Angel series is essential reading for all LGBTQ+ teens, but it is also—in its urgent celebration of love *and* of human difference—essential, life-affirming reading for heterosexual teens, as well. In recognition of this, Block was named the recipient of the 2005 Margaret A. Edwards Award for lifetime achievement in young adult literature.

Published a year earlier than *Baby Bebop*, M. E. Kerr's *Deliver Us from Evie* (1994) is the strongest of her novels with LGBTQ+ content. In it a sixteen-year-old Missouri farm boy, Parr Burrman, tells the reader about his attractive, eighteen-year-old sister, Evie, who—with her short, slicked-back hair—looks like Elvis Presley, is good with machinery, and is jeeringly called Parr's "brother" by the other boys at school.

Evie, though not officially out to anybody, is nevertheless a walking, talking stereotype of the "butch" lesbian. However, she is unapologetically so. As she tells her anxious father, "I don't give a ding-dong-damn what people say about me! Okay?" (57–58). And later, after she comes out to her mother, she says about her appearance, "Some of us *look* it, Mom! I know you so-called normal people would like it better if we looked as much like all of you as possible, but some of us don't, can't, and never will! And some others of us go for the ones who don't, can't, and never will" (86).

This echoes author Kerr's own feelings as expressed in her foreword to Roger Sutton's 1994 book *Hearing Us Out: Voices from the Gay and Lesbian Community*. In recalling how "very early into our own self-acceptance, we [she and other gay and lesbian people] could not yet tolerate those among us who 'looked it.' It took a while to grasp the meaning of gay pride, and that it did not mean looking and acting as straight as possible."[8]

The occasion for Evie's coming-out is her having met and fallen in love with beautiful Patsy Duff, daughter of the local banker. Her mother's first reaction is to question the validity of her daughter's conclusion ("You don't know that for sure, honey" [85]) and then to blame Patsy ("*She* did this to you" [85]). Both parents are heartbroken by their daughter's revelation but do not reject her.

As for Parr—he is less concerned that his sister is a lesbian than he is about her affairs taking her away from the farm and leaving it to him to stay to work the land, something neither he nor their older brother wants to do. After getting drunk with Cord, an older boy who is still smarting from his rejection by Evie, Parr goes along with Cord's plan to publicly post a sign outing Evie and Patsy. Cord justifies this by telling Parr it's for Evie's own good—that it will force Patsy's father to send his daughter away and Evie will, presumably, come to her senses.

As it happens, it is Evie who goes away—to St. Louis—in the wake of the resulting parental firestorm. Ultimately, Patsy follows and the two go to Paris and then move, together, to New York. The book concludes with their reconciling visit home. As Evie says her good-byes and begins to drive away, her mother calls after her, "Don't you two be strangers" (177). And the reader realizes that mutual acceptance of personal differences is a viable and attainable goal, despite the emotional obstacles one must overcome to reach it.

Unlike Evie and Patsy, Jan and Kerry, the two girls who are the coprotagonists of Nancy Garden's second lesbian love story *Good Moon Rising* (1996), initially deny the rumors that they are lovers but, following a campaign of increasingly vicious innuendo that begins to destroy their relationship, courageously choose to come out.

Unlike her earlier *Annie on My Mind*, which is set in New York City, Garden sets this story in a small town in New Hampshire. Jan and Kerry—a new girl in town!—meet when they both audition for their high school's production of Arthur Miller's play *The Crucible*. Their drama teacher, Mrs. Nicholson, explains the theme of the play (and also, the reader realizes, the novel), thus: "It is a play about misguided power and the cruelty of falsehood and about the sin of blindly following the common herd" (36). The equation between the alleged witches in Salem and contemporary gays is underscored when the teacher later gives her cast a pep talk: "I want to weep over this play, over the injustice that is done to these innocent people. I want to be at the edge of my chair by the end of the first act, and in tears by the final curtain" (93).

The element of suspense in Garden's novel is not whether the two girls will realize and acknowledge their attraction to each other; they have already done that by page 75 of this 230-page novel. Nor is it whether guilt or internalized homophobia will poison their new relationship. They know their feelings are rooted in love. And as Kerry says, "I don't see how loving someone can be wrong, like some people say. What could be immoral or sick about love?" (117).

No, the element of suspense comes over whether "the injustice that is done to these innocent people" will destroy their relationship. The injustice is an increasingly strident smear campaign launched by a homophobic senior, Kent, who plays the lead in the play. The climate of fear this creates evokes that of witch-hunting Salem and provides a dramatic and plausible motivation for the two young women's fear of coming out.

Unfortunately their public denial of their feelings begins to poison their relationship and their capacity for being true to themselves. Jan even allows herself to participate in a singularly harebrained scheme proposed by her older friend, Raphael, whom she had met in summer-stock theater. An openly gay man, he is as stereotypical a character as Charlie Gilhooley in *Night Kites*. Improbably, he suggests taking Jan to the cast party where they will pretend to be boyfriend and girlfriend. Jan goes along with this until Kerry arrives at the party, when the charade becomes unbearable to both of them and they publicly declare their love.

The reaction of the other students is generally positive, though both girls recognize, as Jan says, "It's not going to be easy, Kerry, for either of us" (229). Kerry replies, "Nothing worthwhile is easy." And adds, in an echo of the ending of *Annie on My Mind*, "What do we care what people think of us? Some of them will probably never understand. But maybe we can try to show them the truth. Maybe we've already started." Jan has the last word: "Right. Maybe we have" (230).

Like *Annie*, this is another important book about the equation of homosexuality and love and of being open, honest, and truthful about one's feelings. It is not without its flaws, however. Kent seems to lack motivation powerful enough to fuel his almost psychotic behavior, though there are suggestions that he is jealous of Jan's acting abilities and may be afraid that he, himself, is a latent homosexual. For an out gay man, Raphael's suggestion that Jan pretend to be straight seems improbable, though, again, there is some motivation in the story as he tells her of his having been the victim of gay-bashing when he was in high school. His story evokes a similar scene from Scoppettone's *Trying Hard to Hear You*. Finally, the scenes in which the girls express their feelings for each other seem a bit awkward and their dialogue sometimes stilted. However, the sincerity of the author's feelings, the power of her convictions, and the intelligence she brings to her writing make this a book that remains worthy of readers' attention.

Garden published two other books with LGBTQ+ content in the 1990s: *Lark in the Morning* (1991) and *The Year They Burned the Books* (1999). *Lark in the Morning* will be treated in our discussion of the literature of gay assimilation.

First, however, a few words about two of the least successful of the LGBTQ+ books of the nineties, Bette Greene's *The Drowning of Stephan Jones* (1991) and Jack Gantos's *Desire Lines* (1997). Both involve the death of a gay character as the result of the same kind of rabid homophobia rooted in bigotry and religious fundamentalism that first appeared in the problem novels of the 1970s.

The Greene novel charts the course of the persecution of two gay men, Frank and Stephan, lovers who improbably move from Boston to a small town in rural Arkansas to open—of all stereotypical things—"The Forgotten Treasures Antique Shop." Why on earth two gay men would move to a town that the local real estate agent, pointing a "pudgy finger toward the crest of the mountain where a seven-hundred foot high concrete Jesus was visible for miles in any direction," proudly describes it as "the crown jewel on the glittering buckle known as the Bible Belt" is beyond understanding (34). And, once there, why on earth do they stay? They've scarcely arrived in town before locals are calling them "sodomites, faggots, fruit flies" (9–12), and worse, and an outraged local merchant has ordered them out of his store, observing, "Somebody with a little guts would do the whole world a favor if they'd blow both of those fags' brains to smithereens" (13).

His melodramatic declaration is followed by this clumsy bit of foreshadowing: "From the far side of the store, his son thoughtfully took in his dad's words. Removing his hand from the pocket of his chinos, he fashioned a pretend gun with his right hand . . . and announced with an air of finality, 'Bang! You're dead. And bang! You're dead, too'" (13).

Predictably the boy, Andy, becomes the leader of a pack of other teenagers who will hound Stephan, a lapsed Roman Catholic seminarian and the more "sensitive" of the two (it's hard to tell who is more ill served by stereotypical characterization, the two gay men or the small-town residents), to his death by drowning. Though the teens—now called "The Rachetville Five"—will be brought to trial, they will receive a suspended sentence contingent on their doing one hundred hours of community service. The reader is to believe that justice is served, however, when the author has the surviving partner, Frank, approach Andy after the trial and loudly assure him, in the presence of his parents and "more than a dozen members of the press," that he needn't fear "exposure" from him, since the proof of his (i.e., Andy's) affair with Stephan "is no more" (214–17). Of course, Andy had no such affair but his supremely ironic punishment is to be perceived by his family, friends, and neighbors as being gay himself. Clearly, this is intended by the author to be a fate worse than death, and though she surely didn't intend it, this is tantamount to gay-bashing every bit as savage as anything the Rachetville Five did.

Any defects in the Gantos book pale by comparison. Also set in a small southern town, in Florida this time, *Desire Lines* is a story told by Walker, a sixteen-year-old boy who discovers that two of his classmates, Karen and Jennifer, are lovers. This remains his (and their) secret until an itinerant preacher and his son arrive in town, and the son, setting up shop on the high school's playing field, begins a campaign of gay-baiting, with Walker as his principal target. Though Walker is straight, he panics and offers up his secret knowledge about Karen and Jennifer. Unable to cope with being publicly outed, the two attempt suicide. Jennifer succeeds, but Karen survives to confront Walker, accusing him of being the "real" killer of her dead friend.

Although parts of Gantos's book are quite good—especially the richly realized setting, a consistently bleak tone, and a kind of darkly gothic religiosity that evokes Flannery O'Connor—the plot seems contrived, and the girls' instant leap from being outed to attempting a double suicide turns a contemporary, realistic story into Lillian Hellman's dated 1930s melodrama *The Children's Hour.* Overall, homosexual visibility books tell stories of truth, of the positive and negative results when LGBTQ+ characters are honest about their sexual orientation. They are important stories, but fortunately they are no longer the only ones that can be told.

GAY ASSIMILATION

This brings us to our second category of LGBTQ+ literature, gay assimilation, which began to appear more frequently in the nineties. Its hallmark, remember, is the inclusion of characters whose homosexuality is not an issue; it's simply a given and assumes a melting pot of sexual and gender identity. Not surprisingly, though, such stories remained rare in the 1990s. Of the sixty-nine LGBTQ+ novels published during that decade, only a handful could be described as true examples of assimilation. More often, the characters who "happen to" be gay are openly gay for a reason that is central to the purpose of the plot; for example, the character has AIDS—Morris Gleitzman's *Two Weeks with the Queen* (1991), Deborah Davis's *My Brother Has AIDS* (1994), and Theresa Nelson's *Earthshine* (1994)—or is a parent whose open homosexuality poses only a minor but fixable problem for the protagonist. Examples of the latter include A. M. Jenkins's *Breaking Boxes* (where the parent figure is an older brother); Chris Crutcher's short story "A Brief Moment in the Life of Angus Bethune," featuring a boy who has not one but two sets of gay parents; and Carol Dines's story "Lezboy" about a boy with two mothers. A third type is the case of the openly gay secondary character who is necessary to a protagonist's struggle for sexual or personal identity, for example, David in *Peter* or Dirk and Duck in *Witch Baby.*

"Truer" examples of gay assimilation novels with minor secondary characters whose homosexuality is simply an integral part of who they are include Jacqueline Woodson's *The Dear One* (1991), in which a lesbian couple are close friends of the protagonist's mother. (This was only the second novel in the genre to include characters of color who are homosexual, Rosa Guy's *Ruby* being the first.) Other books with unproblematic gay minor characters are Francesca Lia Block's *Missing Angel Juan* (1993) in which an elderly gay couple, Mallard and Meadows, become friends with Witch Baby, and Adele Griffin's *Split Just Right* (1997), which includes a gay neighbor of the protagonist Danny and her mother.

Significant secondary characters who "just happen" to be gay are rarer still but include Waylon, the protagonist's older friend and mentor in Gary Paulsen's novel *The Car* (1994), Barbie's friend Griffin in Block's *I Was a Teenage Fairy* (1998), Pook, one of the three friends featured in Jess Mowry's *Babylon Boyz* (1997), and, most prominently, Gio's friend and unrequited love Marisol in Ellen Wittlinger's Printz Honor Award title *Hard Love* (1999). This last novel is also an example of our third category, queer consciousness/community, and is discussed further in that context below.

In only one novel of gay assimilation from the nineties, Nancy Garden's *Lark in the Morning* (1991), is the protagonist a person whose homosexuality is simply a given. In this case it is Gillian, seventeen, who in a romantic relationship with her longtime best friend Suzanne. The two are apart for the summer—Gillian with her parents at the family's summer cottage in Rhode Island, Suzanne home in New York City—and they are not yet out to their parents. But with Suzanne at a distance, the focus of the novel is Gillian's attempts to help two young siblings, Lark and Jackie, who are on the run from their abusive parents. During the 1990s, realistic novels of gay assimilation were only possible when the LGBTQ+ content was fairly minor *or* when the LGBTQ+ protagonist had more urgent problems to deal with (hiding abused children) than coming out to her likely-to-be-sympathetic parents.

QUEER CONSCIOUSNESS/COMMUNITY

During the 1990s, the idea of queer community also began to appear more frequently in young adult novels, though the community itself was not necessarily any more visible or immediate than before. In fact, the model that had begun to appear in the 1970s, that of the queer community being somewhere offstage, often in the past, sometimes in the future, usually urban, and definitely far from the teen protagonist's home, persisted through the eighties and well into the nineties. This was particularly true for novels that included AIDS as a plot element and that typically involved a gay character and his family dealing with the disease.

One common scenario—always told from the perspective of a young person—involved an older brother or uncle who had made his home in a city with a sizable gay/lesbian community. Before the book opens, however, the character has contracted AIDS and in the course of the story returns to his family of origin to die. This plot first appears in M. E. Kerr's *Night Kites* (1985) and is repeated in other books published throughout the 1990s. In

Penny Durant's *When Heroes Die* (1992), for example, the protagonist is a boy whose uncle has AIDS. In Deborah Davis's *My Brother Has AIDS* (1994), a teenage girl's older brother returns to the family home. In both Melrose Cooper's *Life Magic* (1996) and Gregory Maguire's *Oasis* (1996), the protagonist's uncle is taken in by the protagonist's parent(s). These books provide few details about the gay community except to locate it somewhere else. Since the lives of these gay men, even those whose families fully accept and embrace them, have been led offstage, the gay community exists only in the past and is, thus, entirely invisible.

In other books of the 1990s, the LGBTQ community, though still off-stage, is more optimistically placed in the future. This time the temporal distance is not insurmountable—it's just a matter of getting there. Chris Lynch's *Dog Eat Dog* (1996), the final book in the author's Blue-Eyed Son trilogy, is an example. Over the course of the three books, Toy has been the straight protagonist Mick's friend, a good-looking motorcycle-riding loner whose cool and quiet presence has been a rare constant in Mick's chaotic life. Toy is also gay, and his departure is not unexpected news to Mick:

> Toy began dropping hints that he might not be around anymore once the summer came.
> "What, you mean like a trip, only longer?" I asked hopefully.
> "Ya, like longer," he said.
> "I know I'm not supposed to ask this, but where are you gonna go?"
> Under the straw hat, a big grin pushed his ears up, pushed the hat up.
> "Home," he said, almost sadly. "I'm thinking I'm going to go home."
> This seemed like a lot of information from Toy. I tried not to sound surprised. "Where's home?"
> "I don't know yet," he said. (135–36)

However, even when the queer community is located offstage the reader sometimes gets to see the gay characters *after* they've finally found their kindred spirits. In M. E. Kerr's *Deliver Us from Evie* (1996), for example, the prodigal daughters return to Missouri for a reconciling visit. Still as respectively butch and femme as ever, Evie and Patsy are obviously prospering in the gay-friendly environment of New York City. As Evie's father wryly observes, "You're like the railroad worker's daughter. You made tracks for a better station in life" (175).

In some books, the gay community is actually close enough to visit. In Paul Robert Walker's *The Method* (1990), for example, the reader can observe a community of gay people in their native habitat—in this case a gay-friendly restaurant. As previously noted, Mitch takes the protagonist Albie downtown to watch the gay pride parade, and then to a gay restaurant. "There was an old-fashioned ice-cream parlor in the middle of the next block. It was decorated like something out of the 1890s, with wicker ceiling fans slowly circulating the air. On the walls there were posters of Marilyn Monroe, Bette Davis, and Joan Crawford" (135). As the two friends sit at the counter, Mitch tells Albie that he is gay, and Albie reflects on this news while watching "the gay waiters run up and down the counter, dishing out sundaes and sodas and shakes and banana splits. He watched the gay customers, eating and laughing at the tables" (136).

In another restaurant scene, the young male protagonist of Rodger Larson's *What I Know Now* (1997) visits a pizza parlor with a mixed gay and straight clientele. "These men and women looked comfortable, happy. I believed the men and women in the Gay Nineties Pizza Parlor had interesting thoughts, told funny stories, enjoyed being together. I had a wish then. The wish was to be a part of this group of people, to belong among them, to fit in" (180).

The queer community may also be found at parties, picnics, and get-togethers with friends. In Cristina Salat's *Living in Secret* (1993), for example, Amelia attends a New Year's Eve party with her mother and her mother's partner, Jane. "Denise shares a large house near Golden Gate Park with her brother, Michael, and his boyfriend, Andy. The white-rugged living room is full of people dancing. I notice men are dancing with men, and women are dancing with women. I've never seen so many gay people in one place before. Then I notice that some women are also dancing with men. Nobody seems to mind anyone else. I am amazed. I didn't know gay people and straight people ever hung out together" (94).

Jacqueline Woodson's *From the Notebooks of Melanin Sun* (1995) features Mel, an African American teen, and his mother, EC, who are a tight-knit family of two. When Kristin, who is white, comes into EC's life, Mel is upset by Kristin's racial and cultural difference and what he perceives as her intrusion into his home. After Mel's initial rejection of his mother and Kristin as a couple, EC convinces him to join her and Kristin for a picnic at Jones Beach—and to see what he is gaining rather than what he is losing through his mother's lesbian relationship. "Kristin led us to the area that was mostly gay. It was strange seeing so many of them all coupled up in one place, but it made it feel less weird to be there with Ma and Kristin. We passed a group of people that Kristin knew and she stopped and introduced us." Mel and Kristin walk on the beach, and she tells him how much the two of them have come to mean to her. "'I've always wanted a family,' Kristin was saying, 'I lost mine [when] they found out I'm queer.'" Now she has a different family: "'Not the family I was born into,' she said, 'the family I made for myself. Close friends.'" This need for family and community is underlined in a later conversation. "'Yesterday,' Kristin said. 'I was thinking about buffalo. Can you imagine being the last to die off?' I shook my head. 'I'd want to go in the crowd.' 'Me too,' Kristin said softly, 'Me too'" (132–37).

In all of these books, however, the LGBTQ+ community is a community of adults being observed by a straight teen protagonist. What does such a community look like when it's composed of LGBTQ+ teens themselves? Young adult fiction's first gay/lesbian peer support group appears in Jesse Maguire's 1991 novel *Getting It Right*. In it, Eric, a closeted high school student, mistakenly believes that Josh, one of his classmates, is gay. When Eric queries Josh about his own coming-out story, Josh explodes, "I'm not gay!" After an anguished Eric attempts suicide, a more enlightened Josh and his friends nudge the boy into attending a program sponsored by the high school Gay and Lesbian Alliance, a sketchily rendered group that includes a music geek, a self-described "gay radical," and a lesbian planning to go into the ministry.

Four years later, a much more fully realized gay/lesbian support group is portrayed in R. J. Hamilton's two-volume Pride Pack series, *Who Framed Lorenzo Garcia?* (1995) and *The Case of the Missing Mother* (1995). As typical series books, their plots are predictable, their characters are unidimensional, and much of their dialogue reads like the transcript of a television police drama, but these titles provide an attractive, if perhaps unrealistic, picture of a community that embraces many differences.

In the first title, sixteen-year-old Ramon has been rejected by his family of origin for being gay. After living on the street and in foster homes for two years, he finds an adoptive gay father in police officer Lorenzo Garcia. He also finds a family of friends who hang out together at the Gay and Lesbian Center: Cady, an Asian American lesbian; Aron, whose older brother is gay; Maddie, a Jamaican-born computer genius; Sammi, a lesbian punk rocker; and George, a handsome white athlete. Obviously, some of the teens are gay or lesbian, while others have gay/lesbian family members, but all welcome Ramon into their group, which later becomes the Pride Pack as they begin to investigate drug charges trumped up against Officer Garcia. In the book that follows, *The Case of the Missing Mother*, the Pride Pack investigates the disappearance of a lesbian political activist and discovers that she has been kidnapped by members of a radical right group. The Pride Pack utilizes its members' various skills—from computer wizardry to physical tracking—to locate and release the activist and bring her kidnappers to justice.

Formal groups are certainly useful, but teens may also find their LGBTQ+ peers and a sense of community in informal friendship networks. However, where one gay/lesbian person or a single gay/lesbian couple may go unnoticed in the mainstream world of YA fiction, three or more gays or lesbians can be frightening, discomfiting, or, yes, liberating representations of gay/lesbian people as a community. To closeted teens who are uncomfortable with their own same-sex attractions, such a group of "people like me" is understandably threatening. For example, Cary, the narrator of *Tomorrow, Wendy* by Shelley Stoehr (1998), is struggling with her attraction to her boyfriend's sister. Hence her dismay when the clique she calls "the lesbian collective" sit down at her table in the high school cafeteria. Her discomfort increases when she sees them at the dance club she and her boyfriend frequent:

> I watched the lesbian girls hanging out by the bathroom. A couple of the girls were too heavy for me. One had beautiful hair and a mysterious parched face, but her legs were too spindly-long, and I didn't like the way she dressed. . . . I wouldn't want to be in a clique like that. I mean, in school those girls were never separated. It was like they couldn't stand on their own. I guessed it must be hard, but I still didn't like the almost political force they tried to be, and meanwhile people still laughed at them from across the room. Besides being pathetic, it pissed me off that their public hand-holding and kissing had nothing to do with love. It was more like they were spitting in unison at the rest of us. (32)

Clearly, there is no way Wendy could find this crowd comfortable. But for gay/lesbian teens on the lookout for kindred spirits, meeting not just one, but a whole group of gay/lesbian people can offer the thrill of self-affirmation and at least the promise of community. John, the narrator of *Hard Love* by Ellen Wittlinger (1999), falls in love with Marisol, a self-identified "Cuban American Yankee lesbian" and creator of the zine *Escape Velocity*. Marisol values John's friendship but (gently and firmly) rejects his longing for something more. When the two go to a writers' conference together, they meet a group of lesbians from New York whom John observes warily. "There were four women sitting at the table, three of whom stared intently at Marisol, trying to decide if what they suspected was true. For her part, Marisol locked onto each of them as Bill said their names (Sarah, BJ, June) and she couldn't seem to move past them as the other names were announced" (207). They invite Marisol to return with them to New York City and she joyfully accepts—she's finally reached escape velocity and is traveling on her own toward her future life as part of the community she's been heading for all her life.

Hard Love, a Printz Honor Award winner, was a groundbreaking book not only for its portrayal of a single LGBTQ+ teen seeking out a queer community but also as the first portrayal in young adult fiction of a straight young man falling for a lesbian. Perhaps most importantly, it was the first YA novel with LGBTQ+ content to win a major literary honor. Thus, it set the stage for the next decade's gradual movement of the genre from the literary ghetto to the mainstream of literary acceptance and recognition.

We conclude this chapter with a description of a final nineties text, Marion Dane Bauer's *Am I Blue? Coming Out from the Silence* (1994), a groundbreaking collection of short stories featuring LGBTQ+ characters in narratives that fit into all three categories. This remarkable book also anticipates many of the publishing and narrative trends in LGBTQ+ fiction that began in the nineties and have continued into the twenty-first century. *Am I Blue?* is an anthology of sixteen original short stories with LGBTQ+ content, all by established YA authors. The sixteen stories demonstrate a gender equity and narrative diversity not generally found in this body of literature: half of the stories include gay males, half lesbians, and the LGBTQ+ content is an almost equal mix of nine protagonists and seven secondary characters. By way of comparison, seven YA novels with LGBTQ+ content were also published in 1994. Of the seven novels, only one had a LGBTQ+ protagonist, while six had LGBTQ+ secondary characters. Two of these novels included lesbian characters, while five included gay male characters. All of these characters were Caucasian Americans. In contrast, the sixteen short stories represent a remarkable diversity of characters and genre.

The first (and titular) story is a humorous fantasy; the final story is a memoir of a girl who realized she was "different from other little girls" when she was four years old. Settings include Vietnam, San Francisco, rural Wyoming, a beach on Lake Erie, a summer community on Nantucket island. The LGBTQ characters themselves are likewise diverse, of varying race, class, and cultural backgrounds, and stand in varying relationships to the protagonists. One protagonist is a boy returning from the funeral of his father's lover; another is a girl whose older sister brings home a friend for the summer, a lesbian who has been disowned by her parents. A boy surreptitiously watches a male sunbather on a deserted beach; a girl comes out to her grandmother; a group of gay teens, male and female, staff a literature table for their school's Gay-Straight Alliance at Parents Night. Another group of filmmaking friends includes a gay couple in their movie depicting an unorthodox and touching version of the Nativity; a young lesbian agonizes over her future career options; a boy who has just been gay-bashed is visited by Melvin, a wish-granting fairy godfather.

Taken together, these stories anticipate future trends toward a (slowly) increasing diversity of LGBTQ+ YA fiction in a number of directions: narrative distance, writing style and techniques, genre and language, and setting. In a genre that has so often defined and portrayed "gay" as white, middle class, suburban, and male, *Am I Blue?* heralds an expansion of gender, race, class, and culture variables of YA fiction. Within this collection of sixteen stories, Bauer has created a world that can give all of us hope.

NOTES

1. Michael Cart, *From Romance to Realism*, 3rd ed. (Chicago: ALA/Neal-Schuman, 2016), 177–78.

2. Advocates for Youth, http://www.advocatesforyouth.org .

3. Centers for Disease Control and Prevention (CDC), "Diagnoses of HIV Infection in the United States and Dependent Areas, 2015," *HIV Surveillance Report, 2016*, vol. 27, published

November 2016, https://www.cdc.gov/hiv/group/age/youth/index.html (accessed January 8, 2018).

4. Michael Cart, "A Place for Energy, Activity, and Art," *English Journal* 93, no. 1 (September 2003).

5. For annotated chronological list of the sixty-nine YA fiction with LGBTQ+ content published in the 1990s, see *The Heart Has Its Reasons: Young Adult Literature with Gay/Lesbian/Queer Content, 1969–2004*, by Michael Cart and Christine A. Jenkins (Lanham, MD: Scarecrow Press, 2006), pp. 115–126.

6. Christine Jenkins, "From Queer to Gay and Back Again," *Library Quarterly* 68, no. 3 (July 1998), 301, 304.

7. M. E. Kerr, foreword to *Hearing Us Out: Voices from the Gay and Lesbian Community*, by Roger Sutton (Boston: Little, Brown, 1994), 5.

8. Kerr, foreword to *Hearing Us Out*, 5.

Chapter Five

A New Literature for a New Century

The rapid growth of U.S. young adult publishing that began in the 1990s continued in the first decade of the twenty-first century. One indication of this is the appearance of new publisher imprints created specifically to publish young adult books. This trend began in the 1990s with HarperTempest and Simon Pulse and accelerated in the following decade (2000–2009), when more YA imprints appeared, including Scholastic PUSH, Penguin Putnam Razorbill, Abrams Amulet, Houghton Mifflin Graphia, Simon & Schuster Simon Spotlight Entertainment, Llewellyn FLUX, Aladdin Mix, and Harlequin Kimani TRU.

With the expansion of the genre overall, the number of YA titles with LGBTQ+ content also grew. The book industry keeps no reliable count of the total number of young adult books published annually, but we saw a marked increase in YA titles with LGBTQ+ YA literature, jumping from seventy-eight titles in 1990–1999 to 252 titles in 2000–2009 (see appendix B for publishing trends over time).

Besides growth in sheer numbers, LGBTQ+ titles also mirrored the larger YA literary world in terms of their expanding inclusion of new forms, faces, genres, themes, voices, narrative strategies, and more. During the previous three decades stories with LGBTQ+ characters were commonly relegated to a small and specialized niche on the periphery of the assemblage of YA fiction described as "contemporary realism." However, at the start of the twenty-first century, YA fiction with LGBTQ+ content was moving away from being an isolated or "ghettoized" subgenre and toward becoming a more integrated part of the increasingly varied body of young adult literature as a whole. To demonstrate this, let us briefly consider eight important trends that have informed the growth and enriched the overall content of YA litera-

ture during this decade and examine how each trend is represented by
LGBTQ+ titles.[1]

CROSSOVER TITLES

Whether a book will be classified as adult or young adult is more often a
marketing decision than an editorial one. Though such YA classics as Robert
Cormier's *The Chocolate War* (1972) and Bruce Brooks's *The Moves Make
the Man* (1984) were written as adult titles, their publishers felt they would
find a greater readership as YAs and that, accordingly, was how they were
published and marketed. A similar but slightly different case is Block's
Weetzie Bat (1989). Though it, too, was written as an adult title but published
as a YA, this title successfully blurred the line between YA and adult by
attracting legions of readers who were not only in their teens but also in their
twenties and thirties. A. M. Homes's *Jack*, published in the same year as
Weetzie Bat, is another example of this trend. Called "crossover" books
because they crossed over the traditional boundary separating YA and adult
readerships, these novels heralded the advent of a newly expansive definition
of the term "young adult." This trend was spurred by publishers' growing
attempts to expand the retail market for YA books by publishing titles that
appeal to readers as old as twenty-four and twenty-five, a population now
described as "new adults." Examples of crossover LGBTQ+ young adult
books from 2000 to 2009 that illustrate this trend: *Finding H.F.* by Julia
Watts (2001); *The Shell House by* Linda Newbery (2002); *Sammy & Juliana
in Hollywood* by Benjamin Alire Saenz (2004); *Swimming in the Monsoon
Sea* by Shyam Selvaduri (2005); *The Center of the World* by Andrea Steinhofel (2005); *Refugees* by Catherine Stine (2005); *Life as I Knew It* by Randi
Hacker (2006); *Mistik Lake* by Martha Brooks (2007); *Someday the Pain
Will Be Useful to You* by Peter Cameron (2007); *What They Always Tell Us*
by Martin Wilson (2008); *Twelve Long Months* by Brian Malloy (2008);
Secrets of Truth & Beauty by Megan Frazer (2009); and *Magic and Misery*
by Peter Marino (2009).

LITERARY FICTION

In a departure from traditional problem- and plot-driven YA fiction, a number of publishers have begun issuing literary novels that are character driven
and are enriched by considerations of ambiguity, complex structures, and
nuanced treatment of situation and theme. Such novels respect the maturity
of many contemporary young adult readers and stimulate their emotional and
intellectual development. There was a time when LGBTQ+ content would
have been considered beyond the sophistication of teen readers. And of

course books of literary excellence could have LGBTQ+ content, but some critics assumed that such content was "inappropriate" for books for young adults. Literary excellence in young adult literature was given official recognition in 2000, the inaugural year of the Printz Award, and *Hard Love* by Ellen Wittlinger (1999), a story in which the male protagonist falls in love with a young woman who is an out lesbian, was named a Printz honor book. In 2003 two more books with LGBTQ+ content received Printz Award attention when *My Heartbeat* by Garret Freymann-Weyr (2002) was named a Printz honor book and *Postcards from No Man's Land* by Aidan Chambers (2002) became the first LGBTQ+ YA book to win the Printz Award. (See appendix C for further information about Printz and other literary award winners.)

The year 2003 turned out to be a signal one for YA LGBTQ+ literature, not only in Chambers and Freymann-Weyr receiving Printz recognition, but also in Nancy Garden's receiving the prestigious Margaret A. Edwards Award, which honors an author, as well as a specific body of their work, for making a "significant and lasting contribution to young adult literature." Garden was recognized specifically for *Annie on My Mind* (1982), which the award committee praised as "the first lesbian love story with a positive ending." Thus, the award was an acknowledgment of the importance of LGBTQ+ literature as well as Garden's specific contribution to it.[2]

Garden was neither the first nor the last prolific author of LGBTQ+ YA fiction to receive the Edwards Award. A decade earlier, M. E. Kerr received it, the award citation mentioning *Night Kites* (1986), though not its gay content. More recently, the 2005 Edwards Award went to Francesca Lia Block, and most recently, the 2016 Edwards Award to David Levithan. Both Block and Levithan have made substantial contributions to the visibility of LGBTQ+ content in young adult novels. Interestingly, both of these authors rose to prominence as significant young adult authors with their first published YA titles, Block's *Weetzie Bat* (1989) and Levithan's *Boy Meets Boy* (2003), both of which are now considered must-read classics in LGBTQ+ young adult literature.

In addition to identifying excellence in young adult literature, members of YALSA also began highlighting adult books with YA appeal via the Alex Awards, an annual list of ten books marketed as adult titles but judged to have a special appeal to teen readers. The Alex Awards were first given in 1998, and in 2002 the Alex Award became an official ALA award. The award is so named in recognition of the work of Margaret Alexander Edwards, one of the early leaders of young adult librarianship, who was called "Alex" by her friends. Alex Award winners with LGBTQ+ content from this decade include Brian Malloy's *The Year of Ice* (2003), Bart Yates's *Leave Myself Behind* (2003), Brendan Halpin's *Donorboy* (2004), and David Small's *Stitches: A Memoir* (2009).[3]

It must be noted here that the crossover phenomenon goes both ways, and an increasing number of titles published as adult fiction incorporate the same teen perspective, protagonist, and issues found in YA fiction. One of the first of these was Chbosky's already-discussed *Perks of Being a Wallflower* (1999). Other adult titles with LGBTQ+ content and a YA sensibility include K. M. Soehnlein's *The World of Normal Boys* (2000), Michael Lowenthal's *Avoidance* (2002), Carla Trujillo's *What Night Brings* (2003), and Luis Alberto Urrea's *Into the Beautiful North* (2009).

NEW NARRATIVE TECHNIQUES

Closely related to the trend in more literary fiction is the increasing number of novels that employ new and/or nontraditional narrative techniques rather than assuming that teen readers are best served by straightforward narratives told in chronological order. Aidan Chambers pioneered this strategy within the body of LGBTQ+ YA fiction in *Dance on My Grave* (1982). Ellen Wittlinger experimented with a variety of techniques in her 1999 Printz honor novel *Hard Love* (1999), which is told in a visual collage composed of John's first-person narrative, excerpts from his and Marisol's zines, their letters to their parents and to each other, and the lyrics of the titular song. Wittlinger's *Heart on My Sleeve* (2004), whose characters include the lesbian older sister of the protagonist, is told via e-mails, instant messages, handwritten letters, notes, and postcards. Brian Sloan's *Tale of Two Summers* (2008) is a story told in the alternating voices of two good friends—one straight and one gay—in first-person posts on their mutual blog.

NEW FORMATS—GRAPHIC NOVELS AND COMICS

The use of the sequential visual art to tell stories for young readers has a history that began with newspaper comic strips and came of age in the 1930s when comic books became wildly popular among youth of all ages. Graphic novels began appearing in the late 1980s and early 1990s, when specific titles brought the possibilities of sequential visual art to the attention of a broad audience of teens and librarians serving teens, notably, Art Spiegelman's *Maus I* and *II* (1986, 1991) and Scott McCloud's *Understanding Comics* (1993). During the 2000–2009 decade, two graphic novels with LGBTQ+ content, Judd Winick's *Pedro and Me: Friendship, Loss, and What I Learned* (2000) and Alison Bechdel's *Fun Home: A Family Tragicomedy* (2006) came to the attention of a broad audience via national book awards. (*Fun Home* was also turned into an award-winning Broadway musical.) Chapter 9 of this text examines the history and current status of this medium's inclusion of LGBTQ+ content in stories geared to teen readers.

SHORT-STORY RENAISSANCE

The renaissance of the American short story that began in the 1980s become a major trend in young adult publishing, manifesting itself in (1) collections of stories by a single writer and (2) theme-driven collections of original short stories by different authors. In terms of YA fiction with LGBTQ+ content, this trend was first seen in the 1990s. The earliest example of a single-authored collection in YA literature with LGBTQ+ content is Chris Crutcher's 1991 collection *Athletic Shorts: Six Short Stories,* which included two stories with LGBTQ+ characters. In 2000–2009, more single-author YA short-story collections appeared that included one or more stories with LGBTQ+ characters: Kathi Appelt's *Kissing Tennessee* (2000), Ellen Wittlinger's *What's in a Name?* (2000), Rich Wallace's *Losing Is Not an Option* (2003), Kathy Stinson's *101 Ways to Dance* (2007), and David Levithan's *How They Met, and Other Stories* (2008). Several other single-author collections appeared in which all of the stories had LGBTQ+ characters, including Nancy Garden's *Hear Us Out: Lesbian and Gay Stories of Struggle, Progress, and Hope, 1950 to the Present* (2007); Julie Anne Peters's *grl2grl: Short Fictions* (2007); and Michael Whatling's *Vigil for Joe Rose: Stories of Being Out in High School* (2009).

The earliest example of an LGBTQ+ thematic YA short-story anthology appeared in 1994: Marion Dane Bauer's groundbreaking YA anthology *Am I Blue? Coming Out from the Silence,* a collection of sixteen original short stories written by sixteen different authors of YA fiction. Two other anthologies published in 2000–2009 had a similar overall focus on LGBTQ+ issues: by P-P Hartnett's *The Gay Times Book of Short Stories: The Next Wave* (2001); and Michael Cart's *How Beautiful the Ordinary: Twelve Stories of Identity* (2009), a collection that could be viewed as a successor to Bauer's landmark *Am I Blue?* Cart edited two more YA anthologies in this decade that included one or more stories with LGBTQ+ content: *Love and Sex: Ten Stories of Truth* (2001) and *Necessary Noise: Stories of Our Families as They Really Are* (2003).

POETRY RENAISSANCE

Poetry has become an enormously popular literary form with young adult readers, especially novels written in free verse. Six with LGBTQ+ content were published in this decade: Virginia Euwer Wolff's *True Believer* (2001), Helen Frost's *Kesha's House* (2003), Sonya Sones's *One of Those Hideous Books Where the Mother Dies* (2004), David Levithan's *The Realm of Possibility* (2004), and two novels in verse by Ellen Hopkins, *Impulse* (2007) and *Tricks* (2009).

INTERNATIONALIZATION

Though originally an American contribution to world culture—like the Broadway musical and jazz—young adult literature is now a staple of publishing in virtually every English-speaking country in the world. Editor Marc Aronson pioneered the American publication of YA titles from abroad in the Edge imprint he created when he was at Henry Holt in the 1990s. He has subsequently spoken and written widely on this topic.[4] However, the Edge titles were not the first imported YA books with LGBTQ+ content. As noted in chapter 2, British authors Aidan Chambers, David Rees, and Jean Ure were published in the United States in the 1980s. In the 1990s the small handful of LGBTQ+ imports published in the United States includes Diana Wieler's *Bad Boy* (1992), first published in Canada; Kate Walker's *Peter* (1993) from Australia; and Lutz Van Dijk's *Damned Strong Love* (1995), translated from German and published in Aronson's Edge series

Young adult publishing in 2000–2009 saw a sharp increase in the number and proportion of imported YA titles with LGBTQ+ content. Of the total of 252 YA novels with LGBTQ+ content that appeared in this decade, thirty-six (14 percent) were imports; of those thirty-six, only two (6 percent) were translated titles (*The Center of the World*, by Andreas Steinhofel [2005] and *Girl from Mars*, by Tamara Bach [2008]). Both were originally published in German, then translated and published in English by a U.S. and a Canadian publisher, respectively. This paucity of translated books with LGBTQ+ content reflects an overall lack of translated books from U.S. publishers. The rest of the imports—thirty-four (94 percent) of the thirty-six—were from English-speaking countries: Canada (twenty-two titles), followed by England (eight), Australia (three), and New Zealand (one). Of the twenty-two Canadian titles with LGBTQ+ content, seven were from Orca Press, six from Groundwood, three from Red Deer Press, two from Lorimer, and one each from five other publishers.

Interestingly, during this decade, two of these Canadian presses, Orca and Lorimer, were the *only* publishers in *any* English-speaking country to publish YA titles with LGBTQ+ content that could be classified as "hi-lo"—high-interest fiction (that is, books designed to engage teen readers via contemporary real-life settings, believable and diverse characters, situations, and dialogue) with a relatively brief text (120–150 pages) written at a third- to fifth-grade reading level. Of the five that appeared in 2000–2009, two were in Lorimer's Side Streets series (Tamara Williams's *Truth and Lies* [2002] and Sarah Diersch's *Out* [2009]), two in Orca's Soundings series (Carrie Mac's *Crush* [2006] and Robin Stevenson's *Big Guy* [2008]), and one in Orca's Sports series (Jeff Rud's *Crossover* [2008]).

HISTORICAL FICTION

Historical fiction has been a popular adult genre for generations. Until fairly recently, however, teen fans read the same books as adult fans—*very* few YA fiction titles were set in the past. This is no longer the case, and YA fiction set in the past has become a popular genre in the field. While it's difficult to pinpoint the causes for this trend, we can see it in phenomena like the run-away popularity of the American Girls series and of Scholastic's two historical fiction imprints Dear America and My Name Is America, so it may be that childhood exposure to these and other children's books set in the past (Laura Ingalls Wilder's Little House books, L. M. Montgomery's Anne of Green Gables books, and others) have raised the profile of historical fiction for teen readers. Examples of such historical novels with LGBTQ+ content published in 2000–2009 include George Ella Lyons's *Sonny's House of Spies* (2001), set in the American South in the 1950s; Catherine Jinks's *Pagan in Exile* (2004), set in twelfth-century France; Kim Taylor's *Cissy Funk* (2004), set in the American West during the 1930s; Catherine Stine's *Refugees* (2005), set in New York City and Afghanistan in the months immediately following 9/11; Pat Lowery Collins's *Hidden Voices: The Orphan Musicians of Venice* (2009), set in Venice of the early 1700s; and Liza Ketchum's *Newsgirl* (2009), set in and around San Francisco during the California Gold Rush.

* * *

HOMOSEXUAL VISIBILITY

There was more visible support for real life LGBTQ+ teens in the twenty-first century than in the twentieth. As noted earlier, the first decade of the twenty-first century saw innovations and changes that continued to make YA literature one of the most dynamic areas of publishing. However, one aspect remained a constant in 2000–2009 YA novels with LGBTQ+ content: the preponderance of books that fit into the category of homosexual visibility (HV). The lives of LGBTQ+ teens in twentieth-century YA fiction focused in large part on coming out: first, to themselves, then to their friends and families, and finally in the larger world of their school and community. Certainly the worrisome dilemmas confronting fictional teens of this decade are the same slings and arrows of outrageous homophobia that have confronted LGBTQ+ characters from the earliest years of the genre. But what happens next? Stories that included teen characters' lives *after* coming out were slower to make their way into YA fiction.

For some fictional teens, coming out is not nearly as painful as they anticipated, but it is hard to ignore the worst-case scenarios that spring from a teen's fear of the unknown. The teens in nearly all of these books live in homes with one or both parents on whom they depend on for all their basic needs. Parental rejection may be expressed in silence and/or harsh words, but it can also mean the withdrawal of all material support and homelessness. In fact, research on LGBTQ+ teens indicates that they are significantly overrepresented in the population of homeless teens. In this decade's books, a handful of LGBTQ+ teen characters were homeless as a result of coming out, some of which are described below.

Considerations of sexual identity and occasional gender ambiguity loom large in many titles published in this decade, and these books reflect various attempts to expand upon the category of homosexual visibility, whether or not there is a self-identified gay character. For example, Canadian author Glen Huser's *Stitches* (2003) tells the gender-bending story of Travis, a junior high school boy with a penchant for sewing who aspires to a career as a professional puppeteer. Predictably, this exposes him to charges of being gay, the usual homophobic name-calling and (failed) attempts at gay-bashing. *Stitches* is reminiscent of Mary Sullivan's *What's This about Pete?* (1976), but Travis's narrative is left more open ended with regard to his future life and relationships. Sullivan makes it clear that Pete's worries are groundless and the book closes with an affirmation of his heterosexuality as he looks forward to his upcoming first date with his classmate Barbara. In contrast, *Stitches* ends with Travis happily enrolled in a fine arts high school where "no one seems to mind how different you are" (196), making new friends (one who wants to be a fashion designer, another a musical actress, a third a screenwriter) and continuing to pursue his puppeteer dreams.

Homosexual Visibility and Young(er) Protagonists

The apparent phenomenon of people coming to terms with LGBTQ+ issues and identity (their own or others) at younger ages continued in the twenty-first century. This early awareness is reflected in YA fiction in which middle school age characters begin to recognize their own same-sex attractions. For example, in one of the stories in Kathi Appelt's *Kissing Tennessee* (2000), an eighth-grade boy is wrestling with his feelings for another boy. In *City Girl Country Girl* by Lisa Jahn-Clough (2004), thirteen-year-old Phoebe falls in love with another girl. And in Alex Sanchez's *So Hard to Say* (2004), thirteen-year-old Frederick is questioning his feelings for another boy.

However, LGBTQ+ people of all ages live in a web of connectedness of family (parents, siblings, cousins, aunts/uncles, etc.), friends, neighbors, schoolmates, teammates, and others, so we also see another kind of homosexual visibility in LGBTQ+ YA literature as these younger teens, who may or may not identify as LGBTQ+ themselves, come to terms with learning that people who are already in their lives are in LGBTQ+.

In the 1990s there were books like Morris Gleitzman's *Two Weeks with the Queen* (1991) and Bruce Coville's *The Skull of Truth* (1997), stories about middle-school-age teens coming to terms with the sexual identity of older family members or other adults. This continued in books published in 2000–2009. In Marlene Fanta Shyer's *The Rainbow Kite* (2002), for example, a twelve-year-old boy learns his fifteen-year-old brother is gay. Nancy Garden's *Holly's Secret* (2000) gives us Holly, an eleven-year-old girl protagonist, who is hiding the fact that she has lesbian parents from her friends. In Sarah Withrow's *Box Girl* (2000), thirteen-year-old Gwen's father is gay and it looks like his partner Leon will be moving in with them. Gwen likes Leon, and he is clearly looking forward to living with them as a family, but she fears what her father's homosexual visibility might mean for her own relationships with friends and classmates. In George Ella Lyon's *Sonny's House of Spies* (2004), a thirteen-year-old boy learns that both his father and his surrogate uncle are gay. In A. C. E. Bauer's *No Castles Here* (2007), the eleven-year-old protagonist learns that the Big Brother assigned to him is gay.

Amadeo Kaplan, the sixth-grade protagonist of E. L. Konigsburg's *The Mysterious Edge of the Heroic World* (2007), casually accepts the fact that elderly antique dealers Bert and Ray are a gay couple. But then Amadeo hears the harrowing story of how Johann, father of his beloved godfather Peter, was spirited out of wartime Germany by *his* older brother Pieter, a gay man who wore a pink triangle and died in a labor camp for "social undesirables" in Hitler's Germany. Thus, the revelation of homosexual visibility unlocks the book's central mystery and a new understanding of the very-close-to-home impact that the Nazi persecution of homosexuals has had on the lives of Amadeo and his loved ones.

In Lauren Myracle's *Luv Ya Bunches* (2009), four fifth-grade girls—Violet, Katie-Rose, Camilla, and Yasaman—form a social network they call FFF (Flower Friends Forever). Camilla lives with her two mothers, which raises no alarm with Camilla's friends, but led to a serious conflict between the author and her publisher when Myracle's editor told her that in order for Scholastic to include *Luv Ya Bunches* in their highly profitable Scholastic Book Fairs, she'd need to change Milla's two mothers to a father and a mother as the publisher wanted to avoid letters of complaint from parents. Myracle refused to make this change, stating: "I find that appalling. Over 200,000 kids in America are raised by same-sex parents just like Milla. It's not an issue to clean up or hide away. In my opinion, it's not an issue at all. The issue, as I see it, is that kids benefit hugely from seeing themselves reflected positively in the books they read. It's an extremely empowering and validating experience." As news of this conflict circulated, Scholastic re-

ceived a petition from more than four thousand people who supported Myracle's position, and accordingly reinstated *Luv Ya Bunches* (and Milla's two
mothers).[5]

Homosexual Visibility and Sexual Abuse

Guilt, self-hatred, social opprobrium, and homophobia with their corollary
threats of violence—either self-imposed or imposed by others—remained
fixtures of many homosexual visibility novels throughout this period. One
aspect of violence, though, which had previously received little or no attention—sexual abuse—also began to surface during this period, a reflection,
perhaps, of the higher visibility being accorded this issue by both the media
and society in general. In the five years from 1999 to 2003, five YA novels
were published that focused on these concerns: Catherine Atkins's *When Jeff
Comes Home* (1999); Kathleen Jeffrie Johnson's *Target* (2003); Adam
Rapp's *33 Snowfish* (2003); Brian Doyle's *Boy O'Boy* (2003); and Rebecca
Fjelland Davis's *Jake Riley: Irreparably Damaged* (2003).

Atkins's novel is the story of fifteen-year-old Jeff, who has been returned
to his home after having been kidnapped two and a half years earlier by a
man who calls himself "Ray." During his period of captivity Jeff has routinely been forced to have sex with his captor, who has also photographed the
boy naked. Even after Ray is finally apprehended, Jeff refuses to talk about
what has happened until his former captor, who is about to be released on
bail, insists that Jeff was a willing and complicit sexual partner.

Although it's clear to the reader that Jeff hates himself for unwillingly
submitting to sex with Ray, most other people—including virtually every
student at Jeff's school—believe he must be gay and subject him to horrible,
even gothic, verbal and emotional abuse. Only one of his former friends, Vin,
comes to his defense, but then admits that he himself may be gay and in love
with Jeff. The matter is never pursued further and many readers will, accordingly, view Vin's friendship as potentially suspect, that is, a search for personal gratification.

Similarly, we never see enough of Ray to understand his motivations
beyond his sexual appetite for young boys, which will be enough to convince
many readers that the man is gay. But is he? This blurring of the line between
homosexuality and pedophilia is dangerous, especially when it moves one of
the characters (Vin's mother!) to say, "These faggots that prey on our kids,
they should be strung up, electrocuted, tortured . . ." (102). In the book, as is
often the case in real life, this portrayal of adult gay men as depraved pedophiles goes unchallenged. And the fact that most pedophiles are heterosexuals is never mentioned.

This gay-man-as-child-molester stereotype is seen again in Johnson's
Target, a novel about the consequences of the rape of sixteen-year-old Grady

by two men. This time, however, the motivation for a male's sexual abuse of another male is at least mentioned when the point is made that such attacks are seldom sexually motivated but are, rather, exercises in power and domination. That said, *Target* is a disturbing book that leaves unresolved the relationship between the boy's assault and homosexuality, an issue that is further confused by Grady's terror that his having been singled out for an attack—and his failure to resist that attack—must mean that he himself is gay.

There is no question that the adult pedophile, a heavily stereotyped, effeminate church organist in Doyle's *Boy O'Boy*, is also gay. It is also clear that his interest in the angelically beautiful Martin O'Boy is part of a pattern that the working-class community is aware of but tolerates (the book is set in Canada at the end of World War II)—until, that is, Martin's hero, his older neighbor Buzz Sawyer, returns from the war, learns about the organist, and resolves the problem by threatening the man with violence: "If I ever hear about you again, I've got your address here and we'll come after you, my friends and I, and you'll wind up the sorriest organ player that ever had a fondness for fiddling with choir boys . . ." (157). Once again, a gay man is typecast as a pedophile who must be stopped at all costs. But the only effective solution offered for stopping him is threats and physical violence, while the viability of "curing" violence with more violence is neither addressed nor questioned.

In Davis's book, title character Jake Riley has apparently been sexually abused while in reform school and is thus considered by school counselors to be "irreparably damaged." The irony, however, is Jake's admission that he lied when he said the "bigger boys" made him "do it." "Nobody ever forced me," he admits, "I liked it" (251). The situation is darker and more intense in Adam Rapp's haunting *33 Snowfish*. Here the sexual violence is suffered by a young teen named Custis who has been abused and sexually exploited by the man who, he says, "owns" him. Happily, Custis ultimately escapes and finds the promise of a hopeful future when an elderly man named Seldom gives him sanctuary.

More than any other issue we have addressed, the sexual abuse of young people is one that requires extraordinarily skillful and balanced treatment. Fiction about it can also inform thoughtful discussion and provide teens with knowledge and strategies for recognizing abusive situations they or their friends may encounter.

Homosexual Visibility in Protagonists: Dealing with Difficulties

Our examination of YA literature over time has made it abundantly clear that books published in the 1970s and 1980s included numerous negative experiences suffered by fictional LGBTQ+ teens. Their lives were likely to be fraught with sorrow and strewn with obstacles—including, but not limited to, car crashes. Clearly, gay lives were *not* happy lives. Stories of homosexual visibility were coming-out stories and thus were likely to include problems. Closets can feel safe and coming out of them a risk that cannot be taken lightly. The ongoing stress faced by LGBTQ+ and other minority-status people can make LGBTQ+ lives difficult indeed. Indeed, Eric Rofes titled his 1983 book on LGBTQ+ people and suicide *I Thought People Like That Killed Themselves: Lesbians, Gay Men, and Suicide.*[6]

Other less drastic solutions (such as "reparative therapy") have been proposed and tried, but there are few documented successes or cures for the "problem" of teens' same-sex attractions. Teens themselves may create their own system of driving their same-sex attractions away. For example, in Lee Bantle's *David Inside Out* (2009), we see a high school boy treat his same-sex attractions as a bad habit that can be broken or extinguished via home-made aversion therapy. Whenever he feels such attractions, he snaps a rubber band he always wears around his wrist for just this purpose. However, despite his good-faith efforts to snap the gay out of himself, his feelings continue and he must finally admit to himself that the treatment simply isn't working. Happily, his plan B has a greater probability of success: working on self-acceptance and finding ways to meet other gay teens—and maybe even a boyfriend.

However, in the literature of the early twenty-first century, there are also examples of punishment meted out to LGBTQ+ teens by their adults that are all too real. The statistics are damning, but as teens have begun to come out at younger ages, increasing numbers of LGBTQ+ teens have been kicked out into homelessness by their parents or guardians. A recent study of homeless youth in New York City reported that the average age at which lesbian and gay youth in New York became homeless was 14.4 years, while the average age for homeless transgender youth was 13.5 years.[7] A 2010 study of homeless youth compared the proportion of LGBTQ+ youth in the general population (5–10 percent) to the proportion of LGBTQ+ youth among homeless youth and found that 20–40 percent of homeless youth identified themselves as LGBTQ+ or otherwise gender nonconforming.[8] When homeless young people were asked why they were homeless, the most frequent response was conflict with parents/family, and the most frequent reason given for the conflict was young people's sexual orientation.

A number of YA stories of homosexual visibility end with the teens' unanticipated relief to be truthful about their lives and accepted by their families. Other stories do not follow that path, as teens may have realistic fears as to the negative consequences of coming out to their parents, certain that the results will be disastrous. And sometimes they are right, an outcome rarely depicted in YA fiction. It is not uncommon for homelessness to be a (spoken or unspoken) threat from parents in coming-out stories, but rarely does the threat materialize. But what if the threat is realized?

When parents or guardians tell teens that they are no longer welcome, that their home is now their *former* home, what happens next? Thus far in the twenty-first century, there are significantly more true stories about actual LGBTQ+ young people becoming homeless than there are in the fiction written for young people. But there are a handful of novels from this decade that do explore what happens when the worst-case scenario is realized. In Mayra Lazara Dole's *Down to the Bone* (2008), Cuban American Laura has been in a relationship with Marlena for two years, but when a teacher finds and reads aloud a love letter from Marlena to Laura in class, they are both expelled. Marlena's family sends her back to Puerto Rico to get married; Laura's mother kicks her out of the house, but Laura is a survivor and arranges to move in with her best friend's family.

In like manner, Holland, the seventeen-year-old female protagonist of Julie Anne Peters's *Keeping You a Secret* (2003), has lived with her mother all her life in relative harmony. Holland is having an excellent senior year, with social status as student council president and swim team member *and* a good-looking boyfriend. But then she meets and falls in love with Cece, a new student at her school, a lesbian who is out and proud. At first they are able to keep their relationship secret, but when it is discovered, her mother goes ballistic, and Holland is suddenly homeless and must find ways to support herself during her last semester of high school. With the help of Cece, she persists and endures. Stories of LGBTQ+ teen survivors are more frequent in the second decade of the twenty-first century than they were in the first, but more are needed. Lots more.

Homosexual Visibility in Secondary Characters

A number of other novels dealing with homosexual visibility were published during this period. Many are what has now become such a common plot point (straight protagonist who thinks he or she has never met an LGBTQ+ person meets one and is surprised to learn that the person is gay, either because the protagonist has assumed the gay person is straight, or really never thought about it at all). The former is more often the case with peers; the latter is more common with family members and nonfamilial adults. There are, as we began to see in the 1980s, a number of narratives—including, but not limited to, Hila Colman's *Happily Ever After* (1986) and Ann Rinaldi's *The Good Side of My Heart* (1987)—in which straight female protagonists are interested in a romantic relationship with a boy who is, in fact, gay. In such cases, the revelation of that person's LGBTQ+ identity is greeted with shock, followed by anger, then sorrow, and finally acceptance. During the 1990s we saw this same "hell hath no fury like a woman scorned" scenario as part of a coming-out narrative in Barbara Wersba's *Whistle Me Home* (1997), though in the case of Wersba's protagonist Noli, she gets stuck in the anger phase.

Early in this century, Virginia Euwer Wolff's *True Believer* (2001) provided an innovative approach to the is-my-boyfriend-gay? coming-out story—a girl discovering that the sweet and attractive boy she's been swooning over is gay—artfully told as a novel in verse. Sonya Sones's *One of Those Hideous Books Where the Mother Dies* (2005), another artfully rendered novel in verse—this one interspersed with letters and e-mail—tells another coming-out story as a girl learns that her father is gay.

Similarly, in Ellen Wittlinger's *Heart on My Sleeve* (2006), a girl learns that her older sister is a lesbian, but in a novel told in the form of e-mails, instant messages, and letters. Another book by Wittlinger, *What's in a Name* (2008), is a novel in the form of linked short stories, in one of which a boy comes out and in another of which the reader sees the impact of this action on his older brother, a football star.

In *Dairy Queen* (2006), the first book in Catherine Gilbert Murdock's Dairy Queen trilogy, DJ, who already works long hours on her family's dairy farm, is determined to try out for her high school's football team. She's also starting to get involved with Brian, a neighbor she's been coaching for a starter position on his team, her school's archrival. Then her longtime best friend Amber, who's been upset by all DJ's football guy work, tells DJ that she is gay and has long hoped that she and DJ would eventually be in a full relationship. DJ responds with surprise and sympathy, as she's sorry she's disappointing her best friend. The fact that Amber is gay isn't upsetting in itself, but she worries that she'll lose Amber's friendship. The two stay away from each other for a while, but by the end of the book they have returned to their best friend status. Amber is also a character in the two books that follow—*The Off Season* (2007) and *Front and Center* (2009)—in which she has a female partner, while retaining her status as DJ's best friend.

GAY ASSIMILATION

Just as the heightened visibility of teens and their increased purchasing power led to the dramatic expansion of young adult publishing that started in the 1990s, so, too, has gay assimilation in the new century become more common due—at least in part—to heightened gay visibility and market forces accruing from the discovery of homosexuals as consumers. The expanding presence of gays in commercial advertising (both print and electronic) and as characters in motion pictures—and especially in television programs—has led to their more general assimilation into mainstream culture.

A number of popular television programs with LGBTQ+ content premiered in 2000–2009. NBC's long-running sitcom *Will and Grace* (1998–2006) took a while to catch on, but it drew an increasingly large and enthusiastic audience.[9] The show's success helped pave the way for other popular television shows with LGBTQ+ content, including Showtime's *Queer as Folk* (2000–2005) and *The L Word* (2004–2009) and Bravo's *Queer Eye for the Straight Guy* (2003–2007). Their large audiences throughout this decade suggested that gay and lesbians were indeed everywhere. Equally important, so far as gay and lesbian teens have been concerned, is the routine presence of their LGBTQ+ peers on teen-targeted dramas like *Dawson's Creek* and *Felicity* as well as on MTV's reality series *The Real World*. In 2002 the Supreme Court, in *Lawrence and Garner v. Texas*, overruled a long-standing Texas sodomy law, thus legalizing same-sex sexual conduct and, as the *New York Times* put it, "underlined . . . that the nation's attitudes toward gays and lesbians are radically changing."[10] If history is any indicator, it will be a while before those radical changes become routine staples of young adult literature. But wait! What's going on in Sweet Valley? Yes, in the most commercial of venues—the teen series book—a gay character emerges (and then another and another . . .) and it really is No Big Deal.

Gay Assimilation in the Sweet Valley Universe

Francine Pascal's phenomenally successful Sweet Valley High (SVH) series and the various Sweet Valley spin-offs (Sweet Valley Kids, Sweet Valley Twins, Sweet Valley Junior High, etc.) follow identical twins Elizabeth and Jessica Wakefield from second grade through high school and on into college, careers, and marriages. The stories are told from a third-person limited point of view in numbered chapters that alternate between the perspectives of Jessica and Elizabeth. Like the earlier Sweet Valley series, the Sweet Valley University (SVU) series employs the third-person limited style but from the perspectives of up to five different characters. The multiple narrators provide the reader with a more complex understanding of characters and events and a more nuanced treatment of LGBTQ+ content.

As noted in the previous chapter, only one of the 181 titles in the original SVH series, *SVH #75: Amy's True Love* (1991), contains specific (though minimal) LGBTQ+ content. Two later SVH series have more LGBTQ+ content: Sweet Valley University (1993–2000) and Sweet Valley Senior Year (1999–2003).

LGBTQ+ Content in Sweet Valley University (1993–2000)

The next LGBTQ+ sighting in the Sweet Valley universe occurs when the twins and their friends become students at Sweet Valley University.[11] The SVU narrative covers the Wakefield twins' first two years in college, beginning with their arrival on campus at the start of the fall semester of their first year and concluding at the end of their sophomore year. The LGBTQ+ content emerges during the summer between their first and second school years and continues through the rest of the series.

The LGBTQ+ content first appears as a coming-out (homosexual visibility) narrative, but then shifts to one of gay assimilation. The gay character is introduced in *SVU #48: No Rules* (1999), the first of a three-book sequence that follows the twins (plus friends, of course) on a cross-country road trip competition between six 4-person teams in Winnebago vans. Jessica's team includes the gorgeous Neil Martin, a Stanford student who is described from Jessica's perspective on the book's back cover as "witty, sophisticated, intelligent, and best of all, single." Jessica's first sighting of Neil: "An ocean breeze blew his dark hair into his eye, and he brushed it aside with the sexiest hands Jessica had ever seen. . . . Neil grinned, and Jessica sighed loudly" (25–26). Once they are on the road she also discovers that he's "funny and smart and really knew how to have a good time" (84). The feeling is mutual, as Neil finds that "the more he was around her [Jessica] the more he liked her. She was so funny and alive" (199).

One evening the team decides to stop at a roadside karaoke bar in Wonderlust, South Dakota. Jessica invites Neil to join her in a nighttime stroll. She makes a move to "situate herself in his arms" (*#48:* 214), but he draws away from her with a stricken look.

> "I thought you knew," he said in a choked whisper. Jessica's eyebrows shot up. "Knew? Knew what?" . . . "Jessica," he said slowly. "I'm gay." Suddenly Jessica couldn't breathe. She couldn't speak. She just stared to be sure he'd said what she'd thought he said. This was impossible. She knew men. How could she make such a mistake? How could she not know? . . . Her stomach twisted dangerously, and she covered her mouth with her hand and ran for the door. Bursting out into the still, black night, she gasped for fresh air—any air. *How can I face him again?. . . Was I the only one who didn't know?* (*#48:* 215–16)

She does not return to the bar, and Neil is crushed. Readers can see her thoughts and understand that her response is a combination of social embarrassment (she's made a public fool of herself by pursuing Neil when everyone but her must have known he was gay!) and her own wounded vanity (he turned her down!). Neil blames himself and worries throughout the next book (*SVU #49: Stranded*) and much of the next (*SVU #50: Summer of Love*): "Is Jessica homophobic? Neil asked himself with a small shiver. He hated to think that anyone he liked as much as Jessica—in her happier moods—could be that small-minded, but still, she'd started acting seriously strange right after he'd told her he was gay" (*#49:* 97).

Not until the team's final stop in Key West do Neil and Jessica finally discuss and resolve their conflict:

> [Neil:] "Jessica, I thought you hated me because I'm gay. But now I know you're just mad at me because I said no."
> [Jessica:] "OK . . . but I want you to admit, right this minute, that I'm the most beautiful girl you've ever rejected."
> "You're definitely the most beautiful girl I've ever rejected," Neil promised.
> "Well, all right then," Jessica smiled. "But Neil, why would I hate you because you're gay? That's crazy."
> Neil's face lit up in a big smile. . . . "Never mind that now. We've got to make up for lost time . . . what do you want to do?"
> Neil frowned. He looked at Jessica. And then he smiled. "Shopping!" they cried in unison. (#50: 176)

Neil and Jessica cement their friendship in the SVU books that follow. In *SVU #51: Living Together* (2000), Neil transfers from Stanford to SVU, and Jessica invites him to move into the duplex that she and Elizabeth have rented. He is very relieved to live with his best bud Jessica *and* save on rent. In *SVU #53: Truth or Dare* (2000), Neil, a political science major, runs for student body president with Jessica as his campaign manager, although he worries about being outed during his campaign. Jessica's response to his fear reflects her GA sensibility: "But what I don't understand is, why *does* being outed scare you so much? I mean, what's so bad if every single person on this campus knows you're gay? Who cares, anyway?" (164). He tells his story, ending with his parents' reaction: "They disowned me. Told me I wasn't their son anymore. They totally cut me off, so there was no way I could afford Stanford. They still won't talk to me" (174).

His campaign goes fairly smoothly, but hecklers' shouted questions about his sexual orientation make him increasingly uncomfortable. In his final speech, he decides to come out publicly: "'*I am gay.*' He'd done it. He'd really done it. He'd outed himself. *His* choice. And on his terms" (221). And no, he doesn't win, but he does come in second, and he's passed a significant milestone in his own coming-out process.

In *SVU #57: Who Knew?* (2000), Neil and Jessica are both interested in the same guy, Jason, but neither can tell for sure if the good-looking Jason is straight or gay. Both of them spend time with Jason, but does going running (with Jessica) or going to the library (with Neil) really count as a date? The main drama here is of course between Neil and Jessica, both of whom become certain that they've correctly surmised Jason's sexual orientation. Then one evening Jason invites them both to meet him at a campus eatery—he's finally ready to tell them about himself: *yes*, he is in fact in the process of coming out (sorry, Jessica!), *but* he's not ready for a real relationship (sorry,

Neil!). After Jason leaves, Neil and Jessica give each other a hug, best buds once again.

The final book is *SVU #59: Elizabeth in Love* (2000). Classes end, the Neil + Jessica friendship is definitely on a solid footing, and the housemates host a spontaneous end-of-the-semester party:

> Jessica spun around, in an impromptu boogie. . . . Neil was in the corner, talking to a very hot guy in overalls, but that was cool. She and her best friend were back in the black. Suddenly she felt an arm grab her from behind. Neil grabbed her fingers and dragged her across the party. "I want you to meet someone very special. His name is Logan. And he's definitely gay." Jessica shook Logan's hand, then boogied away, leaving the two lovebirds alone. She was so happy—all of her friends were in one room, finals would be over in mere days, and it would be summer. (228–29)

Ah, youth. Ah, summer. If the series was a single textbook, what might a teen reader learn about LGBTQ+ issues and characters? Homophobic people— including parents—are ignorant, and this ignorance hurts LGBTQ+ people. LGBTQ+ people lead happier lives when they are out, but they don't want to be defined solely by their sexual orientation. Straight women (and men, too) can benefit from having gay friends, and gay guys are talented shoppers. Take one along with you next time you hit the mall!

LGBTQ+ Content in Sweet Valley Senior Year (1999–2003)

The forty-eight books of the final Sweet Valley spin-off series, Sweet Valley Senior Year (SVSY), were published from 1999 to 2003, after most of the Sweet Valley University titles were already in print. SVSY chronicles the social and emotional lives of Jessica and Elizabeth Wakefield and their grow-ing entourage of friends and frenemies during their final year in high school.

As in other Sweet Valley series, the stories utilize a third-person limited style that changes perspective several times in the course of each chapter. Each SVSY title also includes, interspersed throughout the text, clusters of brief first-person diary/e-mail entries from approximately ten characters in fonts that mimic handwriting and contrast with the more traditional font of the narrative chapters. Each book begins with three to five diary entries that provide context and introduce three to five of the lead players. The main body of the story is then told in chapters that alternate with diary entries. The chapters, like those in SVU, consist of three to four vignettes that center on one or more of the diarists plus other characters. These features work togeth-er to create a multivocal narrative collage in which ten or more characters have direct first-person speech, but no single voice or perspective dominates. The technique is particularly effective in presenting stories of gay assimila-tion.

The story begins just weeks after a major earthquake rocks Sweet Valley and surrounding communities.[12] Because the quake caused the collapse of the high school building in El Cerro, a neighboring community, five hundred El Cerro students will spend their next school year at Sweet Valley High. The resulting influx of students brings new friends (and romance, of course) to the Sweet Valley crowd. The LGBTQ+ content is a fairly straightforward story of Andy Marsden, an El Cerro student who becomes a member of the Wakefield entourage.

Andy is a likable and outgoing guy, and his humorous voice enlivens the series. Readers learn more about the other characters via their conversations with Andy, who has a reputation as a good listener, and he figures in nearly every SVSY title. In some books he has a small role, while in others he is one of the featured diarists. New to SVH and interested in meeting other students, he joins the Outdoors Club. There he encounters a girl named Six, who during a hike tries to kiss him (*SVSY #14: Split Decision*). He is nonplussed by his lack of romantic/sexual feeling toward her when she is so obviously attracted to him. His general lack of interest in dating makes him wonder if he might be gay (*SVSY #16: Three Girls and a Guy*).

Throughout the next several books, Andy goes looking for friends to talk to about his sexual orientation, but his friends are so immersed in their own dramas that they don't fully grasp the critical importance that coming out has in Andy's life. For example, when he tells Elizabeth Wakefield and her boyfriend, they tell him they don't care that he's gay—that nothing has changed between them. Not surprisingly, Andy feels like *his* life *has* changed but his friends are too caught up in their own activities and dilemmas to listen to his story. What is a very big deal to Andy—coming out to his parents—has little immediate impact on his friends, which is both an annoyance and a relief. While he is understandably annoyed not to have the immediate attention of his friends, he is also somewhat relieved that the fact of his gay identity is so clearly no big deal to them. (*SVSY #18: As If I Care*; *#19: It's My Life*; *#20: Nothing Is Forever*; *#21: The It Guy*).

Eventually, Andy ends up talking to Six, who turns out to be a sympathetic friend, and she helps him think through coming out to his parents. He does come out to them, it goes well, and their interactions become more honest and relaxed (*SVSY #22: So Not Me*). Andy's own distress lessens over time as his friends finally begin to listen to him. Most respond to his coming out in a positive fashion, and the ones who don't are able to adjust their attitudes with help from his friends who do. Even bad boy Conner, who is in an alcohol rehab center, writes to apologize for neglecting their friendship (*SVSY #23: Falling Apart*).

Andy is the sole gay character in the SVSY series until he meets his boyfriend, Dave Niles (*#36: Tearing Me Apart*). The next volume (*SVSY #37: Be Mine*) focuses on five couples on Valentine's Day, including Andy and Dave. Dave finally comes out to his parents (*SVSY #38: Get a Clue*), and the following week Dave's mother takes Andy and Dave out for a relaxed and conversational dinner (*SVSY #39: Best of Enemies*).

Subsequent SVSY titles with specific LGBTQ+ content feature Andy and Dave as diarists, both individually and in conversation with each other and/or other SV teens and adults. Andy discusses specific LGBTQ+ issues with his friends, such as coming out to parents, but also general topics, such as the pros and cons of taking a "gap year" between high school and college, where to rent a tux for prom, and how to cope with a temperamental parent.

Andy is a quintessential example of gay assimilation. Dave is less comfortable being out than Andy, but all of their Sweet Valley friends are *very* at ease with their relationship. As the seniors near graduation, Dave gets into Columbia University in New York City, which is also Andy's destination as an aspiring stand-up comic. Clearly, their love is no different than that between any other Sweet Valley couple, except perhaps more stable.

Their friends move into and out of relationships at a fairly rapid rate, while Andy and Dave remain together. As they near graduation, it's clear that their circle will begin to scatter, but they are launching their future from their current Sweet Valley community of (straight but not narrow) friends to a new community of LGBTQ+ friends (and allies) in New York City. Yesssss!!!

Gay Assimilation in *Pretty Little Liars* (2006–2014)

Sara Shepard's Pretty Little Liars may be the first mass-market YA series to include a *featured* LGBTQ+ character—in this case one of the series' four titular protagonists. The first title in the sixteen-book series appeared in 2006, and the series immediately took off, with one to two new titles appearing each year until the publication of the final one in 2014. Pretty Little Liars first appeared on the *New York Times Book Review* children's series bestseller list in 2008. By 2012, the series had been on the top ten list for a total of sixty-two weeks.[13] *Pretty Little Liars*, a popular television show based on the series, premiered in 2010 and ran for seven seasons.

The series features five upper-middle-class white girls. Four of the five (the "pretty little liars" Aria, Hanna, Spencer, and Emily) are living; one (Alison, a.k.a. Ali) is dead . . . maybe. They live with their families in Rosewood, an idyllic upper-middle-class bedroom community not far from Philadelphia. All are conventionally pretty (they are represented on each cover as well-dressed Barbie dolls: slim figures, good skin, shoulder-length hair, and beautiful but expressionless faces) and attend Rosewood Day School, a prestigious private secondary school. Despite their advantages, however, their lives are fraught with suspense, mystery, and horror because of the secrets that each is desperate to keep hidden from her family, friends, and community. Hanna is attractive and popular, but is also a bulimic shop-lifter; Spencer is a serious competitor for class valedictorian and her older sister's boyfriends; Aria is a talented visual artist who is having an affair with her English teacher; and Emily is a champion swimmer and a closeted les-bian. Ali, former middle school queen bee and intimate friend of the other four, mysteriously disappeared three years ago and is presumed dead. The individual chapters of each book are told from the perspective of each of the girls in rotation. In the context of the four problem-beset friends, Emily's same-sex attractions are presented as a dark secret comparable to Spencer's and Aria's inappropriate heterosexual attractions or Hanna's criminal acts. Like the others, Emily believes that disclosure will bring her instant ruin.

In the early books, Emily's developmental task is to come out to herself, then her peers, and finally her family. In the later books, the gay assimilation framework emerges, as the Emily's lesbian identity is no longer presented as a shameful stigma but simply a factual—and neutral—description of her sexual orientation.

The series opens at the start of the girls' junior year. Readers learn that three years earlier the friends celebrated the end of their seventh-grade school year with a slumber party. During the course of the evening, Ali stepped outside and never returned. Her inexplicable disappearance is an ongoing stress in the lives of all Rosewood residents. The remaining girls' close friendship has faded over time, but their lives remain fraught with lies and secrets. Ali's family has moved away and the St. Germain family has recent-ly moved into Ali's former house. When Emily delivers a welcome-wagon-type basket, she meets sixteen-year-old Maya St. Germain, and the attraction between them is immediate and mutual. However, this development is put on hold when construction workers find a body buried in the St. Germains' backyard, a body presumed to be that of Ali.

Aria, Spencer, Hanna, and Emily sit together at Ali's memorial service and, in the course of conversation afterward, learn that each of them has recently received anonymous texts and e-mails signed simply "A." The mes-sages threaten to disclose their secrets to their parents and classmates, which each girl believes will lead to certain disaster. Just when the four have con-firmed that this is happening to all of them, each of their phones pings simultaneously. All four see the same text: "I'm still here, bitches. And I know everything.—A." Yikes!

Who is A? The obvious answer is Ali, but she's dead, right? Then who *is* A? Why is A sending them these cruel messages? How should they deal with these threats? And of course the obvious question in a sixteen-book series: What will happen next? In a word: plenty. As they nervously await the next ping that will bring more threats from A, the four girls try to lead normal lives as high schoolers: going to classes, doing homework, juggling prior-ities, hanging out with friends, attending parties, dabbling in romance, and texting. There are secrets upon secrets, revelations upon revelations, as their search for A leads them into dangers that include physical attacks, near drownings, mysterious fires, and other hazards. The plot(s) take innumerable twists and turns as their quest for answers takes them to an isolated mountain hideaway, on a Caribbean cruise, and to points in between. How does A manage to spy on some of their most intimate moments with secret boyfriends or girlfriends? Is A trying to destroy their reputations? Their lives? Tune in to the next thrilling volume of *Pretty Little Liars*.

The reader learns of Emily's same-sex attractions almost immediately, first in her loving memories of Ali, and then through her romance with Maya. In the course of the series, Emily has a succession of girlfriends. Maya is the first, but because she is African American, Emily's racist mother forbids their friendship. When a photo of Emily and Maya kissing is circulated around the community, Emily's parents make plans to send her to Tree Tops, a treatment center that promises to turn gay teens straight. But when Emily meets Becka, who will be her peer counselor at Tree Tops, it's clear that treatment—at least with Becka—hasn't worked. Next, Emily's parents send her to spend the summer with cousins in rural Iowa, where she meets Trista, a girl who "tries to hump anything that moves, girl or guy." From there she heads to Philadelphia, is briefly involved with a guy, gets pregnant, and has a baby that she gives up for adoption. Now she has another secret. Emily heads back to Rosewood and Rosewood Day, but the temptations just keep coming. She meets Kelsey, who celebrates "'girl-on-girl action." The four friends go on a cruise, where Emily falls in love with stowaway Jordan (a.k.a. "the preppy thief"), a thrill seeker who has stolen cars, boats, even planes. But Jordan is caught, found guilty, and sent to a juvenile detention facility, where she is murdered by another prisoner, who appears to be in cahoots with A. A also plays cat and mouse with the other Pretty Little Liars and disrupts their various romances. The girls embark on a complicated quest to unmask the mysterious A, whose machinations now threaten their mental and physical health. The plot twists and turns as others are injured or even killed, but at this point, no one believes the Pretty Little Liars, so they begin working as a team put an end to A's life-threatening activities. Aria, Hanna, and Spencer appear to be aware of Emily's sexual orientation, but it does not hinder their friendship or trust in her as a team member.

In the final book in the series, *Vicious*, Emily is the hero. Ali—still officially considered dead—has gone to ground after managing to frame the four girls for her murder. Emily fakes her own suicide and goes in search of Ali, who they are certain is alive. While the other three are on trial, Emily follows clues that lead to Ali's hiding place, where she confronts Ali and manages to call 911. The police arrive just in time—Ali has a gun and isn't afraid to use it. Meanwhile, the other three girls are found guilty of murder, but when the surprise witness, Emily, and the surprisingly alive murder victim, Ali, are delivered to the courtroom, the Pretty Little Liars are set free. They are featured in *People* magazine as the "Pretty Little Truth-Tellers," while Ali is locked up in an institution for the criminally insane. Happy ending!

The character of Emily grows and matures throughout the series and becomes the hero at the story's climax. Early in the series (Book #2: *Flawless*), she states that she cannot come out because "everyone would make fun of me" (565). But the final pages of the final book (Book #16: *Vicious*) report that Emily is living in California and has come to see her family's disapproval of her lesbianism as *their* problem, not hers. "She would always love them, but it was easier to do so from afar, at least until they came to terms with who she really was. And for now, that was okay. Because she had another family, a *real* family, people who accepted her no matter what. Her friends" (329–30).

Gay Assimilation—Secondary Characters Who "Just Happen to Be" LGBTQ+

One manifestation of gay assimilation is the growing number of secondary characters in YA fiction who "just happen" to be gay. One example is Rachel Cohn's *Gingerbread* (2002), in which protagonist Cyd Charisse (yes, named after the movie star) has lived most of her life with her mother in California. However, her mother wants to get her away from her surfer dude boyfriend, so she sends her to Manhattan to spend the summer with her father, Frank. There she is also introduced to her as-yet-unmet half siblings, the children of her father and his former wife. One is Elspeth, a chilly and humorless adult. The other is Danny, who is openly gay and lives with his partner Aaron. The two of them own a coffee shop in the Village, where CC gets a job as a barista.

Randi Hacker's *Life as I Knew It* (2006) depicts a different take on gay assimilation. Protagonist Angelina Rossini lives with her parents in a small New England town. Her best friend is Jax, who is gay but not out to his family. Her mother's best friend Liz is a lesbian, and Angelina discovers that her bête noire, Celeste, is a lesbian and has a crush on her. There are a significant number of LGBTQ+ characters here, but their LGBTQ+ identities are secondary to the significant roles that each plays in Angelina's life as she and her distant mother struggle to care for her larger-than-life father Andreas, who suffers a stroke that leaves him mute and partially paralyzed in the first pages of this novel.

Two early purpose-driven GA novels, Catherine Atkins's *Alt Ed* (2001) and James Howe's *The Misfits* (2003), include gay characters who are already out but are paying a price for it in peer opprobrium. This ensemble cast is composed of a number of different misfits, each of whom encounter societal discrimination based on their particular difference(s) from the mainstream. For example, *The Misfits* include four teens: one is gay, one is overweight, one is a geek, and one is a working-class "hood." In both of these novels the gay character is one of a group of various types of outsiders who are brought together by their authors for frankly didactic purposes, that is, to educate readers in respecting the differences of others and to discourage any kind of verbal or physical abuse targeted at them. This type of book recalls the "rainbow" books of the eighties and nineties that brought together groups of multicultural characters like those in the "Pride Pack" books from Alyson. And, of course, there are more examples all the time as writers, editors, and publishers fully understand that all teen readers are not automatically homophobic. To be sure, some are, but many teens are fairly comfortable with having LGBTQ+ people in their environment and characters.

In only one title of this decade are gay characters truly—even blithely—accepted and assimilated in a story that beautifully combines elements of gay assimilation and queer community: David Levithan's splendid novel *Boy Meets Boy* (2003). The story opens in a marvelously realized picture of what gay assimilation might look like in a "no difference" setting of magical realism. Levithan's book is discussed more fully below as an example of queer community, but it opens with a glimpse of a world in which the gay assimilation "no difference" model can be a reality. As the reader steps into the utopian hometown of the protagonist and narrator, fifteen-year-old Paul:

> There isn't really a gay scene or a straight scene in our town. They got all mixed up a while back, which I think is for the best. Back when I was in second grade, the older gay kids who didn't flee to the city for entertainment would have to make their own fun. Now it's all good. Most of the straight guys try to sneak into the Queer Beer bar. Boys who love boys flirt with girls who love girls. And whether your heart is strictly ballroom or bluegrass punk, the dance floors are open to whatever you have to offer. This is my town. I've lived here all my life. (1–2)

Within this world, however, are high school students involved in the usual forms of teen angst-ridden romances and friendships.

This is an authentic breakthrough book in the sense that it is the first feel-good gay novel for teens. This is surely the first time that a gay teenage character has ever said—without being ironic—"I'm not used to being hated" (18) or a gay-themed novel could end with the words "And I think to myself, 'What a wonderful world'" (185). Like Block's *Weetzie Bat*, Levithan's novel contains elements of magical realism or wish-fulfilling idealization. It's set in a town and high school where LGBTQ+ folks are totally accepted and are free to be exactly who and what they are. The protagonist Paul and his new boyfriend Noah, for example, walk through town holding hands and, as Paul notes, "If anybody notices, nobody cares" (65–66).

The football team's quarterback, Infinite Darlene, is also the cross-dressing homecoming queen. The school has a Harley-riding biker cheerleading squad, a quiz bowling team whose members score strikes while listing the complete works of the Brontë sisters, there's a school "cover" band, and so forth. The humor agilely skirts the cliff's edge of whimsy without ever toppling over into preciousness.

The real world does intrude in subplots, one of which involves Paul's best friend Tony, the gay son of ultrareligious parents, who manages to be true to himself. A second sees Paul's friend Joni fall in love with a straight (and rather obnoxious) football player; as a result, the two old friends have a falling-out that is never completely repaired. And in a third, Paul's ex-boyfriend Kyle tries to reconcile with him. Paul, believably, makes a bit of a mess of his attempt to deal with this. The heart of the story, though, is Paul's meeting and falling head over heels in love with a new boy, Noah, who is an artist and a free spirit. The two proceed to fall *out* of love (to the reader's distress) but then, sweetly, to fall back in love. There is no sex involved, but there is lots of hugging and kissing and even more heartwarming, deeply satisfying expressions and manifestations of loving and caring. In its acceptance and celebration of human differences, this is one of the most important gay novels since *Annie on My Mind*, and it represents a near revolution in social attitudes and the publishing of YA books with LGBTQ+ content.

QUEER CONSCIOUSNESS/COMMUNITY

The first years of the new century saw significant progress toward a literature of gay assimilation and acceptance, and similar progress was made in terms of queer consciousness and community. Consider that in the earlier decades of young adult novels with LGBTQ+ content, the reader would nearly always find only one or at most two gay/lesbian characters. If there were one, the story would be a coming-of-age/coming-out narrative. If there were two, the story would be either a young adult romance or a story that included a lesbian or gay adult couple. There were exceptions to this pattern, such as Nancy Garden's *Annie on My Mind*, which includes four lesbian characters: one teen couple and one adult couple, but this could also be seen as the same pattern times two. But such exceptions were rare. This meant that readers would almost never see queer community as an ongoing, present-tense entity that was part of the characters' day-to-day lives. Given this history, a novel with three gay/lesbian characters is not just unusual, but groundbreaking.

Alex Sanchez's Rainbow Boys Trilogy:
Queer Community in High School

Alex Sanchez's trilogy, *Rainbow Boys* (2001), *Rainbow High* (2003), and *Rainbow Road* (2005), is about Jason, Kyle, and Nelson—three gay high school friends who are in various stages of coming out. All three novels demonstrate the author's ability to create realistic, sympathetic characters who are on a quest to prove the truth of what another character says early in *Rainbow Boys*: "Coming out means you're no longer ashamed to tell people. It's a question of liking yourself and feeling good about being gay" (7).

Sanchez also has a good ear for the way teens really talk and, at a time when AIDS seems largely forgotten in LGBTQ+ literature, he pays serious attention to the disease and the corollary need for practicing safe sex. Though his characters are sexually active, as are many teens, the author never fails to focus on love as the heart of homosexuality. He also demonstrates that coming out is actually coming into a circle of support and self-acceptance that may, ultimately, lead to a more universal community of acceptance and tolerance.

The lives of Jason, Kyle, and Nelson include Rainbow Youth meetings at a community center and a campaign for a Gay-Straight Alliance in their high school. The presence of community in the book is further emphasized by the supportive friendship and occasional camaraderie that the three provide for each other as they negotiate the treacherous world of high school and their own mercurial relationships with other family members. The story is told from the alternating perspectives of the three classmates, each of whom is wrestling with issues of sexual orientation and personal survival. Jason, a high school jock with a longtime girlfriend, struggles to come out to himself as he acknowledges his strong attraction to men. Kyle, an intelligent but shy ugly duckling with glasses, braces, and a baseball cap, accepts his own gay identity but struggles to quell his seemingly hopeless, longtime crush on Jason. Nelson, Kyle's flamboyant best friend, is an out, "queer and proud" teen whose multicolored hair, multipierced ears, and camp sensibility reflect his longtime acceptance of his own gay identity. Nelson, however, faces perhaps the most overt struggle of the three in his tenacious resistance to the ongoing verbal and physical harassment from his homophobic classmates. Nelson is smart mouthed and irritating and he knows it. As he himself says, "It's not easy being me. Imagine what I have to put up with twenty-four/ seven. At least you can get away from me occasionally" (21).

This story is their story, the narrative is told from behind their eyes, and the fact that there are three gay kids at the novel's core who are friends is revolutionary. The trilogy follows the boys through their senior year and most of post-senior year summer, gives readers the opportunity to see the world from the boys' perspectives as they move in and out of a queer community, attending Rainbow Youth meetings, campaigning for a Gay-Straight Alliance in their school, graduate, and drive together from Washington, D.C., to Los Angeles, and meeting parts of various LGBTQ+ communities along the way, from a clutch of Radical Faeries to a transgender Britney Spears look-alike to a devoted gay couple who have been together for twenty years, and look forward to the large and interesting world that awaits them in their futures.

Maureen Johnson's *On the Count of Three* (a.k.a. *The Bermudez Triangle*): Queer Community in the Larger Community

Maureen Johnson's *On the Count of Three* (2004), formerly titled *The Bermudez Triangle*, is another example of a queer community novel. Three girls—Avery, Mel (Melanie), and Nina—have been best friends since grade school. Think Sisterhood of the Traveling Pants if one of the sisterhood was a lesbian. In the summer before their final year of high school in Saratoga Springs, Nina is in Berkeley while Mel and Avery have summer jobs in a restaurant and slip into a romantic relationship. Not surprisingly, when Nina returns to town, the dynamics among the three have shifted. For Mel the relationship confirms the lesbian identity she has long known but not acted upon; for Avery, dating a longtime friend is warm and comfortable but not exactly electrifying; and for Nina, her new position as a "three's a crowd" outsider makes her the reluctant confidante of both her best friends as they struggle toward the inevitable breakup of their romance. However, once the breakup occurs, Nina embarks on Operation Drag Mel Out of the House. When she sees a notice for a gay and lesbian post-Valentine dance at a nearby high school, she insists that Mel attend it with her.

One common coming-out story of an earlier generation is "the first time I went to a gay bar," which begins with nervous trepidation and ends at the bar surrounded by "people just like me." Mel has the same experience at the dance. After her initial shyness, she looks around her and sees girls with short hair, long hair, and everything in between dancing, talking, and simply standing around. As she says to Nina, "All those people there—they were just being *normal* about it. It made me feel normal" (309). Mel begins to find a new community of LGBTQ+ teens, and learns that she need not give up her existing community of Avery and Nina in order to come out. An LGBTQ+ identity and an ordinary life are not mutually exclusive, and Mel needn't choose between love and family. She needn't sacrifice every element of her current life in order to have a future as a lesbian woman.

One notable feature of this book is that it comes from a packager, 17th Street Productions, which is also responsible for the wildly popular Sisterhood of the Traveling Pants books and is published by Razorbill, a Penguin Putnam YA imprint specializing in commercial fiction. In other words, this may be the first LGBTQ+ novel that is aimed squarely at the mainstream reader and at the retail market, a major development in the publishing of LGBTQ+ fiction, and one that needs to be followed closely.

Brent Hartinger's *The Geography Club*: A "Bloom Where You're Planted" Queer Community

Although actual LGBTQ+ teens often have queer friends of both sexes, this reality is rarely found in young adult novels. Brent Hartinger's *The Geography Club* (2003) breaks free from this confining stereotype. The geography metaphor used throughout describes the variable terrain of risk and safety that the gay narrator and protagonist Russel must negotiate in his search for community. "I desperately wanted to be somewhere where I could be honest about who I was and what I wanted" (11). He begins in an Internet chat room, where he meets another gay teen, Kevin, the handsome jock in his PE class. This discovery gives him the courage to come out to his best friend Min, who reveals that she herself is involved in a romantic relationship with star athlete Terese. These four, plus another gay friend, create a small safe space for themselves by meeting as the after-school Geography Club, a name they hope is sufficiently dull to discourage anyone else from joining. This is an amusing notion, but what is significant is that instead of looking elsewhere for a gay community, the young people set about creating their own. "We were telling each other things we'd never told our best friends before, things we'd never even said out loud. The five of us may have been alone in the pizza place, but we weren't really alone. Not anymore" (42).

At Kevin's urging, Russel joins the school baseball team and finds himself eating lunch at the baseball jocks' lunchroom table "in the Land of the Popular" (159). During the weeks that follow, Russel's odyssey takes him across "the whole terrain of a typical high school," from the Land of the Popular to the Borderlands of Respectability and even to Outcast Island. Some of the club members—among them Kevin, alas—are finally too fearful to come out in their high school. But by the end of the story, a few, including Russel, have formed the nucleus for a new club, the Gay-Straight-Bisexual Alliance, and in so doing have settled in for the long journey toward making a place for themselves in the world of their high school.

"Would we be banished to Outcast Island? Or would we maybe, just maybe, be allowed to stay in the Borderlands of Respectability? (Let's face it: the Land of the Popular was no longer an option.) . . . I didn't care. None of us did. Because wherever we ended up, we'd be there together. And now I knew that even the ugliest place in the world can be wonderful if you're there with good friends" (225).

David Levithan's *Boy Meets Boy* as a Story of Queer Community

As noted earlier, David Levithan's *Boy Meets Boy* (2003) is a story of gay assimilation, since the difference of sexual orientation truly makes no difference here, but we would argue that it is also a story of a queer community as envisioned by LGBTQ+ teens who would just like to hold hands or attend a school dance without getting gay-bashed or facing the peer rejection of Outcast Island.

Like the members of the Geography Club, the LGBTQ+ teen classmates in David Levithan's *Boy Meets Boy* (2003) focus on finding each other, but there is no Outcast Island in Levithan's high school setting. As the story opens, Paul and his friends are heading for a dance at a nearby bookstore. "I move through the crowd with ease, sharing nods and smiling hellos. I love this scene, this floating reality. I am a solo flyer, looking out over the land of Boyfriends and Girlfriends. I am three notes in the middle of a song" (2). In some ways, this community might be likened to Weetzie Bat's Los Angeles. Although this is definitely a town, not a city, its denizens are awash in Weetzie-like sensory detail as they stroll through the park, cruise out to the mall with friends, or move through the halls of their high school on the lookout for who is passing notes to whom, who is at whose locker, and who is looking to catch whose eye.

Noah is the new student who has caught Paul's eye, and Paul leaps at the opportunity to show him around town ("the I Scream Parlor, which shows horror movies as you wait for your double dip . . . the Pink Floyd shrine in our local barber's backyard"). Noah loves what he sees and Paul muses, "I know people always talk about living in the middle of nowhere—there's always another place (some city, some foreign country) they'd rather be. But it's moments like this that I feel like I live in the middle of somewhere. My somewhere" (70).

Will Paul get together with Noah? Will Joni ditch Chuck? Will Tony's parents let him go to the dance? *Boy Meets Boy* is a realistic story of the ins and outs of high school life and relationships, yet it is set in a utopian world in which the difference between heterosexual and homosexual attractions and love are about as significant as the difference between blonds and redheads.

Kim Wallace's Erik and Isabelle Series: The Do-It-Yourself Queer Community

In *Erik and Isabelle: Junior Year at Foresthill High* by Kim Wallace (2006), Erik Pennington, a high school junior, is talking to a college student he's just met at a party. "What's it like being gay in high school?" "It changes from minute to minute. Sometimes it's torture and sometimes it's really okay" (172).

Teens may not have the resources or mobility to actively seek and find an LGBTQ+ community they can join, but instead must create a community for themselves. One of the few exceptions to the segregation of fictional gays and lesbians is Kim Wallace's four-book series featuring Erik and Isabelle, two queer teens who are plowing through their four high school years in a small middle-class community somewhere in the California suburbs. Isabelle is out to everyone in her life, whether they like it or not; Erik acknowledges his same-sex attractions to himself and to Isabelle as he is slowly becoming more confident in his gay identity. Isabelle is an artist whose parents are laid-back former hippies; Erik's a scholar and track star from a military family. Despite their differences, however, their best friendship is a constant in both their lives. The four-book series begins with *Erik and Isabelle: Freshman Year at Foresthill High* (2004) and sees them through their *Sophomore* (2005), *Junior* (2006), and *Senior Year at Foresthill High* (2007). In the four years of high school, Erik does well academically, and is a solid member of the school's track team, but in his freshman year he is the target of harassment at school from a posse of homophobic boys. His solace is an online chat room for gay male teens, where he has long chats with Rainboy, who appears to be a possible kindred spirit. Isabelle is a talented artist, an out and proud lesbian, and a brash extrovert who does not suffer fools gladly. Thus her heart sinks when she is assigned to work on a class project with Mandy, the captain of the cheerleading squad, but their opposites-attract interest in each other is quickly obvious to both of them—and to the rest of the cheerleaders, who are certain that Mandy's association with Isabelle will cause others to assume that the whole squad are (eye roll) lesbians. Their pressure is effective and Mandy breaks off her relationship with Isabelle. Erik, on the other hand, is winning track races and finally meets Rainboy (a.k.a. Jeremy) and, not too surprisingly, they become each other's first boyfriend. Thus ends book one, *Freshman Year*. The three books that follow have a similar narrative structure, with alternating chapters devoted to Erik and to Isabelle as they mature and start to look toward their future adult lives, with frequent conversations as they travel their intense, engaging, and rocky road through secondary school and slowly build a supportive circle of LGBTQ+ friends and allies. Interestingly, these books represent some of the *very* few examples of gay boys and lesbian girls as friends, equals, and coprotagonists.

Julia Watts's *Finding H.F.*: A Rainbow Community for Everyone

In contrast to the slow evolution of a homegrown supportive LGBTQ+ community for Erik and Isabelle, there are other stories for other teens who must leave home to find the LGBTQ+ communities they seek. Julia Watts's *Finding H.F.* (2001) tells the story of teens who seek out their own people in a particularly authentic portrayal of the multiple strands of connection and community in gay/lesbian "families of choice." Abandoned as an infant by her fifteen-year-old mother, H.F. (Heavenly Faith) has been raised in Morgan, Kentucky, by her loving and very religious grandmother, Memaw. As an illegitimate tomboy with a growing attraction to women, H.F.'s sense of difference has been lifelong. Her best friend Bo, a self-described "sissyboy," understandably shares her sense of alienation; both teens dream of the larger landscape that they believe lies outside their small town.

The voice of H.F. is fresh, intelligent, and wryly self-aware, as when she pokes fun at her name: "I never believed those Bible stories were real any more than I believed *The Poky Little Puppy* was real when Memaw read it to me. I didn't believe in those Bible things any more than I believed in talking dogs that ate strawberry shortcake. That's what makes my name so funny. Heavenly Faith, my foot! If I can't see it, hear it, smell it, touch it, or taste it, I don't believe in it" (4). The voice of Bo is likewise humorous, though with a more overtly camp sensibility. In one characteristic exchange, H.F. and Bo explore an unfamiliar path through the woods, H.F. forging ahead while Bo fusses about getting his shoes muddy. H.F. tells the reader in mock exasperation: "I swear, it's like his number one concern in life is being well groomed. The boy irons his jeans, for crying out loud. 'What's the matter, Beauregard? Afraid of messin' up your snazzy new shoes?'" To which he retorts, "Excuse me, sugar, but some people take pride in their personal appearance" (15).

Both of these gender nonconformists are well aware of their deviance from the norms of their small-town high school. As H.F. explains, "The cheerleaders and the jocks and popular kids know I'm different. Different on the inside. Like lions on nature shows that sniff out which giraffe is ripest for the picking, those people can sniff out difference and it's a smell they hate" (80). Yet both are managing to struggle through their adolescence toward a nebulous vision of the terrain outside Morgan, Kentucky.

Just when H.F. is rejected by the girl of her dreams, she finds the address of the mother she's never known and persuades Bo to drive with her to Tippalula, Florida, in search of her. As the two friends make their way from Kentucky to Florida by way of Atlanta, Georgia, they meet three homeless lesbian teens, visit a gay bookstore, attend a gay-friendly church service, and experience the thrill of seeing two men casually walking hand in hand through a public park.

They discover, in short, a community with its own heroes and traditions, gathering places, and lore made up of those elusive people "like us" that they've wondered about but never quite believed in. An older gay couple (Bo marvels "they've been together for longer than we've been alive!" [79]) provides a safe haven for the night and some plainspoken reassurance: "Adolescence sucks, Beauregard. Just wait . . . life'll get easier" (80).

H.F. and Bo return home to the same lives but with a vision of the world that awaits them outside of Morgan: not a utopia by any means, but one that has ample room for H.F., Bo, and all those other "people like us":

> We learned that the world isn't just flooded with meanness—that there are people like us loving each other, living happy lives out in the open. . . . And to me, the rainbow sign God put up in the sky for Noah said pretty much the same thing as the sign I saw at the gay bookstore, at the church, and in the faces and hearts of the rainbow people who are my gay family: "Here you were, thinking it was the end of the world, when it turned out it was only the beginning." (175)

NOTES

1. Michael Cart, "Young Adult Literature Comes of Age," in *Children's Literature Remembered*, ed. Linda Pavonetti (Westport, CT: Libraries Unlimited, 2004).

2. Christine A. Jenkins, "Annie on Her Mind," *School Library Journal* 49 (June 2003): 48–50.

3. Information about the Alex Award and its current and past winners available at http://www.ala.org/yalsa/alex-awards#alex (accessed March 23, 2017).

4. Marc Aronson, *Exploding Myths* (Lanham, MD: Scarecrow Press, 2001).

5. Information on the *Luv Ya Bunches* controversy and resolution available at: https://thinkprogress.org/scholastic-backtracks-on-demand-that-author-change-books-lesbian-parents-to-a-heterosexual-couple-b7cb13c05e1#.mcdjdohdo.

6. Eric Rofes, *I Thought People Like That Killed Themselves: Lesbians, Gay Men, and Suicide* (San Francisco: Grey Fox, 1983).

7. Laura E. Durso and Naomi Goldberg, "Our Juvenile Justice System Is Failing LGBTQ Youth," Rewire, September 14, 2016, https://rewire.news/article/2016/09/14/juvenile-justice-system-failing-lgbtq-youth/.

8. Nico Sifra Quintana, Josh Rosenthal, and Jeff Krehely, "On the Streets: The Federal Response to Gay and Transgender Homeless Youth," June 2010, https://www.americanprogress.org/issues/lgbt/reports/2010/06/21/7983/on-the-streets/ (accessed March 24, 2016).

9. Evan Cooper, "Decoding *Will and Grace*: Mass Audience Reception of a Popular Network," *Sociological Perspectives* 46, no. 4 (2003): 513–33, http://www.csub.edu/~rdugan2/SOC%20577%20Pop%20Culture/decoding%20will%20and%20grace.pdf (accessed March 23, 2017).

10. Linda Greenhouse, "Justices, 6–3, Legalize Sexual Conduct," *New York Times*, June 25, 2003, http://www.nytimes.com/2003/06/27/us/supreme-court-homosexual-rights-justices-6–3-legalize-gay-sexual-conduct.html (accessed March 23, 2017).

11. In addition to the sixty-three titles in the Sweet Valley University, there are eighteen other spin-off titles, including mysteries, holiday stories, and Super-specials, which do not figure in this analysis.

12. Coverage of the earthquake and its immediate aftermath included in the final two volumes of Sweet Valley High Super Editions: *#11: Earthquake* (1998) and *#12: Aftershock* (1998).

13. "Children's Series Best Sellers," *New York Times*, February 5, 2012, https://www.nytimes.com/books/best-sellers/2012/02/05/series-books/.

Chapter Six

Young Adult Literature since 2010

As we entered the twenty-teens, LGBTQ+ literature, like the larger world of YA, was chockablock with change, though continuity, as we will see below, was no stranger to the literature, either. Perhaps not surprisingly, there have been a number of very noticeable changes in this body of literature over the past decades.

The first and foremost change has been the continuing dramatic increase in the sheer number of LGBTQ+ titles that are being published. Consider that from 2000 to 2009 a total of 241 relevant titles were published. Though the following period, 2010–2016, includes four years fewer to consider, the total nevertheless escalated to 592. For some perspective on the remarkable growth of the field, consider that this number is nearly eight times the total published throughout the entire decade of the nineties (seventy-six). It should be noted that this salutary growth is due in part to the entrance into the field of a handful of relatively small publishers specializing in LGBTQ+ materials whose titles began appearing on our lists in 2007 with the advent of Prizm, the YA imprint of Torquere. The following year, it was the turn of Regal Crest titles. Then in 2010 we began seeing books from Bold Strokes and Bella, followed in 2011 by Beanpole and Tiny Satchel Press. In 2012 Harmony Ink—the most prolific of all of these presses—debuted, followed in 2015 by Ylva. Though many of these publishers boasted relatively slender lists, in the aggregate they made a significant contribution to the field. Indeed, in some years they nearly eclipsed titles from major mainstream publishers. In fact, in 2014 fully 63 percent of the ninety-five LGBTQ+ titles on our list emanated from these presses. Their pace of publication has slowed somewhat in recent years as the output of the major publishers has increased significantly. Thus in 2016 only 37 percent of the titles on our list were issued by the specialty presses. Altogether these figures obviously evidence a growing market for the genre but also, perhaps, a growing awareness and acceptance of LGBTQ+ people, who are becoming more and more visible—in both literature and life. This is further evidenced, in part, by the increasing number of GA (gay assimilation) novels: stories in which the gay character is out at the start of the story. Consider that from 2000 to 2004 there were a scant twelve GA (gay assimilation) novels, compared with sixty HV (homosexual visibility) novels—that is, stories in which the character is closeted at the start of the story. From 2004 to 2009 there were eighty-seven GA novels compared with sixty-one HV novels; from 2010 to 2016 there were 170 GA novels compared with 197 HV.

During the current decade there was also a sharp uptick in books with LGBTQ+ protagonists as opposed to LGBTQ+ secondary characters. From 2000 to 2004 there were thirty-nine novels featuring LGBTQ+ protagonists compared with forty secondary characters; from 2005 to 2009 there were fifty-nine compared with seventy-three secondary characters; and from 2010 to 2016 there were 429 compared with 155 secondary characters. Thus, the trend is not only one of more LGBTQ+ books but also a burgeoning one of both out characters and ones who are protagonists. If one of the purposes of young adult fiction is to give faces to every teen, LGBTQ literature can be regarded as being increasingly successful.

Interestingly, one characteristic of the small publishers coincides with one informing YA and LGBTQ literature in general: the increasing presence of so-called crossover books, that is, books with multigenerational appeal. This is partly the result of the recent emergence of a new segment of society, people aged, roughly, nineteen to twenty-five, a generation commonly called new adult or, by some, kiddults or adultescents. As YA literature has become ever increasingly more sophisticated, it has expanded its readership to reach these new adults while, at the same time, books published for adults are now speaking to older YAs; hence, the word "crossover" and the increasingly blurred line between YA and adult. A few examples of YA to new adult crossovers include emily m. danforth's *The Miseducation of Cameron Post* (2015), Robin Talley's *What We Left Behind* (2015), and Jenny Downham's British import *Unbecoming* (2016). Books published in the adult category with YA appeal include Richard Kramer's *These Things Happen* (2012), Meg Howrey's *Blind Sight* (2011), and Ritch C. Savin-Williams's *Becoming Who I Am* (2016).

A second salutary change is the recent growth of books featuring bisexual characters, a change that has become so prevalent that we devote an entire chapter to it. As we will discover in it and elsewhere in this book, there were characters who—before the first book with an authentic bisexual character (M. E. Kerr's 1997 novel *"Hello," I Lied*)—could be said to have manifested bisexual behavior as they struggled to define their sexuality; for example, straight characters who experimented with same-sex love. At this remove, however, we would more likely describe these characters as questioning instead of bisexual.

A third change to which we devote a separate chapter is one now beginning to manifest itself: the remarkable growth of transgender literature. A hallmark of recent books with transgender characters is that readers are able to follow characters through their transition to lives led as openly transgender persons. In the earlier years of this literature, however, characters—as in the case of Julie Anne Peters's *Luna*—were followed only to their decision to come out and begin their transition. In addition to transgender literature, we examine the new presence of intersex literature. Though only three titles in the latter category have appeared to date, it seems likely that this will be an area of expanding interest and coverage.

A fourth change is one that reflects societal changes, that is, the increasing number of LGBTQ+ family members, especially mothers or fathers. Of five recent examples, three—C. Desir and Jolene Perry's *Love Blind* (2016), Kathryn Ormsbee's *Lucky Few* (2016), and Mariko Tamaki's *Saving Montgomery Sole* (2016)—feature lesbian mothers while two—Will Walton's *Anything Could Happen* (2015) and Ellen Wittlinger's *Local Girl Swept Away* (2016)—feature gay fathers. We count eighteen others published since 2010, so many that the phenomenon has become almost routine, a fact so common now as to scarcely be worth comment. Largely gone are the days when such adults were considered unfit to be parents and litigation underscored that. As for other members of the family—for example, sister, brother, aunt, uncle—if we include them, the number mushrooms to thirty-seven, a number that reflects the open presence and increasing acceptance of LGBTQ+ characters in families and society in the real world.

A fifth change is the growth of literary, that is, character-driven, LGBTQ+ fiction. For too many years books with LGBTQ+ content were dismissed as being simply plot- or problem-driven novels that ended with a character's coming out. But no more. Today's more literary novels follow characters through the process of coming out into an examination of their lives as openly gay or lesbian. Since 2010, ALA's Stonewall Awards have honored a children's and young adult book of the year. The 2016 winner was Bill Konigsberg's *The Porcupine of Truth*. Meanwhile such other literary novels as Becky Albertalli's *Simon vs. the Homo Sapiens Agenda*, winner of the 2016 William C. Morris Award for best first novel of the year and Jandy Nelson's *I'll Give You the Sun*, winner of the 2015 Printz Award, are strong indicators that LGBTQ literature has come of age as literature.

A sixth change reflects the fact that for too many years LGBTQ literature has been deadly serious, even grim at times. But, happily, this is no longer the case as the literature has been infused with a welcome dose of humor. We count twenty-two examples of such titles since 2010. Among the more recent are Patrick Ness's *The Rest of Us Just Live Here* (2015), Tim Federle's *The*

Great American Whatever (2016), and S. J. Goslee's *Whatever* (2016). It's worth noting that humor is not confined to novels of realism but is a welcome presence in works of speculative fiction as well. A good example is Rainbow Rowell's delightful *Carry On* (2015) and much of the work of Cassandra Clare and Jenna Black. If not every one of these is laugh-out-loud funny, they all, nevertheless, offer a benign, lighthearted view of the universe evocative of David Levithan's modern classic *Boy Meets Boy* (2003).

A seventh powerful change acknowledges that historically LGBTQ+ titles have been almost exclusively novels of contemporary realism, but no more. LGBTQ+ literature has increasingly become home to work of speculative fiction and magic realism. We find fifty-five such novels published since 2010. Among the best of these are Maggie Stiefvater's Raven Boys Quartet (2012–2016), Holly Black's *The Darkest Part of the Forest* (2015), Andrew Smith's *Grasshopper Jungle (*2014), and Patrick Ness's *The Rest of Us Just Live Here* (2015).

An eighth change is the increasing appearance of people of color in a literature that historically has been almost exclusively white and middle class. This is no longer the case, though characters of color are still underrepresented. Since 2010 we count eighteen books featuring black, Latino/a, or Asian characters: books such as Bill Konigsberg's *Porcupine of Truth* (2015), Hannah Moskowitz's *Not Otherwise Specified* (2015), Rafi Mittelfehldt's *It Looks Like This* (2016)—all African American—and Adam Silvera's *More Happy Than Not* (2016), Gloria Velasquez's *Tommy Stands Tall* (2016), e. E. Charlton-Trujillo's *Fat Angie* (2013) and Bil Wright's *Putting Makeup on the Fat Boy* (2011)—all Latino—and Paul Yee's *Money Boy* (2011) and C. B. Lee's *Not Your Sidekick* (2016)—both Asian. At the same time, there has been an increase in what we call "melting pot" books in which the race or ethnicity is only indicated via appearance or feature, such as brown skin or almond-shaped eyes. In some cases this might be labeled tokenism, but in others it could be viewed as a demonstration of community. In the meantime, the world populated by LGBTQ folks has expanded nearly exponentially. We count twenty-one books since 2010 featuring characters from such disparate places as Iran, Pakistan, Germany, Australia, Armenia, and more. Most of these novels are set in the United States, but a handful are set in foreign countries, including Iran (Sara Farizan's *If You Could Be Mine* [2013]) and Russia (Daria Wilke's *Playing a Part* [2015]). Yes, these numbers are relatively small and growing far too slowly, but they are significantly larger than in the past and may (or may not) point toward a more inclusive literature to come—time will tell.

A ninth change is the appearance of novels with ensemble casts—often told from multiple points of view—that include one LGBTQ+ character as a member of a group of teens. This phenomenon was present to a limited degree in the eighties and nineties, but it is only recently that it has become significant in LGBTQ+ fiction. We're a bit ambivalent about this change—as with characters of color, there is the risk of tokenism, such that the inclusion of the queer character is superficial diversity rather than genuine inclusion. However, at its best it is a welcome change, reminding us that LGBTQ+ people are increasingly prominent, visible members of the general population and a literature of realism needs to acknowledge that fact. Among recent exemplary titles that fall into this category are Carolyn Mackler's *Infinite In Between* (2015), Celia Carter's *Tumbling* (2016), and Laura Nowlin's *This Song Is (Not) for You* (2016).

A tenth change is rooted in the fact that LGBTQ+ literature is filled with examples of girls who fall in love with gay teens and are heartbroken when they discover the truth. Early examples are Hila Colman's *Happily Ever After* (1986) and Ann Rinaldi's *Good Side of My Heart* (1987). Happily, thanks to the introduction of humor in the literature, this discovery is no longer treated as tragic but as less consequential, often greeted with good humor, even laughter, and the two characters in question can even become good (nonromantic) friends (e.g., S. J. Goslee's *Whatever* [2016]) and sometimes can—as Francesca Lia Block so memorably put it—go "duck hunting" together or have a friendly rivalry for the same would-be object of their affections.

An eleventh change sees the emergence of books with younger protagonists, that is, youth in middle or elementary school. Earlier instances of such books were confined to picture books. Some recent examples include Richard Peck's *The Best* Man (2016), Tim Federle's *Better Nate Than Ever* (2013) and *Five Six Seven Nate* (2014), and Alex Gino's *George* (2015).

And, lastly our twelfth change is evident in the increasing number of LGBTQ+ protagonists. In recent years there had been a trend toward secondary characters supplying the LGBTQ+ presence, often being friends (or even friends of friends) of straight protagonists or supernumeraries who were momentarily visible in what could be viewed as more of a nod to than an embrace of multiculturalism. Starting in 2012, however, this situation did a dramatic—and salutary—about-face, and recent titles have LGBTQ+ protagonists far outnumbering LGBTQ+ secondary characters. This may be due in part to the growth of the small and specialty presses, most of whose books focus on LGBTQ+ protagonists. Be that as it may, the 2016 titles featured 102 protagonists compared with only thirty secondary characters.

CONTINUITIES: GETTING PAST SNIPS AND SNAILS AND SUGAR AND SPICE

As for the consideration of continuity, the literature continues to be deficient in its inclusion of lesbian characters compared with those who are gay males.

From 2005 to 2009 there were fifty-three novels with lesbian content compared with 109 with gay male content. The trend continued from 2010 to 2016 when there were 134 novels featuring lesbians and 215 including gay male characters. This imbalance has been a feature of LGBTQ+ literature since its beginnings and sadly suggests that male chauvinism is alive and well in the field. That the imbalance lessened somewhat from 2010 through 2016, though, may presage a change toward a more balanced treatment. One can only hope.

Another instance of truly unfortunate continuity is the ongoing segregation of the sexes in LGBTQ+ literature, that is, titles include either lesbians *or* gay males but only very rarely will both be represented in the same book. In examining the publishing output for 2000–2016, we counted 588 novels with LGBTQ+ content and were startled to find that only ten (1.7 percent) of those titles included both a gay *and* a lesbian teen character. We find this odd because in the real world we live in, it is not uncommon for gays and lesbians to be friends (the coauthors of this book being an example!), work together to establish GSAs, and share a sense of community, as reflected in Nina LaCour and David Levithan's *You Know Me Well* (2016). Needless to say, we hope that future LGBTQ+ YA fiction will become more realistic in depicting the relationships and alliances that commonly exist between actual male and female LGBTQ+ teens.

It is hard not to be daunted by the depth and persistence of the continuities identified above. However, the vitality and growth we have seen in the positive changes in this literature over time are equally persistent. If those changes evidence nothing else, they are surely indicators that LGBTQ+ literature is increasingly lively and dynamic, reflecting not only literary but also societal changes and that is, perhaps, the most important change of all.

HOMOSEXUAL VISIBILITY

As noted above, there is currently an increasingly large literature of gay assimilation (GA); that said, there remains a core group of novels of homosexual visibility (HV), novels in which protagonists or secondary characters are initially in the closet and then bravely come out or are forced out. This is so common that two recent novels turn the trope on its head: Bill Konigsberg's *Openly Straight* (2013) and Jaye Robin Brown's *Georgia Peaches and Other Forbidden Fruit* (2016) feature out teens who—for their several reasons—go back into the closet. Konigsberg's protagonist, tired of being the prototypical out boy at his school, enrolls in a new one where no one knows him and tries to become just one of the (straight) boys. Brown's female protagonist is unapologetically out, but when her minister father moves the family to a new community, she is asked by him to be more, well, discreet.

It should be noted that—unlike earlier HV novels where the coming out was the denouement—today's HV tends to follow the consequences of coming out; in this regard HV comes very close to being GA.

As young people are coming out at younger and younger ages, we are beginning, in these twenty-teen years, to see LGBTQ+ books featuring them and targeted at them. We have observed examples of them in our chapter on transgender literature, but we might note here Tim Federle's two delightful books about his stagestruck protagonist Nate (*Better Nate Than Ever* and *Five Six Seven Nate*) (2013, 2014). In many of these younger books the gay or lesbian character or characters is adult.

For example, in Richard Peck's *The Best Man* (2016), fifth grader Archer Magill's student teacher is the movie-star handsome Mr. McLeod. Archer and his classmates adore him, but there's something about him they don't know until the day three sixth-grade boys tie up Archer's classmate Russell and write the word "gay" on his forehead with a pink magic marker. Mr. McLeod confronts the three in front of their entire sixth-grade class, demanding they say the word they've branded Russell with. They demur, but one of them finally mutters, "Gay." Another of them protests, "It was just a word. It was . . . random."

> "Gay's not a random word," Mr. McLeod said. "It's an identity."
> "Whatever," Perry mumbled.
> "It's my identity," Mr. McLeod said.

Peck describes what happens next: "Silence fell. You could have heard breathing, but there wasn't any" (112).

Mr. McLeod, whose first name, for the record, is Ed, has outed himself and the moment is electric. Soon thereafter the revelation goes viral. (It needs to be explained here that on Mr. McLeod's first day at school, he showed up in his National Guard uniform; the school secretary, not the sharpest knife in the drawer, seeing an unexpected man in a uniform, calls the police; the school goes into lockdown and the media, expecting a juicy story, arrive in droves. There's even a helicopter. As a result, the handsome Mr. McLeod becomes a celebrity, so the press is primed for another story about him.) The weekend edition of the *Chicago Tribune* runs a picture of the teacher with a headline that says it all: SORRY, LADIES.[1]

But wait; there's more. Archer has an uncle named Paul. And here he is when Archer gets home that memorable day:

> Filling the doorway was Uncle Paul, since it was getting on for Friday evening [the 6'4" Uncle Paul has dinner with Archer's family every Friday evening]. Uncle Paul, large as life: hundred-dollar haircut, manscaped stubble, a whiff of Tom Ford aftershave.

"Can you believe it?" Uncle Paul said. "Ed McLeod outs himself with no
escape plan? I knew by ten o'clock and North America knew by noon."
Uncle Paul? (117)

Hundred-dollar haircut? Manscaped stubble? Hmmmm . . . And guess who's
with him? That's right, Mr. McLeod whom he's brought along for dinner.
Double hmmmm . . .

Sure enough. Not long after Mr. McLeod's outing it's Uncle Paul's turn.
He and Archer are sitting in the center-field bleachers at Wrigley Field (Uncle P. does public relations for the Cubs) when the boy wonders why his
mother had wanted them to talk, thinking it had to do with Mr. McLeod's
being gay.

"Maybe she wanted to talk about *me* being gay," Uncle Paul said.
Whoa. The sun stopped at the top of the sky.
"You knew I was gay, right?"
"Sure," I said. "I guess. Not really. No."

A moment passes and Archer says, "Uncle Paul, do you think I might be
gay?" This is a not uncommon reaction for a young person to have when
confronted by the homosexuality of a family member.

"'I don't know,' he said. 'Do you moisturize?'" (332).

It's a retort worthy of Ron Koertge's Uncle Wes. Indeed, Peck's book is
evocative of *The Arizona Kid*, though targeted at a younger readership.

Be that as it may, the conversation between nephew and uncle isn't over
yet: "You love men, right?" Archer asks.

Without missing a beat, Uncle Paul inscrutably replies, "I love one man"
(133).

Readers will tumble to that one man's identity long before naïve Archer
does. It's Mr. McLeod, of course. The two men quickly become a couple, but
there will be a few missteps on the way to the altar, because Uncle Paul has a
propensity to cut and run. However, love finds the way, and the two are
married with Archer as the best man dressed in a snazzy blue Ralph Lauren
suit.

Quite aside from being a charming, funny, feel-good read, *The Best Man*
is historic, being the first LGBTQ+ novel to feature a gay wedding. (Michael
Wilhoite's *Daddy's Wedding* [1996] preceded it but was a picture book.)
Kudos to Peck, who demonstrates that a light touch is often the most effective way to deal with weighty issues.

Three other gay novels with a similarly sanguine view of coming out are
S. J. Goslee's *Whatever* (2016), Becky Albertalli's *Simon vs. the Homo Sapiens Agenda* (2015), and Rainbow Rowell's *Carry On* (2015).

Goslee's novel is seriously delightful. In large part that's due to the droll
cast of characters she's created and her wonderful sense of the ironies and

occasional idiocies of adolescence. Her star is sixteen-year-old Mike Tate, whose three favorite things are his little sister Rosie, his garage band, and his sort of girlfriend Lisa. But now Lisa has broken up with him—sort of. That's bad but not fatal because she's still his BFF until she brings up the gay thing. But Mike's not gay . . . is he? Surely (as Lisa claims) he didn't really make out with another boy at a party while he was seriously wasted, so wasted he can't remember it? And surely Rook Wallace, his longtime bête noire, is still his enemy. Isn't he? Even though he's being suspiciously, improbably . . . nice. What next? Well, for one, if Mike *is* gay, there's the horrifying prospect of actually coming out (if he hasn't already outed himself at that party). Sure, a few girls know, but among his friends only Jason witnessed the infamous event; as for the rest, "[Mike's] just not sure he wants even more people to know about something he doesn't even really know about himself yet . . ." (58). But Mike does summon the moxie to talk with the aforementioned Jason about it: "Jesus Christ. I'm fucked up." "Hey, no," Jason replies. "You're in no way fucked up." Whew! But what will the rest of his friends think if Mike reveals the awful truth to them? Before he can find that out, his mother says, "So, Michael. Anything you want to tell me?" (111). Uh-oh. The following conversation is brief and the word "gay" is never invoked, but it's obvious to Mike that his mom knows his secret without his telling her. It leaves him thinking. "He just sort of came out to his mom and it went pretty fucking great" (113). But, still, what about his friends? Before he can find that out, the unthinkable happens: at a party Rook Wallace kisses him! And Mike—though in denial—finds himself kissing him back!! "I'm really sorry you're not gay," Rook says ironically and saunters away (127). Well, *that* was weird, but before it's resolved, Mike finally comes out to his best friend Cam Scott. The exchange goes like this: "So," Mike says, "I'm pretty sure I like guys." This is followed by an awful, pregnant silence, which is then broken by Cam's saying, "Sexual deviancy, dude. I totally approve" (161). Phew! The reaction of Mike's nana, a retired army colonel, is slightly differ- ent. "Your mother tells me you're queer now," she barks. "She did not," Mike replies, horrified. "She used the term bisexual," Nana continues, "but no grandson of mine is going to be indecisive" (188). His grandmother then outs him to the rest of his family. Is there anyone left who *doesn't* know Mike is gay? Well, yes; there are the rest of his friends. But, before they are told, Mike and Rook finally come to their senses and hook up, but then Mike realizes "he's going to have to *tell people*" (203). And "once everyone knows, there's no going back. There's no changing his mind, no brushing it off" (204). And so it's especially disquieting when Mike finally does tell his friends—Meckles and Omar—and they react badly for their individual rea- sons. This sends Mike into an emotional tailspin that threatens his new rela- tionship with Rook. All of this invests the feel-good story with just the apposite amount of angsty drama to enliven its final pages as the story reaches its heartwarming end.

If Mike's life has occasionally been hard, Goslee's take on it is easy— easy to like. How to describe her story about Mike's tentative steps toward self-awareness? Well, *she* doesn't make a single false step. Everything about her book is just right: the tone, the style, the right-on dialogue, the character-ization, and the pace of the unfolding, genuinely sweet-spirited story. In the context of homosexual visibility the story is sui generis in that Mike doesn't come out just once but, rather, a handful of times. And the tale not only takes a close look at the process but also at its wake.

In the excellent *Simon vs. the Homo Sapiens Agenda*, seventeen-year-old, closeted Simon has mixed feelings about the process of coming out. "The whole coming out thing doesn't really scare me," he muses (2). "It's a giant holy box of awkwardness and I won't pretend I'm looking forward to it. But it probably wouldn't be the end of the world. Not for me" (2), although he acknowledges that there are several boys who are out at school "and people definitely give them crap. Not like violent crap. But the word 'fag' isn't exactly uncommon" (21). However, things change when straight Martin, "a little bit of a goober nerd" (4), discovers his secret and uses it to blackmail Simon, who is in love with an anonymous boy who calls himself Blue. The two boys know each other only through the e-mails they pseudonymously exchange. But that is enough for Simon to fall head over heels in love with Blue. And "what would it mean for Blue," Simon thinks, "if [I] were outed. The thing about Blue is he's kind of a private person" (3). So Simon feels he has no choice but to go along with Martin, whose price for silence is an introduction to Simon's friend, the beautiful (and desirable) Abby Suso. Of course, it's not that simple. Simon puts it off as long as possible, for starters, while Martin drops evil hints that if something doesn't happen soon, the cat will be well and truly out of the bag. But then perhaps all of this becomes moot, for Simon—first swearing her to secrecy—comes out to Abby. "So the thing is, I'm gay" (124). In the revelation's wake Abby says, "Simon, I'm really honored." Then she asks if he plans to tell other people. "I don't know," he says. "I mean, eventually, yeah." "Okay, well I love you," she says in one of the sweetest coming-out scenes since Dirk's in *Weetzie Bat*. But about telling people other than Abby? The answer is at hand, for not too much later—on Christmas Eve, actually—rejected by Abby and unjustly blaming Simon for it, Martin poses as Simon and posts the following mes-sage on the school's Tumblr account: "Dear all dudes of Creekwood, With this missive I hereby declare that I am supremely gay and open for business. Interested parties may contact me directly to discuss arrangements for anal butt sex. Or blow-jobs. But don't give me blue balls. Ladies need not apply. That is all" (158–59). When, in response to this, Simon's younger sister says, "You could deny it," Simon responds, "Okay, I'm not going to deny it. I'm not ashamed of it" (160). And so then, on Christmas Day, he comes out to his parents, who are instantly supportive and loving. Yes, there are a few isolated but obnoxious incidents at school in the wake of the post, yet nothing too serious. But might this reveal Simon's identity to Blue? And what will happen if the two boys discover their true identities? The answers must remain a secret in this spoiler-free zone. But as for coming out: this superlative gay romance reflects the new and heartening reality that coming out and being out no longer need to be deeply traumatic or to invite havoc in their wake. Indeed, it can be almost as natural as breathing.

Next we have Rainbow Rowell's superlative fantasy *Carry On*, which is told in multiple voices and comes with an interesting backstory: its three principal characters first appeared in two incarnations in one of her previous novels, *Fangirl* (St. Martin's Griffin, 2013). First, the three were central characters in a Harry Potter–like series; then, they found new life in *Fangirl*'s protagonist Cath's slash fan fiction. Now they have their own novel. The three are Simon Snow, arguably the greatest magician who has ever lived even if he can't always control or direct his magic; Tyrannus Basilton Grimm-Pitch, better known simply as Baz, who is widely regarded as being a vampire; and Simon's best friend the stalwart Penelope (Penny) Bunce. The three are students at the Watford School of Magicks. Though sworn antagonists, Simon and Baz, now eighteen, have been roommates since they were magically assigned this relationship when they were eleven and first-year students at Watford. What has been done, can't be undone even as the two visit difficulties on one another. When they were fifth-year students, for example, Baz unleashed a chimera on Simon and the two boys barely survived the encounter. This is just one of three times Baz has attempted to kill Simon. As for Simon himself, he ruefully thinks, "I'm probably gonna have to kill him someday" (165). The most recent contretemps that has them at figurative swords' points is more mundane: Simon has seen Baz holding hands with his (Simon's) putative girlfriend, the beautiful Agatha. As a result, Simon and Agatha have broken up, well, sorta. More dramatically, Baz has gone missing, not showing up for the first day of the new school year. Eight weeks later he is still missing, and the absence is driving Simon crazy. Where could Baz be? How could he be missing? After all, Simon muses, "Baz is . . . indelible. He's a human grease stain" (88). "How was I supposed to eat and sleep knowing he was out there, plotting against me?" (170). When Baz finally shows up, it turns out he had been kidnapped by rocklike creatures called numpties, though he keeps this fact secret from Simon. Also a secret—this time from Baz—is the identity of the person who hired the numpties to do the deed.

Meanwhile, something vastly more serious is going on. Something called the Insidious Humdrum is roaming the English countryside devouring magic, leaving holes in the atmosphere like dead spots where magic can't exist, and posing a mortal threat to the entire Mage world. And what's this? The Humdrum looks exactly like an eleven-year-old Simon! Ironically it may be up to Simon—with the arguable help of Penny and Baz—to defeat the Humdrum, for Simon is the Chosen One, the Greatest Mage, the Power of Powers. As *the* Mage, the school's powerful headmaster, says to Simon: "[The Humdrum] is our greatest threat. And you are our greatest hope" (47).

Things take a wildly different turn when Baz, watching Simon sleep one night, thinks, "I (hold) on to the one thing I'm always sure of—Blue eyes. Bronze curls. The fact that Simon Snow is the most powerful magician alive. That nothing can hurt him, not even me. That Simon Snow is *alive.* And I'm hopelessly in love with him" (176).

"I wish I'd never figured it out," he continues. "That I love him. It's only ever been a torment" (177). While Baz continues to agonize over this seemingly hopeless situation, the two boys declare a truce in the interest of cooperating in an effort to eradicate the Humdrum. But there will be more than a truce, for when, sometime later, Baz, in a frenzy of suicidal self-hatred, admits to Simon that he's a vampire, Simon . . . kisses him! "I wonder how long he's wanted this?" Simon thinks. "I wonder how long *I've* wanted it?" (347).

Later, the two discuss their new relationship: "I didn't think you were gay," Baz says. "I don't know," Simon responds. "I guess I've never thought much about what I am. I've got a lot on my plate."

"That makes me laugh," Baz says.

> "A lot on your plate?" I repeat.
> "Are *you* gay?" he [Simon] asks. . . .
> "Yeah," I say. "Completely." (354)

Whether he is gay or not (and it becomes increasingly obvious to readers that he is ["I suppose I am gay," Simon finally admits to himself] [515]), Simon and Baz begin a relationship ("I want to be your boyfriend," Simon tells Baz [390])—a relationship that is at once tender and stormy and, for the reader, deeply satisfying. It is also secret until, at the book's end, at a school party, the two come out, as they dance together and Simon kisses Baz.

There is, of course, more going on while all this is happening The Humdrum is still busily gobbling up magick; the revolutionary Mage is carrying on an unofficial war against the established families like Baz's; Simon encounters the Humdrum in a wonderfully dramatic set-to, and more. But what underlies and survives all of this is the boys' love for each other. And so *Carry On* is not only an epic fantasy, it is also a beautifully realized romance.

But enough of fantasy, back to realistic fiction now and a more sober view of coming out in Jenny Downham's British import *Unbecoming.* Katie hates the claustrophobia of her small hometown, "a place where once rumors began, they easily spread" (8). At the root of this feeling is the fact that Katie has, unbidden, kissed her best friend Esme, been betrayed by her, and made a social pariah. "They think I'm a freak," she says ruefully of Esme's gaggle of girlfriends (61). This is bad enough, but to make matters worse, her elderly grandmother, who suffers from Alzheimer's, has come to live with her, her mother, and her brother after an absence of many years. Once this fact is established, the main narrative then moves back and forward in time to portray the grandmother's childhood and early adulthood. As for *Katie's* secretive present life (her mother doesn't know about Esme), she feels that if it is to improve, she has to get her best friend back. But how? Encountering Esme at a party as she had hoped, Katie tries to engage her in conversation. "I miss you," Katie says. "I thought we were friends." "My friends don't jump me," Esme replies coldly. "I didn't. You know I didn't. Why are you telling everyone that?" When Esme doesn't respond, Katie continues: "I miss us. There's so much you don't know" (121). Esme's response is to say that Katie has been observed hanging out at a café where a girl named Simona, an out lesbian, works. Katie tries to explain she goes there because her grand-mother, Mary, likes the place. "See, this just sounds like lies," Esme retorts. "So, I'm guessing you've decided that's what you are now. Someone like Simona Williams, I mean" (122). "What? No," Katie insists. But Esme re-fuses to believe her, and the conversation ends badly. Several days later Simona invites Katie for coffee. A shocked Katie says no and, panicked, runs for her life but soon finds herself questioning who she is. And finds herself actually talking with Simona about her uncertainties and finally saying, "Teach me. I want to be sure. Teach me about love with a girl" (210). Just as they kiss, Esme and her boyfriend Lukas approach and Katie slinks away before they can see her, implicitly rejecting Simona in the process. "Go home," a weary Simona later says, "it's probably best." But then she adds a cautionary "To thine own self be true" (218).

Life goes on much as before until Katie and her mother have a terrible quarrel about Katie's grandmother. In its wake Katie gives her mother the journal she has been keeping and asks her to read it. "There are things you don't know about me," she says. "Oh, Christ," her mother replies. "What am I going to find out?" (304).

Katie leaves before her mother can read the book to meet up with Jamie, the boy she's been dating—perhaps to prove to herself she isn't a lesbian—and after several false starts tells him the truth about herself. "What I'm telling you, Jamie, is that I don't really fancy boys. I like you loads, but I don't think we should see each other anymore" (309).

Jamie is devastated, though Katie is quick to tell him, "Jamie, if I didn't have these feelings for girls, I would totally snap you up. I'd marry you, in fact. You're gorgeous and funny and kind and I wanted so badly to fancy you" (310).

Wounded, he merely shrugs and walks away.

Next Katie goes to the coffee shop where Simona works and tries to effect a rapprochement with the angry girl but with no success. Now it is Katie's turn to be devastated. She returns home to find her mother in tears. When the woman recovers herself, they talk—or attempt to. The mother asks Katie if she has simply been experimenting. "I'm not experimenting, Mum," Katie answers. "Not in the way you mean. I've felt it for ages. It was just difficult to admit." To Katie's surprise her mother is accepting, but what about Simona? Is there any chance they might reconcile? The short answer is yes, though not without some emotional heavy lifting, and the book ends with Katie fantasizing about their having a future together.

Perhaps this complex novel reminds us more immediately than the other books we've discussed that before you can come out to others, you must first come out to yourself, a process that may be as frightening and painful as sharing your truth with others. As Simona tells Katie when they have their first serious conversation, "Most people will go to ridiculous lengths to deny who they are" (209).

And finally we have emily m. danforth's *The Miseducation of Cameron Post*. Cameron's parents are killed in a car crash when she is a girl, and she is sent to live with her grandmother and conservative Aunt Ruth. As she grows into her teenage years, she discovers she is a lesbian and begins a clandestine affair with her bisexual best friend Coley. When their affair is discovered, Coley blames Cameron for their relationship and Aunt Ruth arranges for Cameron to be sent to God's Promise, a church camp that claims to "cure" young people of their homosexuality. Set in eastern Montana, a setting that is vividly realized, the novel then follows Cameron's experiences at the camp. Such "religious conversion therapy" is rooted in reality; in fact, it has recently been declared to be illegal in the states of California and New Jersey. A coming-of-age novel, danforth's *Miseducation of Cameron Post* is a work of literary fiction that is notable for its characterization and its intelligent treatment of its thematic content. It was shortlisted for the William C. Morris Award, which is presented annually by ALA's Young Adult Library Services Association for the best first novel of the year.

GAY ASSIMILATION

As noted earlier, novels of gay assimilation now equal in number or outpace those of homosexual visibility. Here are five typical examples of the GA genre.

In Jaye Robin Brown's *Georgia Peaches and Other Forbidden Fruit*, rising senior Joanna Gordon is comfortably out and presumably proud when her popular radio preacher father marries for the third time and moves the family from urban Atlanta to rural Rome, Georgia, where, Joanna frets, "queer girls go to die." Speaking of which, once they're ensconced in Rome, her father has a disquieting request: "I want you to lie low. Don't be so boldly out of the closet up here" (13).

"I can't even process this nugget," the baffled Joanna thinks. "My father, the one who's said he supports me one hundred percent, is taking some percentage of that back. This isn't something he should ask. It's completely freaking wrong. 'I can't believe this,'" she tells him (13).

They debate the issue a bit before Joanna agrees on one condition: that her preacher father will give her the radio show she has wanted so she can minister to outsider teens like herself. He gives in, and the deed is done. And Joanna's "new" life as being ostensibly straight begins . . . swimmingly, as she soon finds herself one of the popular girls, and, "I'd never admit it to my dad but there's a part of me that feels okay being incognito" (64). Joanna takes one small step out of her newly self-imposed closet when she meets nerdy but sweet-natured George and, learning he has two moms, comes out to him on the condition he absolutely keep her secret. For in the meantime she has met the beautiful and enchanting Mary Carlson; the two are becoming BFFs, and Joanna is determined that nothing will compromise their relationship even though she thinks she's crazy for falling for a straight girl. Or is Mary Carlson straight? There are just enough innuendos to drive Joanna crazy with wondering. "This whole Rome experience," she thinks exasperatedly, "is tilting my equilibrium, and I'm not sure what's fact or what's fiction" (188). So it should be perfection when Mary Carlson comes out to her and acknowledges that "I like you" (199). But is it? To acknowledge her own homosexuality and feelings would be to go against her father's wishes. But to deny her feelings would be personally devastating. Perhaps there's a third way? "The one that plays along and admits some mutual feelings but maybe doesn't share the all of it" (200). Easier said than done, for Joanna quickly finds herself in a full-blown secret relationship. But how long will it be secret? "I can tell, even after just two weeks," she thinks, "[Mary Carlson's] antsy to let the world know" (216). But Joanna can't come out; she has promised her father she won't, and so the two girls break up with recriminations on both sides. In the wake of the breakup, Mary Carlson comes out and is embraced by her friends. Then it's Joanna's turn. Following an impassioned talk with her father, he approves her exit from the local closet, and she comes out to the circle of her best friends who embrace her as they did Mary Carlson. And then Joanna comes out to the world when she acknowledges being a lesbian on her new radio show. And finally, finally, she and Mary Carlson reconcile. Cue the happy ending.

The paradox of an out girl's going back into the closet and then struggling to stay there is an intriguing and offbeat one that will remind readers of Bill Konigsberg's *Openly Straight*. It's bound to satisfy readers.

And then there's David Levithan's antic *Hold Me Closer*. He's baaack: Tiny Cooper, the larger-than-life and definitely out costar of Levithan's *Will Grayson, Will Grayson* (coauthored with John Green), now claims center stage in the author's latest, which—according to its title page—is "a musical in novel form (Or, A novel in musical form)." Either way, the book is presented as being the script—in two acts—for Tiny's epic autobiographical musical, *Hold Me Closer*. Act 1 charts his childhood and his struggle to come out to his family and friends who are less than surprised or disturbed by the revelation, Tiny being, as his friend Will observed in *Will Grayson, Will Grayson* (2009), "the world's largest person who is really, really gay and also the world's gayest person who is really, really large" (3). Tiny offers paradigmatic evidence that gay crushes can start well before puberty. With an outsize personality to match his physicality, the out Tiny is flamboyant and fabulous and, as we learn in act 2, also a hopeless romantic, so much so that he has fallen in love eighteen times. And, yes, all eighteen of his exes put in an appearance. Meanwhile the action is propelled by twenty-five songs with such titles as "The Ballad of the Lesbian Babysitter," "Oh! What a Big Gay Baby," and "Summer of Gay." This is all as much fun as it sounds, but it has its serious side, too, in its sober examination of the nature of love, its joys and its sorrows. Does it have a happy ending? That remains for readers to decide, but there is no doubt that the accomplished Levithan has turned in another star turn with a book that is witty and wise, and demonstrates that being out can be a catalyst to imagination rather than degradation. This novel is worthy of an encore.

Next, consider Bill Konigsberg's *The Porcupine of Truth* (2015). Seventeen-year-old Carson has come from New York City to Billings, Montana, to spend the summer with his father, whom he hasn't seen in fourteen years and who is now dying. Things are different in Billings, Carson soon discovers. For one thing, it's quiet; for another, there are no animals in the Billings Zoo—well, there is a depressed Siberian tiger "with a look of existential despair in his eyes" (2), but otherwise, nada. However, all is not lost, for it is at the zoo that Carson meets Aisha and falls instantly in love: "A ridiculously beautiful girl is organizing the greeting card display. In terms of attractiveness, she is in the 999th percentile of zoo employees. I can't take my eyes off her" (3). The two talk, and Carson discovers that the girl sometimes sleeps there outdoors in a sleeping bag. Puzzled, he asks why. "Another time," she says mysteriously. "Long story" (13). The next afternoon when he takes her for coffee, he finds out why. It begins when Aisha is outed by a barista who is her bête noire. "How do you like living on the streets, dyke sauce? Couldn't have happened to a nicer man-girl" (40). "I feel as if someone stole the air from my chest," the love-struck Carson thinks. "I'm sorry," he says. "You're sorry?" Aisha replies. "What for? Because some asshole called me a name? Because I'm a dyke? Because my dad found out and kicked me out and I'm sleeping in the fucking zoo? I'm at the end of my rope here and you're sorry?" (41).

Happily, she soon calms down and tells Carson her story in more detail. It turns out her very religious father had gotten suspicious a week earlier because she was away from home a lot. "So he tracked my cell phone," she continues. "He rang the doorbell and scared the crap out of my girlfriend, Kayla. He barged into Kayla's room and I was in her bed and I'm like 'Dad.' Shit. Well, this ain't great" (42). The father roughly takes her home and the next day announces he's sending her to Flowing Rivers in Mesa, Arizona. "And this place," she tells Carson, "is going to make me straight, through the Jesus" (43).

When she refuses to go, the man kicks her out of the house, and so it is that the zoo has become her home away from home.

When Carson discovers she has no place to go, he brings her home; his father lets her move into the basement and the two become fast friends, forming an easy, bantering relationship. Together they set off in search of Carson's grandfather who vanished when Carson's dad was a teenager. Their goal is to bring the dying man closure. But their search seems quixotic, filled with secrets and surprises that will test their friendship. And the truth, when it emerges, may be as thorny as, well, a porcupine! In the wake of their quest, Aisha strikes out on her own, determined to find herself and her future as an out lesbian in San Francisco. Carson is bereft, but Aisha assures him, "I'll call you every day. This isn't good-bye, Carson. I mean, it will be in a few days. But you will never be without me. I'm gonna be there on your phone and on your Skype 'til you're sick of my ass" (322). And the reader has the sense that she will, and their friendship will endure even though a continent will separate them.

In his third novel Konigsberg employs an attractive, colorful style (a day is "warm, like bread just out of the oven" [5]) and crafts fascinating, multidimensional characters, both teens *and* adults. A friendship between a straight boy and a lesbian is relatively rare in YA fiction—though one thinks of Wittlinger's *Hard Love*—and is, accordingly, exceedingly welcome in this altogether memorable novel.

Adam Silvera's *History Is All You Left Me* is another example of gay assimilation. After the out Griffin and his boyfriend Theo break up, after Theo moves to California for college, even after Theo finds a new boyfriend in Jackson, Griffin continues to believe that their endgame will be to find their way back to each other, however impossible that seems at the moment. But then Theo drowns, and all that is left for Griffin is their now fugitive history together. Griffin's affecting account of that history is told partly in flashbacks that are simultaneously elegiac and melancholy. As for the present, it finds him bereft, grieving but discovering, perhaps, a weird sort of comfort in continuing to speak to the dead Theo, reliving their past while sharing what is happening in the here and now. But will Griffin, who is so stuck in the past, find a future? Perhaps a future with Jackson? Silvera's splendid second novel (his first is *More Happy Than Not* [2015]) is filled with tantalizing questions about lies and honesty, love and loss, past and present, but answers are gradually revealed through Griffin's growth and change as well as the evolution of the other characters who populate this beautifully realized, character-driven work of literary fiction. *History Is All You Left Me* leaves its readers enriched and challenged to join Griffin in questioning the meaning of life and love and finding it in the unsparing honesty that brings closure to the novel and to Griffin's openly gay quest to let go of the past and embrace the future. It demonstrates unequivocally that when a character is openly gay, the story can transcend that simple fact and embrace more complex—and arguably more satisfying—territory.

And, lastly, Patrick Ness's *The Rest of Us Just Live Here* (2015). This is the satirical story of teenager Mikey who suffers from obsessive-compulsive disorder and whose best friend Jared is not only openly gay but also one-quarter god—the god, as it happens, of cats—which explains why he can cozy up to mountain lions. Mikey has a huge crush on the beautiful girl Henna and is distraught when a new boy in their circle of friends appears to have his cap set for her. In the department of comic misunderstandings, it turns out that the object of the boy's affections is not Henna after all but, rather, Jared! Meanwhile, in this novel of magic realism, beings called the Immortals are attempting to infiltrate Mikey's town to take over the earth. Yikes! This is one of a small handful of LGBTQ+ novels in which a straight protagonist has a gay best friend and one, at that, who is openly gay with no repercussions. Others in this genre include April Lurie's *The Less Dead* (2010), Hannah Moskowitz's *Marco Impossible* (2013), Tim Federle's *The Great American Whatever* (2016), and Benjamin Alire Saenz's *The Inexplicable Logic of My Life* (2016).

QUEER CONSCIOUSNESS/COMMUNITY

Of our three categories, QC is by far the least represented. In fact, we count only twenty-five such titles published between 2010 and 2016. This may be due to the fact that out teens are now simply presumed to have a sympathetic unofficial community of friends both gay and straight whether or not they have access to formal communities like school Gay-Straight Alliances (GSAs) or teen LGBTQ+ centers. Adult gays and lesbians have bars and clubs in which to find community, but such opportunities typically don't exist for teens, though a gay bar does provide a partial setting for one of these QC novels: Hannah Moskowitz's *Not Otherwise Specified* (2015), which is addressed at some length in our chapter on bisexuality. While, as noted,

GSAs often provide the element of community, it is the theater that more often does. In fact, sixteen of the twenty-five QC titles feature the world of drama, among them such titles as Maria Boyd's *Will* (2010), Emily Horner's *A Love Story Starring My Dead Best Friend* (2010), Julie Williams's *Drama Queens in the House* (2014), Becky Albertalli's *Simon vs. the Homo Sapiens Agenda* (2015), and Linus Alsenas's *Beyond Clueless* (2016).

Gay-Straight Alliances figure prominently in *The Alliance, The Fight, The Mariposa Gown,* and *Starting from Here. The Alliance* and *The Fight* are two volumes in Darby Creek's Surviving Southside series. In the first, *The Alliance* by Gabriel Goodman (2013), two Southside students, Scott and Carmen, team up to start a GSA in the wake of the suicide of a gay friend. Unfortunately they meet resistance from other students, teachers, and the school's administration. Despite this, it appears their efforts are about to reach fruition when a group of parents, getting wind of the effort, complain to the school board which meekly quashes the two teens' efforts. In the sequel, *The Fight* by Elizabeth Karre (2013), which takes place at the same school a year later, Bella, witnessing a case of gay-bashing that a teacher refuses to stop, decides to join the GSA, only to discover it exists only unofficially, in large part because the school has a so-called neutrality policy that prevents teachers from taking a stand. Zoe, one of the GSA members, explains, "There's something going on. . . . The teachers are totally freaked out about anything having to do with gay people" (24). Despite—or because of—this, Bella and Zoe then launch a community-wide effort to change the policy. Both of these books are highly didactic but nevertheless provide opportunities for teaching tolerance and empathy, something the coprotagonists of *The Mariposa Gown* by Rigoberto Gonzalez (2012) also search for, finding it in the informal, tight-knit community of support they give each other. Finally, in *Starting from Here* by Lisa Jenn Bigelow (2012), sixteen-year-old Colby's girlfriend leaves her for a boy. As a result, Colby withdraws and avoids not only her friends but also the GSA meetings at school. It isn't until she discovers and adopts a three-legged dog that she is able to reexamine her life and accept help and support from her friends in the Rainbow Alliance.

Arguably the most interesting of these novels—*Fan Art* by Sarah Tregay (2014)—offers the least GSA content. The story: A high school senior, the gay but closeted Jamie, is horrified when he realizes that he is in love with his straight best friend Mason. While he longs to come out to Mason, he doesn't for fear the act would destroy their friendship, the most important thing in the world for Jamie. In the meantime he is nonplussed to realize that a gaggle of girls in his art class have intuited that he is gay. When he asks one of them, Eden, how this can be, she says, simply, "They've got good gaydar" (77). They also have decided that Jamie and Mason make an ideal pair. Eden has even drawn a picture of them kissing, a picture that will have a dramatic impact later in the novel. One of the other girls is Challis, an out lesbian who is president of the school's GSA. "I admire Challis," Jamie thinks, "maybe even wish I was more like her—out, proud, and in the GSA" (26). Nevertheless, he settles for an informal community among the girls in his art class, especially Eden, who, it turns out, is a lesbian. When Jamie inadvertently outs himself to her, he finds something of a soul mate in the girl. Be that as it may, the plot then becomes more complex when Challis submits a graphic novel–type story with gay content to the school magazine, which Jamie serves as art editor. Fearful of losing funding, the editorial board—against Jamie's wishes—rejects the story. Jamie then takes it upon himself to surreptitiously work with the printer to ensure the story is, indeed, included, his feeling being that the magazine is for the entire school, not just the editorial board, and that includes LGBTQ+ students. Having done this, however, Jamie is terrified when he considers the consequences: that he will have outed himself to the entire school, especially since, as Eden points out, the two boys in Challis's story look like Jamie and Mason. Nevertheless, Jamie is determined to make the magazine a success and attends a meeting of the GSA to sell copies to the students there and to create a word-of-mouth campaign. Uncertain what to do next, Jamie elects to do nothing except lie low, avoiding Mason and any possible confrontation. Then, as we fast-forward to graduation day, something almost unimaginable happens: arriving at the ceremony, Jamie discovers that someone has stapled a copy of Eden's compromising picture in every commencement program. It turns out that someone is Eden's Neanderthal brother, who unjustifiably blames Jamie for his having been discovered as being complicit in a high school prank. Devastated by the thought that people will now think Mason is gay, Jamie is beside himself with anxiety and grief until the ceremony is completed and Mason finds him in the audience and, yes, kisses him! It turns out that Mason is gay and loves Jamie in turn. Fade to a happy ending.

Other novels with unofficial communities of support include Carolyn Mackler's *Infinite in Between* (2015), which has an ensemble cast of five teens whom we follow through their four years in high school. One of their number is gay and finds support from his four friends. David Levithan's *Two Boys Kissing* (2015) is the story of two boys who, in the wake of a gay-bashing, attempt to set a world record for the longest sustained kiss. As word of their effort spreads, it attracts a huge online community of support as well as a large crowd of people who come to the event to offer visible support. More important, however, is the chorus of gay survivors of the eighties whose voices tell the story and provide a contextual link to the larger community of gay men who have preceded today's gay teens.

Speaking of online, that is where closeted Will finds his community in Michael Harris's *Homo* (2013). One of the supporting characters in *Two*

Boys Kissing also finds community in this electronic venue, though with less than salutary results.

AND MORE

A number of already established characteristics and hallmarks of LGBTQ+ literature continued to manifest themselves during the twenty-teens. Among them: friendship between LGBTQ+ and straight characters. Chief among these were the friendships of a straight girl and a gay boy. We find twenty of these titles. As for a straight boy and a lesbian, though, we count only two. For a straight girl's friendship with a lesbian, we find three and for a straight boy's friendship with a gay, five. We believe we will see more examples of out gay and lesbian teens no longer being sad-eyed loners but, instead, having firm friendships with self-described straight kids.

As for love relationships, a long-established trope is the straight girl in love with a gay boy, though the number of these titles is in decline and, as previously noted, is now often told with humor rather than tragedy; there are only four such that we find during this period. A new trend, however, is the gay boy in love with a straight boy. There was only one of these pre-2010; however, from 2010 to 2016, we find seven. As with some other trends, there seems to be no accounting for this one, but it will be important to watch to see if it continues. As for gay girls in love with straight ones, we find only two.

Another familiar trope is the use of drama and the arts (dance and music) as settings—sometimes as a summer drama camp, sometimes a high school theater production, sometimes individual aspiration to a professional career. Whichever, these books show an opportunity for community for teens who might otherwise be regarded as outsiders. Together they find a place where talent, dedication, hard work, and individuality are rewarded with companionship and collegiality. Happily, we find sixteen such books published between 2010 and 2016. Among them are Becky Albertalli's *Simon vs. the Homo Sapiens Agenda* (2015), Elizabeth Hand's *Radiant Days* (2012), Laura Goode's *Sister Mischief* (2013), and Emily Horner's *A Love Story Starring My Dead Best Friend* (2010).

Unfortunately, violence directed at the LGBTQ character continues to manifest its ugly self. We find fifteen titles in this category (there were thirteen between 2004 and 2009). This trope has a fraught relationship with reality. On the one hand, one hopes that the violence dramatized exaggerates a real-world decline; on the other, we continue to need such books to expose empathetic teen readers to the horrors of violence.

Lastly, there continues to be an abundance of short-story collections with LGBTQ+ themes and content; fourteen, in fact, since 2010.

Others signs of progress in YA literature—the growing visibility of transgender, intersex, and bisexual teens; the increasing presence of LGBTQ+ characters in comics and graphic novels, and the state of nonfiction with LGBTQ+ content—are all covered in other chapters.

NOTE

1. Evidence of how far LGBTQ literature has come since its inception is the remarkable difference between two McLeods: the sunny, gregarious, out Ed McLeod and the dour, closeted martinet Justin McLeod of Isabelle Holland's *The Man without a Face* (1972).

Part II

Breaking Down the Barriers

Chapter Seven

Bisexual Inclusion in
Young Adult Literature

According to the website bisexual.org, the concept of bisexuality—an individual's attraction to both sexes—emerged from the famous Kinsey Reports of 1948. While some people continue to believe that persons who claim to be bisexual are actually only lesbians and gays manqué, there is a sizable population who would disagree, claiming bisexuality is, indeed, their condition of being. The number of people who self-identify as bisexual is growing according to a Pew Research report.[1] Another study, conducted by the Williams Institute at UCLA, found that of the 3.5 percent of the population that identified as LGBT, more than half were bisexual.[2] Unfortunately, despite this robust figure, the number of YA novels having bisexual content is depressingly small. Only twenty-one titles with such content have appeared since the first, M. E. Kerr's pioneering *"Hello," I Lied*, was published in 1997.[3]

Set on Long Island during one fateful summer, the story is told by Lang, a seventeen-year-old, self-identified gay teen who is in a relationship with twenty-one-year-old Alex. But Alex is away doing summer-stock theater and Lang is disconcerted to find himself attracted to a visiting French girl, Huguette. She returns his interest, and the two give physical expression to their mutual attraction. Their relationship predictably ends with the summer, and Lang and Alex happily reunite, even as Lang unregretfully acknowledges, "I knew that I'd always think of it as the summer that I loved a girl" (171).

It must be noted that the book didn't appear until twenty-eight years after John Donovan's groundbreaking *I'll Get There. It Better Be Worth the Trip* (1969)—a long time to wait. A full list of YA novels with bisexual content is provided at the end of this chapter.

While all of the novels with teen characters who identify as bisexual are excellent in their respective ways, five stand out as paradigmatic: Maureen Johnson's *The Bermudez Triangle* (2004), Alex Sanchez's *Boyfriends with Girlfriends* (2011), Andrew Smith's *Grasshopper Jungle* (2015), Carrie Mesrobian's *Cut Both Ways* (2015), and Hannah Moskowitz's *Not Otherwise Specified* (2015).

Consider first *The Bermudez Triangle* (retitled *On the Count of Three* in 2013). The self-styled Bermudez Triangle consists of three BFFs: the eponymous Nina Bermudez, Avery Dekker, and Melanie Forrest. The three have been inseparable forever, until the summer before their senior year when Nina goes to a leadership camp at Stanford University. There she meets and falls for Steve, a West Coast environmentalist. Happy with that, she returns home to find, to her horror, that in her absence Mel and Avery have become lovers. Her first thought on learning this is to wonder if her friends are suddenly bisexual; her second is to wonder if they're lesbians. Either way, the long-standing "Bermudez Triangle" is sundered, now a thing of the past. Though Nina doesn't know it, her friends' relationship had begun with a kiss from Mel, whom Avery has previously mused has universal appeal "like baby seals and koala bears" (40). Who better to try this experiment with? Avery thinks. After all, "here was someone she knew and truly loved, really and truly and totally. No surprises. No hidden agenda. This was someone she could trust. It would be secret" (40). In fact, Avery likes keeping her relationship with Mel a secret. "She wanted to be the only one who knew what it was like to be with Mel—to be able to look at her and know that Mel was all hers, and she was all Mel's, and no one else with all their posturing had *any idea* what that meant" (121–22). But Nina, who has discovered her two friends kissing, knows that it's more than mere kissing: the two are in a relationship. It's hard to keep a relationship a secret, and soon it's common knowledge that the two girls are a pair. With the secret out at school, the novel then follows the three girls and their new friend Parker throughout the course of their senior year as Nina's long-distance relationship begins to fray and Avery begins to question her homosexuality and her attraction to Mel, who is unquestionably a lesbian. As for Avery, "I'm not gay," she declares (151). "Okay," Mel says, "you're bi" (152). Wrong answer. "Stop trying to tell me what I am!" Avery snaps. "Mel stepped back in shock. She could understand that Avery might not feel comfortable being labeled gay—Mel still had trouble with this sometimes—but being bi wasn't exactly something she could deny" (152). But Avery can try: "This isn't the same as other people. The bi girls, they go back and forth. We're just . . . together" (152). But for how long, because things get even more complicated when Nina then discovers Avery making out with a (gasp) boy. This presages a sexual sea change as Avery suddenly has "guys on the brain" (191). But things are, yes, complicated. Avery tells Nina that she isn't sure if she's gay or straight or bi or what. "Maybe you should have thought that one through before you started dating Mel," Nina says tartly (186). "It's not that simple," Avery replies, continuing, "I definitely like Mel. I like . . . the things that go along with dating. I mean, I have those feelings. But I think it might just be Mel that I like that way" (186). "You like guys, too?" Nina asks. "Avery felt her skin flushing. Something about that question made her feel like . . . a glutton. Like she wanted *everyone.* Guys, girls, dogs, cats, populations of whole cities" (186). Despite all of this and her reiterated declaration to the boy she's been seeing that she's not gay, Avery tentatively suggests that she and Mel might get back together, a notion that Mel wisely(?) rejects. "I think that's a bad idea," she says. "Why?" Avery asks. "Because you're not gay." "I'm some-thing," Avery replies. "What are you then?" Mel demands. "Avery didn't have an answer" (282).

In the meantime, a number of things happen because Nina has inadver-tently outed Mel to her family. It does not go well at first, though her father tells her he will love her no matter what. Nina's friend Steve has ended their relationship, telling her he's dating someone else. Parker has declared his feelings for Nina, who thinks they should just be friends, a notion that is reinforced when the changeable Steve then declares he wants to get back together with her. Mel and Avery reconcile—as friends. Nina forgives Avery for her infidelity and, presto, the Bermudez Triangle is restored.

A few lingering questions remain, though. What will happen to the bereft Parker (although it appears he may have found a girlfriend)? And what, exactly, is Avery? Avery herself doesn't seem to know, so it's a question that must remain unanswered. However, it's obvious that she is attracted to both girls and boys and is, for all practical purposes, bisexual. One thing remains certain: it's complicated, a word that gets quite a workout in the context of this agreeably romantic coming-of-age novel, which is notable for being one of the first LGBTQ novels to be targeted at the retail market.

In *Boyfriends with Girlfriends,* Sergio and Lance meet online and make a date to meet in person and bring along their respective best friends, Kimiko and Allie. The first meeting is sweetly awkward; the boys hit it off all right but there's a problem: Sergio is bisexual, and Lance isn't sure he can handle that or if he even believes it is possible to be attracted to both boys and girls. As he says to his friend Allie before meeting Sergio, "I guess that [his stated bisexuality] means he's still coming out. Like in the saying *bi now, gay later?*" (3). Is this a problem? Well, actually there are several: Sergio is still smarting from having been dumped by his erstwhile girlfriend Zelda and isn't sure if he wants to undertake a new relationship. Although he acknowl-edges he's out at school as bisexual, girls usually accept his bi-ness, while with guys it often seems like the kiss of death as it may, too, with the somewhat dubious Lance, who finds it hard to believe Sergio's claims that he is turned on by both guys and girls. "But you admit you're attracted to guys?"

Lance asks. "Yeah . . . ," Sergio says. "But I'm also attracted to chicks" (8).
Lance is still dubious, wondering: "Why didn't he just take the next step and
say he was gay? Maybe he [Sergio] wasn't as mature as [Lance] had hoped"
(8). Sergio has some doubts of his own. As he later tells Kimiko, "I like him.
I'm just not sure he gets the bi thing" (11).

Sergio explains the "bi thing" to readers: "Guys and girls brought out
different feelings in him. With boys, he liked the rough-and-tumble play,
their earthy smells and no-nonsense talk, the fact that in so many ways they
were the same as he was. With girls he liked everything the opposite: their
soft tender touch, their flowery scents, the way they flirted and teased, their
difference and mystery. By the time he'd finished grade school, he'd scored
kisses from three boys and three girls. The teams were tied, even-steven"
(33–34). But when, in high school, he meets Zelda, she becomes the only
person he thinks about "almost each and every moment" (36). Sadly, Zelda
ultimately ends the relationship because of Sergio's bisexuality. "I'm always
wondering: Are you thinking about me or about a guy?" she asks (38). This,
of course, echoes Lance's own reservations. He still can't quite wrap his
mind around the concept of bisexuality: "But if you're attracted to guys,
doesn't that make you gay?" he asks Sergio. "I mean, straight guys aren't
attracted to other guys—right?" (61). "Yeah," Sergio agrees. "But neither are
gay guys attracted to girls—right? I mean," he tellingly asks Lance, "are
you?" (61). Lance is *still* not convinced: "I don't believe there really is such a
thing as being bi" (64). "I just don't understand how somebody can switch
between guys and girls like that." "It's not 'switching,'" Sergio replies. "It's
just accepting different sides of myself" (65). Lance: "It feels sort of unfair
that you have that choice and I don't." What Lance increasingly wants is for
Sergio to choose him and eschew his attraction to girls, especially, perhaps,
because, as he later tells Allie, "Apparently he truly is bi." "I thought you
didn't believe in bi people," Allie observes. "Now I do," Lance admits. "He's
already had full-on sex with both guys and girls." To make sure she gets the
point, he repeats: "*And girls!*" (79). And yet, despite this assertion, Lance is
still dithering: "It's like there's this straight part of him that I'll never be able
to connect with—and I don't *want* to connect with it" (80). Ultimately, Lance
feels there is only one way to resolve his doubts: to make his burgeoning
relationship with Sergio monogamous. Unfortunately, Sergio is not ready to
take such a step and Lance, accordingly, ends the putative relationship. If his
head dictates that he take this step, Lance's heart dictates otherwise, and the
two boys reconnect, this time as a couple. Their problem is resolved and
perhaps, for the reader, this is the solution to the problem (if we may put it
that way) of dating a bisexual—to insist on a monogamous relationship. As
for Allie, she is unsure about this: "So do all bi people have open relationships?" she asks Kimiko (123). "I guess some do," is Kimiko's inconclusive
answer. "Sergio doesn't." The question arises from Allie's growing suspicion

that *she* is bi. Kimiko is a lesbian who has crushed on Allie who—though she has a devoted boyfriend—is now questioning, as she finds herself increasingly attracted to her new friend. Kimiko thinks Allie may simply be bi-curious until Allie kisses her. Then things get complicated. Like Lance, Allie begins to want a relationship. Like Sergio, Kimiko is unsure of this, not because she has reservations about Allie's emerging bisexuality but because she feels she isn't good enough for Allie who, she believes, is out of her league.

How will these four engaging kids ultimately resolve the mixed messages their hearts are sending to their brains? Leave it to Lambda Literary Award winner Sanchez to sort it all out. He's written another innovative, important book that explores with empathy and sympathy largely ignored aspects of teen sexual identity. While lip service is routinely given to these aspects of sexual identity in the acronym "LGBTQ," there have been, as noted above, only a relative handful of novels that so plausibly and dramatically bring the nature of bisexuality and sexual questioning to life. Sanchez does both, establishing in the process welcome possibilities for other authors to explore.

Andrew Smith in his *Grasshopper Jungle* is one of these. Welcome to the apocalypse. Best friends Austin and Robby are inadvertent witnesses to a clutch of bullies who unwittingly unleash a deadly, genetically engineered plague on their small Iowa hometown, a plague that results in the creation of six-foot-tall, carnivorous bugs that look like praying mantises. The book is a feast for those who hunger for black humor. The action follows the gigantic carnivores around town while they copulate with each other and chow down on its hapless inhabitants. In the meantime, on the human front, Austin's oft-repeated mantra is "I'm so confused"; and so it seems he is, for he's in love with both Robby and also his girlfriend Shann, dreaming of three-ways. "I wondered if it made me homosexual to even think about having threesomes with Robby and Shann" (23). Homosexual or not, Austin is horny as a hop toad. A veritable encyclopedia of things make him horny, a word that seems omnipresent in the narrative. "I wondered," Austin muses, "if I would ever not be horny, or confused about why I got horny at stuff I wasn't supposed to get horny at" (19). "Thinking about me and Robby going to Sweden made me horny" (20). "Shann always kissed Robby on the mouth after she kissed me. It made me horny" (23). "Thinking about having sex on the floor of the Ealing Coin Wash Launderette made me horny" (40). "Thinking about getting drunk for the first time with Robby made me feel horny" (43). And—well, you get the idea.

All three kids are wonderfully engaging as they dodge those pesky, insatiable bugs, finally finding an underground bunker called Eden that may or may not offer them sanctuary while all hell continues to break loose in the world above them. But if they're in Eden, there's trouble in paradise. Robby is gay (he came out in the seventh grade) and when he asks to kiss his friend, Austin complies and finds he likes it. As for Robby, his reaction is touching:

"I think that was the best moment of time in my entire life, Austin" (46). He then adds, "I don't want you to hate me." "How could I hate you?" Austin responds. The fact is that he is unequivocal about loving Robby. Robby: "I do love you though." Austin: "I love you, Robby" (121). But still Austin is confused. What does his declaration of love make him? "Robby was homosexual. I didn't know if I was anything. I wondered what I was. None of that mattered" (70). And so when Shann later tells Austin that she thinks Robby is in love with him, Austin can find no fault in that and acknowledges that he has kissed Robby. Shann, in a fury, storms away and later sends him a text saying, simply, "I hate you." She then sends the same message to Robby. Earlier Austin had said that Shann was jealous of Robby, "possibly to the point of being a little curious about my sexuality. I know, maybe that was also my confusion as well" (29–30). Later Austin, in a tit-for-tat way, will believe that Robby is jealous of Shann. Nevertheless, throughout, Austin continues to wonder "how it was possible to be sexually attracted and in love with my best friend, a boy *and* my other best friend, a girl—two completely different people, at the same time" (162). And yet, when the three had earlier danced together, Austin couldn't resist: "I love you, Shann. I love you, Robby," he tells his friends (188). And yet Austin stubbornly remains a study in uncertainty: "I was pretty sure I was not exactly queer. But I was not certain" (210). "I was confused. How could I be in love with a girl *and* a boy, at the same time? I was trapped forever" (306). An answer may be forthcoming: "Robby shrugged. 'They have a name for guys like you, you know, Austin?' 'Um. Bisexual?'" Austin hazards (the only time in the book the "bi" word is invoked). Robby's answer is startling: "No. The word is *selfish*. You don't really care about me *or* Shann." "It was like bombs had been dropped," Austin says with a wince, "and the biggest one just landed on my chest" (340). Robby quickly apologizes if he hurt Austin, and the two are reconciled, but the notion that being bisexual is selfish is one that recurs in the literature. Things get even more complicated when Shann and her parents show up in the bunker, and Austin and Shann, having reconciled, have sex, leaving Shann pregnant, though neither of the two teens knows it at the time.

As the devastation continues, Robby and Austin bravely venture out of the bunker determined to exterminate the bugs, using Robby's blood, which—they have determined—is toxic. They are successful until they discover that the eggs, which the female bug has laid, are hatching and the earth is becoming infested with myriads of the monsters. The boys beat a hasty retreat to the bunker. At book's end they have been living there for five years with Shann, her parents, Robbie's mother, and a local cook. Austin and Shann's son, Lucky, is now four years old; he and his father live together, though both Robby and Shann want the two to live with them. Nevertheless, the living arrangements evidence Austin's lingering confusion, though he has come to terms with it. "I no longer care to ask the question, 'What am I going to do?'" (383).

Indeed, the book leaves that question unresolved, and perhaps there is no resolution to it. There is no changing one's bisexual nature, any more than there is any way of changing one's homosexuality. Love is love, and it is not to be denied.

Grasshopper Jungle is wildly entertaining as it examines these questions and may remind readers of the work of Kurt Vonnegut Jr. It's more than just the "I'm so confused" and "You know what I mean" leitmotifs, it's the book's askew attitude toward the world and its absurdities. It's a 2015 Printz honor book and a BFYA selection (Best Fiction for Young Adults).

Consider, now, Carrie Mesrobian's novel *Cut Both Ways*. Will's gay best friend Angus surprises him with a kiss. Will is even more surprised when he kisses him back. After all, he thinks, "I'm not gay. I'm not gay" (16). So why does he get a partial erection from the kiss? "Can Angus tell?" he wonders (18). The next thing you know, Will is chatting up Brandy, a cute sophomore. And then—most natural thing in the world—they're making out in Will's bedroom. It goes no further than petting but still. . . . Nevertheless, he can't stop thinking of Angus, but he's not gay, he continues to insist to himself, "because Angus didn't get me off" (31). But that's about to change. When Brandy briefly leaves town, Will winds up at Angus's house, spends the night, and finds himself in bed with his friend, and this time they *do* get each other off! And then before you can say Ican'tbelievethisishappening, Will and Brandy have sex. "Didn't earn this," a dazed Will thinks. "No way. But I take it anyway. Of course I take it" (78). Some days later when Will hears Angus sing at an appearance with his band, Will has an epiphany: "Right that minute I know that I love Angus. That I'm in love with him and I'll always love him. I'm as gay as any gay choir boy. As gay as any theater kid. Gay. And holding my girlfriend's hand" (Will has brought Brandy to the gig with him [194]). Things get even more complicated when Angus later tells Will that *he* loves *him* (266). Which leads Will to think, "I'm embarrassed of how much I want to have them both. Brandy and Angus, forever, separately, but forever, always. I can't stop it, can't stand it; the way I have to tuck that inside myself so no one sees how much I want. How much I always, always, want" (268).

Another thing Will wants is for his alcoholic father to turn his life around. Will's parents are divorced and—significantly—Will splits his time between them just as he splits his time between Angus and Brandy. Can he bring the disparate elements of his bifurcated life together?

Does he even regard himself as being bisexual? He never uses the word. But perhaps more importantly, earlier he invoked another word, "cheat," for the first time. "I never thought of myself as a cheater. Cheating at first seemed mainly like lying. Which is nothing great. But why do liars lie?

Because they're greedy. They want everything without admitting it. I don't think about it too much or I'll fucking go crazy myself" (290).

And then, inevitably, it is Brandy's turn to say, "I love you, Will. I love you so much" (297). Significantly, Will doesn't tell her he loves her. This comes in the wake of their having had unprotected sex for the first time and, yes, it appears that Brandy then becomes pregnant. But happily, it's a false alarm. Unhappily, when she calls to tell Will this, he's in bed with Angus who hears the whole conversation and doesn't respond well. But there's worse to come: One of Will's little half sisters then discovers his phone and, on it, naked pictures of Will that Angus had taken and sent him. Will's stepfather goes berserk; his mother, less so, though both are aghast that they have trusted Will. Before this can be resolved, something else catastrophic happens. Will's father's newly remodeled house burns, and Will is crushed by the loss of his emotionally fragile father's hard work. And that, essentially, is the end of the book, leaving every major situation unresolved. For readers who have come to care deeply for Will, it's a devastating denouement. Some may feel Will is being punished for being attracted to both Brandy and Angus, for having made love with both of them, for having kept this fact of love secret from the two. On the novel's last page Will muses that his father will rebuild the house (and arguably his life). "And all of this will go on, between him and my mom, between him and me. Between me and myself whoever I turn out to be, years from now. Between me and Brandy. And me and Angus. Maybe one of those conversations will stop. Sooner rather than later. I can't decide what I think of that" (340). Most readers will have the same feeling.

Appended to the melancholy novel is an author's note in which Mesrobian discusses the genesis of the book: "I wanted to explore how some teenagers might come to define themselves as bisexual." She continues: "Do they land on 'gay' or 'lesbian' first? Would they assume they were bisexual to begin with?" (341). Interestingly, Mesrobian goes on to claim she doesn't know what Will's identity is, though this seems a bit disingenuous, for surely most readers will presume he is, indeed, bisexual (a word that, again, is never used in the book). "What I do know," the author concludes, "is that we need to work for a world where it is easier for kids like him" (342).

Finally we have Hannah Moskowitz's *Not Otherwise Specified*. Seventeen-year-old Etta has broken up with her boyfriend Ben even as she has started eating disorder treatment, though she's not sure if *Dump the boyfriend who weighs less than you* is a completely rational application of her counselor's admonition to cut out toxic influences. And, oh, yes, the bisexual Etta is seriously on the outs with her lesbian friends—even her best friend and heart's desire Rachel—for having dated a boy. As a result, she fits in neither the gay nor the straight worlds: "I'm never gay enough or straight enough," she laments (57). While talking with a friend, she acknowledges a popular misperception about bisexuals: that they are all sluts. "Like, everyone thinks that just because we're into both we're into everybody" (31).

If that's the bad news, the good—well, somewhat better—news is that auditions are being held for a scholarship to New York's prestigious Brentwood, one of the best arts high schools in the country. Imagine: both New York *and* an escape from Nebraska, for, as Etta says, "Getting out of Nebraska is like the first dream a Nebraskan baby has" (34). But, oh, those auditions: Etta has no delusions about her voice, and as for dancing, she's given up ballet. "Black girls aren't supposed to be ballerinas," she says (47). And there's also the consideration of size. "You don't have to be skinny for tap," her younger sister says, but "apparently you don't have to love it either," Etta thinks glumly (73). But she feels it's essential to win a scholarship to get out of Nebraska, where her life is increasingly a nightmare, thanks to her eating disorder and the savage bullying she's experiencing from her former friends.

In the meantime she's met wispy, fascinating, anorexic fourteen-year-old Bianca, who is in her eating disorder group. "She's the Tiny Tim of our group," Etta thinks (19), unsure of exactly how she feels about the girl who will also be auditioning for Brentwood but, unlike Etta, has a glorious voice. As it turns out, Etta, Bianca, and Bianca's older brother James all make it through the first round of auditions. But there are now further complications. James is gay and Bianca, whose family is deeply religious, has mixed feelings about this, especially when James meets a boy at their audition and begins a relationship with him, suddenly vanishing from his sister's life. Deeply disturbed, Bianca fails to make the cut during the second round, though Etta and James both do, just as Etta begins to find a tentative rapprochement with Rachel, though not with the other girls. Then it's time for the final auditions. James has dropped out to stay in Nebraska with his sister. As for Etta, her plan now is to get to New York—not to go to Brentwood but instead to look for dance schools. But first she has to get to the Big Apple. And she does, winning a place in the school and a possible future as a Broadway actress, leaving Nebraska behind as she has dreamed. Meanwhile Bianca, whom Etta has begun to regard as a little sister, has gone into inpatient care for her eating disorder, and her prognosis is positive. Indeed, there are hopeful if not entirely happy endings for all involved, and Etta may have the makings of a new relationship with a girl in New York.

While these books examine various aspects of bisexuality, they all leave a common impression: being bisexual is frustratingly—and sometimes painfully—confusing for the persons in question, who can't themselves understand how they could be attracted to both males and females. Furthermore, if they act on their impulses or even make them public, they may be perceived by their potential partners as inherently promiscuous, sluttish, or selfish, or cheats. There seems to be no remedy for this, except for the bisexual person to choose a partner of one sex, eschewing his or her attraction to the other.

Whether this may offer a permanent solution is moot, because bisexuality is a condition of being, not a matter of choice. And that, of course, is why we need a literature that examines the world of such young people and deals with their issues. May we have more books about bisexual teens.

BOOKS WITH BISEXUAL CONTENT

1997

Kerr, M. E. *Hello, I Lied.* New York: Harper & Row, 1997.

2001

Ryan, Sara. *Empress of the World.* New York: Viking, 2001.

2003

Freymann-Weyr, Garret. *My Heartbeat.* Boston: Houghton Mifflin, 2003.
Hartinger, Brent. *The Geography Club.* New York: HarperCollins, 2003.

2004

De Olivera, Eddie. *Lucky.* New York: Scholastic PUSH, 2004.
Johnson, Maureen. *On the Count of Three.* [Original title: *The Bermudez Triangle.*] New York: Razorbill, 2004.

2010

Cohn, Rachel. *Very La Freak.* New York: Random, 2010.

2011

Sanchez, Alex. *Boyfriends with Girlfriends.* New York: Simon & Schuster, 2011.

2012

Peters, Julie Anne. *It's Our Prom, So Deal with It.* Boston: Little, Brown, 2012.

2013

Lo, Malinda. *Inheritance.* Boston: Little, Brown, 2013.

2014

Smith, Andrew. *Grasshopper Jungle.* New York: Dutton, 2014.

2015

Davey, Douglas. *Switch.* Calgary: Red Deer, 2015.
Hall, Sandy. *Signs Point to Yes.* New York: Swoon, 2015.
Mesrobian, Carrie. *Cut Both Ways.* New York: HarperCollins, 2015.
Moskowitz, Hannah. *Not Otherwise Specified.* New York: Simon & Schuster Pulse, 2015.
Summers, Elizabeth. *Trust Me. I'm Trouble.* New York: Delacorte, 2015.

2016

Hall, Sandy. *Been Here All Along.* New York: Swoon, 2016.
Keplinger, Kody. *Run.* New York: Scholastic, 2016.
Lindstrom, Eric. *A Tragic Kind of Wonderful.* Boston: Little, Brown Poppy, 2016.
Selzer, Adam. *Just Kill Me.* New York: Simon & Schuster, 2016.
Wallace, Kali. *Shallow Graves.* New York: HarperCollins/Tegen, 2016.

NOTES

1. www.pewresearch.org//search/?query=bisexuality.
2. Williamsinstitute.law.ucla.edu.
3. Between the 1980 publication of Norma Klein's *Breaking Up* and 1997's *"Hello,"* I *Lied*, nine novels appeared in which marriages end because of the homosexuality of one of the partners. A case could be made that at least some of these adults are bisexual, though it is more likely that they are actually homosexual and married because of social constraints and fear of opprobrium. Like most issues involving bisexuality, this is complicated, and we raise it for readers' consideration.

Chapter Eight

Transgender and Intersex Inclusion in Young Adult Literature

Though transgender individuals[1] had appeared previously in popular culture—think *M. Butterfly*, *The Rocky Horror Picture Show*, and *The Crying Game*—it was the very public transition of the character played by actress Laverne Cox in the critically hailed television series *Orange Is the New Black* that first drew widespread attention to transgender people. (An excellent biography of the actress is *Laverne Cox* by Erin Staley [New York: Rosen, 2016].) Subsequently the 2016 transition of former athlete Bruce Jenner to Caitlyn Jenner in 2016 further focused the nation's attention on transgender people and transgender issues. Among the latter are some alarming statistics that came to light as they refer to the plight of young people: 89.5 percent of transgender students report feeling unsafe at school; and no wonder, for 55 percent of them say they're being physically harassed because of their gender expression; 23 percent report being physically abused, while 11 percent are physically assaulted; 81 percent report being sexually harassed because of their gender transition, and 82 percent report that faculty/staff either never intervened or sometimes intervened when they heard other students make derogatory remarks.[2]

Such transphobia is rampant not only in America's schools but in society as well, where it is increasingly being codified. For example, the state of Mississippi's controversial—and subsequently struck down—"religious freedom" bill HB 1523 sought to severely compromise LGBT rights, identifying three religious beliefs for special protection: (1) marriage is or should be recognized as the union of one man and one woman; (2) sexual relations are properly reserved to such a marriage, and (3) [man] or [woman] refer to "an individual's immutable biological sex as objectively determined by anatomy and genetics by time of birth."[3] The ACLU's reaction? "This means discrim-

161

ination against the very existence of transgender people."[4] A similar bill, North Carolina's HB2 law, barred local governments from extending civil rights protections to gay and transgender people. Further, the law required individuals to use public restrooms that correspond with the sex listed on their birth certificates, thus barring transgender persons from using the restrooms corresponding with their gender expression.[5]

(The issue of bathroom accessibility has become increasingly thorny and widespread; two good sources of information about this include www.genderspectrum.org and, secondly, Toilet Training Companion Guide for Activists and Educators, a video and toolkit from the Sylvia Rivera Law Project: https://srlp.org/wp-content/uploads/2012/08/2010-toolkit.pdf.)

Meanwhile, more information about transgender teens is urgently needed, and such information is available in young adult books. Happily, a small but rapidly growing number of YA novels featuring transgender characters have begun appearing, thirty-five to date. And beginning around 2011, a small group of book-length nonfiction titles also started appearing. Historically, however, this was not the case; the first transgender/transsexual character did not appear in young adult fiction until 1996, twenty-seven years after the first gay character appeared. The character in question was featured in Francesca Lia Block's short story "Dragons in Manhattan," which was included in Block's *Girl Goddess #9* (1996).

It should be noted that, though the story was published in a YA book, the male-to-female (MtF) transsexual character is an adult, "transsexual" referring to a person who has had gender affirmation surgery. The first transsexual teen would not appear until 2015 in Meredith Russo's book *If I Was Your Girl* (q.v.). Sadly, Block's story didn't exactly open the floodgates to a wave of similar stories about transgender people for teens. Indeed, the next one, Emma Donoghue's "The Welcome," published in Michael Cart's collection *Love and Sex: Ten Stories of Truth* (2001), didn't appear for another five years. This one also features a male-to-female transgender person, but this time the character is a teen.

It wasn't until another three years had passed that the first YA *novel* to feature a transgender character appeared: it was Julie Anne Peters's 2004 book *Luna*. Luna is a girl who can only be seen by moonlight, for during the day she's a boy named Liam who is, yes, a transgender person. She has known since she was six—a not uncommon age for such a realization as we will see—that she's a girl trapped in a boy's body. The strain of pretending to be a boy has made her often depressive and suicidal. "I want to be free," she tells her younger sister Regan. "I want to transition" (21). Her ultimate goal, she avers, is sex affirmation surgery. No longer able to live as Liam, the tormented boy then shows up at school as Luna; not surprisingly, she is assaulted by a boy who has always been an enemy. Then, on her birthday, she arrives at the breakfast table as Luna. Her father is at first disbelieving, then furious, angrily rejecting her. "Dad's lips receded over his teeth like a snarling dog. 'You're sick,' he hissed. 'You are sick'" (222). As for Luna's mother, it turns out she has always known the truth but has refused to deal with it. Given these sorry circumstances, Luna leaves home, bound for Seattle, where a successful transgender woman she has met has promised to give her a place to live.

Though Peters and her publisher are to be commended for their courage in addressing this previously taboo subject, the novel suffers from a situation common to groundbreaking fictional treatments of previously unacknowledged issues: it tends to be driven by the "problem" instead of by more literary concerns and is occasionally melodramatic. And because this is the first book-length treatment of being transgender, it is perhaps unfortunate that Luna's parents are shown rejecting her and that, to truly be herself, she has to leave home. Nevertheless, the novel is always heartfelt and many readers will be moved by and informed about a life circumstance that then as now needs broader exposure and understanding.

Unfortunately three more years would have to pass before the appearance of another transgender character, this one in Ellen Wittlinger's 2007 novel *Parrotfish*. (The title refers to a tropical fish that changes gender from female to male as the fish population dictates.) As we will see throughout this chapter, society likes to label people, and high school junior Angela McNair is no exception. The label it applies to her is "gender dysphoria." What this means in a human context is that Angela occupies the wrong body, though this is an oversimplification; many transgender people say that this is more of a disaffiliation with the body a person is in than necessarily a straightforward narrative of the wrong body. Be that as it may, Angela, born a girl, knows that she is really a boy. And so she bravely begins transforming herself into a male. She cuts her hair short, buys men's clothing, and announces that his name is now "Grady." Grady's transition—though bold—is surprisingly easy; Some readers, in fact, may find his transition too easy to be completely believable, but there is no question that Wittlinger does a superb job of untangling the complexities of gender identity and producing a reasoned approach to what was then still a controversial, hot-button issue. Most importantly, this is a groundbreaking work in being the first to feature a female-to-male (FtM) character. Happily, unlike Luna, Grady does not have to flee town to find acceptance and community; indeed, at book's end he plans to start a Gay-Straight Alliance at his high school.

Unfortunately, after *Parrotfish*, the appearance of transgender characters in YA literature continued to proceed at a snail's pace; two years passed before the next such novel appeared, Brian Katcher's *Almost Perfect* (2009). High school senior Logan is instantly smitten when he meets Sage, the new girl in school. When Sage then begins to flirt with him, Logan finds his feelings becoming serious, and they kiss. Then it is that Logan discovers the truth: Sage is a male-to-female transgender person. Logan's immediate reaction is revulsion: "I had never been so disgusted" (100). Furthermore, he is terrified by the possibility that someone might think he is gay for having made out with a person he considers to be a boy ("That made me a fag, didn't it?" [100]); this erroneous notion is one that will unfortunately prove to be common in the literature.

To get back at him, Sage goes on a date with another boy. Unfortunately, when Sage tells him her truth, he assaults her, beating her so savagely she must be hospitalized. This episode recalls the real-life case of Brandon Teena, whose life and death were the subject of the 1999 movie *Boys Don't Cry*. It should be noted, though, that while the threat of violence is never entirely absent from these books, Sage's is a relatively extreme case. In the wake of the beating, Sage leaves town, instructing her sister never to tell Logan where she has gone. The boy finally receives a letter from Sage in which she tells him the bittersweet fact that she will probably never see him again ("And don't wait for me, I may never be back" [354]).

So we have another MtF book like *Luna* with a protagonist who must go away, though not, this time, to find a community but rather, one might say, to survive with no suggestion that she will ever find happiness. On the contrary, her case suggests that even if one does find love, it will be fleeting; moreover, that life is dangerous, threatening the possibility of being physically assaulted—or even killed—simply for being who you know you are.

The year 2009 turned out to be a signal one, for it saw not only the publication of *Almost Perfect* but also the appearance of not one but two other books with transgender content: Michael Cart's short-story anthology *How Beautiful the Ordinary; Twelve Stories of Identity* (2009) and Adam Rapp's novel *Punkzilla* (2009).

How Beautiful contains three relevant stories: in order of appearance they are Jacqueline Woodson's "Trev," Francesca Lia Block's "My Virtual World," and Jennifer Finney Boylan's "The Missing Person." Let us examine these three, beginning with "Trev." From the age of six, tall, androgynous Trev has known she is different, that "I'm wrong down there" (68). But Trev is a survivor and on the second day of first grade, she is allowed to use the boys' bathroom. "When I stepped inside and closed the stall door, I smiled. I was home" (72). Trev is exceptional at finding herself and in being the youngest transgender character in YA literature.

In "My Virtual World" by Francesca Lia Block, two teens, a boy who calls himself "blue boy" and a girl who calls herself "ms. r. r.," begin an online correspondence. Readers get a first hint of blue boy's situation when he writes, "I was having a hard time. they were about not feeling integrated in my body" (76). As the teens' correspondence continues, they learn each other's names—Garret and Rebecca—and Garret acknowledges that he was born a girl but at age twenty-one, he began hormone therapy and elected to have surgery. "It helped but there is a lot of shame I still feel . . ." (88). Rebecca challenges him: "Why do you feel shame? There is nothing shameful about you. You are a beautiful person. In some cultures you would be revered as a representative of both sexes" (88). In an echo of *Almost Perfect*, though, Rebecca does at one point ask Garret: "I'm wondering if a straight girl involved with a boy who was born a girl is really a lesbian?" (85). In the end, though, Garret and Rebecca put aside any doubts and become a couple whose happiness is genuine though a bit idealized.

Jennifer Finney Boylan's "The Missing Person" is the story of "the summer I gave up on being a boy and became a girl, instead" (154), says the unnamed protagonist of Boylan's story. The summer in question is the one between eighth and ninth grades. The catalyst for the change comes one day when the boy's family are all gone and he fearfully decides to put on lipstick and his sister's clothes and go to the local horse show. The act is liberating: "I felt like someone who had been released from jail, like someone who'd spent her whole life in prison only to be unexpectedly paroled, at the age of fourteen, and set loose upon the world" (161). It's worth noting that Boylan is a transgender woman and this is apparently an autobiographical story told in her protagonist's first-person voice.

Adam Rapp's *Punkzilla* includes a transgender secondary character who plays a minor, albeit affecting, role. En route to Memphis, fourteen-year-old Jamie, a.k.a. Punkzilla, meets a "weird guy wearing a black silky on his head" (150). The man's name is Lewis and he's living at a run-down motel, which he says is "a transitional place" (157). When Jamie inquires "from what to what," the man explains that he has had top surgery. "What's top surgery?" Jamie innocently asks (158), and Lewis explains that he is transitioning to become a man. Jamie finds him likable and hospitable, but the next day he is back on the road and doesn't see Lewis again.

The next year, 2010, also saw the publication of three books with transgender content: the novels *I Am J* by Cris Beam; *F 2 M: The Boy Within* by Hazel Edwards and Ryan Kennedy; and *Jumpstart the World* by Catherine Ryan Hyde. To discuss them in order we begin with *I Am J.*

Cris Beam, *I Am J* (2010)

Seventeen-year-old J is desperate to take testosterone and begin his transition from the girl he was born as to the straight boy he has known he is since he was five. But there's a problem: because he isn't yet eighteen, he needs parental permission to receive testosterone, and his parents don't yet know the truth about him. At best they think he might be a lesbian, as does his closest friend Melissa, with whom he is secretly in love. J, who is Jewish and Puerto Rican (one of the very few non-majority-status transgender characters in this literature), reflects on this: "Being trans wasn't special, and yet it was. It was just good and bad and interesting and fucked-up and very human like everything else" (211).

Hazel Edwards and Ryan Kennedy, *F 2 M: The Boy Within* (2010)

"Just because I'm a butch girl doesn't make me a lesbian," eighteen-year-old Skye boldly asserts (20). In fact she has been diagnosed with gender identity disorder (a subsequently discredited term); that is, she is an FtM transgender person, a boy trapped in a girl's body. She takes an important first step toward transitioning when she starts calling herself Finn; the next step is to change the name officially. Then there is the matter of coming out to friends and family. Finn gains their acceptance—more or less—and prepares to face the as-yet-unknown future.

Catherine Ryan Hyde, *Jumpstart the World* (2010)

The day fifteen-year-old Elle's mother improbably moves her into an apartment of her own, the girl meets her next-door neighbor, sweet, gentle, thirty-something Frank. Elle is instantly smitten until a group of her friends meet Frank and—more perceptive than she—tell her he is an FtM transgender person. Elle is devastated, at first refusing to believe the truth of what they have said, but when it finally becomes obvious to her that they are right, she rejects Frank. When he is subsequently injured in a freak accident, she repents, but Elle is not always a sympathetic character. Some readers may even think she's a bit misguided: at one point she says, of Frank, "It's not like I was judging him for his life choices . . ." (96). But is Frank's condition of being really a choice or an imperative, instead? Unfortunately Hyde doesn't explore this issue (which is also raised below in *Father Son Father*). It's worth noting that this is the only book since Block's "Dragons in Manhattan" and "My Virtual World" to feature an adult transgender person who is in a relationship.

Inexplicably, after two relatively rich publishing years, 2011 featured only one book with transgender content: Libba Bray's *Beauty Queens* (2011), which tells the offbeat story of aspiring teen beauty queens who are marooned on a tropical island. One of the members of this ensemble cast, Miss Rhode Island, is revealed to be an MtF transgender person. Though a relatively minor character, she is at least accorded the same limited attention as most of the other members of the large cast.

Happily, 2012 went 2011 two better, featuring three relevant books: Kirstin Cronn-Mills's *Beautiful Music for Ugly Children*, Rachel Gold's *Being Emily*, and Tanita S. Davis's *Happy Families*.

Kirstin Cronn-Mills, *Beautiful Music for Ugly Children* (2012)

Liz has a secret: he is a female-to-male transgender person, who is just beginning his transition, calling himself Gabe and being out only to his unsupportive family and his best friend Paige. Gabe's goal is to keep his head down till the end of his senior year in high school and then start a new life in the Twin Cities. Meanwhile, he has secretly gotten a job as "Gabe" serving as a late-night DJ. His radio show, *Beautiful Music for Ugly Children*, becomes a cult fave, leading him to muse that being transgender is like being a record with both an A and B side, a motif that he uses to good effect on his radio program.

Rachel Gold, *Being Emily* (2012)

Seventeen-year-old Christopher has known since kindergarten that she is a girl trapped in a boy's body, a girl she has named Emily. She has managed to keep her condition a secret, but she has now decided she can no longer remain silent and comes out to her girlfriend, Claire. Though at first disbelieving and inevitably wondering, "If I keep loving him, what am I?" (49), Claire accepts Emily's truth and becomes a staunch ally. When a parent-dictated bout of therapy then fails (the doctor insists that Emily's condition can be "cured" in the same way that some erroneously claim homosexuality can be "cured" by reparative therapy), Emily's father finally agrees to take her to see an endocrinologist, who starts her on Spironolactone and Premarin. This is the most clinical story yet about the condition of being a transgender person and of the difficult process of transitioning.

Tanita S. Davis, *Happy Families* (2012)

Justin is in high school when he learns that his father is an MtF transgender person. This book is significant for being one of the few such novels to feature characters of color (the family is African American) and to focus on the impact a parent's transition has on the entire family. When Justin notices a familiar-looking woman in the audience at one of his debate tournaments, he realizes that it is his father in women's clothing, which leads to the discovery that his father is a transgender person. In the wake of this, the father leaves the family, but circumstances dictate that Justin and his twin sister must spend spring break with him, leading them to an understanding of the man and his condition of being.

Happily, the following year saw two more YA books with transgender content: *FreakBOY* by Kristin Elizabeth Clark (2013) and *Two Boys Kissing* by David Levithan (2013).

Kristin Elizabeth Clark, *FreakBOY* (2013)

Clark's *FreakBOY* is written in verse from three different first-person per-spectives: of Brendan, a high school senior who is confused about his gender identity; his girlfriend Vanessa; and Angel, a twenty-year-old MtF transgen-der person. Angel has been on hormones but hasn't yet had sex affirmation surgery, although "my junk doesn't dictate who I am," she tartly says (188). Meanwhile, Brendan finds himself increasingly wanting to be a girl, while hating himself and his own body, a feeling exacerbated by the occasional dream in which he is a girl, waking to wonder, desperately, if this means he's gay. "I'm a freak and my future / is totally screwed" (98). When his secret is compromised, everyone at school erroneously thinks he's gay, even Vanessa, who, realizing she still loves him, anxiously wonders, "What does that make me?" (348). Now alone, Brendan miserably thinks, "I'm Freakboy and / there will never / be a place for me" (379). Following a long talk with Angel, who first suggests he is genderqueer or perhaps gender fluid, Brendan sensibly decides to begin therapy, and the book ends with the words "There is / No Tidy Ending / for Someone / Like Me" (427).

David Levithan, *Two Boys Kissing* (2013)

David Levithan's *Two Boys Kissing* features a blue-haired boy, Ryan, and a pink-haired one, Avery, who meet at a gay prom. "Pink-haired Avery," Levi-than tells us, "was born a boy that the rest of the world saw as a girl." Happily, "with his parents' help and blessings, if not always comprehension, Avery charted a new life, was driven many miles to get the hormones that would set his body in the right direction. And it's worked" (12). It's unclear at this point how far Avery's transition has come. As he tells Ryan his story, he talks "about the surgeries that have happened and the surgeries that are going to happen" (55). But his main concern is this: "Now that Ryan knows, is Avery still a boy in his eyes?" (55). The answer is an unqualified yes, and with this promise of a future together, their story ends happily.

The following year saw five more books with transgender content, two of which are significant titles: Kim Fu's *For Today I Am a Boy* (2014) and Ami Polonsky's *Gracefully Grayson* (2014).

Rachel Eliason, *The Best Boy Ever Made* (2014)

This self-published book tells the story of Alice, who comes from a conser-vative rural background but makes the decision to remain loyal to her best friend Sam when Sam comes out as a female-to-male transgender person. But what will happen when Alice finds herself attracted to him?

Kim Fu, *For Today I Am a Boy* (2014)

This book is significant for its portrayal of the ways in which its protagonist Peter must navigate gender identity within the context of her strict Chinese immigrant family and the familial emphasis on gender roles. This is one of the few books to feature such an intersectional and heartfelt description of identity.

Rachel Gold, *Just Girls* (2014)

Prolific author Gold tells the story of a girl named Jess, who steps up when word starts to spread that a girl in her dormitory is a transgender person. Figuring she has nothing to lose since she's an out lesbian—and hoping to save someone possible persecution—Jess claims to be the person in question.

Ami Polonsky, *Gracefully Grayson* (2014)

Sixth grader Grayson knows that she is, in fact, a girl trapped in a boy's body. Her life changes when she tries out for the class play, as she decides to read for the female part. To her surprise she gets the role. In the wake of this, two boys become her bêtes noires, routinely bullying her until the day of the play, when one of them pushes her down the stairs and she fractures her wrist. Happily, it doesn't stop her from being in the play (wearing a pink cast on her arm!), and she is a triumph. This is another groundbreaker, the first full-length transgender novel to feature an elementary-school-age protagonist.

Jeannie Wood, *A Boy Like Me* (2014)

Peyton was born a girl but has been living as a boy when, in the eighth grade, he meets Tara and falls in love. Determined to win her, he masters the drums and becomes a basketball player, but can he survive the prejudice of their small hometown?

The following year boasted a total of four books having transgender content: Alex Gino's *George* (2015), Ellen Hopkins's *Traffick* (2015), Evan Jacobs's *Father Son Father*, and Robin Talley's *What We Left Behind*. We begin our analysis with *George*, which, like *Gracefully Grayson*, breaks new ground.

Alex Gino, *George* (2015)

Everyone thinks that ten-year-old George is a boy, but inside she knows she's really a girl. When her fourth-grade class prepares to mount a dramatic production of *Charlotte's Web*, George knows that she desperately wants to play the part of Charlotte, the spider, a plot point that echoes *Gracefully Grayson*. Gino's first novel is a sensitive, insightful portrayal of a transgender child coming to terms with gender identity. Gino has done an excellent job of introducing factual information into the narrative and crafting an accessible and appealing story that features the youngest transgender character since Woodson's Trev.

Ellen Hopkins, *Traffick* (2015)

This story is told in five voices by five teenage prostitutes. A minor transgender character—an aspiring model—is savagely beaten.

Evan Jacobs, *Father Son Father* (2015)

When sixteen-year-old Jeff's ill father must be hospitalized, the teen is horrified to discover that the man's nurse/therapist is a transgender woman named Andrea. However, when Jeff sees the excellent care she gives his father, he gradually warms to her.

Robin Talley, *What We Left Behind* (2015)

Toni has an imperative question: Who—and what—is she? She has come out to her girlfriend Gretchen as being genderqueer, but what does that mean? There is no other book thus far that gives such attention to language; every conceivable word in the transgender vocabulary is bandied about, dissected and analyzed, as Toni tries to make up her mind as to which words she wants to use—or not use; "I still haven't found a label that feels exactly right for me," she laments (73). Indeed, she vacillates between genderqueer, gender nonconforming, and gender fluid (73) and even thinks about using nonbinary and multigender. Eschewing gendered pronouns altogether ("I wish pronouns had never been invented" [128]), she begins using recently created pronoun substitutes (ze and hir), later she uses "they"; and still later finally settles on he, his, and him as Toni grows to believe she is a man. "Maybe I'm not gender variant," Toni muses, "maybe I'm, well, a guy. It's just—does it have to be an either/or thing? Why is this all so confusing? Am I really the only person in the world who thinks this stuff is complicated?" (137). The reality is that these issues *can* be confusing, a cardinal reason we need good books with transgender content to illuminate and explicate the realities of the situation.

    If 2015 were a good year for transgender literature, 2016 was a banner one, with a total of twelve relevant titles: Megan Atwood's *Raise the Stakes*, Kristin Elizabeth Clark's *Jess, Chunk, and the Road Trip to Infinity*, Eric Devine's *Look Past*, Corinne Duyvis's *On the Edge of Gone*, Donna Gephart's *Lily and Dunkin*, Sarah N. Harvey's *Spirit Level*, M. G. Hennessey's

The Other Boy, C. B. Lee's *Not Your Sidekick*, Anne-Marie McLemore's *When the Moon Was Ours*, Meredith Russo's *If I Was Your Girl*, Brie Spangler's *Beast*, and Lisa Williamson's *The Art of Being Normal*. We begin our analyses with *Raise the Stakes* by Megan Atwood.

Megan Atwood, *Raise the Stakes* (2016)

This is the third in a series of five linked novellas. In this one, Colin, whose family has financial problems, agrees to enter a contest sponsored by a mysterious man that promises the winner $10 million, which he hopes will enable Colin's transgender sister to have the surgery necessary to make her fully female.

Kristin Elizabeth Clark, *Jess, Chunk, and the Road Trip to Infinity* (2016)

Road trip! Jess and her best friend Christophe, nicknamed Chunk for his size, are on their way from San Jose to Chicago to crash the second wedding of Jess's dad. Jess, who is transitioning from Jeremy, hopes to confront her father—whom she regards as transphobic—with the real her. Along the way she realizes she is in love with her best friend, who can't possibly return her feelings . . . can he? Yes, he can! Chunk does, indeed, return her feelings, and there is an implicit promise that the two will have a happy love relationship. It's a salutary step forward to have a book in which the straight character is actually in love with the transgender character and isn't afraid to show and accept it without reservation.

Eric Devine, *Look Past* (2016)

Avery is a female-to-male transgender person who came out in middle school. Now seventeen, he continues his transition, taking testosterone. His family is loving and supportive, but the town where he lives is not; to its residents he is universally known as "the freak." And now his friend Mary, whom he loves dearly, has been brutally murdered. The assailant remains unknown but has sent Avery a text explaining that Mary was murdered because she refused to repent of loving him. Avery immediately suspects Mary's father, the ultraconservative pastor of a local church, who had routinely beaten his daughter. But is he guilty, or is it Mary's former boyfriend who had sex with her and then abandoned her? Or is it someone with no known connection to Mary? Avery is determined to find out, even though the murderer has made it clear that he will be the next to die unless he repents and returns to living as a girl. This mystery is one of the few genre titles to feature a transgender protagonist. And though often clumsy and melodramatic, it does viscerally present the worst-case scenario of a transgender teen who is so universally loathed for openly being who he is (the pastor's church members consider him an abomination) that he would be threatened with murder. Too over the top to invite complete credibility, *Look Past* does nevertheless remind readers that given the climate of opinion in some quarters, it can still be dangerous to openly express oneself. One hopes for better days.

Corinne Duyvis, *On the Edge of Gone* (2016)

This postapocalyptic novel includes an MtF supporting character, who, contributing nothing to the narrative, might as well not be. But perhaps that's the point. Just as we've wanted an LGB literature where a character just happens to be gay, so we now have one where a character just happens to be a transgender person. More cause for celebration and less for criticism, perhaps.

Donna Gephart, *Lily and Dunkin* (2016)

"I guess everyone has secrets," thirteen-year-old Tim muses. His is known only to his family and his best friend Dare. Born a boy, Tim knows she is really a girl, whom she has named Lily. Enter her new friend Norbert, whom she has nicknamed Dunkin, acknowledging his passion for Dunkin Donuts. We learn early on that Lily has known about her condition since she was five, but her real problem is the imperative need to start taking hormone blockers to avoid entering Tanner Stage II (when her body will enter puberty) (35). Nevertheless, her father refuses to accept and approve this. When Lily's mother finally persuades her still reluctant husband to go to a psychologist with her and Lily, he abruptly changes his mind about Lily's transition, leading Lily to wonder what the doctor has said to him behind a closed door. At the end of the book we learn the psychologist has told Lily's father the statistics for transgender kids' suicides and attempted suicides. "Would you rather have a dead son or a live daughter?" she asks (324). In the meantime, Lily is tormented by bullies, but she doesn't tell her parents this. She does finally tell Dunkin, who is understanding and sympathetic, wondering why Vasquez (the chief bully) calls Lily "fag" all the time. "Does Vasquez know about Tim being transgender?" Dunkin wonders. "But if he does, 'fag' isn't the right word anyway. One thing has nothing to do with the other" (283). At book's end, Lily, dressed as her true self, goes to the school's dance and meets Dunkin there. The two friends dance together and Lily spots her previously disapproving father, who has come to the dance proudly wearing a T-shirt that says "I love my DAUGHTER!" (323).

Sarah N. Harvey, *Spirit Level* (2016)

Alex is an FtM character with whom the unknowing protagonist Harry (short for Harriet) falls in love. When Harry learns the truth, she at first receives the news with remarkable equanimity. "You thought I would freak out?" she asks Alex, who laughs. "Yeah, even you. It's kind of a big deal" (134). Indeed it is; he goes on to tell her the horrors of his coming out: he wound up in the hospital after his father beat him with a baseball bat; his brother and his friends jumped and stabbed him; his mother took him to this "crazy" Pentecostal exorcist when he was twelve. And his brother told everyone at school he was gay, which he clearly is not. It was, to say the least, not an easy transition. Nor is his new relationship with Harry all that easy, either. As Harry thinks at book's end, "there's the whole trans thing. . . . It's not exactly simple" (229). Will their relationship survive this uncertainty?

M. G. Hennessey, *The Other Boy* (2016)

Now twelve, Shane has known since the age of three that she is a boy, even though he was born in a girl's body. When he turned nine, he started getting implants of a hormone blocker and now that he is twelve, he is about to begin taking testosterone, provided his father, who has joint custody (his parents are divorced), will agree to it. At first the father refuses, concerned that the results are irreversible, but when he understands how important this is to his son, he reluctantly agrees. Shane is elated, but things change dramatically when a bully at school learns the secret that Shane has kept from even his best friend, Josh—that he is a transgender person. Soon the entire school knows, and Shane's mood shifts from elation to desolation. He quits the baseball team, for which he is the star pitcher, and retreats into himself, refusing to go to school and even ignoring Josh's texts. Things look bleak until Josh shows up at Shane's house uninvited on the day of a big game demanding to know why Shane isn't in his uniform. Shane is nonplussed, especially when he discovers that the entire team has accompanied Josh and all are insisting he suit up. Bemused, he does, strikes out the bully and wins the game. Hero time!

C. B. Lee, *Not Your Sidekick* (2016)

This is a rare science fiction genre title for this body of literature. In this dystopian superhero story, protagonist Jessica Tran narrates her adventures, many of which include her FtM sidekick, Bells.

Anna-Marie McLemore, *When the Moon Was Ours* (2016)

His name is Samir. Coming from Pakistan, he is a *bacha posh*, a girl who secretly lives as a boy. She is Miel, a girl who seems to have sprung from the water of a toppled water tower, a girl with roses growing from her wrist, roses the four Bonner girls, who are regarded locally as witches, desire to restore their waning powers. Though Miel knows Sam's secret, she falls in love with him and he with her, and the two quickly become a couple. This sweet spirited, beautifully written love story is the only novel of magic realism to feature a transgender character.

Meredith Russo, *If I Was Your Girl* (2016)

Eighteen-year-old Amanda has a closely guarded secret. At her old school she was Andrew. But following sex affirmation surgery, Amanda is an MtF transgender person who has come to live with her father, hoping to spend her last year in her new school as invisible as possible. But then she meets sweet, gentle Grant and finds herself falling in love. It's obvious that the boy returns her feelings, but what will happen if Grant learns the truth? The answer is predictable: "But what's that say about me then?" he thinks. "Does that—does that make me gay?" (238). Like Boylan (above), the author is a transgender woman, and she writes with authority and empathy, giving her readers not only an intellectual but also an emotional understanding of Amanda and her compelling story. There is a sense of foreboding to this book that underscores a thread common to all these titles: the potential danger of being openly transgender/transsexual. We know that Amanda was savagely attacked before changing schools. "I was never really safe," she thinks (15), so it is a triumph for her that she finally overcomes her fears and accepts the fact that Grant loves her. The book concludes with Amanda's saying, "I deserved to find love. I knew now—I believed, now—that I deserved to be loved" (287). This novel was the winner of the 2016 Stonewall Award.

Brie Spangler, *Beast* (2016)

At fifteen, Dylan is tall (6'4"), all meat and muscle and with enough body hair to, as he wryly puts it, "insulate a small town" (1). Predictably, he's been cruelly nicknamed "the Beast." When—after a bad day at school—he falls off a roof—perhaps not altogether accidentally—and breaks a leg, he finds himself remanded to therapy for self-harmers. There he meets an enchanting girl named Jamie and finds himself falling in love. The attraction is mutual until Dylan discovers that Jamie is a male-to-female transgender person and things become problematic. Loosely based on the classic fairy tale "Beauty and the Beast," *Beast* brings together two memorable teens in a beautifully written and memorable romance.

Lisa Williamson, *The Art of Being Normal* (2016)

Here's a rarity, a novel with *two* transgender characters, one MtF, the other FtM. This is the only English import on the list (*F 2 M* is from Australia).

* * *

Readers learn a number of things from these books: for one, the discussion of gender affirmation surgery tends to be oversimplified, not mentioning—for example—the nearly prohibitive cost of such surgeries and the required counseling that must precede them. Too, there is not enough acknowledgment of the highly regulated use of hormones. There is also some criticism that such texts devalue youth who are unable—or don't wish to—elect surgery. It should be stressed that teens need more self-love and a sense of community, and less notions of being "fixed" by outside forces. Teens often gather information from their reading of fiction, so the question of how transgender and gender-nonconforming teens identify their options is an important one, but sadly one that is rarely addressed in these books. All this said, most kids seem to first become aware that they are transgender at around the age of five but quickly learn they mustn't express their true identities. Sometimes they hate themselves and their bodies as they grow up; some hate the circumstances preventing them from expressing their true gender identity. They may bitterly regard themselves as being freaks. Many of them feel as if they are in prison. It is not uncommon for the transgender character to leave home at the book's end which is often, accordingly, bittersweet. Transgender kids are not necessarily gay; indeed, the two conditions of being are not synonymous. However, kids who are attracted to transgender teens often worry that *they* are gay. The language of being transgender is important but very complicated and often confusing, demanding careful attention from readers. Transgender kids can expect to be verbally bullied and even physically assaulted. Despite this, there is a possibility they will be accepted and loved. In addition to learning about chest binding and wearing non-gender-specific clothing, readers also learn some of the more technical aspects of transitioning: taking hormones—testosterone, estrogen, and so forth—with or without parental consent, having breast surgery, and electing sex affirmation surgery, though both of the latter—while often discussed—are rare in actual execution and there is no discernable pattern as to what age this might happen. As to when characters begin their transition, this typically takes place when they are in their midteens, though in at least four cases (Trev, Grayson, George, and Shane) it happens earlier. The possibility that being a transgender person is hereditary is raised only once, and there are contrasting opinions as to whether transitioning is a choice or not. Most of these books, like those in the early days of LGB literature, are coming-out stories and a few might be described as problem novels. Finally, to put it in theatrical terms, all of the transgender characters whom readers meet are major players in their dramas, with the exception of supporting characters in *Punkzilla*'s Lewis, *On the Edge of Gone*'s Iris, and *Not Your Sidekick*'s Bells, and minor characters ("walk-ons") in Libba Bray's *Beauty Queens* and Ellen Hopkins's *Traffick*.

* * *

"Intersex" is a general term used for a variety of conditions in which a person is born with a reproductive or sexual anatomy that doesn't seem to fit the typical definitions of female or male. For example, a person might be born appearing to be female on the outside, but having mostly male-typical anatomy on the inside. Or a person may be born with genitals that seem to be in-between the usual male and female types—for example, a girl may be born with a noticeably large clitoris, or lacking a vaginal opening, or a boy may be born with a notably small penis, or with a scrotum that is divided so that it has formed more like labia. Or a person may be born with mosaic genetics, so that some of her cells have XX chromosomes and some of them have XY.—Intersex Society of North America

If it took twenty-seven years for the first transgender character to appear in young adult literature, it would take another decade until the appearance of the first intersex character in the 2014 novel *Double Exposure*.

Bridget Birdsall, *Double Exposure* (2014)

"I wonder who wouldn't hate a body that wants to be half of one thing and part of another?" fifteen-year-old Alyx thinks bitterly. Born intersex, Alyx has "the dysfunctional organs of both genders" (46). Though her "politically correct" parents decided they shouldn't elect a gender for their newborn baby, leaving the decision to the child to make at an appropriate age, they have essentially raised Alyx as a boy. Unfortunately, the androgynous teen is regarded as being gay and has been the regular target of bullies. "Why didn't you just make me a girl?" she hotly demands of her mother. "That's what everyone else does with their ambiguous babies, right?" (10). After one attack too many, Alyx begs his mother to move and so they do, from California to Milwaukee, where he has now determined to become a girl, though his endocrinologist has stipulated he has to live as a girl for two years before electing any surgeries; however, he does start Alyx on a low dose of hormones. "Someday," she thinks, "I'll be a girl. A real girl. My outsides will match my insides" (47). Starting a new life may give her the new identity she longs for, although she continues to worry that she may not look sufficiently like a girl (she's over six feet tall) and identifies as being genderqueer (66). Because the only time she has felt as if she fit in was when she was playing basketball, she joins her new school's girls' basketball team. For some reason, though, one of the other players, Pepper, takes an instant dislike to her. Somehow Pepper discovers Alyx's past and during a game of truth or dare at a raucous party reveals the truth. Puzzlingly, it doesn't seem to register with the other partygoers and things go on as before—until a letter arrives from the district's interscholastic sports commissioner advising, "It has come to my attention . . ." and it goes on to note Alyx's past history, asking for proof that she is, indeed, a girl. Otherwise her team will be disqualified from playing in the state tournament. In the wake of this bombshell, Alyx muses, "I always want to run. But I know that I can't—not anymore. I'm not going down without a fight" (211). Despite her brave words, she can't help herself: "I sigh—wishing my life wasn't so damn complicated, wishing I'd been born like other kids, either a boy or a girl and not some friggin' abnormality with an extra X chromosome that doesn't quite fit anywhere" (213). Yet she finds comfort in her doctor's telling her she's definitely not alone, that "2 percent of the babies born in the United States are gender fluid, or intersex, and many scientists believe there are more than two genders" (223). Happily, at the last minute, she is declared eligible to play and her team goes on to win the state championship.

In the wake of *Double Exposure*, two more books with intersex characters appeared the next year, 2015: Alyssa Brugman's *Alex as Well* and I. W. Gregorio's *None of the Above*. Let us examine them in turn, beginning with *Alex as Well*.

Alyssa Brugman, *Alex as Well* (2015)

This import from Australia tells the sometimes hard-edged, sometimes darkly humorous story of Alex who, born intersex, has been raised as a boy (he was born with a penis but no testes, having ovaries, instead). Now fourteen, Alex declares he's a girl ("I've been a girl in my head since as long as I can remember" [25]) and stops taking his medicine (testosterone). He then takes it upon himself to enroll in a new school as a girl without telling her parents. There's only one hitch: she needs to show her birth certificate, which presently declares she is a boy. To remedy that, Alex consults an attorney. When the man investigates, he discovers that a first birth certificate was issued declaring Alex to be a girl but was annulled six months later in favor of one stating he was a boy. But "I'm not a boy on the inside," Alex declares (15). "They [his parents] knew," she later says bitterly. "They *made* me a boy" (161). When her parents refuse to support her, Alex begins legal proceedings to become emancipated. In the meantime, Alex has been outed, and the truth about her being intersex becomes common knowledge at school. The girls who had been her friends reject her, all but one, Amina, who tells Alex she is brave, and the two become close friends. There is no reconciliation with Alex's parents, however, and she moves out of their house and into an apartment owned by her attorney. The book ends at that point with no indication of what kind of future Alex can expect. However, though she has more than once described herself as a freak, she now seems to approach her life with more equanimity, saying at book's end: "I laughed because people are always going to give me a hard time. I might even get beaten up now and again. But there are worse things than people you don't care about not liking you."

I. W. Gregorio, *None of the Above* (2015)

When high school senior Kristin and her boyfriend Sam attempt to have sex, the process is so painful for Kristin that they're unable to continue. Troubled, she consults her OB-GYN and discovers, to her horror, that she has AIS, androgen insensitivity syndrome; "I think you might be what some people call a hermaphrodite" (38), the doctor says but quickly corrects herself. "I shouldn't have used that term—it's quite antiquated. The better term to use is *intersex*" (40). Semantics, unfortunately, are small comfort to Kristin, who becomes increasingly uneasy when she learns she has no uterus or cervix; what she does have are two undescended testes. When she subsequently consults a specialist, she is relieved to learn that she is, indeed, a girl and not a boy as she had at first feared; she does have a body filled with testosterone, though, and her chromosomes are XY. Given her condition, she will be unable to have children, although, with dilation, she will be able to have sex. Despite this reassurance, she nevertheless bitterly calls herself a freak (47), wondering "what kind of boy could ever love a freak like me?" (60). When she goes to a party with Sam and gets drunk, the two succeed in having sex, though it's still painful for her. But when Sam falls asleep, a weeping Kristin shares her secret with her best friend Vee, and soon the news is all over the school. An angry Sam then rejects Kristin, savagely whispering, "I thought I loved you, you fucking man-whore. And you've been lying to me. I have nothing to say to you. Ever. Again" (114). In the wake of these betrayals, Kristin thinks, "All I wanted was for everything to be okay again" (120). But that's not going to happen. She is a gifted runner, but her track coach tells her that two of the other teams in their division have filed complaints and that she won't be permitted to run "until we get things straightened out" (129). In the wake of these setbacks and uncertainties, Kristin has a gonadectomy (the surgical removal of her testicles) and takes a six-week leave of absence from school. To satisfy her community service requirements, she begins volunteering at a clinic with her faithful friend Darren. Vee speaks for the reader when she then gruffly tells Kristin, "I'm talking about you *getting over yourself.*

Krissy, it's time to *move on*" (284). To her credit Kristin begins to take tentative steps in that direction, but it takes a near assault for her to realize that her friend Darren is in love with her and she with him. A happy ending for a previously troubled girl. Of the three intersex books we've discussed, this is by far the most clinical. Gregorio is a doctor who has professional experience with the intersexed, and her expertise is evident throughout.

* * *

Taken together, the three novels succeed in dramatizing the challenging complexities of being intersex, including—as in the case of being gay or transgender—the attendant dangers of ignorance, the inevitability of bullying, and the threat of violence. Parents apparently tend to further cloud circumstances by choosing wrongly which gender to raise their child as, resulting in the child's rampant self-hatred. Reflecting real-world events, two of the three protagonists are athletes whose continued participation in their respective sports may be compromised by confusion over their real gender. One hopes for more novels like these that can educate and enlighten readers who urgently need the information they contain. In the meantime, three nonfiction sources are invaluable for further information:

1. Laurel Golio and Diana Scholl's *We Are the Youth* (2014), based on an online photojournalism project that shares the stories of LGBTQ+ youth in the United States. [6]
2. Kate Bornstein's *Hello, Cruel World: 101 Alternatives to Suicide for Teens* (2006), a self-described "one of a kind guide to staying alive outside the box . . . a catalog of 101 alternatives to suicide." [7]
3. Mary L. Gray's *Out in the Country: Youth, Media, and Queer Visibility in Rural America* (2009), one of the few sources to turn the focus from urban to rural youth. [8]

NOTES

1. Transgender: "A word to describe anyone whose identity or behavior falls outside of stereotypical gender norms. More narrowly defined, it refers to an individual whose gender identity does not match their assigned birth gender. Being transgender does not imply any specific sexual orientation (attraction to people of a specific gender)." https://www.genderspectrum.org.

2. Further information is available from the Gender Diversity website: http://www.genderdiversity.org/.

3. Neely Tucker, "Emails Show Outside Group's Influence on Mississippi's 'Religious Freedom' Bill," *Washington Post*, July 21, 2016.

4. Further information is available from the GLAAD website, http://www.glaad.org/.

5. Tim Bontemps, "NBA Will Move 2017 All-Star Game from Charlotte over HB2 Law," *Washington Post*, July 21, 2016.

6. Laurel Golio and Diana Scholl, *We Are the Youth* (New York: Space-Made, 2014).

7. Kate Bornstein, *Hello, Cruel World: 101 Alternatives to Suicide for Teens* (New York: Seven Stories, 2006).

8. Mary L. Gray, *Out in the Country: Youth, Media, and Queer Visibility in Rural America* (New York: New York University Press, 2009).

Chapter Nine

Comics and Graphic Novels with LGBTQ+ Content

We start with a few words of definition: By "comics" we mean comic strips and comic books. Comic strips, usually published in newspapers or, increasingly online, contain sequential panels that tell a mini-story, a joke, or a serial. Comic books, on the other hand, are a combination of pamphlet and magazine; they're typically single-issue publications that usually appear monthly and are stapled rather than bound and are seldom longer than thirty-six pages. In addition to comic strips and comic books we will address graphic novels, a form popularized in the mid-1980s with the publication of such work as Art Spiegelman's *Maus* and Frank Miller's *Dark Knight Returns*. The graphic novel is different from the comic book by virtue of its longer length and its sturdier format, being square bound and containing original, never-before-published, book-length stories or collections of previously unpublished short stories. They are a medium, not a genre.

With this noted, we acknowledge that there was a time, not so long ago, when comics were dismissed as disposable entertainment, here today, gone tomorrow, and good riddance. That situation has changed dramatically over the course of the past twenty years. Comics have now become aesthetically pleasing constructions of text and sequential art and share shelf space with graphic novels. Their content, once limited to the adventures of men in tights and capes, has become infinitely more various, and LGBTQ+ content, once entirely absent, has become more common. This was not always the case.

For example, during the late 1940s and early 1950s, a tremendous wave of social anxiety focused on juvenile delinquency and crime. Federal hearings were held, witnesses were called, experts were consulted, and comics became a scapegoat for a number of developments in the broader American society, including (among other things) that the youth of America were a grave danger to themselves and others. There was a perceived increase in crime and gang activity among juveniles, communist infiltration of schools, and homosexuals eager to recruit youth to their deviant activities. This anxiety was exacerbated by the publication of Dr. Fredric Wertham's best-selling book *Seduction of the Innocent*,[1] which posited a relationship between juvenile delinquency and comics. Though now largely discredited, it was quite influential in its time. Indeed, in reaction to it and in order to prevent legal censorship of comics, the Association of Comic Book Publishers opted, in 1954, for self-censorship by creating and implementing a "voluntary" Comics Code that controlled language, costumes, religion, portrayals of authority figures, and a section titled "Marriage and Sex," which contained several rules that spoke directly to such issues as the depiction of homosexuality. More specifically, the Code contained the following language:

> Illicit sex relations are neither to be hinted at or portrayed. Violent love scenes, as well as sexual abnormalities are unacceptable.
> The treatment of love-romance stories shall emphasize the value of home and the sanctity of marriage.
> Sex perversion or any inference to same is strictly forbidden.

The Code did *not* apply to comic strips, however, and one of the first openly gay characters, Andy Lippincott, appeared in Garry Trudeau's *Doonesbury* in 1976, reappearing as a gay activist in 1982 and again in 1989 when he suffered from AIDS, dying in 1990. Another celebrated appearance of a gay character in a comic strip took place in 1993 in Lynne Johnston's *For Better or for Worse* when teenager Lawrence, Michael's friend and neighbor, came out as gay.[2] The immediate response was less than salutary, and a number of newspapers ran replacement strips or canceled the comic altogether. However, Johnston was honored in 1994 as one of three "nominated finalists" for that year's Pulitzer Prize for Editorial Cartooning, cited for having "sensitively depicted a youth's disclosure of his homosexuality and its effect on his family and friends."[3]

Of course, a handful of exclusively LGBTQ+ comic strips have been syndicated over the years, largely to counterculture newspapers and magazines. Transgressive and envelope pushing, they were inherently controversial. A landmark in this context was *Gay Comix*, a comic book that debuted in 1980, published by Kitchen Sink Press and edited by Howard Cruse. A number of significant artists contributed work to *Gay Comix*; in addition to Cruse and Tim Barela, they included the likes of Mary Wings, Roberta Gregory, Jerry Mills, Burton Clarke, Jennifer Camper, Jon Macy, and Alison Bechdel.

Gay Comix included the first appearance of noteworthy strips *Wendel* (1983–1989) by Howard Cruse and Tim Barela's *Leonard and Larry*

(1984–2003). Another very prominent contributor was Alison Bechdel, whose *Dykes to Watch Out For*[4] ran from 1983 to 2008. Both Bechdel and Cruse are established, award-winning masters of the comics and graphic novel forms. Bechdel won the prestigious Eisner Award for her autobiographical work *Fun Home: A Family Tragicomic*, recently adapted as a Broadway musical that garnered multiple Emmy Awards.

Bechdel grew up in a small Pennsylvania town where her closeted father doubled as a high school English teacher and a mortician. His children dubbed the funeral home in which they resided "the fun home," hence the book's title. The book charts not only Bechdel's early work as an artist but also her growing awareness that she is a lesbian. Indeed, it is when she comes out to her father that she learns about his own homosexuality and discovers that he has had sex with his students and with the young man who worked as the children's babysitter. Not long after Bechdel learns this, her father is killed in an accident that was most probably a suicide. *Fun Home*, which has been compared to Proust and Joyce, is a beautifully rendered, psychologically astute work of art.

As for Cruse, his masterwork is inarguably the modern classic *Stuck Rubber Baby*. This semiautobiographical novel is the story of a young white working-class man named Toland Polk, who is coming of age in the South during the civil rights era. Struggling with the fact of his homosexuality, he becomes involved with the black community and has a brief affair with a black man. Like *Fun Home*, this is a psychologically acute story that defies easy categorization. Cruse has said of the book, "My goal was to create the kind of novel that is too full of incident for someone to simply summarize in their mind to one sentence."[5] He has succeeded brilliantly.

COMIC BOOKS

Although strictly forbidden by the Code, LGBTQ+ content has nevertheless been present by innuendo for years—Wonder Woman or Batman and Robin, anyone? Indeed, to quell rumors of Batman's being gay, the comic's publisher, DC, introduced the character of Batwoman, Kathy Kane, to provide a love interest. Some fifty years later in 2006, as Kate Kane, she was revealed to be a lesbian! Holy irony, Batman! She has since become a fixture of the DC Universe, starring in 2013's *Batwoman Volume 1: Hydrology*, in which she and her lover, the beautiful police detective Sawyer, undertake a paranormal adventure involving La Llorona, the legendary Weeping Woman. Through 2015 the series grew to six volumes.

DC had introduced its first gay character, the Peruvian magician Extrano, in 1988; however, though he demonstrated stereotypical gay characteristics, calling himself "Auntie," for example, he never came out. After the Comics

Code Authority's strictures were loosened in 1989, Marvel introduced its first openly gay character, Northstar a.k.a. Jean-Paul Beaubier, in 1992. Northstar had originally appeared in 1979 with no indication that he was gay. After 1992's outing, he went on to become one of the X-Men and later was one of the first LGBTQ+ comic characters to be married to his partner, when, in 2012, he and Kyle Jinadu tied the knot. Another Marvel first took place in 2002 when an established character, the Rawhide Kid, was revealed to be gay and became the first openly gay comic book character to star in his own series. (At one point in 1994 Northstar featured in a limited four-volume series, but it ignored his homosexuality.) In 2011 the first lesbian superhero, DC's Batwoman, received her ongoing solo series.

The same year the Code loosened, 1989, saw another important advance: the character of Negative Man in the Doom Patrol series was revealed to be transgender. Another transgender character, the trans woman Kate Goodwin, was subsequently introduced in 1993, becoming the superhuman Coagula. The British author Neil Gaiman in his Sandman books has included a number of trans characters, many of whom, unfortunately, are summarily killed off. Much more recently, in 2013, DC introduced the transgender character Alysia Yeoh, roommate of Batgirl, making Yeoh the first major transgender character in American comics.

Over the years there have been many other lesser-known characters who could be perceived as being transgender simply because they are shape-shifters, switching from male to female and back again at whim. Xavin, who comes to earth to marry the lesbian Karolina of the Runaways, is one such; another is Benjamin Deeds of the Uncanny X-Men series; *Flutter*, the story of fifteen-year-old Lily who transforms into a boy to win the girl, is a more recent example.

MANGA

Shape-shifting is a feature not only of American comics but also, routinely, of Japanese manga. Speaking of Japanese comics: since the 1970s they have included in their ranks Yaoi (boys' love) and Yuri (girls' love) comics. Mainstream manga have also featured LGBTQ+ characters, notably Sailor Neptune—a friend of Sailor Moon—and Sailor Uranus. Two other mainstream offerings are particularly notable here. One is Moto Hagio's *The Heart of Thomas*; the second is Shimura Takako's multivolume *Wandering Son*. The former, set in Germany, records the enigmatic death of a fourteen-year-old boy named Thomas, who leaves a note declaring his love for another boy, Juli. The story then follows the troubled friendships of Juli and the rebellious Oskar and, later, a transfer student, Erich, who looks exactly like Thomas! The latter book is the story of two fifth graders, Nitori Shuichi and

Takatsuki Yoshino. Both children have a secret: the boy Shu wants to be a girl and the tomboy Yoshino wants to be a boy. The two gradually begin expressing their wish, experimenting with cross-dressing and gradually feeling more comfortable in their new roles. Unlike the rest of the books we've been discussing, this is targeted at a middle school readership.

GAY TEENS IN COMICS

In 2005 Marvel's the Young Avengers series of comic books introduced the gay teen lovers Hulking and Wiccan. Other Avengers include the group's founder Iron Lad, Patriot, and Hawkeye. Another Marvel teen series, the Runaways, featured a lesbian character named Karolina Dean. In later issues she began a relationship with a shape-shifting alien named Xavin, who came to earth expressly to marry her. The Runaways are all children of supervillains collectively known as the Pride. They discover they have inherited the superpowers of their parents and set out to defeat them. Another ensemble, the Teen Titans, included the gay characters Bunker and Power Boy. Then there is Iceman a.k.a. Bobby Drake, the youngest member of the original X-Men.

The most celebrated gay teen of the moment, however, is surely Kevin Keller, who became Archie Comics' first gay character when he moved to Riverdale in 2010 and has been a fixture of the series ever since. "Kevin is the All-American teenager who just happens to be gay," reads the introduction to *Archie's Pal Kevin Keller*. Immediately popular with his new schoolmates, Kevin is elected class president, and in a future installment, which finds him an adult, he marries his boyfriend. This is clearly not your father's Riverdale nor your father's Archie, for that matter. According to Gregory Schmidt, writing in the *New York Times*, "Jon Goldwater felt the need to modernize Archie Comics when he came aboard as publisher. 'It was crystal clear that Archie was not diverse. It was a cultural decision and business decision. They go hand in hand.'"[6] And, in this case, are equally successful.

GRAPHIC NOVELS

As Kevin so clearly evidences, not every teen LGBTQ+ character in comics and graphic novels is a superhero. Consider, for example, the adolescent gay brothers in Raina Telgemeier's charming graphic novel *Drama*. Jesse and Justin are identical twins, but their personalities are radically different, Jesse being high spirited and openly gay, while Justin, who is more reserved, is apparently not gay—or is he? A different type of ambiguity informs another graphic novel, Abby Denson's *Tough Love: High School Confidential*. In it two boys, Brian and Chris, meet at their high school karate class and are instantly attracted to each other, although Chris is still recovering from the end of his relationship with Li, whose parents, after discovering his homosexuality, have sent him to live in China. Following a failed suicide attempt, Li returns to the United States determined to resume his relationship with Chris. Will he succeed and what will happen with Brian? Another exercise in ambiguity is Ilike Merey's *a + e 4EVER*. Eulalie and Asher wonder why everyone has to call themselves either gay or straight. "Why do I have to call it anything?" the androgynous Asher asks. An artist, he is widely regarded at school as being gay, while the tall, tough-minded Eu is presumed to be a lesbian, though she occasionally dates boys. So what does that make them?

In Mariko Tamaki and Jillian Tamaki's *Skim*, the question that drives the narrative turns out to be: Is she suicidal or not? The "she" in question is Kim (whom everyone calls "Skim," hence the title). Kim is in love with her teacher Ms. Archer, who unexpectedly departs for another school, leaving Kim bereft. Meanwhile, a local boy who is gay commits suicide, and Kim's best friend Lisa worries that Kim might herself be suicidal. This is a very dark coming-of-age story that succeeds as a mood piece that is greatly enriched by the fluid black-and-white illustrations that perfectly capture the saturnine mood and tone of the text. Less ambiguous and significantly sunnier are the girls in Noelle Stevenson and Shannon Watters's antic series *Lumberjanes*, one of whom, Jo, is transgender. "We wanted to have queer characters but not oversexualize them," Watters tells the *New York Times*, continuing, "The normalization of queer young people was important."[7]

That normalization doesn't guarantee a happy ending. A case in point is French comics creator Hubert's *Adrian and the Tree of Secrets*. Set in a small town, this is the story of an outsider who attends a Catholic high school where he is dogged by rumors about his homosexuality, bullied by his fellow soccer players, and chastised by the school's principal who regards the rumors as evidence that Adrian is sick. Everyone seems against him except Jeremy, the coolest kid in school, who befriends a dazzled Adrian. The two boys begin a relationship and Adrian falls in love, until Jeremy's girlfriend sees the two boys together and Jeremy withdraws, leaving Adrian bereft and alone.

Not all of the queer young people in the literature have appeared exclusively in fiction. One notable work of graphic nonfiction is Judd Winick's *Pedro and Me: Friendship, Loss, and What I Learned*. Winick and Pedro Zamora were roommates on MTV's reality show *The Real World: San Francisco*. This is the affecting story of the friendship that ensued, of Zamora's work as an AIDS educator, and, sadly, of his death from AIDS at twenty-two. The book continues with the story of Winick's own subsequent work as an AIDS educator. Also covered are his evolution as a cartoonist and his falling in love with another cast member, Pam Ling. It's a memorable book, beautifully executed in Winick's black-and-white art. Another autobiographical series of graphic novels is Ariel Schrag's high school chronicles *Awkward and Definition, Potential,* and *Likewise* (2008–2009). Begun when the artist/author was still a student at Berkeley (California) High School, the series chronicles the everyday experiences of an unusually perceptive teen, who is struggling to deal with her identity as a lesbian.

Another autobiographical story worth noting here is Cristy C. Road's *Spit and Passion.* It portrays the Cuban American author at twelve as she deals with coming-of-age issues, notably her emerging homosexuality. She is not yet out, for, as she says, "I liked to see my closet as a safe and alternate universe of us vs. them and now vs. later" (24). She finds comfort and inspiration in the band Green Day.

CURRENT TRENDS

LGBTQ+ characters continue to make headlines. In 2012, Alan Scott, the original Green Lantern, who first appeared in 1940, returned, now openly gay. He is not the only old-timer who has been reincarnated as gay or lesbian: consider Catwoman, who also debuted in 1940 and was recently revealed to be bisexual, and Miss America, who first appeared in 1943. In 2011 she reemerged as the lesbian Latina character America Chavez.

In February 2015, Midnighter captured headlines when he became the first openly gay superhero to have his own monthly series ("Midnighter is not in the closet about anything," his creator Steve Orlando tells the *New York Times*).[8] In August 2015 Wonder Woman officiated at a lesbian wedding; in October Alysia Yeoh, the transgender friend of Batgirl, married her girlfriend; Iceman came out (technically he was outed) in November 2015; and in June 2016 DC Comics announced that erstwhile lovers Midnighter (whose solo series ended in May 2016) and Apollo, analogues for Batman and Superman, respectively, would return in a six-issue miniseries to debut in the fall of 2016. (Apollo, who debuted in 1993, was one of the first gay superheroes.) The two were formerly married and adopted a little girl. Whether the new series means they will reconcile is anybody's guess. For some time Midnighter has had a flirty relationship with Dick Grayson; yes, *that* Dick Grayson, Robin to Bruce Wayne's Batman!

"The industry is catching on pretty quickly to the fact that diversity can improve sales of comics," Josh Siegel, founder of Geeks Out, recently told the *New York Times*. "So," he continued, "publishers are evolving their lines of books to showcase queer characters in a number of interesting ways. Both lead characters and supporting cast members are now openly queer in many comics, allowing stories to explore different kinds of queer themes."[9]

One way to measure how far LGBTQ comics have come is to assess how many queer characters now populate their pages. Not surprisingly, estimates vary. Comic Book Resources' (CBR) estimate—sixty-three—is limited to Marvel and DC characters, a gratifyingly large number for the formerly conservative titans of the field. "It is very encouraging to see the decision that DC and Marvel have made in giving marginalized creators more of a platform to tell their stories," Boom! Studios Shannon Watters tells the *New York Times*.[10] Wikia's LGBTQ Project casts a wider net than CBR, listing 158 such characters: ninety-eight gay and sixty lesbian.[11] Here, it's interesting that this imbalance reflects that of traditional LGBTQ+ literature. Gayleague.com lists 260,[12] while Comic Vine claims a whopping 292.[13] How many comics and graphic novels chronicle their gay and lesbian characters' adventures is impossible to estimate, though surely Goodreads' list of 311 is a paltry guess. However you measure it, surely it is true as Gregory Schmidt writes in the *New York Times*: "Industry insiders say the trend mirrors the country's evolving attitudes toward gays and lesbians." "The population of America has changed," Milton Griep, chief executive of industry observer ICv2, confirms. "A good story is enjoyable to everybody."[14]

Nevertheless, it sometimes seems that for every step forward, the industry takes two steps backward. For example, before DC's spring 2016 Rebirth launch, it featured four ongoing solo titles starring Catwoman, Constantine: The Hellblazer, Harley Quinn, and Midnighter. Post-Rebirth, only Harley Quin and Hellblazer remain. As for Marvel, it has a large cast of queer characters, but all of them are supporting players. The likes of Wiccan, Mystique, Hercules (if he's actually gay), Prodigy, Shatterstar, Rictor, Karma, Julie Power, Ms. America, Anole, Daken, and others still await their turn in the spotlight. Also awaiting their turn in the spotlight are more female characters. Like the larger world of comics and graphic novels, too many of the queer characters are male, presuming a predominantly male audience. But that is changing rapidly.

One of the most exciting trends in the current industry is the rapid growth of a female audience and the increasing number of female authors and illustrators working in the field. An early example of this is Paige Braddock, creator of the mainstream comic *Jane's World*, the first gay-themed comic to be distributed by a national media syndicate (Universal Press Syndicate). It follows the sometimes ordinary, sometimes extraordinary life of its protagonist Jane Wyatt, a young lesbian who gets fired from her job at a newspaper, goes to work at a convenience store, shares her trailer home with her straight male friend Ethan, while her hamster hires a lawyer(!), and more. It was nominated for an Eisner Award in 2006.

Despite its deficiencies, the industry *is* changing. Queer comics and their creators are increasingly visible presences at that annual behemoth, San Diego's Comic Con, while several other Cons devoted entirely to the queer field are now appearing, including New York's Flame Con and San Francisco's Queer Comics Expo. The field changes but, happily, excellence remains. In addition to the numerous characters, comics, and graphic novels we've already discussed, here, to conclude this chapter, are some notable others:

Alphabet (2016). Jon Macy and Tara Madison Avery, eds. Stacked Deck Press. A generous collection of graphic stories by LGBTQ+ creators from Prism Comics. Diversity rules!

Buffy the Vampire Slayer (1998–). Going the TV series one better, Buffy experiments with a different kind of love.

Enigma (1993). This features arguably the first gay kiss in a mainstream comic book. It is ranked #15 on the Comics Alliance list of the fifty most important LGBTQ+ books and characters of all times.

Enormous (2012–). A postapocalyptic setting starring a lesbian of color.

The Sandman: A Game of You (1993). An apartment house full of the otherworldly creatures. One of Neil Gaiman's best.

Hack/Slash (2004–). Teens' bad decision puts them in jeopardy. Dedicated to dealing with bisexuality.

Hopeless Savages (2001). Meet the Hopeless Savage family featuring Twitch, who is gay.

Hothead Paisan (1991–). Homicidal lesbian terrorist. Violent but funny underground comic.

The Invisibles (1994–2000). Stars the fabulous transgender Shaman Lord Fanny.

Love and Rockets (1982–). The Hernandez brothers at their best. Maggie and Hopey fans are grateful.

The Marvels (2015). Scholastic. An ambitious combination graphic novel and traditional novel, *The Marvels* tells the story of a family of actors and of a boy whose gay uncle is mourning the death of his beloved from AIDS.

Pied Piper (First appeared in 1959). Gay musical prodigy born deaf who later recovers his hearing. Originally the Flash's bête noire, he later reforms.

The Pride (2014–). Basically a gay Justice League.

Scott Pilgrim (2012: the first six volumes). Canadian slacker Scott's roommate is the gay, witty, and wry Wallace Wells.

Seven Miles a Second (1996). The autobiography of gay artist David Wojnarowicz.

Shade, the Changing Man (1990–1996). As the title suggests, Shade, a policeman from another world, is a shape-shifter, easily transforming into a woman.

Strangers in Paradise (1993–). Terry Moore's triumph. Featuring Katchoo (Gesundheit!).

X Factor #3 (2005–2013). Featuring the gay couple Rector and Shatterstar.

Young Bottoms in Love (2007). Anthology series by various hands that originally ran as a web comic.

NOTES

1. Fredric Wertham, *Seduction of the Innocent* (New York: Rinehart, 1954).

2. http://www.fborfw.com/char_pgs/lateryears/friends/index=php?page=poirers.

3. http://www.pulitzer.org/prize-winners-by-year/1994.

4. http://www.dykestowatchoutfor.com.

5. Michael Cart and Christine A. Jenkins, *Top 250 LGBT Books for Teens: Coming Out, Being Out, and the Search for Community* (Chicago: Huron Street Press/ALA Editions, 2015), 115.

6. Gregory Schmidt, "As Archie Nears 75, Riverdale Gets a Youthful Infusion," *New York Times*, December 14, 2014.

7. Gregory Schmidt, "Pow! Gay Comic Book Characters Zap Stereotypes," *New York Times*, July 5, 2015.

8. George Gene Gustines, "Coming Out as Gay Superheroes," *New York Times*, December 23, 2015.

9. Gustines, "Coming Out as Gay Superheroes."

10. Schmidt, "Pow!"

11. lgbt.wikia.com/wiki/Main_Page.

12. https://www.gayleague.com.

13. http://comicvine.gamespot.com/.

14. Schmidt, "Pow!"

Chapter Ten

Desperately Seeking Information: Young Adult Nonfiction with LGBTQ+ Content

When teens seek LGBTQ+ information, where do they look and what do they find? In this chapter, we survey nonfiction publishing for teens on LGBTQ+ topics. Books designated by publishers as YA literature are overwhelmingly fiction titles, but of course teens also read mysteries, westerns, romances, fantasy, and other fiction genres that are not specifically written for or marketed to a young adult audience. The nonfiction works that teens encounter are even less likely to be YA focused. In fact, in many public libraries nonfiction books for teens and for adults are shelved together. Thus, in this chapter we include books that engage and inform teens, regardless of their designations for marketing or cataloging purposes.

The universe of nonfiction is in continual flux as new issues and events come to the fore and old ones become less compelling, then less visible, and finally disappear from view. Outdated books are replaced by new titles about the same subjects that reflect new facts and interpretations. It would be impossible to survey the entire universe of nonfiction with LGBTQ+ content for teen readers in a single chapter, so we must paint the picture with a broad brush that will, we hope, provide an accurate image of the dynamic world of LGBTQ+ nonfiction for teens.

Nonfiction books for young adults are judged by the same criteria as nonfiction for adults—accuracy and objectivity—as well as the appeal of their topics, texts, and images to teenage readers. In addition, the problematic criterion of age appropriateness is commonly applied. All of these standards (information accuracy, reader appeal, suitability for a YA audience) are fluid and have changed over time, yet highly subjective concerns about a book's "appropriateness" or "suitability" have often stymied the provision of LGBTQ+ nonfiction writing for teen readers.

Until the final decades of the twentieth century, intimate same-sex love was absent from nearly all YA books. As author David Sedaris notes in a memoir of his teen years, "My school had no information on gay people, and neither did the public library, not even in novels. Perhaps it was different for kids in big cities but in Raleigh, North Carolina, in the late '60s and early '70s, I honestly believed I was the only homosexual on earth."[1]

Adults (authors, publishers, librarians, parents) possess the authority and power to limit teens' access to LGBTQ+ information, but their urge to censor meets its match in the prodigious, persistent curiosity of teens determined to learn what *they* want to learn. Teens itch to open the Pandora's box of LGBTQ+ information and they will, despite (and, paradoxically, often because of) censorship by their elders.

We see this thirst for knowledge in fictional accounts of teens' coming out. For example, Liza and Annie, the protagonists of Nancy Garden's classic young adult novel *Annie on My Mind* (1982),[2] first meet at New York City's Metropolitan Museum. The girls spend increasing amounts of time with each other, including a day walking in the New York Botanical Garden, another place dedicated to knowledge and discovery. After wandering through the garden hand in hand with Annie, a realization comes crashing in on Liza: "*You're in love with another girl, Liza Winthrop, and you know that means you're probably gay. But you don't know a thing about what that means.*" Her first thought is to look for information in the family's encyclopedia:

> I looked up homosexuality, but that didn't tell me much about any of the things I felt. What struck me most, though, was that, in that whole long article, the word "love" wasn't used even once. That made me mad; it was as if whoever wrote the article didn't know that gay people actually love each other. The encyclopedia writers ought to talk to me, I thought as I went back to bed; I could tell them something about love. (143)

The next day she tells Annie what she found—or, actually, *didn't* find— in the encyclopedia. "'Encyclopedias are no good,' she [Annie] said, going to her closet and pulling out a battered, obviously secondhand book. *Patience and Sarah*, it said on the cover, by Isabel Miller" (143). (Miller's historical novel is based on the lives of two actual women who made a home with each other in early nineteenth-century New England.)[3] Liza reports:

> I did read the book, and Annie reread it, and it helped us discuss the one part of ourselves we'd only talked around so far. We read other books, too, in the next week, trying to pretend we weren't there when we checked them out of the library, and we bought—terrified—a couple of gay magazines and news-

papers. I felt as if I were meeting parts of myself in the gay people I read about. (144)

Liza and Annie find the information they need in fiction, a common and useful resource for unearthing emotional truths, and clearly more reassuring than a dry encyclopedia article. Importantly, the fictional *Patience and Sarah* has the power to affirm Annie and Liza's love in part because it is based on a *true* story. Although fiction and nonfiction are typically treated as distinct categories, the genres overlap, and both play a role in reassuring LGBTQ+ teens and their allies that they are not alone and in supplying meaningful information about their own lives and futures.

Fortunately, teens are not limited to resources specifically identified as "young adult." Even before the Internet, there was a far larger field of books for the "general" reader that were considered basic resources for teens in school and public libraries, namely, the reference books that students were continually urged to consult, such as the encyclopedia that Liza turned to.

ENCYCLOPEDIAS: LOOK IT UP!

Generations of American elementary school students have been routinely taught to use encyclopedias in their classrooms and school libraries. Owning the current year's edition of the *World Book Encyclopedia*, which was first published in 1917, was a measure of a public library's ability to serve information seekers of all ages. The popular *World Book* offered clearly written entries enhanced by attractive photos, maps, and charts, all printed on invitingly glossy, sturdy paper. The *World Book* is still published in print format, while its online product is a respected alternative to *Wikipedia* and other noncommercial information sources.

Despite the centrality of encyclopedias as trusted factual sources, up until relatively recently, encyclopedias commonly found in libraries for teens contained very little information on homosexuality.[4] In fact, there was no entry under "Homosexuality" in the "H" volume or the index of the *World Book Encyclopedia* until the 1973 edition, when a seven-hundred-word entry appeared. The neutral language of the entry is notable for its time, beginning with "Homosexuality is sexual activity between persons of the same sex. Both men and women may be homosexual. Female homosexuals are sometimes called lesbians. Scientists estimate that 4 per cent of the adult males in the United States feel sexually attracted primarily to members of their own sex." The text goes on to cover causality (various theories, but no one knows), treatment (unlikely to be successful), history (since ancient times), and legal status. The entry's final words are upbeat: "In 1961, Illinois became the first state in the United States to abolish its laws against homosexual acts. Since the 1960s various homosexual organizations—sometimes called gay liberation groups—have worked in a number of countries to urge society to adopt more tolerant attitudes."[5] Not surprisingly, *World Book*'s coverage of this topic expanded over time. The 2017 edition, for example, includes entries under Gay rights movement, Homosexuality, Civil union, Same-sex marriage, and Transgender. The 2017 edition's index also includes LGBTQ+ content in articles on Adolescence (establishing a sexual identity), AIDS (history), Boy Scouts (organization), California (the 2000s), Civil rights (major changes), Drama (later United States drama), Family (varieties of family), Marriage (laws concerning marriage), Obama, Barack (military ends gay ban), Sexuality (sexual orientation), and Vermont (recent developments).[6]

LGBTQ+ CONTENT IN YOUNG ADULT NONFICTION: THE EARLY YEARS

In this chapter, we cover nonfiction texts published specifically for young adults from the 1970s to 2016. However, we must emphasize that inquiring teens would certainly have consulted information sources that were not published specifically for them. For example, daily newspapers typically run advice columns that are followed by readers of all ages. Two of the best known purveyors of advice in the last half of the twentieth century were the identical twin sisters Esther Pauline (Eppie) Lederer (writing as Ann Landers) and Pauline Esther (Popo) Phillips (writing as Abigail Van Buren), whose columns debuted in 1955 and 1956, respectively. Each columnist received five to seven thousand letters per day from advice seekers, and each day's column featured three to four letters with Ann's or Abby's responses. Their syndicated columns reached upwards of eighty to ninety million readers of all ages across the country. Both were noted for boldly tackling sensitive issues; the broaching of a taboo subject in their columns could spark widespread discussion of it.

Most of the letters published in their columns came from adult readers, but both Ann and Abby were well aware that many of readers of their newspaper columns and book-length column collections were teens. Indeed, early books by both columnists were addressed specifically to teens: Abby's first book was titled *Dear Teen-Ager* (1959),[7] while Ann's second full-length book was *Ann Landers Talks to Teen-Agers about Sex* (1963).[8] Abby did not take on the topic of same-sex love in her book,[9] but Ann boldly plunged into the topic of same-sex love in an eleven-page chapter titled "What You Should Know about Homosexuality," which begins with her acknowledgment of the regrettable lack of information on homosexuality available to teens in the early 1960s. "They need constructive information, but they don't know where to get it. Many teen-agers who write to me expressing the fear that they might be homosexual say they would 'rather die' than discuss the problem with someone they know. In my search for background material I found pitifully little that has been written in terms a teen-ager could understand."[10] In keeping with her image as a straight-shooting advice giver, Ann provides information regarding stereotypes (generally untrue), social history (extends back to ancient Greece and Rome), and theories of causality (no one really knows). She also urges her (presumably heterosexual) teen readers toward sympathy for the less fortunate homosexuals who "want desperately to be like everyone else." She holds out little hope for a "cure" for the condition, but notes that psychiatric therapy could help homosexuals toward social adjustment and self-acceptance, and ends by addressing her (heterosexual) teen readers directly:

> Be thankful that you have been blessed with healthy, normal sex drives, and remember that not all boys and girls are so fortunate. When you encounter people who are "different," remember that their lives are probably unbelievably difficult and that they are faced with the enormous problem of adjustment. You can help by understanding.[11]

This well-intentioned but condescending advice was in fact the best that teens were likely to find during the 1960s.[12] Nonfiction for readers of all ages generally portrayed teens with same-sex attractions the same way they were portrayed in the early YA fiction: sad-eyed loners who wisely kept their sexual orientation tucked away in the furthest reaches of their closets.

YOUNG ADULT NONFICTION WITH LGBTQ+ CONTENT: A MILESTONE

As noted earlier, the first YA fiction title with LGBTQ+ content was published in 1969. The field of YA LGBTQ+ nonfiction was slower to emerge. The first YA title, Frances Hanckel and John Cunningham's *A Way of Love, a Way of Life: A Young Person's Guide to What It Means to Be Gay*, finally appeared in 1979.[13] On the first page, Hanckel and Cunningham introduce themselves as "active members of the Gay Liberation Movement" and explain their reason for writing this book:

> Too often we have heard stories and read books that describe gay people as though they were strange or flawed, unhappy or disturbed. In response, gays are beginning to speak out for themselves, to tell people the facts about what it means to be gay. However, little is available specifically written for young people.[14]

The authors assert that this is a book for everyone—"You don't have to be gay to wonder what it means to be gay"—while clearly identifying the primary audience as "young people who are either gay or uncertain of their sexual orientation." Their goal was "to provide information and support that will help young gay men and women develop self-confidence and positive feelings about themselves."[15]

Before this time, authors of YA sex ed books that included LGBTQ+ content drew upon their academic credentials and their professional experience in the helping professions (as a psychologist, a science writer for young readers, a psychiatrist, a secondary school educator, a Methodist clergyman, and an advice columnist) for their knowledge of LGBTQ+ people and issues.[16]

Hanckel and Cunningham also had academic credentials and professional experience in the helping professions (a health care administrator and a public librarian, respectively), but their book was the first one written from the perspective of insiders with firsthand knowledge of LGBTQ+ lives and informed by their own experiences as teens, plus those of dozens of other lesbians and gay men.

The book prompts readers to examine their preexisting knowledge and assumptions about gay/lesbian people, and then provides practical information teens can use as they explore homosexuality for themselves, including how to meet other gay/lesbian people and come out to friends and family. The final chapter of the book presents first-person accounts of twelve people (six men and six women, four couples and four single people) who were members of Philadelphia's gay/lesbian community. The remarkable and forthright openness of the text is echoed in the candid photos that normalize gays and lesbians as regular people and reinforce the message that gay teens are not alone. Another fine feature of *A Way of Love, A Way of Life* is its extensive annotated resource list. In an online review titled "This Book Saved My Life," a reader who discovered the book as a teen recalled:

> I found this book, and it was like having some friendly person sit down and talk to me openly and non-judgmentally about what was happening with me. Someone understood. And I wasn't the only one. What I remember most are the biographies at the end of the book. They featured people of all shapes, sizes, colors and ages, some single and some coupled, and all gay or lesbian and leading happy, healthy, productive lives. There was hope. That's what I got out of this book. Those three things. Someone understood. I wasn't the only one. There was hope. This book helped me believe that this life was possible, and inspired me to go out and find it for myself.[17]

Young, Gay, and Proud, edited by Sasha Alyson, a book first published in Australia and then in the United States by Alyson Press in 1980 (with revised editions in 1985, 1991, and 1995), provides much of the same information as *A Way of Love, a Way of Life*, but in the form of a collection of essays by teens describing their own experiences and lives. Perhaps the chief difference between the two texts is that Hanckel and Cunningham wrote with the hindsight of adults, while the essays in *Young, Gay, and Proud* were written by younger authors during or shortly after their own teen years. These are not competing but complementary visions of the world of gay teens. Both titles sought to inform, educate, and support their readers, and both offered an insiders' view of "what it means to be gay."

Since those early years, the body of LGBTQ+ YA nonfiction has grown. Many more titles are now available, and their scope has broadened to include a range of content areas. These areas include (but are not limited to) self-help/advice books; first-person autobiographies and memoirs; individual and collective biographies; LGBTQ+ history; and LGBTQ+ issues. What follows is a survey of the some of the titles within the growing universe of YA nonfiction with LGBTQ+ content.

LGBTQ+ Information: Self-Help/Advice Books for Teens

A number of self-help books for LGBTQ+ teens were written in the 1990s. Despite the absence of omnipresent information technology in the lives of 1990s teens (no cell phones, no social media), little of the advice on coming out has become dated. Earlier titles most readily available to teens included *Passages of Pride: Lesbian and Gay Youth Come of Age* by Kurt Chandler (Times Books, 1995); *Joining the Tribe: Growing Up Gay and Lesbian in the '90s* by Linnea Due (Anchor, 1995); *The Journey Out: A Guide for and about Lesbian, Gay and Bisexual Teens* by Rachel Pollack and Cheryl Schwartz (Viking, 1995); *The World Out There: Becoming Part of the Lesbian and Gay Community* by Michael Thomas Ford (New Press, 1996); and *Free Your Mind: The Book for Gay, Lesbian, and Bisexual Youth—and Their Allies* by Ellen Bass and Kate Kaufman (HarperCollins, 1996).

The publishing of self-help YA books with LGBTQ+ content continued in the new century, but at a slower pace. One of the first of these twenty-first-century books was one of the very few titles to focus exclusively on a single sex: *Growing Up Gay in America: Informative and Practical Advice for Teen Guys Questioning Their Sexuality and Growing Up Gay* by Jason Rich (Franklin Street Books, 2002). The first edition of *GLBTQ: The Survival Guide for Queer and Questioning Teens* by Kelly Huegel was published in 2003; a second edition was published in 2011 with the revised title *GLBTQ: The Survival Guide for Gay, Lesbian, Bisexual, Transgender, and Questioning Teens* (Free Spirit Publishing). *Queer: The Ultimate LGBT Guide for Teens* by Kathy Belge and Marke Bieschke (Zest Books) was also published in 2011. The most recent title in this genre is *This Book Is Gay* by Juno Dawson (Sourcebooks, 2015).[18]

FIRST-PERSON NARRATIVES: AUTOBIOGRAPHY/MEMOIRS

As noted by the Amazon reviewer quoted above in "This Book Saved My Life," part of the value of *A Way of Love, a Way of Life*, in addition to the self-help advising, is the opportunity to meet twelve lesbian and gay individuals via their photos and brief (two- to three-page) biographies. Such first- and third-person narratives of various lengths that tell the stories of LGBTQ+ lives have proliferated since 1979. The first-person narratives include interviews, memoirs, and autobiographical accounts. The third-person narratives vary in length from the half-page summaries in biographical dictionaries to book-length biographies of notable LGBTQ+ figures throughout history.

LGBTQ+ Teen Lives: Book-Length Autobiographies

The earliest teen-focused autobiography/memoir of an LGBTQ+ teen was the widely read *Reflections of a Rock Lobster: A Story about Growing Up Gay*, by Aaron Fricke (Alyson Publications, 1981). In the spring of 1980 Fricke successfully challenged his Rhode Island high school in U.S. District Court for the right to bring a same-sex date to the prom.[19] The prom, which was covered in the national media, took place with no incident. As the plaintiff in a precedent-setting case (*Fricke v. Lynch*, May 28, 1980), Fricke became a celebrity in the gay press, and his autobiography was published the following year by Alyson Publications, at that time a gay-oriented small press in Boston.

There are a number of YA nonfiction collections of adults' memories of growing up LGBTQ+, but few full-length memoirs of LGBTQ+ teens written for a teen audience have appeared since Fricke's pioneering book. Memoirs of LGBTQ+ adults commonly include some account of their childhood and adolescence, but the great majority are written by those who made their mark on the world as adults and are aimed at an adult audience.

As with Aaron Fricke, LGBTQ+ youth may be pulled into the national spotlight via their involvement in significant public events. Unlike Aaron in his successful court case, some enter the public eye when their lives are touched by criminal events. Thus, two memoirs of LGBTQ+ youth are by those whose lives were changed by two brutal events in the national news: the murder of Matthew Shepard in 1998 and the attempted assassination of Arizona representative Gabby Giffords in 2011.

Romaine Patterson, a twenty-year-old lesbian and good friend of Matthew Shepard, took action on behalf of Matthew's family in the aftermath of Matthew's murder in Laramie, Wyoming. Upon learning that the antigay Westboro Baptist Church would be picketing the trial of Matthew's murderers, she organized Angel Action, a local group whose members donned large angel wings to encircle the picketers and visually shield Shepard's family from the sight of their "God Hates Fags" and "Matthew in Hell" placards. *The Whole World Was Watching: Living in the Light of Matthew Shepard* (2005) is Patterson's memoir of her life before, during, and after Matthew's death.

Daniel Hernandez was twenty years old when he went to work as an intern for Arizona representative Gabby Giffords. When a shooter opened fire on Giffords and others at a neighborhood meet-and-greet event, his quick thinking and actions saved her life. He tells his story of growing up in Tucson as a gay Mexican American in *They Call Me a Hero: A Memoir of My Youth* (2013), which was published in both an English- and a Spanish-language edition. Hernandez is now a member of the Arizona House of Representatives!

Other LGBTQ+ young people are noted for their exceptional talent; their memoirs focus largely on their public careers but also include their personal lives. Laurie Rubin, who is blind from birth, is a brilliant mezzo-soprano, an internationally known opera singer, and a lesbian. Her disability, her voice, and her fame would make her a likely candidate for a memoir of vision loss overcome via determination and talent, but woven into her narrative of artistic struggle and success is also her growing awareness of herself as a lesbian, as told in Rubin's *Do You Dream in Color? Insights from a Girl without Sight* (2012).

Another recent memoir of a talented "happens to be gay" teen is by Jack Andraka, whose painstaking analysis of blood chemistry resulted in an inexpensive screening test for early-stage pancreatic cancer. In *Breakthrough: How One Teen Inventor Is Changing the World* (2015), Andraka relates his year-by-year progress through secondary school as a self-identified science nerd, an award-winning researcher, and an out-and-proud gay high school student. His frank acknowledgment of his gay identity disconcerted many high school peers, but, in Andraka's words, "I'm openly gay and one of my biggest hopes is that I can help inspire other LGBT youth to get involved in STEM [science, technology, engineering and mathematics]. I didn't have many role models [i.e., gay scientists] besides Alan Turing."[20]

One significant and positive factor in the lives of both Rubin and Andraka has been the unconditional support they received from their parents. But parents can also play a negative role in the lives of their nonconforming adolescent children. In these cases, even well-intentioned and loving parents can also be obstacles when their priorities are in direct conflict with those of their children. For example, Aaron Hartzler's *Rapture Practice: My One-Way Ticket to Salvation* (2013) and Alex Cooper's *Saving Alex: When I Was Fifteen I Told My Mormon Parents I Was Gay, and That's When My Nightmare Began* (2016) are memoirs of LGBTQ+ teens from devout Christian families whose parents are determined to protect their children from the secular world via rigid religious schooling (Aaron) and confinement to a so-called reparative treatment facility (Alex). Both resist these misguided efforts and tell their stories as twenty-something gay (Aaron) and lesbian (Alex) adults. It is interesting to note that both of these titles were originally published as adult nonfiction. Were the publishers' decisions made because of the perceived controversial nature of their stories (negative portrayals of parental power? depictions of harsh "for your own good" discipline as seen by the teens being disciplined?). Whatever the reason, both books would certainly be of interest to teens.

In 2014 Simon & Schuster published a pair of memoirs by transgender teens: Arin Andrews's *Some Assembly Required: The Not-So-Secret Life of a Transgender Teen* and Katie Rain Hill's *Rethinking Normal: A Memoir in Transition.* Arin is FtM (female-to-male) transgender, and Katie is MtF (male-to-female). Both grew up in the Tulsa area, where they met in a transgender support group while both were in their late teens and in the process of transitioning. They become friends—and then romantic partners—and were featured on a segment of television's *20/20* in 2013. That segment, plus other interviews of the two, quickly went viral. Each tells their story of childhood gender dysphoria and of their later experiences as instant celebrities on television and YouTube.

Jazz Jennings's *Being Jazz: My Life as a Transgender Teen* (2016) is another first-person account of lifelong gender dysphoria as a child with a male body but a female identity. Her youth, plus her photogenic beauty and well-honed interview skills, have made her a popular and engaging spokesperson for transgender youth. In addition to her memoir, she is featured in *I Am Jazz*, a picture book by Jennifer Herthel (Dial 2014) and a TLC television reality show.

Finally, Zach Wahls is not LGBTQ+ himself, but as the son of two lesbians, he sees himself as part of the LGBTQ+ community. His book *My Two Moms: Lessons of Love, Strength, and What Makes a Family* (2012) was originally published as adult nonfiction, but is definitely accessible to teens. Wahls's eloquent testimony in 2011 before the Iowa State Legislature on behalf of same-sex marriage was captured on a video that quickly went viral and led to his book.

LGBTQ+ Lives: Memoir Collections

The social isolation felt by LGBTQ+ teens is a recurring theme running through both YA fiction and nonfiction in the early years of this literature. As isolated young people are in the process of coming out, they commonly begin searching for community, for kindred spirits, and simply for "people like me." But where to find them? Negative stereotypes of gay men and lesbians were ubiquitous, and any gay people who did *not* resemble those stereotypes were simply presumed to be heterosexual. Given that before 1962, a sexual act between two people of the same sex could be prosecuted as a felony in all fifty states,[21] gay people commonly opted for the invisibility of the closet. The closet was an uncomfortable place to live, but the people who found that invisibility particularly troubling were individual LGBTQ+ teens longing to know that they were not alone.

One pioneering media event that signaled the opening of that closet door to teens and, indeed, to mainstream society, was the November 1977 premiere of *Word Is Out: Stories of Some of Our Lives*, a 120-minute documentary film composed of interviews with twenty-six (thirteen male, thirteen female) self-identified gay and lesbian Americans ranging in age from eighteen to seventy-seven. The twenty-six were likewise diverse in race, class, culture, and life experience. *Word Is Out* was subsequently released to theaters and aired on PBS stations in January 1978. As later noted in the *New York Times*, "Understated though it was, *Word Is Out* had a remarkable impact, coming at a time when images of homosexuals as everyday people, as opposed to psychopaths or eccentrics, were rare."[22]

The film reached an audience beyond its viewers via the filmmakers' book based on the film, which was published in 1978 in both hardcover and paperback editions. Each of the book's twenty-six chapters begins with a full-page photo of one of the interviewees followed by an eight- to twelve-page excerpted transcript of their interview illustrated by other candid photos. The film and the book gave faces to ordinary lesbian and gay people, a fact that not only provided LGBTQ+ teens with role models, but also with the assurance that if these ordinary people were gay or lesbian, then there were certainly others in their own schools, neighborhoods, towns, counties, and cities. The message? "You are not alone."

In 1979, lesbian writer and cartoonist Alison Bechdel, then a student at Oberlin College, was struggling to come out to herself. In her autobiographical graphic novel *Fun Home: A Family Tragicomedy*, she pictures herself at age nineteen perusing the shelves of a bookstore. There she experiences a personal revelation when she finds and opens a copy of *Word Is Out*. "That volume led quickly to others. A few days later I screwed up my courage and bought one. This book referred to other books, which I sought out in the library. One day it occurred to me that I could actually look up Homosexuality in the card catalog. I found a four-foot trove in the stacks which I quickly ravished. And soon I was trolling even the public library, heedless of the risks."[23]

Word Is Out was marketed to a general readership, but Bechdel's immediate engagement with the book as a teen demonstrates its appeal to teen readers: crisp, candid photos of the subjects' expressive faces and body language, accompanied by personal stories told in accessible prose. *Word Is Out* was the first in a long line of YA nonfiction collections of real LGBTQ+ people telling real stories from their lives.

Collections of interviews and first-person accounts have been and remain a mainstay of YA nonfiction with LGBTQ+ content. The first such collection for a young audience, Ann Heron's *One Teenager in Ten: Writings from Gay and Lesbian Youth*, contained pieces by twenty-five contributors and appeared in 1983. Others followed, including Roger Sutton's *Hearing Us Out: Voices from the Gay and Lesbian Community* (1994), and a second revised and enlarged edition of Heron's book with more contributions and a less lonely title, *Two Teenagers in Twenty* (1995). These were followed by a number of others.

Collections vary in length, format, content, and diversity. Some are text only, while others have photographic portraits of LGBTQ+ teens and adults accompanied by interview transcripts, essays, and/or explanatory notes (indicated by "photo illus." in bibliographic entry). Two of these—Adam Mastoon's *The Shared Heart* (1997) and Rachelle Lee Smith's *Speaking Out* (2015)—include handwritten texts by the teens portrayed.

A number focus exclusively on teen voices. For example, *We Are the Youth* by Laurel Golio and Diana Scholl (2014) depicts LGBTQ+ young people via photos and personal essays. The two editions (2006, 2016) of *The Full Spectrum*, edited by David Levithan and Billy Merrell, contain autobiographical essays, stories, and poetry, all written by youth under age twenty-three. Other texts include a range of ages; *Born This Way: Real Stories of Growing Up Gay* by Paul Vitagliano (2012) is a playful collection of LGBTQ+ adults' childhood photos from the 1950s to the 2000s with accompanying autobiographical notes that anticipate their future sexual identities.

There are also collections that focus on specific groups within the larger LGBTQ+ population, such as transgender youth in Jackson Wright Schultz's *Trans/portraits: Voices from Transgender Communities* (2015), and homeless youth in Sassafras Lowrey's *Kicked Out* (2010), an enlightening collection of contributions (memoirs, interviews, essays, and research) by and/or about homeless LGBTQ+ youth, who comprise approximately 40 percent of all homeless youth.

Keith Boykin's *For Colored Boys Who Have Considered Suicide When the Rainbow Is Still Not Enough* (2012) is a collection of memoirs and autobiographical essays by African American men on their own experiences growing up LGBTQ+ as a black male, and addressed, directly and/or indirectly, to young black men who are LGBTQ+ and seeking kindred spirits.

It Gets Better: Coming Out, Overcoming Bullying, and Creating a Life Worth Living, edited by Dan Savage and Terry Miller (2011), could be classified as a self-help book for teens, but the book's one-hundred-plus essays, drawn from the It Gets Better website (www.itgetsbetter.org)—written by people of all sexual orientations—relate stories of the lives of former and current LGBTQ+ teens and their allies.

Like *Word Is Out*, most collections are designed to reflect diverse voices, and all reflect an awareness of a teen audience. For example, in Candace Gingrich's introduction to Rachelle Lee Smith's *Speaking Out* (2015), she states, "Just because there has been visibility doesn't mean the voices of LGBTQ people are being heard."[24] This is particularly true for teens from marginalized populations. From *Word Is Out* to today, the ongoing presence of these and similar collections demonstrates that these articulate LGBTQ+ voices are speaking out and, hopefully, will continue to be heard.

LGBTQ+ People: Individual Biographies

Until relatively recently, biographies of LGBTQ+ people written for a YA audience rarely included any overt indication of the subjects' sexual orientation. All too often well-known figures who were openly gay had their life stories "tidied up" and were portrayed as bachelors or spinsters, either too busy with their accomplishments to have time for romance, or in lifelong mourning for an early lost love (of the opposite sex).

A comparison of two early YA biographies of the African American author James Baldwin, who was openly gay throughout his life, provides a vivid illustration of this phenomenon. The first book, *James Baldwin* by Lisa Rosset (1989), was a volume in Chelsea House Publishers' Black Americans of Achievement series;[25] the second, also titled *James Baldwin*, by Randall Kenan (1994), was a volume in the same publisher's series Lives of Notable Gay Men and Lesbians.[26] Rosset makes no mention of Baldwin's same-sex romantic relationships. Kenan, while covering the same highlights of Baldwin's life and literary achievements, weaves in Baldwin's experience of coming out as a gay man, his several significant romantic interests, and the various ways his gay identity impacted other events in his life.[27] Of course, speculation about the private sexuality of public figures has no place in reputable biographies and, unless subjects are known primarily as LGBTQ+ activists, their sexual identity should not overshadow other aspects of their lives and achievements. However, the omission of such information from the biography of a subject who self-identified as gay casts serious doubt on the overall text as an accurate representation of Baldwin's life.

Chelsea House Publishers: A Trail Blazed and Abandoned

Kenan's *James Baldwin* was the first volume in Chelsea House's groundbreaking biographical series Lives of Notable Gay Men and Lesbians. As the first publisher to launch a YA biographical series about lesbian and gay subjects, Chelsea House provides an example of the hopes and disappointments that LGBTQ+ teens and their allies experienced as this body of literature slowly took shape.

Chelsea House Publishers (now an imprint of Infobase Learning) has focused largely on thematic nonfiction series within the general area of social studies. In the 1990s Chelsea House was noted for publishing biographical series of notable historical figures who, as members of minority-status groups, had received minimal coverage in standard biographies or histories for teens.[28]

Late in 1992, announcements began to circulate of two new Chelsea House series for teen readers, Lives of Notable Gay Men and Lesbians (biographies) and Issues in Lesbian and Gay Life (social, political, and cultural histories).[29] Both series were to be edited by noted historian and scholar Martin Duberman. Those who had searched in vain for honest YA biographies of LGBTQ+ subjects greeted the news with cheerful anticipation.[30] In spring 1994, Chelsea House announced that Lives of Notable Gay Men and Lesbians would include thirty volumes, and Issues in Lesbian and Gay Life, twenty-five volumes.[31] This promised bounty of LGBTQ+ nonfiction for YA readers was unprecedented.

The first volumes in the series were released in 1994. In addition to Kenan's excellent work on James Baldwin, four more biographical volumes appeared (*Willa Cather* by Sharon O'Brien; *John Maynard Keynes* by Jeffrey Escoffier; *Sappho* by Jane McIntosh Snyder; and *Oscar Wilde* by Jeff Nunokawa). In 1995, four more were published (*Marlene Dietrich* by W. K. Martin; *T. E. Lawrence* by Daniel Wolfe; *Liberace* by Raymond Mungo; and *Martina Navratilova* by Gilda Zwerman). The tenth and final volume in the series (*k. d. lang* by Paula Martinac) was published in 1997. Projected volumes on Jane Addams, Alvin Ailey, Federico Garcia Lorca, Lorraine Hansberry, Tennessee Williams, and fifteen others were never published.[32] Issues in Lesbian and Gay Life, the other announced series, was likewise short lived: of the twenty five volumes originally projected, only four were published. The publisher shared no news on the fate of either series, but after 1997, the flow of new volumes ceased.

Duberman's memoir, *Waiting to Land: A (Mostly) Political Memoir, 1985–2008* (New Press, 2009), includes some details of his difficulties spearheading the project.[33] When Duberman was first approached in 1992 about editing a series of YA biographies on notable lesbian and gay people in history, he had misgivings due to his numerous other writing and teaching projects, but he finally succumbed to the project's "missionary appeal" as he envisioned a series of books that would provide gay teens with reliable information on gay/lesbian lives and culture.[34] He was promised full authority to recruit authors from among scholars, writers and activists he thought best suited for the subjects. However, once Duberman agreed to this project and began reaching out to prospective authors, he ran into immediate objections from the publisher, who was unfamiliar with many of the authors Duberman proposed and urged him instead to pursue celebrity authors (Madonna could write about Janis Joplin!). Contracts for twenty titles were finally signed, and the first volume, Kenan's *James Baldwin*, was released to positive reviews. However, the owner of Chelsea House then became concerned that the texts' reading level would be too high for teens, and he called a halt to further contracts until they saw how the first titles sold.[35] The already-contracted manuscripts began arriving at Chelsea House, but authors' payments were delayed by many months, even years, and Duberman was chagrined by the poor treatment the authors received. In 1995, after over a year of silent avoidance, the owner announced that both series were being canceled due to slow sales. Duberman's reaction: "The project, despite having fourteen books in print, was dead in the water. Was it killed by Chelsea House ineptitude? By homophobia among school officials and librarians? Was the caliber of the writing too high and the sexual discussion of the subject's life too explicit for high school students (and their teachers) to handle? I was at a loss for how to parcel out appropriate shares of blame."[36] It's possible that the series' cancellation influenced other publishers, a conclusion that could be drawn from the relative absence of book-length YA biographies of LGBTQ+ subjects; certainly, there have been no projects of this size and scope in the twenty-plus years since then.[37]

With twenty-twenty hindsight we can point to the overall political climate with regard to LGBTQ+ issues and youth in the early and mid-1990s as one factor that worked against the success of LGBTQ+ publishing for young adults. In 1990 the Supreme Court ruled that the Boy Scouts of America could expel gay members. In November 1992 Colorado voters approved Amendment 2, which would eliminate antidiscrimination legislation on behalf of LGBTQ+ people. In 1993 the military implemented Don't Ask Don't Tell; DOMA (the Defense of Marriage Act) was signed into law in 1996. As Duberman observes, "The Chelsea House morass reflected, in miniature, some of the broader currents of the day. [The owner's] alternating beneficence and contempt mirrored the increasingly conflicted attitude of the general public toward gay people in general."[38]

Twenty-First-Century LGBTQ+ Biographies for Teens: Slow Progress

The majority of full-length YA biographies of LGBTQ+ people are series books. This mode of publishing has several advantages in reaching teen readers. First, the individuals selected for treatment are typically people who are already well known to teen audiences, who may in turn seek out the books themselves out of their own personal interest. The format of each volume in the series is consistent and designed for maximum readability. Covers are eye catching, the writing is clear, and texts include numerous photos and and/or boxed side bars with further information, as well as a glossary, a list of resources, and an index.

Formulaic content and a cookie-cutter format make series books more approachable, especially for so-called reluctant readers. But because they are based on secondary sources, these series biographies are more likely to provide an introduction to the subject rather than a full picture. Furthermore, subjects are people in the media spotlight at the time of publication. Reader engagement with current celebrities is just about automatic, but once the subjects are no longer utterly contemporary, the interest of teen readers may wane.

For example, four of the six volumes in Rosen Publishing's 2015 series, Remarkable LGBTQ Lives, profile current media figures in television (television hosts Rachel Maddow and Ellen DeGeneres) and Hollywood films (actors/performers Jane Lynch and Zachary Quinto). Similarly, all four of the figures profiled in Rosen's 2016 series, Transgender Pioneers, are prominent media personalities: television star Laverne Cox (*Orange Is the New Black*), Hollywood film director Lana Wachowski (*The Matrix*), and celebrities Caitlyn Jenner and Chaz Bono.

A few outstanding treatments of LGBTQ+ figures have been published in biographical series on related topics, such as Morgan Reynolds Publishing's series Civil Rights Leaders, a collection of individually authored biographies for teens that includes two excellent volumes featuring LGBTQ+ icons: Calvin Craig Miller's *No Easy Answers: Bayard Rustin and the Civil Rights Movement* (2005); and David Aretha's *No Compromise: The Story of Harvey Milk* (2009). Miller's aptly titled *No Easy Answers* is a straightforward look at the life of Bayard Rustin (1912–1987), the African American activist and astute political strategist who masterminded Dr. Martin Luther King Jr.'s 1963 March on Washington but remained behind the scenes, because as a "known homosexual" his public presence in the movement was a potential liability. Aretha's *No Compromise* features politician and gay rights activist Harvey Milk (1930–1978). Milk was elected to San Francisco's Board of Supervisors in 1977. He served a single year before he was assassinated, but his astute understanding of the power of LGBTQ+ visibility has had a lasting impact. More recently, *Harvey Milk: Pioneering Gay Politician*, by Corinne Grinapol (Rosen, 2015), appeared as a volume in the publisher's series "Remarkable LGBTQ Lives" as a biography for slightly younger readers.

Several full-length biographies stand apart from series. For example, Jan Greenberg and Sandra Jordan's *Andy Warhol: Prince of Pop* (Delacorte, 2004) provides an immersive picture of the New York City pop art scene of the 1960s and the life of Andy Warhol (1928–1987) that includes his impoverished childhood and early evidence of his artistic talent, his restless determination to succeed as both artist and celebrity, and his lifelong attraction to other men.

Two biographies of gay British mathematician Alan Turing (1912–1954) were published in 2016 in graphic novel format. Interest in Turing's life exploded with the Hollywood release of *The Imitation Game* in 2014. Jim Ottaviani's *The Imitation Game: Alan Turing Decoded* (Abrams, 2016) and Arnaud Delalande's *The Case of Alan Turing: The Extraordinary and Tragic Story of the Legendary Codebreaker* (Arsenal Pulp Press, 2016) are both aimed at a general audience, but teens will definitely appreciate the ironic tale of Turing's groundbreaking cryptographic work on behalf of his government during the 1940s and his arrest and conviction for homosexuality by the same government in the 1950s.

A final biography of note is Tam O'Shaughnessy's *Sally Ride: A Photobiography of America's Pioneering Woman in Space* (Roaring Brook, 2015). The author, Ride's longtime life partner, provides a vivid, fully realized portrait of scientist-astronaut Sally Ride (1951–2012) in an engaging text enriched by numerous color photos. In addition to her work at NASA, Ride's career included work as a physicist and a science educator, and this conversational text recounts both Ride's public career and her personal life with family, close friends, and O'Shaughnessy, her partner of nearly thirty years.

Such in-depth stories are still rarely told to young adult readers. The early promise of the canceled Chelsea House series has yet to be fulfilled. What seemed too innovative for commercial success in the 1990s, however, may be just what today's LGBTQ+ teens and their allies long to read. The high quality of the most recent additions to this small body of literature is encouraging. We hope that other publishers' plans for book-length biographies of LGBTQ+ subjects will continue full speed ahead.

LGBTQ+ People: Collective Biographies

As noted earlier, there are comparatively few truthful YA biographies of LGBTQ+ people. However, the number of collective biographies and biographical dictionaries detailing the lives of LGBTQ+ public figures for teen and adult readers has grown over time. Although the terms "collective biography" or "biographical dictionary" may seem about as scintillating as "telephone directory," the texts themselves are in fact stories of accomplished LGBTQ+ people of the past and present that can definitely be read for pleasure.

Three recent collective LGBTQ+ biographies are aimed at a teen audience. Sarah Prager's *Queer, There and Everywhere: 23 People Who Changed the World* (HarperCollins, 2017) confirms the ubiquity of queer people in a chronology that ranges from the ancient Roman Empire to the twenty-first century. An introductory survey of the queer aspects of societies over time and throughout the world is followed by chapters that introduce and contextualize historical figures. The breezy, conversational text presents Jeanne D'Arc, Queen Christina of Sweden, Abraham Lincoln, Bayard Rustin, George Takei, and eighteen other intriguing figures.

Kathleen Archambeau's *Pride & Joy: LGBTQ Artists, Icons and Everyday Heroes* (Mango, 2017) is based on the author's interviews with thirty contemporary subjects active in a range of fields. The ten artists profiled include singers, musicians, dancers, and writers. The ten icons are political activists, scholars, and religious, business, and IT (information technology) leaders. Everyday heroes include a bookseller, firefighters, scientists, athletes, and social activists. Barbra Penne's *Transgender Role Models and Pioneers* (Rosen, 2017) is the first collective biography for teens to focus exclusively on the lives and contributions of early and current transgender activists. The author's chronological approach begins with Christine Jorgensen, followed by accounts of the lives of Marsha P. Johnson and Sylvia Rivera, who were participants in the Stonewall riots and leaders of New York City's increasingly visible transgender community in the 1960s and 1970s. Current-day transgender media figures, including Chaz Bono, Caitlyn Jenner, Laverne Cox, and others, are featured in the book's final pages.

Earlier LGBTQ+ collective biographies were aimed at an adult or general audience, but will certainly appeal to teens who wish to acquaint themselves with past and current LGBTQ+ public figures. For example, Erin McHugh's *The L Life: Extraordinary Lesbians Making a Difference* (Abrams, 2011) features two- to five-page profiles of twenty-six lesbians who are currently public figures in business, government, law, media, or the arts. McHugh visited and interviewed each of them, which allows profiles to include interview transcripts and memorable color photos in addition to biographical information.

Robert Aldrich's *Gay Lives* (Thames & Hudson, 2012) also offers striking visual images in the one- to three-page biographical entries for seventy-four LGBTQ+ people. The author is a professor of European history, and his scholarly but highly readable text is by far the most international collection of people profiled. Entries are enlivened by contemporaneous portraits, photos, and artifacts. Paul Elliott Russell's *The Gay 100: A Ranking of the Most Influential Gay Men and Lesbians, Past and Present* (Carol Publishing, 1995) highlights the one hundred (primarily European and American) people whom Russell, a scholar in literature and gay/lesbian studies, judges to be the most significant contributors to twentieth-century gay/lesbian culture. Each entry's three- to four-page text makes a persuasive and well-researched case for the subject's significance in shaping twentieth-century LGBTQ+ identity.

Given the size, alphabetical arrangement, and multiple indexes of several collective LGBQ+ biographies, they could be considered biographical dictionaries—but definitely more fun to browse than most. For example, Michael J. Tyrkus's *Gay and Lesbian Biography* (St. James Press, 1997) contains 275 biographies of LGBTQ+ people, and indexes them by nationality and occupation, and "general subjects." The six-hundred-plus pages of Keith Stern's *Queers in History: The Comprehensive Encyclopedia of Historical*

Gays, Lesbians, Bisexuals, and Transgenders (BenBella, 2009) contain over nine hundred biographical sketches of people ("from 2450 BC to today") rumored to be LGBTQ+. Scholarly history this isn't, but (despite its cover description as "history and dish garnished lavishly with innuendo") this is a rich resource for readers curious about the (sketchy/factual) reasons behind a public figure's queer reputation. The entries are indexed by profession, nationality, birthplace, and birth year.

LGBTQ+ HISTORY AND ISSUES

Do young adults seek out historical nonfiction? On the one hand, teens may dismiss history in general as an academic subject centered on such dull topics as tariffs and treaties from long ago and far away. On the other hand, teens may feel compelled to explore LGBTQ+ history because they feel a personal connection with LGBTQ+ issues but have learned exactly nothing about it in their history classes (or anywhere else, for that matter). Historical works not only spotlight significant figures who are members of the many and diverse LGBTQ+ communities, but also reveal how LGBTQ+ people, who have nearly been invisible in standard accounts of history, have in fact been here all along. Indeed, the first YA nonfiction title with LGBTQ+ content, Hanckel and Cunningham's *A Way of Love, a Way of Life* (1979), devotes a full chapter to history ("From Plato's Academy to the National Gay Task Force"). Early YA nonfiction titles with LGBTQ+ content would commonly include historical highlights, such as the event known variously as the Stonewall rebellion, uprising, or riots (with "riots" currently leading the pack). Sabra Holbrook's *Fighting Back: The Struggle for Gay Rights* (Dutton, 1987) was the earliest YA nonfiction title to focus exclusively on this area of twentieth-century U.S. history, particularly the events, people, and organizations that played key roles in the early history of the movement.

LGBTQ+ History: Stonewall

A number of nonfiction accounts of the Stonewall riots have been published. The earliest were published as adult titles: *Stonewall* by Martin Duberman (Dutton, 1993) and *Stonewall: The Riots That Sparked the Gay Revolution* by David Carter (St. Martin's, 2010). In more recent years, however, a number of titles have been published for a young adult audience. They include *The Stonewall Riots and the Gay Rights Movement, 1969* by Betsy Kuhn (Twenty-First Century Books, 2011); *Stonewall: Breaking Out in the Fight for Gay Rights* by Ann Bausum (Viking, 2015); *The Stonewall Riots*, by Laurie Collier Hillstrom (Omnigraphics, 2016); and *The Stonewall Riots: The Fight for LGBT Rights* by Tristan Poehlmann (Abdo, 2016).

The Stonewall riots occurred in June 1969, but the riots/uprising/rebellion is commemorated every year in late June with parades, rainbow flags, and general hoopla. Two excellent books appeared in 2016 that provide an exuberant and colorful visual record of these annual celebrations. Robin Stevenson's *Pride: Celebrating Diversity & Community* (Orca, 2016) is a joyful rendition of the celebration from its Stonewall origins to current-day pride celebrations in countries in Africa, Asia, Australia, Europe, and North and South America. Jurik Wajdowicz's *Pride & Joy* (New Press, 2016) provides a history of pride in New York City with a wealth of color photos, celebratory words from forty-five LGBTQ+ activists and public figures, and a chronology of relevant political, legal, social, and historical events and milestones.

LGBTQ+ History: Marriage Equality

There are a number of recent, accessible titles on the knotty legal and political struggle that established marriage equality for same-sex couples in the United States. This dramatic story has been told from several different angles by the various players involved. *Love Unites Us* by Kevin Cathcart and Leslie J. Gabel-Brett (New Press, 2016) tells this story from the long-view perspective of Lambda Legal, the nonprofit LGBTQ+ legal advocacy organization active in the struggle since early same-sex marriage cases in the 1970s.[39] Marriage in the United States has traditionally been under the legal jurisdiction of the states, and Marc Solomon's *Winning Marriage* (ForeEdge, 2015) tells the story from that perspective by focusing on the legal and political battles in Massachusetts and New York. Roberta Kaplan's *Then Comes Marriage* (Norton, 2015) tells the story from her perspective as lawyer for Edie Windsor in her suit against the federal government. Windsor and her longtime partner Thea Spyer married legally in Canada, but when Thea died, the federal government's refusal to recognize Edie as Thea's widow forced her to pay inheritance tax on property that would have been untaxed if they had been a heterosexual married couple. The successful challenge of this inequality before the U.S. Supreme Court (*Windsor v. U.S. 2013*) brought down a key section of the Defense of Marriage Act (DOMA). Debbie Cenziper and Jim Obergefell's *Love Wins* (Morrow, 2016) tells the story from the perspective of Obergefell and his legal team, who fought to have him listed as next of kin on his longtime partner's death certificate. In *Obergefell v. Hodges 2015*, the U.S. Supreme Court ruled that all states must grant and recognize same-sex marriages. Nathaniel Frank's *Awakening* (Belknap, 2017) begins the story in the late 1940s to provide the perspective of ordinary LGBTQ+ people—activists and bystanders alike—whose personal lives had long felt the impact of marriage inequality. The author is a legal scholar, and the courtroom scenes are riveting. Finally, in *From the Closet to the Court-*

room (Beacon, 2010), legal scholar Carlos Ball tells the story of marriage equality as part of a broader struggle for LGBTQ+ rights with regard to families, harassment, discrimination, sexual acts, and marriage. All of these books were marketed as adult titles but would definitely meet the information needs and reading interests of young adults.

This section would be incomplete without an observation about the disconnect between publishing for the general/adult audience and a teen/young adult audience. During the past decade, marriage equality was frequently in the news with various legal battles leading up to the Supreme Court's game-changing decisions in 2013 and 2015. Not surprisingly, the drama surrounding these events has received extensive coverage in the press and stimulated a flurry of book publishing, and our coverage here reflects both powerful courtroom drama and compelling stories of love and loss.

While this certainly has been—and will continue to be—a controversial area, the struggle for same-sex marriage has had a profound effect on the lived experiences of the many thousands of same-sex couples and their families, who have been affected by the positive legal provisions put in place by the institution of same-sex marriage. The paucity of young adult titles is especially confounding when there has been such a recent flowering of excellent adult books on the subject of same-sex marriage.

For example, the records of WorldCat, the global online catalog of library collections (www.worldcat.org), identify fewer than a dozen young adult nonfiction titles on "same-sex marriage" or "marriage equality" produced by U.S. publishers from 2005 to the present. Nearly all are volumes in YA series with titles such as "Opposing Viewpoints," "Hot Topics," and "Controversy!" Thus, if teens are looking outside the frame of controversy for basic information about same-sex marriage or marriage equality, they will need to consult general/adult audience books such as the engaging ones described above. Which is fine, of course, but the implied "don't touch!" caveat of the "controversial issues" label leaves teen readers and researchers with limited objective information about the topic, except that it has been controversial, which would certainly be old news to teens.

LGBTQ+ History: The Big Picture

In the course of this chapter's survey of YA nonfiction, it is clear that many titles have focused on the specific people and events who have played a role in our personal, local, national, and international history. Thus, it behooves us to consider what we might call the Big Picture. Happily, a number of scholars have taken on this task. What follows is a somewhat idiosyncratic tour of outstanding books—most recent, some older—that present aspects of LGBTQ+ history likely to be of interest to teen readers. We note that recent titles have benefited from innovations in printing technology with regard to economical reproduction of photos and other images that enhance a book's visual appeal. Some titles are specifically YA, but many are aimed at a general audience, which would include teens as well as adults.

The earliest teen-friendly nonfiction title on LGBTQ+ history was Vern L. Bullough's *Homosexuality: A History* (New American Library, 1979). The book's jacket copy accurately describes the span of its coverage "from ancient Greece to gay liberation," and it is one of the few titles in this section that includes societies and events beyond North America. R. B. Parkinson's *A Little Gay History: Desire and Diversity across the World* (Columbia University Press, 2013) goes further in offering a more international focus on queer culture from ancient Egypt to the present, enhancing the information with color photos of contemporaneous art and artifacts depicting same-sex love in the cultures and time periods covered by the text.

We also want to highlight Ken Setterington's *Branded by the Pink Triangle* (Second Story Press, 2013), a YA title on the Holocaust that documents a very specific event in LGBTQ+ history. The Holocaust is now studied in schools across the United States, but many do not realize that the Nazis rounded up other groups as well as Jews, and one of these groups was gay men. Although the story is a grim one, the fact that *Branded by the Pink Triangle* was written for and marketed to a young adult audience is an encouraging sign.

Neil Miller, author of *Out of the Past: Gay and Lesbian History from 1869 to the Present* (Vintage Books, 1995), begins his account of nineteenth- and twentieth-century LGBTQ+ history with the earliest documented use of "homosexuality" in 1869 to create a highly readable narrative of this history in the United States and Europe. Michael Bronski's *Queer History of the United States* (Beacon Press, 2011) begins with the earliest European exploration of the New World and encounters with Native American culture to create a saga of five-hundred-plus years of queer history in North America.

One of the most congenial accounts for teens is Linas Alsenas's *Gay America: Struggle for Equality* (Abrams, 2008), which documents the back-and-forth progress of LGBTQ+ civil rights in the United States. The book's narrative begins in the Victorian era, and proceeding through the twentieth century; it is a clear and readable chronology with numerous images that bring the stories vividly alive.

The Right Side of History: 100 Years of Revolutionary LGBTQI Activism and Radical Agitation for Equal Rights, edited by Adrian Brooks (Cleis Press, 2015), is an anthology of historical/biographical accounts by a number of journalists and historians that focus on key figures—from Isadora Duncan to Diana Nyad—to offer a social history of the United States and of the pioneers and radicals that made it happen.

Vicki L. Eaklor's *Queer America: A People's GLBT History of the 20th Century* (New Press, 2008) covers roughly the same span of years as

Brooks's book, but views LGBTQ+ history through the lens of the larger trends and events in U.S. history and focuses on larger social movements rather than individual movers and shakers.

In contrast to the other books featured here, Jerome Pohlen's *Gay and Lesbian History for Kids: The Century-Long Struggle for LGBT Rights; With 21 Activities* (Chicago Review Press, 2016) is directed to a younger audience and is clearly tailored to classroom use.

Susan Stryker's *Transgender History* (Seal Press, 2008) is a visually engaging treatment of a history that began in the years immediately following World War II. The author directs her text to a general audience in tracing the shifting medical, legal, political, and cultural attitudes regarding gender roles on individuals and groups in U.S. society and introducing the reader to movement leaders, positions, and issues.

Stand by Me: The Forgotten History of Gay Liberation by Jim Downs (Basic Books, 2016) focuses on the political and social movements within the LGBTQ+ community in the 1970s—a period overlooked by many as simply being the decade between Stonewall and the AIDS epidemic.

And finally, Molly McGarry's *Becoming Visible: An Illustrated History of Lesbian and Gay Life in Twentieth-Century America* (Penguin Studio, 1998) is a well-documented and visually engaging text based on an exhibit at the New York City Public Library to commemorate the twenty-fifth anniversary of the Stonewall riots. It remains to be seen how the publishing world will mark the fiftieth anniversary of the Stonewall riots in 2019.

Teens and LGBTQ+ Issues: Finding Their Way to Information

A number of publishers of juvenile nonfiction issue most of their titles in topical series (such as those on states, countries, planets, U.S. presidents, mammals, and so on). Today's series books typically include color photos, sidebars, and other visual elements to enhance reader engagement. The uniformity of their reading level, style, length, chapter arrangement, and other features provides a predictable reading experience that makes them unlikely pleasure reading, but useful as information resources. Readers who become familiar with the format of one volume can more easily use the other volumes in that series. Predictability is often viewed as a flaw in fiction, but in nonfiction it enables information seekers to find what they are looking for with minimal assistance. This is desirable because teens are rarely comfortable asking for help in finding LGBTQ+ information—if they can't find it independently, they won't find it. Coming-out stories in (pre-Internet) YA fiction commonly featured visits to libraries and/or bookstores where teens would surreptitiously comb the catalog and shelves for books with LGBTQ+ content. In these narratives, the teens are eager, even desperate, for information, but they *never* consult the librarian or bookseller.

As a former middle school librarian, Christine recalls her weekly "search and rescue" missions as she walked through the library's stacks looking for nonfiction titles with LGBTQ+ content. The books were rarely checked out (no one wanted their name in the circulation record or to be seen carrying them around), but were clearly read by a number of students, who would look up "homosexuality" in the library catalog, find the books on the shelves, read them in a study carrel or other private location, and then leave them unshelved. By finding and reshelving the library's LGBTQ+ nonfiction, she enabled the next information seekers to locate the books they sought, which, of course, is exactly what the Dewey Decimal System was designed to facilitate—particularly helpful when you don't want anyone else to know what you are looking for. Thank you, Melvil Dewey![40]

LGBTQ+ Issues: Social, Political, Cultural, Mental/Physical Health, Other

As noted earlier, Martin Duberman edited two series for Chelsea House, one of biographies and one of LGBTQ+ issues. Unfortunately, Issues in Lesbian and Gay Life (1994–1997) was as short lived as its companion series, Lives of Notable Gay Men and Lesbians (1994–1997). The first volume in the Issues series appeared in 1994 (*Lesbians and Gays and Sports*, by Perry Deane Young). Two more volumes appeared in 1995 (*Psychiatry, Psychology, and Homosexuality* by Ellen Herman; and *Gay Men, Lesbians, and the Law* by Ruthann Robson). The fourth (and, alas, final) volume was published in 1997 (*Beyond Gay or Straight: Understanding Sexual Orientation* by Jan Clausen). Clausen's book is particularly notable, a model for titles in the Issues series that might have followed had the publisher not discontinued it.[41]

When a contentious social issue or event comes into the public eye, people with a variety of stands and perspectives publish their opinions in online forums and print-on-paper newspapers and periodicals. If the issue is deemed of sufficient interest for teen readers, these pieces may be gathered into collections that can provide a useful overview of a range of positions on that issue. Sometimes the title itself signals the debate format, such as Laura Friedman's *Gay Marriage: Opposing Viewpoints* (Greenhaven, 2010) or Tricia Andryszewski's *Same-Sex Marriage: Granting Equal Rights or Damaging the Status of Marriage?* (Twenty-First Century Books, 2014). In other cases, the volume's title may be neutral (*Gays in the Military, Gay Rights, Same-Sex Marriage*), but the publisher's series title—Pro-Con (Grolier); Point-Counterpoint (Chelsea House); Ethical Debates (Rosen); Introducing Issues with Opposing Viewpoints (Greenhaven); Hot Topics (Lucent)—indicates that the text will provide a range of opinions, but may or may not provide basic factual information.

Although there is much to be learned from the arguments put forth in persuasive writing, the writer's goal is to convince the reader that his or her position is the correct one. The goal of expository writing, on the other hand, is to present factual information with a minimum of bias. Although this may be more an ideal than a reality in these days of "fake news," it nonetheless remains the aim of expository writing. For example, a book may provide information about the history and current status of transgender people in the military (expository writing), or it may provide a range of opinions/arguments as to whether transgender people should be permitted or prevented from serving in the military (persuasive writing). LGBTQ+ teens and their allies who are looking for information may or may not find what they are looking for in texts that present a range of opposing viewpoints. Knowing your enemy is a key strategy for resisting the status quo, but solid facts are essential.

Teens Confronting Homophobia

Sadly, verbal and/or physical expressions of homophobic prejudice are "business as usual" for many teens. Books can't punch out a bully, but they can provide information and support to LGBTQ+ teens and their allies. For example, *"You Can Tell Just by Looking" and 20 Other Myths about LGBT Life and People*, by Michael Bronski, Ann Pellegrini, and Michael Amico (Beacon Press, 2013), addresses common (and erroneous) assumptions that many people (including LGBTQ+ people themselves) hold. Two 2013 titles in Scarecrow Press's It Happened to Me series also offer valuable information for teens facing anti-LGBTQ+ prejudice: Kathlyn Gay's *Bigotry and Intolerance: The Ultimate Teen Guide* provides a broader context for dealing with prejudice directed toward teens themselves, and Eva Apelqvist's *LGBTQ Families: The Ultimate Teen Guide* offers strategic support for straight and gay teens who must deal with anti-LGBTQ+ prejudice directed toward members of LGBTQ+ families. Two books from Canada's Lorimer Press in graphic novel format provide a lighter touch for resisting anti-LGBTQ+ prejudice via humor, irony, and sass: Steven Solomon's *Homophobia: Deal with It and Turn Prejudice into Pride* (2013) and J. Wallace Skelton's *Transphobia: Deal with It and Be a Gender Transcender* (2016).

Other books that provide valuable perspectives for LGBTQ+ teens and their allies—Eric Marcus's *What If? Questions about What It Means to Be Gay and Lesbian* (Simon & Schuster, 2013); Sarah Moon's *The Letter Q: Queer Writers' Notes to Their Younger Selves* (Scholastic, 2012); and Dan Savage and Terry Miller's *It Gets Better* (Plume, 2012)—provide assurance to teens that there is life after high school; and Sue Hyde's *Come Out and Win: Organizing Yourself, Your Community, and Your World* (Beacon, 2007)

is a handbook for teens who are looking for ways to make a positive difference *right now.*

In addition, two books aimed at a general or professional audience of
adults who work with teens can useful in expanding teen readers' understanding of how homophobia affects LGBTQ+ youth. Stuart Biegel's *The
Right to Be Out: Sexual Orientation and Gender Identity in America's Public
Schools* (University of Minnesota Press, 2010) looks at the very specific
issues and challenges that LGBTQ+ youth (and their teachers) face in school
settings. David E. Newton's *LGBT Youth Issues Today* (ABC-CLIO, 2014),
is a one-stop-shopping handbook that addresses a broad range of issues that
are of specific concern to LGBTQ+ teens, which may help readers identify
their own critical LGBTQ+ issues and, more importantly, discover the range
of advocacy organizations available to LGBTQ+ youth.

HIV/AIDS

HIV/AIDS is a topic that has gone through a number of changes as scientific
research and medical information have advanced and have demonstrated not
only that silence is deadly but that information is power. The earliest book
for young readers on the subject was *AIDS* (Watts, 1986) by Alan E. Nourse,
a medical doctor who wrote a number of science books for young readers.
We now have a clearer picture of what HIV/AIDS is, how to prevent it, how
to diagnose and treat it, and how to live with it, but there are surprisingly few
recent YA nonfiction titles about it. Kim Chilman-Blair and John Taddeo's
Medikidz Explain HIV (Rosen, 2010), Carol Sonenklar's *AIDS* (Lorimer,
2011), and Kathy Furgang's *HIV/AIDS* (Rosen, 2015) all present information
clearly and make good use of visual elements within the text but need to be
updated. If teens are taught anything about HIV/AIDS, it is how to avoid
HIV infection. This is fine as far as it goes, but there is also a need for teen-
friendly resources on living with HIV/AIDS. John G. Bartlett and Ann K.
Finkbeiner's *The Guide to Living with HIV Infection*, 6th ed. (Johns Hopkins
Press, 2006) will provide teens with information that is both practical and
accessible. However, up-to-the-minute information about HIV/AIDS is essential for teen information seekers, which affirms the usefulness of online
resources.

LGBTQ+ Lives: Transgender, Bisexual, Asexual, Other

Chapters 7 and 8 of this book reflect the growth of YA fiction with bisexual,
transgender, and intersex characters and content. There are now increasing
numbers of YA nonfiction titles that examine these issues, including several
YA nonfiction series. Mason Crest Publishing currently publishes two inclusive nonfiction series on this subject: The Gallup's Guide to Modern Gay,

Lesbian and Transgender Lifestyle (2010–2011) is a fifteen-volume series that was the first to feature specific coverage of transgender issues, and *Living Proud! Growing Up LGBT* (2016–2017) is a similar but more current ten-volume series. Rosen Publishing also produces two series relevant to LGBTQ+ issues: *Teens: Being Gay, Lesbian, Bisexual, or Transgender* (2010) is a four-volume series that focuses on LGBTQ+ issues; *Transgender Life* (2016) is a five-volume series that focuses exclusively on transgender issues. In addition to being lesbian, gay, bisexual, transgender, queer, or questioning, there are a number of other modes of expressing/enacting one's gender/sexuality orientation, such as genderqueer, nonbinary, gender fluid, or pansexual. Ashley Mardell's *The ABC's of LGBT+* (Mango Media, 2016) is a thorough introduction to what can be a confusing subject, while Meg-John Barker and Julia Scheele's *Queer: A Graphic History* (Icon, 2016) provides an approach to this topic in graphic novel format. The title and subtitle of Laura Erickson-Schroth's *"You're in the Wrong Bathroom!" and 20 Other Myths and Misconceptions about Transgender and Gender Non-conforming People* (Beacon, 2017) provide a succinct description of its content and the author's clear and conversational explanations. The focus on athletes in Kirstin Cronn-Mills's *LGBTQ+ Athletes Claim the Field: Striving for Equality* (Twenty-First Century Books, 2017) introduces readers to people whose lives have been impacted by erroneous assumptions about their gender/sexuality. Julie Sondra Decker's *The Invisible Orientation: An Introduction to Asexuality* (Carrel Books, 2014) and Shiri Eisner's *Bi: Notes for a Bisexual Revolution* (Seal Press, 2013) also provide much-needed information about asexuality and bisexuality. Finally, teen readers may find the interactive workbook format of two books—*My New Gender Workbook* by Kate Bornstein (Routledge, 2013) and *The Gender Quest Workbook* by Rylan Jay Testa, Deborah Coolhard, and Jayme Peta (Instant Help/New Harbinger, 2015)—helpful for determining what they themselves believe about the complex topics of gender and identity.

NOTES

1. David Sedaris, "Drop Dead, Warlock," in *It Gets Better: Coming Out, Overcoming Bullying, and Creating a Life Worth Living*, ed. Dan Savage and Terry Miller (New York: Dutton, 2011), 110–11.
2. Nancy Garden, *Annie on My Mind* (New York: Farrar, Straus & Giroux, 1982).
3. Isabel Miller, pseud., *Patience and Sarah* (New York: McGraw-Hill, 1971). The author, Alma Routsong, wrote her early novels under her own name. Her later novels, all of which featured lesbian protagonists, were published under her pen name, Isabel Miller.
4. Edmund Frank Santavicca, "The Treatment of Homosexuality in Current Encyclopedias" (PhD diss., University of Michigan, 1977).
5. Carlfred Broderick, "Homosexuality," *World Book Encyclopedia*, vol. 8 (H) (Chicago: Field Enterprises, 1973), 275–76.
6. *World Book Encyclopedia* (Chicago: World Book, 2017).

7. Abigail Van Buren, *Dear Teen-Ager* (New York: B. Geis, dist. by Random House, 1959).

8. Ann Landers, *Ann Landers Talks to Teen-Agers about Sex* (New York: Prentice Hall, 1963).

9. *Dear Teen-Ager* (1959) steered clear of questions about same-sex attractions or homosexuality, but Abby's newspaper columns and book-length compilations offered frank and positive advice regarding homosexuality from the 1960s on. For example, in a column that appeared in April 1970, Abby responded to a reader who worried he might be gay by stating that homosexuality was not a disease. "It is the inability to love at all which I consider an emotional illness." See Wenzel Jones, "Justifying Our Love," *Advocate*, November 12, 2002, 85, https://www.thefreelibrary.com/Dear+Abby+April+1970%3a+advice+columnist+Dear+Abby+speaks+out+in+favor...-a094598285.

10. Landers, *Ann Landers Talks*, 84.

11. Landers, *Ann Landers Talks*, 94.

12. In the years that followed, Ann Landers's words on this subject in her daily newspaper columns would become decidedly more negative. For example, in 1973 her column carried a letter from a gay male reader who asked, "Why must people like me sneak around the backs of parents and relatives so that we don't shame or 'disgrace' them? Why can't I hold hands with my lover in public and dance with him the way heterosexual lovers do?" Ann responded in her usual flinty manner, "Because homosexuality is unnatural. It is, in spite of what some psychiatrists say, a sickness, a dysfunction. . . . I do not believe that homosexual activity is normal human behavior" (Ask Ann Landers, *Lawrence [KS] Journal-World*, January 8, 1973. 8). In a 1976 column she wrote, "I do NOT believe that homosexuality is 'just another life style.' I believe that these people suffer from a severe personality disorder. Granted, some are sicker than others, but sick they are" (Ann Landers, *St. Petersburg Times*, July 21, 1976, 3D).

13. Here we want to acknowledge that there were in fact two other nonfiction titles aimed at a teen audience published at roughly the same time as Hanckel and Cunningham's book *Homosexuality: Time to Tell the Truth to Young People, Their Families and Friends* by Leonard P. Barnett (Gollancz, 1975) and *Gay: What You Should Know about Homosexuality* by Morton Hunt (Farrar, Straus & Giroux, 1977). Barnett was a Methodist clergyman in England whose work focused largely on creating and sustaining church youth groups. Like *A Way of Love, A Way of Life*, his book is aimed at "young adults, their families and friends," but it was published by a British press and available in Great Britain only. Hunt was a science writer with a background in psychology who wrote popular articles and books on social psychology. Hunt's book, a nonfiction title on homosexuality, was considered a general (adult) title and marketed as such (though receiving some reviews as a YA title). A revised edition of Hunt's book was published in 1987 and marketed as a young adult title, but of course at that point, it was no longer a first.

14. Frances Hanckel and John Cunningham, *A Way of Love, a Way of Life: A Young Person's Guide to What It Means to Be Gay* (New York: Lothrop, Lee & Shepard, 1979), 15.

15. Hanckel and Cunningham, *A Way of Love*, 16.

16. Chronology of early sexual information books (1963–1979) with LGBTQ+ content accessible to teens: author, title, publisher, and date, plus the professional background of each book's author(s):

> 1963—Ann Landers, advice columnist: *Ann Landers Talks to Teen-Agers about Sex* (Prentice Hall, 1963)
>
> 1968—Eric W. Johnson, secondary school educator: *Love and Sex in Plain Language* (Lippincott, 1968)
>
> 1968—Wardell Pomeroy, psychologist and sex researcher: *Boys and Sex* (Delacorte, 1968)
>
> 1969—Wardell Pomeroy, psychologist and sex researcher: *Girls and Sex* (Delacorte, 1969)
>
> 1969—David Reuben, psychiatrist: *Everything You Always Wanted to Know about Sex but Were Afraid to Ask* (Random House, 1969)
>
> 1970—Eric W. Johnson, secondary school educator: *Sex: Telling It Straight* (Lippincott, 1970)

1975—Leonard Barnett, Methodist clergyman and church youth group organizer: *Homosexuality: Time to Tell the Truth to Young People, Their Families and Friends; An Introduction* (Gollanz, 1975)

1977—Morton Hunt, science writer and social psychologist: *Gay: What You Should Know about Homosexuality* (Farrar, Straus & Giroux, 1977)

1979—Frances Hanckel, health care administrator (professional org. work: APHA [American Public Health Association] project on gay youth) and John Cunningham, public librarian (professional org. work: ALA [American Library Association] Gay Task Force, Philadelphia Gay Hotline volunteer): *A Way of Love, a Way of Life: A Young Person's Introduction to What It Means to Be Gay* (Lothrop, Lee & Shepard, 1979)

17. Terrance H. Heath, "This Book Saved My Life," February 26, 2002, https://www.amazon.com/Way-Love-Life-PersonsIntroduction/dp/0688519075/ref=sr_1_1?s=books&ie=UTF8&qid=1501641952&sr=1-1, accessed July 27, 2017.

18. *This Book Is Gay*, by James Dawson, was first published in Great Britain in 2014 by Hot Key Books. In 2015 Dawson announced her intention to undergo gender transition on her website (http://www.junodawson.com/about/). Thus, the U.S. edition was published the following year as *This Book Is Gay*, by Juno Dawson (Sourcebooks, 2015).

19. Fricke was represented by GLBTQ Legal Advocates & Defenders (GLAD), a nonprofit legal rights organization in the Boston area. GLAD later became Lambda Legal, whose lawyers played a key role in arguing the case for same-sex marriage before the U.S. Supreme Court.

20. Wilber Stuart, "Standing on the Right Side of History: 16 Year Old Jack Andraka is 'The Edison of Our Times,'" The New Civil Rights Movement (online news site), http://www.thenewcivilrightsmovement.com/standing_on_the_right_side_of_history_16   year_old_jack_andraka_is_the_edison_of_our_times/news/2013/03/23/61683, accessed June 7, 2017.

21. In 1961 Illinois became the first state to decriminalize consensual same-sex sexual activity. In the 1970s, twenty more states decriminalized; in the 1980s, four more followed. Kentucky became the twenty-sixth state to decriminalize private homosexual conduct in 1992, the year in which a slim majority of states finally held that otherwise law-abiding gays were no longer criminals.

22. David Dunlop, "Peter Adair, 53, Director, Dies. Made Films with Gay Themes," *New York Times*, June 30, 1996.

23. Alison Bechdel, *Fun Home: A Family Tragicomedy* (Boston: Houghton Mifflin, 2006), 75–76.

24. Candace Gingrich, introduction to *Speaking Out: Queer Youth in Focus*, by Rachelle Lee Smith (Oakland, CA: PM Press, 2015), 8.

25. Lisa Rosset, *James Baldwin*, Black Americans of Achievement (New York: Chelsea House, 1989).

26. Randall Kenan, *James Baldwin*, Lives of Notable Gay Men and Lesbians (New York: Chelsea House, 1994).

27. For example, Kenan states that Baldwin considered artist Lucien Happersberger, whom he met in 1949, to be the love of his life. They were briefly lovers and remained close friends. Happersberger named his son after Baldwin, and he was among the author's inner circle of at-home caregivers when he was dying of cancer in 1987. Despite ample evidence of their abiding love, there is no mention of Happersberger in Rosset's book, which simply states that Baldwin "spent his final days" at his home in rural France.

28. Among the biographical series that Chelsea House debuted in the 1990s were American Women of Achievement, Black Americans of Achievement, and Great Achievers: Lives of the Physically Challenged.

29. Nadine Brozan, "Chronicle," *New York Times*, November 24, 1992, http://www.nytimes.com/1992/11/24/style/chronicle-607092.html.

30. Later in 1993, the excitement grew further with the announcement that a book on Tennessee Williams by the playwright Terrence McNally would be part of the biographical series. Sarah Lyall, "Book Notes," *New York Times*, September 22, 1993, http://www.nytimes.com/1993/09/22/books/book-notes-059893.html.

31. *GLTF Newsletter: A Publication of the Gay and Lesbian Task Force of the Social Responsibilities Round Table of the American Library Association* 6, no. 1 (Spring 1994).

32. Kenan, *James Baldwin*, front matter.

33. Martin B. Duberman, *Waiting to Land: A (Mostly) Political Memoir, 1985–2008* (New York: New Press, 2009).

34. Duberman, *Waiting to Land*, 131.

35. Duberman, *Waiting to Land*, 134.

36. Duberman, *Waiting to Land*, 188.

37. In 2005, without fanfare, Chelsea House released a six-book series titled Gay and Lesbian Writers. Three of the titles are revised editions of titles originally part of the Notable Gay Men and Lesbians series (*James Baldwin*, *Sappho*, and *Oscar Wilde*); each of the new editions has a smaller page size, fewer illustrations, and a coauthor. The other three (*Allen Ginsberg* by Neil Heims, *Adrienne Rich* by Amy Sickels, and *Walt Whitman* by Arnie Kantrowitz) were new titles. As literary biographies, the focus of all six is more on the writers' works than on their lives.

38. Duberman, *Waiting to Land*, 136.

39. https://www.lambdalegal. "Founded in 1973, Lambda Legal is the oldest and largest national legal organization whose mission is to achieve full recognition of the civil rights of lesbians, gay men, bisexuals, transgender people and everyone living with HIV through impact litigation, education and public policy work." As a 501(c)3 nonprofit organization, Lambda Legal does not charge clients for legal representation or advocacy and receives no government funding. Lambda Legal is supported via contributions from supporters around the country. https://www.lambdalegal/about-us.

40. The two books that traveled around the library in the early 1980s exemplify the small number of YA and general audience titles available to teens at that time: (1) the earliest YA nonfiction title with LGBTQ+ content, Hanckel and Cunningham's *A Way of Love, A Way of Life* (Lothrop, Lee & Shepard 1979); and (2) a clearly written and relatively brief general audience title with YA appeal, Vern L. Bullough's *Homosexuality: A History from Ancient Greece to Gay Liberation* (New York: New American Library, 1979).

41. In addition to the four that were published, Chelsea House's Issues in Gay and Lesbian Life series was projected to include volumes on "African-American Lesbian and Gay Culture; AIDS and Other Health Issues; Asian-American Lesbian and Gay Culture; Coming Out; Growing Up Lesbian or Gay; Homophobia; Latin-American Lesbian and Gay Culture; Lesbian and Gay Communities; Lesbian and Gay Couples and Parenting; Lesbian and Gay Culture; Lesbian and Gay Literature; Lesbian and Gay Protest and Politics; Lesbian and Gays in Other Cultures; Lesbian and Gays in Theater and Film; Lesbian and Gays in the Holocaust; Lesbian and Gays in the Media; Lesbian and Gays in the Military; Lesbians, Gays, and Spirituality; Lesbians, Gays, and the World of Business; Neither Male nor Female: Third-Gender Figures; Race and Class in the Lesbian and Gay World; Reclaiming the Lesbian and Gay Past: The Ancient World; Reclaiming the Lesbian and Gay Past: The United States; and Transvestites and Transsexuals" (front matter of *Lesbians and Gay and Sports* by Perry Dean Young).

Conclusion

What a Wonderful World?

There's an old saying, "Bit by bit our sweaters we knit," that says a lot about the evolution of LGBTQ+ literature. Like the knitting of a sweater or a sock, it has been a similarly slow, sometimes tedious, and often incremental process plagued by more than a few dropped stitches. But despite occasional setbacks, progress has been made. In the area of queer consciousness, for example, even geographically and socially isolated teens now have a wide variety of social media for building community. As for stories of homosexual visibility, they continue to be written, but their treatment has become more expansive and, as a result, readers now get to observe the increasing opportunities for assimilation that occur after the dramatic moment of coming out. And thanks to the growing visibility of LGBTQ+ people in motion pictures and especially in series television, YA literature is now including more and more characters who "just happen" to be LGBTQ+ and whose sexuality is no longer presented as being a "problem" but, instead, a condition of almost quotidian being.

What advances remain, though, to be made? In *The Heart Has Its Reasons* (2006), we called out the need for more LGBTQ+ books featuring characters of color, more bisexual characters, more transgender youth, and more characters with same-sex parents. Happily, there has been positive movement in these areas and awareness of these issues continues to grow.

Yet the literature still needs to be even more all-inclusive to offer a better depiction of the complexities of the real world anent homosexuality and to ensure that all readers might see their faces reflected in it. We must redress the imbalance between gay and lesbian characters, we must acknowledge that young people are grappling with their sexual identity at younger ages than in the past—though progress has been made here, too—and that lesbians and gays and others from across the gender/sexuality spectrum do not live on separate planets but, instead, go to the same schools, hang out at the same LGBTQ+ centers, belong to the same Gay-Straight Alliances, and often form friendships.

By definition, young adult literature will always feature rite-of-passage and coming-of-age experiences involving the sometimes arduous task of discovering one's sexual identity and dealing with it. However, there is more to life than sex, more to human identity than one's preference in sexual partners. And so LGBTQ+ needs to be—and is now becoming—more than a literature confined to coming-out stories. It urgently needs to include more stories about young people of color and about those whose homosexuality is simply a given and who are dealing with other issues and challenges like straight kids—emotional, intellectual, physical, social, developmental, and so forth.

Unfortunately, homophobia and gay-bashing are still with us (for up-to-date information about this sad reality in the lives of LGBTQ+ youth visit the websites of such organizations as GLSEN [www.glsen.org], PFLAG [www.pflag.org], and Advocates for Youth [www.advocatesforyouth.org]), but happily many teens now make the transition from the closet to an out life without peril, often with the help of caring adults in organizations like GLSEN and PFLAG or peers in Gay-Straight Alliances. Surely it is time for LGBTQ+ literature to abandon the traditional and too-easy equation between homosexuality and violent death. We note that suicide has more or less disappeared from the pages of LGBTQ+ novels as this fiction has made the transition from problem novel to contemporary realistic fiction. Now, like the rest of young adult literature, it must continue to come of age *as literature.*

Yes, it still needs to be evaluated on the basis of the authenticity of its portrayal of LGBTQ+ adults and teens and the world they inhabit, but it also needs to be evaluated as literature. Does it offer multidimensional characters? Does it have a setting rich in verisimilitude? Does it have not only an authentic but an original voice? Does it offer fresh insights into the lives of LGBTQ+ people? Does it offer other innovations in terms of narrative strategy, structure, theme? Or is it the same old story, told in the same old way that readers have encountered too many times in the past? In short, LGBTQ+ literature must be not only an inclusive and authentic literature, it must be an artful literature as well.

We close with these words, which we believe are as relevant today as they were in 2004 when they concluded *The Heart Has Its Reasons*:

> Nonfiction gives us information for our minds. But we need good LGBTQ+ fiction, too, because novels give us information for our hearts. It is not enough to comprehend the homosexual experience on a cognitive level; we must de-

velop an empathetic understanding as well. Don't forget: the heart has its reasons that the mind cannot know. And if we are to insure that love—not ignorance and its evil twin hatred—wins, then it is imperative that good books on the homosexual experience be read not only by gay and lesbian teens but also by their heterosexual peers. Ignorance demonizes those who are different. Good books bestow knowledge by showing us the commonalities of our human hearts.

Appendix A

Bibliography of LGBTQ+ Titles: Fiction, Comics and Graphic Novels, and Nonfiction

Note that we use the following abbreviations: "G" identifies fiction with gay male characters; "L" identifies fiction with lesbian characters. "Bi-F" and "Bi-M" identifies fiction with female or male bisexual characters, respectively. "MtF-Transgender" and "FtM-Transgender" identifies fiction with transgender characters who are male-to-female and female-to-male, respectively. "M-xdress" identifies fiction with male characters who choose to dress in female-gendered clothing. Other identities are spelled out in full.

"HV" stands for homosexual visibility; "GA" stands for gay assimilation; "QC" stands for queer consciousness/community. Books may have more than one designation, depending on the plot. For further information on codes, see appendix D.

"Pro" indicates that the book's protagonist is LGBTQ+, though other characters may be as well; "Sec" indicates that the protagonist is not LGBTQ+, but one or more secondary—or supporting—characters are. "Pro/Sec" indicates an LGBTQ+ protagonist *and* one or more secondary character(s). A title coded "Pro/Sec" may be a short story collection or a novel.

LGBTQ+ YA FICTION OF THE 1960s

1969

Donovan, John. *I'll Get There. It Better Be Worth the Trip.* New York: Harper & Row, 1969. G HV Pro

LGBTQ+ YA FICTION OF THE 1970s

1972

Holland, Isabelle. *The Man without a Face*. New York: Lippincott, 1972. [filmed in 1993 minus its gay content] G HV Pro

1974

Scoppettone, Sandra. *Trying Hard to Hear You*. New York: Harper & Row, 1974. G HV Sec

1976

Guy, Rosa. *Ruby*. New York: Viking, 1976. L HV Pro
Sullivan, Mary W. *What's This about Pete?* New York: Nelson, 1976. G HV Pro

1977

Hall, Lynn. *Sticks and Stones*. Chicago: Follett, 1977. G HV Sec
Kerr, M. E. *I'll Love You When You're More Like Me*. New York: Harper & Row, 1977. G GA Sec

1978

Hautzig, Deborah. *Hey, Dollface*. New York: Greenwillow, 1978. L HV Pro
Scoppettone, Sandra. *Happy Endings Are All Alike*. New York: Harper & Row, 1978. L HV Pro

1979

Rees, David. *In the Tent*. London: Dobson Books, 1979. [Boston: Alyson, 1985]. G QC Pro

LGBTQ+ YA FICTION OF THE 1980s

1980

Hanlon, Emily. *The Wing and the Flame*. Scarsdale, NY: Bradbury, 1980. G HV Pro
Klein, Norma. *Breaking Up*. New York: Random House, 1980. L HV Sec
Reading, J. P. *Bouquets for Brimbal*. New York: Harper, 1980. L HV Sec
Tolan, Stephanie S. *The Last of Eden*. New York: Warne, 1980. L HV Sec

1981

Barger, Gary W. *What Happened to Mr. Forster?* New York: Clarion, 1981. G HV Sec
Futcher, Jane. *Crush*. Boston: Little, Brown, 1981. L HV Sec
Levy, Elizabeth. *Come Out Smiling*. New York: Delacorte, 1981. L HV Sec
Snyder, Anne, and Louis Pelletier. *Counterplay*. New York: New American Library, 1981. [reissued in 1987 as *The Truth about Alex*] G HV Sec
St. George, Judith. *Call Me Margo*. New York: Putnam, 1981. L HV Sec

1982

Bunn, Scott. *Just Hold On*. New York: Delacorte, 1982. G HV Pro
Chambers, Aidan. *Dance on My Grave*. New York: Harper & Row, 1982. G HV Pro
Garden, Nancy. *Annie on My Mind*. New York: Farrar, Straus & Giroux, 1982. L HV/QC Pro/ Sec
Hulce, Larry. *Just the Right Amount of Wrong*. New York: Harper & Row, 1982. G HV Sec
Rees, David. *The Milkman's on His Way*. London: Gay Men's Press, 1982. G HV/QC Pro

1983

Ecker, B. A. *Independence Day*. New York: Avon, 1983. G HV Sec
Kesselman, Wendy. *Flick*. New York: Harper & Row, 1983. L HV Pro
Mosca, Frank. *All-American Boys*. Boston: Alyson, 1983. G HV/QC Pro
Singer, Marilyn. *The Course of True Love Never Did Run Smooth*. New York: Harper & Row, 1983. G HV Sec

1984

Ireland, Timothy. *Who Lies Inside*. London: Gay Men's Press, 1984. G HV Pro
L'Engle, Madeleine. *A House Like a Lotus*. New York: Farrar, Straus & Giroux, 1984. L HV Sec
Rees, David. *Out of the Winter Gardens*. London: Olive, 1984. G HV/QC Sec
Ure, Jean. *You Win Some, You Lose Some*. New York: Delacorte, 1984. G HV Sec

1985

Bess, Clayton. *Big Man and the Burn-Out*. Boston: Houghton Mifflin, 1985. G HV Sec

1986

Colman, Hila. *Happily Ever After*. New York: Scholastic, 1986. G HV Sec
Kerr, M. E. *Night Kites*. New York: Harper & Row, 1986. G HV Sec
Meyer, Carolyn. *Elliott and Win*. New York: Atheneum, 1986. G HV Sec
Sakers, Don. *Act Well Your Part*. Boston: Alyson, 1986. G HV Pro
Ure, Jean. *The Other Side of the Fence*. New York: Delacorte, 1986. G/L HV/GA Pro/Sec
Wersba, Barbara. *Crazy Vanilla*. Harper & Row, 1986. G HV Sec

1987

Klein, Norma. *My Life as a Body*. New York: Knopf, 1987. L/G GA Sec
Rinaldi, Ann. *The Good Side of My Heart*. New York: Holiday House, 1987. G HV Sec

1988

Klein, Norma. *Now That I Know*. New York: Knopf, 1988. G HV Sec
Koertge, Ron. *The Arizona Kid*. Boston: Little, Brown, 1988. G GA/QC Sec
Wersba, Barbara. *Just Be Gorgeous*. New York: Harper & Row, 1988. G HV Sec

1989

Block, Francesca Lia. *Weetzie Bat*. New York: Harper & Row, 1989. G HV/QC Sec

Brett, Catherine. *S.P. Likes A.D.* Toronto: Women's Press, 1989. L HV/QC Pro/Sec
Childress, Alice. *Those Other People.* New York: Putnam, 1989. G HV Sec
Homes, A. M. *Jack.* New York: Macmillan, 1989. G HV Sec
Rees, David. *The Colour of His Hair.* Exeter, UK: Third House, 1989. G HV/QC Pro
Shannon, George. *Unlived Affections.* New York: Harper & Row, 1989. G HV Sec

LGBTQ+ YA FICTION OF THE 1990s

1990

Levy, Marilyn. *Rumors and Whispers.* New York: Ballantine, 1990. G HV Sec
Sweeney, Joyce. *Face the Dragon.* New York: Delacorte, 1990. G HV Sec
Walker, Paul Robert. *The Method.* New York: HBJ Gulliver, 1990. G HV/QC Sec
Westall, Robert. *The Kingdom by the Sea.* New York: Farrar, Straus & Giroux, 1990. G HV Sec

1991

Block, Francesca Lia. *Witch Baby.* New York: Zolotow/HarperCollins, 1991. G HV/GA Sec
Crutcher, Chris. *Athletic Shorts.* New York: Greenwillow, 1991. [short stories] G HV/GA Sec
Garden, Nancy. *Lark in the Morning.* New York: Farrar, Straus & Giroux, 1991. L GA Pro
Gleitzman, Morris. *Two Weeks with the Queen.* New York: Putnam, 1991. G GA Sec
Greene, Bette. *The Drowning of Stephan Jones.* New York: Bantam, 1991. G HV Sec
Maguire, Jesse. *Getting It Right.* New York: Ivy/Ballantine, 1991. G HV QC Sec
Pascal, Francine. *Amy's True Love.* Sweet Valley High #75. New York: Scholastic, 1991. G HV Sec
Woodson, Jacqueline. *The Dear One.* New York: Delacorte, 1991. L GA Sec

1992

Durant, Penny Raife. *When Heroes Die.* New York: Atheneum, 1992. G HV Sec
Isensee, Rik. *We're Not Alone.* Fairfield, CT: Lavender, 1992. L/G HV Pro
Wieler, Diana. *Bad Boy.* New York: Delacorte, 1992. G HV Sec

1993

Bess, Clayton. *The Mayday Rampage.* Lookout, 1993. G HV Sec
Block, Francesca Lia. *Missing Angel Juan.* New York: Harper, 1993. G/MtF-Transgender Sec
Dhondy, Farrukh. *Black Swan.* Boston: Houghton Mifflin, 1993. G HV Sec
Kaye, Marilyn. *Real Heroes.* Boston: Gulliver/Harcourt, 1993. G HV Sec
Mullins, Hilary. *The Cat Came Back.* Tallahassee, FL: Naiad, 1993. L HV Pro
Murrow, Lisa Ketchum. *Twelve Days in August.* New York: Holiday House, 1993. G HV Sec
Salat, Cristina. *Living in Secret.* New York: Bantam, 1993. L HV/QC Sec
Walker, Kate. *Peter.* Boston: Houghton, 1993. G HV/GA Sec

1994

Bauer, Marion Dane. *Am I Blue? New York:* HarperCollins, 1994. [short stories] G/L HV/GA/QC Pro/Sec
Davis, Deborah. *My Brother Has AIDS.* New York: Atheneum, 1994. G GA Sec
Donovan, Stacey. *Dive.* New York: Dutton, 1994. L HV Pro
Kerr, M. E. *Deliver Us from Evie.* New York; HarperCollins, 1994. L HV/QC Sec

McClain, Ellen Jaffee. *No Big Deal.* New York: Lodestar, 1994. G HV Sec
Nelson, Blake. *Girl.* New York: Simon & Schuster, 1994. G HV Sec
Nelson, Theresa. *Earthshine.* New York: Orchard, 1994. G GA Sec
Paulsen, Gary. *The Car.* New York: Harcourt, 1994. G GA Sec

1995

Bantle, Lee F. *Diving for the Moon.* New York: Macmillan, 1995. G GA Sec
Block, Francesca Lia. *Baby Bebop.* New York: HarperCollins, 1995. G HV QC Pro
Brown, Todd D. *Entries from a Hot Pink Notebook.* New York: Washington Square, 1995. G HV Pro
Crutcher, Chris. *Ironman.* New York: Greenwillow, 1995. G HV Sec
Fox, Paula. *The Eagle Kite.* New York: Orchard, 1995. G HV Sec
Hamilton, R. J. *Who Framed Lorenzo Garcia?* Pride Pack series #1. Boston: Alyson, 1995. G/L GA/QC Pro/Sec
———. *The Case of the Missing Mother.* Pride Pack series #2. Boston: Alyson, 1995. L GA/QC Sec
Springer, Nancy. *Looking for Jamie Bridger.* New York: Dial, 1995. G HV Sec
Van Dijk, Lutz. *Damned Strong Love.* New York: Holt, 1995. G GA Pro
Velasquez, Gloria. *Tommy Stands Alone.* Houston, TX: Arte Publico, 1995. G HV Pro/Sec
Woodson, Jacqueline. *From the Notebooks of Melanin Sun.* New York: Scholastic, 1995. L HV/QC Sec

1996

Block, Francesca Lia. *Girl Goddess #9.* New York: HarperCollins, 1996. [short stories] G MtF-Transgender HV Sec
Cart, Michael. *My Father's Scar.* New York: Simon & Schuster, 1996. G HV Pro Sec
Cooper, Melrose. *Life Magic.* New York: Holt, 1996. G HV Sec.
Garden, Nancy. *Good Moon Rising.* New York: Farrar, Straus & Giroux, 1995. L/G HV Pro/Sec
Lynch, Chris. *Dog Eat Dog.* Blue Eyed Son Trilogy. New York: Harper Trophy, 1996. G HV Sec
Maguire, Gregory. *Oasis.* New York: Clarion, 1996. G HV Sec
Pausacker, Jenny, ed. *Hide and Seek: Stories about Being Young and Gay/Lesbian.* Victoria, Australia: Mandarin, 1996. [short stories] G/L HV/GA/QC Pro/Sec
Zalben, Jane Breskin. *Unfinished Dreams.* New York: Simon & Schuster, 1996. G HV Sec

1997

Coville, Bruce. *The Skull of Truth.* A Magic Shop Book. New York: Harcourt, Brace, 1997. G HV Sec
Dines, Carol. *Talk to Me.* New York: Delacorte, 1997. [short stories] L GA Sec
Donoghue, Emma. *Kissing the Witch: Old Tales in New Skins.* New York: Cotler/HarperCollins, 1997. [short stories] L HV/GA/QC Pro
Gantos, Jack. *Desire Lines.* New York: Farrar, Straus & Giroux, 1997. L HV Sec
Griffin, Adele. *Split Just Right.* New York: Hyperion, 1997. G GA Sec
Jenkins, A. M. *Breaking Boxes.* New York: Delacorte, 1997. G HV/GA Sec
Kerr, M. E. *"Hello," I Lied.* New York: HarperCollins, 1997. Bi-M/G HV Pro
Ketchum, Lisa. *Blue Coyote.* New York: Simon & Schuster, 1997. G HV Pro
Larson, Rodger. *What I Know Now.* New York: Holt, 1997. G HV/QC Sec
Mowry, Jess. *Babylon Boyz.* New York: Simon & Schuster, 1997. G GA Pro
Wersba, Barbara. *Whistle Me Home.* New York: Holt, 1997. G HV Sec
Woodson, Jacqueline. *The House You Pass on the Way.* New York: Delacorte, 1997. L HV Pro

1998

Block, Francesca Lia. *I Was a Teenage Fairy.* New York: HarperCollins, 1998. G GA Sec
Revoyr, Nina. *The Necessary Hunger.* New York: St. Martin's, 1998. L HV Pro
Stoehr, Shelley. *Tomorrow Wendy: A Love Story.* New York: Delacorte, 1998. L HV Sec

1999

Atkins, Catherine. *When Jeff Comes Home.* New York: Putnam, 1999. G HV Sec
Bechard, Margaret. *If It Doesn't Kill You.* New York: Viking, 1999. G HV Sec
Boock, Paula. *Dare Truth or Promise.* New York: Houghton, 1999. L HV Pro
Chbosky, Stephen. *The Perks of Being a Wallflower.* New York: MTV/Pocket, 1999. G HV/
  GA Sec
Durbin, Peggy. *And Featuring Bailey Wellcom as the Biscuit.* Port Orchard, WA: Little Blue
  Works, 1999. G HV Sec
Garden, Nancy. *The Year They Burned the Books.* New York: Farrar, Straus & Giroux, 1999. L/
  G HV/QC Pro
Naylor, Phyllis Reynolds. *Alice on the Outside.* New York: Atheneum, 1999. L HV Sec
Nolan, Han. *A Face in Every Window.* New York: Harcourt, 1999. G HV Sec
Taylor, William. *Blue Lawn.* Boston: Alyson, 1999. G HV Pro
———. *Jerome.* Boston: Alyson, 1999. G/L HV Sec
Torres, Laura. *November Ever After.* New York: Holiday House, 1999. L HV Sec
Wittlinger, Ellen. *Hard Love.* New York: Simon & Schuster, 1999. L GA QC Sec
Yamanaka, Lois-Ann. *Name Me Nobody.* New York: Hyperion, 1999. L HV Sec

LGBTQ+ YA FICTION OF THE 2000s

2000

Appelt, Kathi. *Kissing Tennessee, and Other Stories from the Stardust Dance.* New York:
  Harcourt, 2000. [short stories] G HV Sec
Ferris, Jean. *Eight Seconds.* New York: Harcourt, 2000. G HV Sec
Garden, Nancy. *Holly's Secret.* New York: Farrar, Straus & Giroux, 2000. L HV/QC Sec
Hines, Sue. *Out of the Shadows.* New York: Avon Tempest, 2000. L HV Sec
Wittlinger, Ellen. *What's in a Name?* New York: Simon & Schuster, 2000. G HV/QC Sec
Wright, Bil. *Sunday You Learn How to Box.* New York: Simon & Schuster, 2000. G HV Pro

2001

Cart, Michael, ed. *Love & Sex: Ten Stories of Truth.* New York: Simon & Schuster, 2001.
  [short stories] "The Acuteness of Desire," by Michael Lowenthal, G HV Pro; "The Wel-
  come," by Emma Donoghue, L/MtF-Transgender HV Pro
Hartnett, P-P, ed. *The Gay Times Book of Short Stories: The Next Wave.* London: Gay Times
  Books, 2001. [short stories] G HV/GA/QC Pro/Sec
Howe, James. *The Misfits.* New York: Simon & Schuster, 2001. G HV/GA Sec
Killingsworth, Monte. *Equinox.* New York: Holt, 2001. L HV Sec
Reynolds, Marilyn. *Love Rules.* Buena Park, CA: Morning Glory, 2001. L HV Sec
Ryan, Sara. *Empress of the World.* New York: Viking, 2001. L/Bi-F HV/GA Pro
Sanchez, Alex. *Rainbow Boys.* New York: Simon & Schuster, 2001. G HV/GA/QC Pro
Taylor, Kim. *Cissy Funk.* New York: HarperCollins, 2001. L HV Sec
Thibou, F. *The Foul Line.* San Jose, CA: Writers Club, 2001. L HV Pro
Toten, Teresa. *The Game.* Markham, ON: Red Deer, 2001. G HV/GA Sec
Vande Velde, Vivian. *Alison, Who Went Away.* Houghton Mifflin, 2001. G HV Sec

Watts, Julia. *Finding H.F.* Los Angeles: Alyson, 2001. L/G QC Pro
Withrow, Sarah. *Box Girl.* Toronto: Groundwood/Douglas & McIntyre, 2001. G HV Sec
Wittlinger, Ellen. *Razzle.* New York: Simon & Schuster, 2001. G GA Sec
Wolff, Virginia Euwer. *True Believer.* New York: Atheneum, 2001. G HV Sec

2002

Alphin, Elaine Marie. *Simon Says.* New York: Harcourt, 2002. G HV Sec
Chambers, Aidan. *Postcards from No Man's Land.* New York: Dutton, 2002. G HV/GA/QC
Pro
Cohn, Rachel. *Gingerbread.* New York: Simon & Schuster, 2002. G GA Sec
Desai Hidier, Tanuja. *Born Confused.* New York: Scholastic, 2002. L GA Sec
Freymann-Weyr, Garret. *My Heartbeat.* New York: Houghton Mifflin, 2002. G/Bi-M HV Sec
Lowenthal, Michael. *Avoidance.* St. Paul, MN: Graywolf, 2002. G HV Pro
Malloy, Brian. *The Year of Ice.* New York: St. Martin's, 2002. G HV Pro
Newbery, Linda. *The Shell House.* New York: Random House, 2002. G HV Pro
Plum-Ucci, Carol. *What Happened to Lani Garver.* New York: Harcourt, 2002. MtF-Transgen-
der HV Sec
Shimko, Bonnie. *Letters in the Attic.* Chicago: Academy Chicago Press, 2002. L HV Pro
Shyer, Marlene Fanta. *Rainbow Kite.* Tarrytown, NY: Marshall Cavendish, 2002. G HV Sec
Wallens, Scott. *Exposed.* Sevens, Week 2. New York: Puffin, 2002. G HV Pro
Williams, Tamara. *Truth and Lies.* Toronto: James Lorimer, 2002. G HV Sec
Wilson, Barbara. *A Clear Spring.* New York: Girls First/Feminist, 2002. L GA Sec

2003

Atkins, Catherine. *Alt Ed.* New York: Dutton: 2003. G HV Sec
Benduhn, Tea. *Gravel Queen.* New York: Simon & Schuster, 2003. L HV Pro
Brennan, Herbie. *Faerie Wars.* London: Bloomsbury, 2003. L HV Sec
Cart, Michael, ed. *Necessary Noise: Stories about Our Families as They Really Are.* New York:
HarperCollins/Cotler, 2003. [short stories] "Sailing Away," by Michael Cart. G HV Pro
Davis, Rebecca Fjelland. *Jake Riley: Irreparably Damaged.* New York: Harper Tempest, 2003.
G HV Sec
Doyle, Brian. *Boy O'Boy.* Toronto: Groundwood, 2003. G HV Sec
Frost, Helen. *Keesha's House.* New York: Farrar, Straus & Giroux, 2003. G HV Sec
Hartinger, Brent. *Geography Club.* New York: Harper Tempest, 2003. G/L HV/QC Pro
Huser, Glen. *Stitches.* Toronto: Groundwood Books, 2003. G HV Pro
Johnson, Kathleen Jeffrie. *Target.* Brookfield, CT: Roaring Brook, 2003. G HV Pro
Levithan, David. *Boy Meets Boy.* New York: Knopf, 2003. G GA/QC Pro
Matthews, Andrew. *The Flip Side.* New York: Delacorte, 2003. G HV Pro
Murray, Martine. *The Slightly True Story of Cedar B. Hartley.* New York: Scholastic, 2003. G
GA Sec
Myracle, Lauren. *Kissing Kate.* New York: Dutton, 2003. L HV Pro
Oates, Joyce Carol. *Freaky Green Eyes.* New York: Harper Tempest, 2003. G HV Sec
Peters, Julie Anne. *Keeping You a Secret.* Boston: Little, Brown, 2003. L HV/QC Pro
Rapp, Adam. *33 Snowfish.* Cambridge, MA: Candlewick, 2003 G HV Sec
Ripslinger, Jon. *How I Fell in Love and Learned to Shoot Free Throws.* New York: Roaring
Brook, 2003. L HV Sec
Sanchez, Alex. *Rainbow High.* New York: Simon & Schuster, 2003. G HV/QC Pro
Taylor, William. *Pebble in a Pool.* Los Angeles: Alyson, 2003. G HV Pro
Trujillo, Carla. *What Night Brings.* Willimantic, CT: Curbstone, 2003. L HV Pro
Wallace, Rich. *Losing Is Not an Option.* New York: Knopf, 2003. [short stories] G HV Sec
Yates, Bart. *Leave Myself Behind.* New York: Kensington, 2003. G HV Pro

2004

Cohn, Rachel. *Pop Princess*. Simon & Schuster, 2004. L HV Sec
De Oliveira, Eddie. *Lucky*. New York: Scholastic, 2004. Bi-M HV/QC Pro
Earls, Nick. *48 Shades of Brown*. Boston: Graphia/Houghton, 2004. L HV Sec
Halpin, Brendan. *Donorboy*. New York: Villard, 2004. G GA Sec
Hite, Sid. *The King of Slippery Falls*. New York: Scholastic, 2004. G HV Sec
Jahn-Clough, Lisa. *Country Girl, City Girl*. Boston: Houghton, 2004. L HV Pro
Jinks, Catherine. *Pagan in Exile*. Cambridge, MA: Candlewick, 2004. G HV Sec
Johnson, Maureen. *The Bermudez Triangle*. [Retitled *On the Count of Three* in 2013.] New
    York: Razorbill/Penguin, 2004. L/Bi-F HV/QC Pro
Kaslik, Ibi. *Skinny*. New York: Walker Books, 2004. Bi-F GA Pro
Kemp, Kristen. *The Dating Diaries*. New York: Push/Scholastic, 2004. L HV/GA Sec
Levithan, David. *The Realm of Possibility*. New York: Knopf, 2004. G/L HV/GA Pro
Lyon, George Ella. *Sonny's House of Spies*. New York: Atheneum, 2004. G HV Sec
MacLean, Judy. *Rosemary and Juliet*. New York: Alice Street Editions, 2004. L HV Pro
Martin, Ann M. *Here Today*. New York: Scholastic, 2004. L HV Sec
Peters, Julie Anne. *Luna*. Boston: Little, Brown, 2004. MtF-Transgender HV Sec
Sáenz, Benjamin Alire. *Sammy and Juliana in Hollywood*. El Paso, TX: Cinco Puntos, 2004. G
    HV Sec
Sanchez, Alex. *So Hard to Say*. New York: Simon & Schuster, 2004. G HV Pro
Sones, Sonya. *One of Those Hideous Books Where the Mother Dies*. New York: Simon &
    Schuster, 2004. G HV Sec
Wallace, Kim. *Erik & Isabelle Freshman Year at Foresthill High*. Sacramento, CA: Foglight,
    2004. G/L HV/QC Pro Sec
Wittlinger, Ellen. *Heart on My Sleeve*. New York: Simon & Schuster, 2004. L HV Sec
Wyeth, Sharon Dennis. *Orphea Proud*. New York: Delacorte, 2004. L HV Pro

2005

Amateau, Gigi. *Claiming Georgia Tate*. Cambridge, MA: Candlewick, 2005. G HV Sec
Burchill, Julie. *Sugar Rush*. New York: Harper Tempest, 2005. L GA Pro
Cirrone, Dorian. *Dancing in Red Shoes Will Kill You*. New York: HarperCollins, 2005. G GA
    Sec
Coy, John. *Crackback*. New York: Scholastic, 2005. G HV Sec
Hartinger, Bret. *The Order of the Poison Oak*. New York: Harper Tempest, 2005. G/L GA Pro
Hoffman, Alice. *The Foretelling*. Boston: Little, Brown, 2005. L GA Sec
Howe, James. *Totally Joe*. New York: Atheneum, 2005. G HV Pro
Jacobson, Jennifer Richard. *Stained*. New York: Atheneum, 2005. G HV Sec
Koertge, Ron. *Boy Girl Boy*. New York: Harcourt, 2005. G GA Sec
Koja, Kathe. *Talk*. New York: Farrar, Straus & Giroux, 2005. G HV Pro
Larochelle, David. *Absolutely, Positively Not*. New York: Scholastic, 2005. G HV Pro
Limb, Sue. *Girl (Nearly) 16, Absolute Torture*. New York: Delacorte, 2005. G GA Sec
Manning, Sarra. *Pretty Things*. New York: Dutton, 2005. G/L GA Pro
Papademetriou, Lisa, and Christopher Tebbetts. *M or F?* New York: Razorbill/Penguin, 2005.
    G GA Sec
Peters, Julie Anne. *Far from Xanadu*. [Retitled *Pretend You Love Me* in 2007.] Boston: Little,
    Brown, 2005. G/L GA Pro
Pierce, Tamora. *The Will of the Empress*. New York: Scholastic, 2005. L HV Sec
Poole, Blair. *Breathe*. Princeton, NJ: Burrows, 2005. G HV Pro
Roth, Matthue. *Never Mind the Goldbergs*. New York: Push/Scholastic, 2005. G GA Sec
Ruditis, Paul. *Rainbow Party*. New York: Simon Pulse, 2005. G HV Sec
Sanchez, Alex. *Rainbow Road*. New York: Simon & Schuster, 2005. G GA Pro
Selvadurai, Shyam. *Swimming in the Monsoon Sea*. Toronto: Tundra Books, 2005. G HV Pro
Sloan, Brian. *A Really Nice Prom Mess*. New York: Simon & Schuster, 2005. G HV/QC Pro
Steinhöfel, Andreas. *The Center of the World*. New York: Delacorte, 2005. G GA Pro

Stine, Catherine. *Refugees.* New York: Delacorte, 2005. G HV Sec

Wallace, Kim. *Erik & Isabelle Sophomore Year at Foresthill High.* Sacramento, CA: Foglight, 2005. G/L HV/GA/QC Pro Sec

Weyn, Suzanne, and Diana Gonzalez. *South Beach Sizzle.* New York: Simon Pulse, 2005. G GA Sec

Withrow, Sarah. *What Gloria Wants.* New York: Groundwood, 2005. G GA Sec

2006

Barnes, Derrick D. *The Making of Dr. Truelove.* New York: Simon Pulse, 2006. L GA Sec

Bildner, Phil. *Playing the Field.* New York: Simon & Schuster, 2006. G GA/QC Sec

Burch, Christian. *The Manny Files.* New York: Atheneum, 2006. G GA Sec

Carlson, Melody. *Bright Purple: Color Me Confused.* Colorado Springs, CO: NavPress/Tyndale, 2006. L HV/GA Sec

Cohn, Rachel, and David Levithan. *Nick and Norah's Infinite Playlist.* New York: Knopf, 2006. G GA Sec

Embree, Michelle. *Manstealing for Fat Girls.* Brooklyn, NY: Soft Skull, 2006. L GA Pro

Friend, Natasha. *Lush.* New York: Scholastic, 2006. G HV Sec

Fullerton, Alma. *In the Garage.* Calgary, AB: Red Deer, 2006. L HV Pro

Goobie, Beth. *Hello, Groin.* Victoria, BC: Orca Books, 2006. L HV Pro

Hacker, Randi. *Life as I Knew It.* New York: Simon Pulse, 2006. G/L HV/GA/QC Sec

Hall, John. *Is He or Isn't He?* New York: Avon, 2006. G GA Pro

Hartinger, Brent. *Grand & Humble.* New York: HarperTeen, 2006. G GA Sec

Hyde, Catherine Ryan. *Becoming Chloe.* New York: Knopf, 2006. G GA Pro

Korman, Gordon. *Born to Rock.* New York: Hyperion, 2006. G HV Sec

Levithan, David. *Wide Awake.* New York: Knopf, 2006. G,/L GA Pro

Lockhart, E. *Fly on the Wall: How One Girl Saw Everything.* New York: Delacorte, 2006. G GA Sec

Mac, Carrie. *Crush.* Vancouver, BC: Orca Books, 2006. L GA Pro

Murdock, Catherine Gilbert. *Dairy Queen.* Houghton Mifflin, 2006. L GA Sec

Nelson, Blake. *Prom Anonymous.* New York: Viking, 2006. G GA Sec

Peters, Julie Anne. *Between Mom and Jo.* Boston: Little, Brown, 2006. L GA Sec

Reisz, Kristopher. *Tripping to Somewhere.* New York: Simon Pulse, 2006. L GA Pro

Sanchez, Alex. *Getting It.* New York: Simon & Schuster, 2006. G GA Pro

Shaw, Tucker. *The Hookup Artist.* New York: HarperCollins, 2006. G GA Pro

Sloan, Brian. *Tale of Two Summers.* New York: Simon & Schuster, 2006. G HV Pro

Wallace, Kim. *Erik & Isabelle Junior Year at Foresthill High.* Sacramento, CA: Foglight, 2006. G/L HV/QC Pro Sec

2007

Bauer, A. C. E. *No Castles Here.* New York: Random, 2007. G HV Pro

Berman, Steve. *Vintage: A Ghost Story.* New York: Haworth, 2007. G GA Pro

Bildner, Phil. *Busted!* New York: Simon & Schuster, 2007. G HV Sec

Blank, Jessica. *Almost Home.* New York: Hyperion, 2007. G GA Sec

Brooks, Martha. *Mistik Lake.* New York: Farrar, Straus & Giroux, 2007. L HV Sec

Cameron, Peter. *Someday This Pain Will Be Useful to You.* New York: Farrar, Straus & Giroux, 2007. G HV Pro

Chambers, Aidan. *This Is All: The Pillow Book of Cordelia Kenn.* New York: Amulet/Abrams, 2007. G GA Sec

Chase, Dakota. *Changing Jamie.* Round Rock, TX: Prizm/Torquere, 2007. G HV/QC Pro

Clare, Cassandra. *City of Bones.* New York: Simon & Schuster, 2007. G HV/GA Pro/Sec

Cohn, Rachel. *Cupcake.* New York: Simon & Schuster, 2007. G GA Sec

Cohn, Rachel, and David Levithan, *Naomi and Ely's No Kiss List.* New York: Knopf, 2007. G GA Pro

Felin, M. Sindy. *Touching Snow*. New York: Atheneum, 2007. L HV Pro
Garden, Nancy. *Hear Us Out: Lesbian and Gay Stories of Struggle, Progress, and Hope, 1950 to the Present*. New York: Farrar, Straus & Giroux, 2007. [short stories] L/G HV/GA/QC Pro/Sec
Golden, Christopher. *Poison Ink*. New York: Delacorte, 2008. L GA Sec
Hartinger, Brent. *Split Screen: Attack of the Soul-Sucking Brain Zombies / Bride of the Soul-Sucking Brain Zombies*. New York: HarperTeen, 2007. G/L HV/GA/QC Pro
Hopkins, Ellen. *Impulse*. New York: Margaret K. McElderry, 2007. G GA Pro
Imes, Jarold. *5 Miles to Empty*. Winston-Salem, NC: Abednego's Free, 2007. G GA Sec
Jones, Carrie. *Tips on Having a Gay (Ex) Boyfriend*. St. Paul, MN: Llewellyn, 2007. G HV/GA Sec
Juby, Susan. *Another Kind of Cowboy*. New York: HarperTeen, 2007. G HV/GA Sec
Kizer, Amber. *Gert Garibaldi's Rants and Raves: One Butt Cheek at a Time*. New York: Delacorte, 2007. G HV Sec
Knowles, Jo. *Lessons from a Dead Girl*. Somerville, MA: Candlewick, 2007. L HV Pro
Konigsburg, E. L. *The Mysterious Edge of the Heroic World*. New York: Atheneum, 2007. G HV Sec
Lockhart, E. *Dramarama*. New York: Hyperion, 2007. G GA Sec
Mac, Carrie. *The Beckoners*. Vancouver, BC: Orca, 2007. G GA Sec
Medina, Nico. *The Straight Road to Kylie*. New York: Simon Pulse, 2007. G GA Pro
Moore, Perry. *Hero*. New York: Hyperion, 2007. G HV/GA Pro
Murdock, Catherine Gilbert. *The Off Season*. New York: Houghton Mifflin, 2007. L GA Sec
Penny, Patricia G. *Belinda's Obsession*. Not Just Proms & Parties series. Toronto: Lobster, 2007. L GA Pro
Peters, Julie Anne. *grl2grl: Short Fictions*. Boston: Little, Brown, 2007. [short stories] L HV/GA/QC Pro/Sec
Reynolds, Marilyn. *No More Sad Goodbyes*. Hamilton High. Buena Park, CA: Morning Glory, 2007. L GA Sec
Ryan, P. E. *Saints of Augustine*. New York: HarperTeen, 2007. G HV Pro
Ryan, Sara. *The Rules for Hearts*. New York: Viking, 2007. L GA Pro
Sanchez, Alex. *The God Box*. New York: Simon & Schuster, 2007. G HV/GA/QC Pro
Stinson, Kathy. *101 Ways to Dance*. Toronto: Second Story, 2007. [short stories] G/L HV/GA/QC Pro/Sec
St. James, James. *Freak Show*. New York: Dutton, 2007. G GA Pro
Trueman, Terry. *7 Days at the Hot Corner*. New York: HarperTeen, 2007. G GA Sec
Vickers, Lu. *Breathing Underwater*. Los Angeles: Alyson, 2007. L HV/GA Pro
Wallace, Kim. *Erik & Isabelle Senior Year at Foresthill High*. Sacramento, CA: Foglight, 2007. G/L/MtF-Transgender HV/QC Pro Sec
Weinheimer, Beckie. *Converting Kate*. New York: Viking, 2007. G HV Sec
Whittall, Zoe. *Bottle Rocket Hearts*. Toronto: Cormorant Books, 2007. L GA Pro
Wittlinger, Ellen. *Parrotfish*. New York: Simon & Schuster, 2007. FtM-Transgender HV Pro

2008

Bach, Tamara. *Girl from Mars*. Translated by Shelley Tanaka. Toronto: Groundwood, 2008. L HV Pro
Berman, Steve. *Vintage: A Ghost Story*. Maple Shade, NJ: Lethe, 2008. G HV Pro
Brooks, Kevin. *Black Rabbit Summer*. New York: Penguin, 2008. G HV Sec
Brothers, Meagan. *Debbie Harry Sings in French*. New York: Henry Holt, 2008. M-xdress HV Sec
Burch, Christian. *Hit the Road, Manny*. New York: Atheneum, 2008. G HV/GA Sec
Chase, Dakota. *Changing Jamie*. Round Rock, TX: Prizm, 2008.G HV Pro
Clanton, Barbara L. *Out of Left Field: Marlee's Story*. Clarksonville series #1. Port Arthur, TX: Regal Crest, 2008. L HV Pro
Clare, Cassandra. *City of Ashes*. New York: Simon & Schuster, 2008. G HV Sec
Dole, Mayra Lazara. *Down to the Bone*. New York: HarperCollins, 2008. L GA Pro

Dunnion, Kristyn. *Big Big Sky.* Calgary, AB: Red Deer, 2008. L HV/GA Pro
Ford, Michael Thomas. *Suicide Notes.* New York: HarperTeen 2008. G HV Pro
Geerling, Marjetta. *Fancy White Trash.* New York: Viking, 2008. G HV Sec
Golden, Christopher. *Poison Ink.* New York: Delacorte, 2008. L GA Sec
Goldman, Steven. *Two Parties, One Tux and a Very Short Film about the Grapes of Wrath.* New York: Bloomsbury, 2008. G GA Pro
Hardy, Mark. *Nothing Pink.* New York: Front Street, 2008. G HV Pro
Harmon, Michael. *The Last Exit to Normal.* New York: Knopf, 2008. G GA Sec
Harris, Gina. *I Kiss Girls.* Round Rock, TX: Prizm/Torquere, 2008. L HV Pro
Jones, Carrie. *Love (and Other Uses for Duct Tape).* Woodbury, MN: Flux, 2008. G GA Sec
Kluger, Steve. *My Most Excellent Year: A Novel of Love, Mary Poppins & Fenway Park.* New York: Dial, 2008. G HV Pro
Konigsberg, Bill. *Out of the Pocket.* New York: Dutton, 2008. G HV Pro
Lecesne, James. *Absolute Brightness.* New York: Geringer/HarperCollins, 2008. G GA Sec
Levithan, David. *How They Met, and Other Stories.* New York: Knopf, 2008. [short stories] G/L HV/GA/QC Pro/Sec
Lieberman, Leanne. *Gravity.* Vancouver, BC: Orca, 2008. L HV Pro
Malloy, Brian. *Twelve Long Months.* New York: Scholastic, 2008. G HV Sec
Mazer, Norma Fox. *The Missing Girl.* New York: HarperCollins, 2008. L GA Sec
McLaughlin, Lauren. *Cycler.* New York: Random House, 2008. L GA Sec
McMahon, Jennifer. *My Tiki Girl.* New York: Dutton, 2008. L HV Pro
Medina, Nico. *Fat Hoochie Prom Queen.* New York: Simon & Schuster, 2008. G GA Sec
Rosen, Selina. *Sword Masters.* N.p.: Dragon Moon, 2008. L HV/QC Sec
Roth, Matthue. *Losers.* New York: Push/Scholastic, 2008. G HV Sec
Rud, Jeff. *Crossover.* Vancouver, BC: Orca, 2008. G HV Pro
Ruditis, Paul. *Entrances and Exits.* New York: Simon Pulse, 2008. G GA Pro
Schmatz, Pat. *Mousetraps.* Minneapolis, MN: Carolrhoda Books, 2008. G HV Sec
Smith, Emily Wing. *The Way He Lived.* Woodbury, MN: Flux, 2008. G GA Pro
Stevenson, Robin. *Big Guy.* Vancouver, BC: Orca, 2008. G GA Pro
Wallace, Rich. *Dishes.* New York: Viking, 2008. G GA/QC Sec
Wilson, Martin. *What They Always Tell Us.* New York: Delacorte, 2008. G HV Pro
Wittlinger, Ellen. *Love & Lies: Marisol's Story.* New York: Simon & Schuster, 2008. L/G GA Pro
Woodson, Jacqueline. *After Tupac and D Foster.* New York: Putnam, 2008. G GA Sec

2009

Amateau, Gigi. *A Certain Strain of Peculiar*, 2009. Somerville, MA: Candlewick, 2009. L HV Pro
Bantle, Lee. *David Inside Out.* New York: Henry Holt, 2009. G HV/QC Pro
Beck, P. V. *Sweet Turnaround J.* Fairfield, CA: Fletching Books/Bedazzled Ink, 2009. L HV Pro
Bjorkman, Lauren. *My Invented Life.* New York: Henry Holt, 2009. L GA Sec
Borris, Albert. *Crash into Me.* New York: Simon Pulse, 2009. L GA Sec
Bray, Libba. *Going Bovine.* New York: Delacorte, 2009. G HV Sec
Burd, Nick. *The Vast Fields of Ordinary.* New York: Dial Books, 2009. G HV Pro
Cart, Michael, ed. *How Beautiful the Ordinary: Twelve Stories of Identity.* New York: HarperTeen, 2009. [short stories] G/L HV/GA/QC Pro/Sec
Carter, Timothy. *Evil?* Woodbury, MN: Flux, 2009. G GA Pro
Ceci, Louis Flint. *Comfort Me.* Round Rock, TX: Prizm/Torquere, 2009. G HV Pro
Clanton, Barbara L. *Art for Art's Sake: Meredith's Story.* Port Arthur, TX: Regal Crest, 2009. L HV Sec
———. *Quite an Undertaking: Devon's Story.* Port Arthur, TX: Regal Crest, 2009. L HV Pro
Clare, Cassandra. *City of Glass.* New York: Simon & Schuster, 2009. G GA Sec
Collins, Pat Lowery. *Hidden Voices: The Orphan Musicians of Venice.* Somerville, MA Candlewick, 2009. L HV Pro

Cronn-Mills, Kirstin. *The Sky Always Hears Me and the Hills Don't Mind.* Woodbury, MN: Flux, 2009. L HV Pro
Crutcher, Chris. *Angry Management.* New York: Greenwillow, 2009. G GA Sec
D'Arcangelo, Lyndsey. *The Crabapple Tree.* Green Bay, WI: Alpha World, 2009. L HV Pro
Diersch, Sandra. *Out.* Victoria, BC: Orca, 2009. G GA Sec
Ehrenberg, Pamela. *Tillmon County Fire.* Grand Rapids, MI: Eerdmans, 2009. G GA Sec
Frazer, Megan. *Secrets of Truth & Beauty.* New York: Disney Hyperion, 2009. L/G HV/QC Sec
Garsee, Jeannine. *Say the Word.* New York: Bloomsbury, 2009. L GA Sec
Going, K. L. *King of the Screwups.* New York: Harcourt, 2009. G GA Sec
Gonzalez, Rigoberto. *The Mariposa Club.* Boston: Alyson, 2009. G GA/QC Pro
Harding, Robyn. *My Parents Are Sex Maniacs: A High School Horror Story.* Toronto: Annick, 2009. G HV Sec
Hartinger, Brent. *Project Sweet Life.* New York: HarperTeen, 2009. G GA Sec
Hopkins, Ellen, *Tricks.* New York: Margaret K. McElderry, 2009. G HV/GA Pro
Hurwin, Davida Wills. *Freaks and Revelations.* Boston: Little, Brown, 2009. G GA Sec
Katcher, Brian. *Almost Perfect.* New York: Delacorte, 2009. MtF-Transgender HV Sec
Ketchum, Liza. *Newsgirl.* New York: Viking, 2009. L GA Sec
Levithan, David. *Love Is the Higher Law.* New York: Knopf, 2009. G GA Pro
Lo, Malinda. *Ash.* Boston: Little, Brown, 2009. G GA Pro
Marino, Peter. *Magic and Misery.* New York: Holiday House, 2009. G GA Sec
Murdock, Catherine Gilbert. *Front and Center.* Houghton Mifflin, 2009. L GA Sec
Myracle, Lauren. *Luv Ya Bunches: A Flower Power Book.* New York: Amulet/Abrams, 2009. L GA Sec
Pearce, Jackson. *As You Wish.* New York: HarperTeen, 2009. G GA Sec
Peck, Dale. *Sprout.* New York: Bloomsbury, 2009. G GA Pro
Peters, Julie Anne. *Rage: A Love Story.* New York: Knopf, 2009. L GA Pro
Rapp, Adam. *Punkzilla.* Somerville, MA: Candlewick, 2009. G GA Sec
Ryan, P. E. *In Mike We Trust.* New York: HarperTeen, 2009. G HV Pro
Sanchez, Alex. *Bait.* New York: Simon & Schuster, 2009. G HV Sec
Stevenson, Robin. *Inferno.* Vancouver, BC: Orca Books, 2009. L GA Pro
Walliams, David. *The Boy in the Dress.* Illus. by Quentin Blake. New York: Razorbill, 2009. M-xdress HV Pro
Whatling, Michael. *Vigil for Joe Rose: Stories of Being Out in High School.* Bloomington, IN: iUniverse, 2009. [short stories] G HV/GA/QC Pro/Sec
Wilkinson, Lili. *Pink.* New York: HarperTeen, 2009. L HV Pro

LGBTQ+ YA FICTION FROM 2010 TO 2016

2010

Agell, Charlotte. *The Accidental Adventures of India McAllister.* New York: Holt, 2010. G GA Sec
Appelt, Kathi. *Keeper.* New York: Atheneum, 2010. G HV Sec
Barnes, David-Matthew. *Mesmerized.* Johnsonville, NY: Bold Strokes Books, 2010. G GA Sec
Black, Holly, ed. *Zombies vs. Unicorns.* New York: Margaret K. McElderry Books, 2010. G GA Sec
Block, Francesca Lia. *Frenzy.* New York: HarperCollins, 2010. G HV Sec
Boyd, Maria. *Will.* New York: Knopf, 2010. G HV/QC Sec
Clanton, Barbara L. *Tools of Ignorance: Lisa's Story.* Clarksonville series #2. Maryville, TN: Regal Crest, 2010. L GA Pro
Cohn, Rachel. *Very LeFreak.* New York: Knopf, 2010. Bi-F GA Pro
Colasanti, Susane. *Something Like Fate.* New York: Viking, 2010. G HV Sec
danforth, emily m. *The Miseducation of Cameron Post.* HarperCollins/Balzer + Bray, 2012. L HV Pro

Diaz, Alexandra. *Of All the Stupid Things.* Copenhagen, Denmark: Egmont, 2010. L HV Pro
Donley, Jan. *The Side Door.* Minneapolis, MN: Spinsters, 2010. L GA Pro
Eagland, Jane. *Wildthorn.* New York: Houghton Mifflin Harcourt, 2010. L HV Pro
Edwards, Hazel, and Ryan Kennedy. *F2M: The Boy Within.* Collingwood, Victoria, Australia: Ford Street, 2010. FtM-Transgender. GA Pro
Gonzalez, Rigoberto. *Mariposa Club.* Maple Shade, NJ: Tincture/Lethe, 2010. G GA/QC Pro
Green, John, and David Levithan. *Will Grayson, Will Grayson.* New York: Dutton, 2010. G GA Pro
Horner, Emily. *A Love Story Starring My Dead Best Friend.* New York: Dial, 2010. L GA/QC Pro
Hubbard, Jennifer R. *The Secret Year.* New York: Viking, 2010. G HV Sec
Hyde, Catherine Ryan. *Jumpstart the World.* New York: Knopf, 2010. FtM-Transgender GA Sec
Ignatow, Amy. *The Popularity Papers: Research for the Social Improvement and General Betterment of Lydia Greenblatt and Julie Graham-Chang.* New York: Amulet, 2011. G GA Sec
Klise, James. *Love Drugged.* Woodbury, MN: Flux, 2010. G HV Pro
Lurie, April. *The Less Dead.* New York: Delacorte, 2010. G GA Sec
McCaughrean, Geraldine. *The Death-Defying Pepper Roux.* HarperCollins, 2010. G HV Sec
Murray, Jill. *Rhythm and Blues.* Toronto: Doubleday Canada, 2010. G GA Sec
Murray, Yxta Maya. *Good Girl's Guide to Getting Kidnapped.* New York: Razorbill/Penguin, 2010. L HV Pro
Olsen, Nora. *The End: Five Queer Kids Save the World.* Round Rock, TX: Prizm/Torquere, 2010. G/L GA/QC Pro
Rainfield, Cheryl. *Scars.* Lodi, NJ: Westside Books, 2010. L HV Pro
Rivers, Diana. *City of Strangers.* Tallahassee, FL: Bella Books, 2010. L GA Sec
Shrya, Vivak. *God Loves Hair.* N.p.: Self-published, 2010. G HV Pro
Stuart, Sebastian. *The Hour Between.* New York: Alyson Books, 2010. G HV Pro
Williams, Lori Aurelia. *Maxine Banks Is Getting Married.* New York: Roaring Brook, 2010. L HV Sec
Wilson, Jacqueline. *Kiss.* New York: Roaring Brook, 2010. G HV Sec
Wilson, Martin. *What They Always Tell Us.* New York: Delacorte, 2010. G HV Pro

2011

Adams, S. J. *Sparks: The Epic, Completely True Blue (Almost) Holy Quest of Debbie.* Woodbury, MN: Flux/Llewellyn, 2011. L HV Pro
Barnes, David-Matthew. *Swimming to Chicago.* Valley Falls, NY: Bold Strokes, 2011. G GA Pro
Beam, Cris. *I Am J.* Boston: Little, Brown, 2011. FtM-Transgender GA Pro
Belgue, Nancy. *Soames on the Range.* New York: HarperCollins, 2011. G GA Sec
Bell, Jay. *Something Like Summer.* Los Gatos, CA: Smashwords, 2011. G GA Pro
Berman, Steve, ed. *Speaking Out: Stories of Overcoming Adversity and Experiencing Life after Coming Out.* Valley Falls, NY: Bold Strokes Books, 2011. [short stories] L/G GA/QC Pro
Bray, Libba. *Beauty Queens.* New York: Delacorte, 2011. MtF-Transgender/L HV/GA/QC Sec
Brezenoff, Steve. *Brooklyn Burning.* Minneapolis, MN: Carolrhoda, 2011. Sex unspecified GA Pro
Cameron, Sam. *Mystery of the Tempest.* Valley Falls, NY: Bold Strokes Books, G HV Pro
Clare, Cassandra. *City of Fallen Angels.* New York: Simon & Schuster, 2011. G GA Sec
Cohen, Joshua C. *Leverage.* New York: Dutton, 2011. G HV Sec
Cook, Trish, and Brendan Halpin. *Notes from the Blender.* New York: Egmont, 2011. G GA Sec
Cooper, Michelle. *The FitzOsbornes in Exile: The Montmaray Journals, Book II.* New York: Knopf, 2011. G GA Sec
DeKalb-Rittenhouse, Diane. *Immortal Longings.* Philadelphia: Tiny Satchel, 2011. L/Bi-F GA Pro

Diemer, Sarah. *The Dark Wife*. N.p.: CreateSpace, 2011. L GA Pro
Farrey, Brian. *With or Without You*. New York: Simon Pulse, 2011. G HV Pro
Goode, Laura. *Sister Mischief*. Somerville, MA: Candlewick, 2011. L GA/QC Pro
Hartinger, Brent. *Shadow Walkers*. New York: HarperTeen, 2011. G GA Pro
Herren, Greg. *Sleeping Angel*. Valley Falls, NY: Bold Strokes Books, 2011. G GA Pro
Hopkins, Ellen. *Perfect*. New York: Simon & Schuster, 2011. L HV Sec
Ignatow, Amy. *The Popularity Papers: Book 2: The Long Distance Dispatch between Lydia
    Greenblatt & Julie Graham-Chang*. New York: Amulet, 2011. G GA Sec
————. *The Popularity Papers: Book 3: Three Words of (Questionable) Wisdom from Lydia
    Greenblatt & Julie Graham-Chang*. New York: Amulet, 2011. G GA Sec
Kizer, Amber. *Seven Kinds of Ordinary Catastrophes*. New York: Delacorte, 2011. G HV Sec
Knowles, Jo. *Pearl*. New York: Henry Holt, 2011. L GA Sec
Lo, Malinda. *Huntress*. Boston: Little, Brown, 2011. L HV Pro
Meehl, Brian. *You Don't Know about Me*. New York: Delacorte, 2011. G HV Sec
Mulder, Michelle. *Out of the Box*. Victoria, BC: Orca, 2011. L GA Sec
Myracle, Lauren. *Shine*. New York: Amulet, 2011. G GA Sec
Payne, K. E. *365 Days*. Valley Falls, NY: Bold Strokes Books, 2011. L HV Pro
Perkins, Stephanie. *Lola and the Boy Next Door*. New York: Penguin, 2011. G HV Sec
Peters, Julie Anne. *She Loves You, She Loves You Not*. Boston: Little, Brown, 2011. L HV Pro
Reed, Amy. *Clean*. New York: Simon Pulse, 2011. G HV Pro
Rice, M. L. *Who I Am*. Valley Falls, NY: Bold Strokes Books, 2011. L HV Pro
Rice-Gonzalez, Charles. *Chulito: A Novel*. New York: Magnus Books, 2011. G GA Pro
Ryan, Patrick. *Gemini Bites*. New York: Scholastic, 2011. G GA Pro
Sanchez, Alex. *Boyfriends with Girlfriends*. New York: Simon & Schuster, 2011. G/L/Bi-M
    GA Sec
Scott, Elizabeth. *Between Here and Forever*. New York: Simon Pulse, 2011. L HV Pro
Smith, Andrew. *Stick*. New York: Feiwel and Friends/Macmillan, 2011. G GA Sec
Smith, Julie. *Cursebusters!* Valley Falls, NY: Bold Strokes, 2011. G HV Sec
Volponi, Paul. *Crossing Lines*. New York: Viking, 2011. G GA Sec
Watts, Julia. *Revived Spirits*. N.p.: Beanpole Books, 2011. F HV Pro
Wilkinson, Lili. *Pink*. New York: HarperCollins, 2011. L HV/GA Pro
Wright, Bil. *Putting Makeup on the Fat Boy*. New York: Simon & Schuster, 2011. G GA Pro
Yee, Paul. *Money Boy*. Toronto: Groundwood, 2011. G HV/QC Pro

2012

Backes, M. Molly. *The Princesses of Iowa*. Somerville, MA: Candlewick, 2012. G HV Sec
Berman, Steve, ed. *Boys of Summer*. Valley Falls, NY: Bold Strokes, 2012. G HV/GA Sec
Bigelow, Lisa Jenn. *Starting from Here*. New York: Amazon Children's Publishing/Marshall
    Cavendish, 2012. L GA/QC Sec
Calin, Marisa. *Between You & Me*. New York: Bloomsbury, 2012. L HV Pro
Cameron, Sam. *The Secret of Othello*. Valley Falls, NY: Bold Strokes, 2012. G HV Pro
Cashore, Kristin. *Bitterblue*. New York: Penguin, 2012. L HV Sec
Clanton, Barbara L. *Going, Going, Gone: Susie's Story*. Clarksonville series #3. Nederland,
    TX: Regal Crest, 2012. L HV/GA Pro
Clare, Cassandra. *City of Lost Souls*. New York: Simon & Schuster, 2012. G GA Sec
Cordoba, Jax. *Fate Lends a Hand*. Tallahassee, FL: Harmony Ink, 2012. G GA Pro
Cronn-Mills, Kirstin. *Beautiful Music for Ugly Children*. Woodbury, MN: Flux, 2012. FtM-
    Transgender HV Pro
danforth, emily m. *The Miseducation of Cameron Post*. New York: Balzer + Bray/HarperCol-
    lins, 2012. L HV Pro
Davis, Tanita. *Happy Families*. Random House, 2012. MtF-Transgender GA Sec
DeKelb-Rittenhouse, Diane. *Immortal Longings*. Philadelphia: Tiny Satchel, 2012. L HV Sec
Erich, James. *Dreams of Fire and Gods*. Tallahassee, FL: Harmony Ink, 2012 G HV Pro
————. *Seidman*. Tallahassee, FL: Harmony Ink, 2012. G HV Pro
Erno, Jeff. *Bullied*. Tallahassee, FL: Harmony Ink, 2012. G HV/GA Pro

Franklin, Emily, and Brendan Halpin. *Tessa Masterson Will Go to Prom.* New York: Walker, 2012. L GA Pro

Gaines, Sara. *Noble Falling.* Tallahassee, FL: Harmony Ink, 2012. L HV Pro

Gant, Gene. *The Thunder in His Head.* Tallahassee, FL: Harmony Ink, 2012. G GA Pro

Gennari, Jennifer. *My Mixed-Up Berry Blue Summer.* Boston: Houghton Mifflin, 2012. L GA Sec

George, Madeleine. *The Difference between You and Me.* New York: Penguin, 2012. L HV/GA Pro

Gold, Rachel. *Being Emily.* Tallahassee, FL: Bella Books, 2012. MtF-Transgender HV Pro

Gonzalez, Rigoberto. *Mariposa Gown.* Maple Shade, NJ: Tincture/Lethe, 2012. G GA/QC Pro

Goode, John. *Distant Rumblings.* Lords of Arcadia, Book 1. Tallahassee, FL: Harmony Ink, 2012. G GA Sec

———. *End of the Innocence.* Tales from Foster High. Tallahassee, FL: Harmony Ink, 2012. G GA Sec

———. *Eye of the Storm.* Lords of Arcadia, Book 2. Tallahassee, FL: Harmony Ink, 2012. G GA Sec

Graham, H. Rachelle. *Cursed.* Tallahassee, FL: Bella Books, 2012. L GA Pro

Griffin, Molly Beth. *Silhouette of a Sparrow.* Minneapolis, MN: Milkweed Editions, 2012. L HV Pro

Hand, Elizabeth. *Radiant Days.* New York: Viking, 2012. L HV Pro

Harrington, Hannah. *Speechless.* Don Mills, ON: Harlequin Teen, 2012. G HV Sec

Hartman, Brett. *Cadillac Chronicles.* El Paso, TX: Cinco Puntos, 2012. G GA Sec

Herren, Greg. *Sara.* Valley Falls, NY: Bold Strokes, 2012. G GA Pro

———. *Timothy.* Valley Falls, NY: Bold Strokes Books, 2012. G GA Pro

Hesik, Annameekee. *The You Know Who Girls: Freshman Year.* Valley Falls, NY: Bold Strokes Books, 2012. L GA Pro

Hoole, Elissa Janine. *Kiss the Morning Star.* New York: Amazon Children's Publishing/Marshall Cavendish, 2012. L GA Pro

Hopkins, Ellen. *Tilt.* New York: Margaret K. McElderry Books, 2012. G GA Sec

Hopkinson, Nalo. *The Chaos.* New York: Margaret K. McElderry Books, 2012. L HV Sec

Ignatow, Amy. *The Popularity Papers: The Rocky Road Trip of Lydia Greenblatt and Julie Graham-Chang.* New York: Amulet, 2012. G GA Sec

Jackson, Corrine. *If I Lie.* New York: Simon Pulse, 2012. G HV Sec

Johnson, Angela. *A Certain October.* New York: Simon & Schuster, 2012. G GA Sec

King, A. S. *Ask the Passengers.* Boston: Little, Brown, 2012. L HV Pro

King, Jeremy Jordan. *In Stone.* Valley Falls, NY: Bold Strokes Books, 2012. G GA Pro

Knowles, Jo. *See You at Harry's.* Somerville, MA: Candlewick, 2012. G HV Sec

Kokie, E. M. *Personal Effects.* Somerville, MA: Candlewick, 2012. G HV Sec

Lavoie, Jennifer. *Andy Squared.* Valley Falls, NY: Bold Strokes, 2012. G HV Pro

Lecesne, James. *Trevor.* New York: Seven Stories, 2012. G GA Pro

Lenk, J. R. *Collide.* Tallahassee, FL: Harmony Ink, 2012. G/Bi-M HV Pro

Lo, Malinda. *Adaptation.* Boston: Little, Brown, 2012. L HV Pro

Lowrey, Sassafras. *Roving Pack.* Brooklyn, NY: PoMo Freakshow, 2012. MtF-Transgender HV Pro

Lucombe, Jeffrey. *Shirts and Skins.* New York: Chelsea Station Editions, 2012. G HV Pro

Magoon, Kekla. *37 Things I Love (in No Particular Order).* New York: Henry Holt, 2012. L HV Pro

Michaels, Robbie. *Don't Judge a Book by Its Cover.* Tallahassee, FL: Harmony Ink, 2012. G HV Pro

———. *Go West, Young Man.* Tallahassee, FL: Harmony Ink, 2012. G GA Pro

Moskowitz, Hannah. *Gone, Gone Gone.* New York: Simon Pulse, 2012. G HV Pro

Neff, Beth. *Getting Somewhere.* New York: Viking, 2012. L GA Sec

Nelson, Lisa R. *Drifting.* Philadelphia: Tiny Satchel Press 2012. L HV Sec

Payne, K. E. *ME@YOU.COM.* Valley Falls, NY: Bold Strokes, 2012. L HV Pro

Peters, Julie Ann. *It's Our Prom (So Deal with It).* Boston: Little, Brown, 2012. L/G/Bi-M GA/QC Pro

Radclyffe and Katherine E. Lynch, eds. *OMG Queer.* Valley Falls, NY: Bold Strokes, 2012.
  [short stories] G/L HV/GA/QC Sec
Rainfield, Cheryl. *Hunted.* Lodi, NJ: WestSide Books, 2012. L GA Sec
Rice, M. L. *Pride & Joy.* Valley Falls, NY: Bold Strokes Books, 2012. L GA Pro
Roman, J. *Heartless.* Tallahassee, FL: Harmony Ink, 2012. G GA Pro
Rudetsky, Seth. *My Awesome/Awful Popularity Plan.* New York: Random, 2012. G HV Pro
Ryan, Tom. *Way to Go.* Victoria, BC: Orca Books, 2012. G HV Pro
Saenz, Benjamin Alire. *Aristotle and Dante Discover the Secrets of the Universe.* New York:
  Simon & Schuster, 2012. G HV/GA Pro
Saldin, Erin. *The Girls of No Return.* New York: Arthur A. Levine, 2012. L HV Pro
Schemery, Bean. *The 7th of London.* Tallahassee, FL: Harmony Ink, 2012. G HV Pro
Thorne, Hayden. *The Winter Garden and Other Stories.* Glen Allen, VA: Queerteen/JMS
  Books, 2012. [short stories] G HV/GA Pro
Tomas, J. *Boys, Boys, Boys.* Glen Allen, VA: Queerteen/JMS Books, 2012. G HV/GA Pro
Tregay, Sarah. *Love & Leftovers.* New York: HarperCollins, 2012. G GA Sec
Wise, Tama. *Street Dreams.* Valley Falls, NY: Bold Strokes, 2012. G HV Pro
X, Sulaman. *King of Storms.* Tallahassee, FL: Harmony Ink, 2012. G GA Pro
———. *Tears of a Dragon.* Tallahassee, FL: Harmony Ink, 2012. G GA Pro

2013

Astruc, R. J. *Banned Books.* Tallahassee, FL: Harmony Ink, 2013. G HV Pro
Barnes, David-Matthew. *Wonderland.* Valley Falls, NY: Bold Strokes, 2013. G/L GA Pro
Barson, Kelly. *45 Pounds (More or Less).* New York: Viking, 2013. L GA Sec
Block, Francesca Lia. *Love in a Time of Global Warming.* New York: Henry Holt, 2013. G GA/
  QC Sec
Bonaste, Sophie. *The Sacrifices We Make.* Tallahassee, FL: Harmony Ink, 2013. G GA Pro
Bowler, Michael J. *Children of the Night.*Tallahassee, FL: Harmony Ink, 2013. G HV Pro
Burton, Hallie. *Tapestry.* Tallahassee, FL: Harmony Ink, 2013. G HV Pro
Cameron, Sam. *Kings of Ruin.* Valley Falls, NY: Bold Strokes Books, 2013. G HV Pro
———. *The Missing Juliet.* Valley Falls, NY: Bold Strokes Books, 2013. L GA Pro
Carter, Caela. *Me, Him, Them, and It.* New York: Bloomsbury, 2013. L GA Sec
Charlton-Trujillo, e. E. *Fat Angie.* Somerville, MA: Candlewick, 2013. L HV/QC Sec
Clanton, Barbara L. *Stealing Second: Sam's Story.* Clarksonville series #4. Belton, TX: Regal
  Crest, 2013. L HV Pro
Clark, Kristin Elizabeth. *FreakBOY.* New York: Farrar, Straus & Giroux, 2013. MtF-Transgen-
  der/Gender fluid HV/GA Sec
Demcak, Andrew. *If There's a Heaven Above.* n.p.: JMS Books, 2013. G/L GA Pro
Dos Santos, Steven. *The Culling.* Woodbury, MN: Flux, 2013. G GA Pro
Dunne, Amy. *Secret Lies.* Valley Falls, NY: Bold Strokes Books, 2013. L HV Pro
Easton, Eli. *Superhero.* Tallahassee, FL: Harmony Ink, 2013. G/Bi-M GA Pro
Egloff, Z. *Leap.* Ann Arbor, MI: Bywater Books, 2013. L GA Pro
Erich, James. *Dreams of Fire and Gods: Fire.* Tallahassee, FL: Harmony Ink, 2013. G GA Pro
———. *Dreams of Fire and Gods: Gods.* Tallahassee, FL: Harmony Ink, 2013. G GA Pro
Erno, Jeff. *You Belong with Me.* Tallahassee, FL: Harmony Ink, 2013. G HV Pro
Farizon, Sara. *If You Could Be Mine.* New York: Algonquin Young Readers, 2013. L HV Pro
Federle, Tim. *Better Nate Than Ever.* New York: Simon & Schuster Books for Young Readers,
  2013. G HV/QC Pro
Finneyfrock, Karen. *The Sweet Revenge of Celia Door.* New York: Viking, 2013. G GA Sec
Fishback, Jere' M. *Tyler Buckspan.* Waldo, AR: Prizm, 2013. G HV Pro
Frangione, Lucia. *Leave of Absence.* Vancouver, BC: Talon Books, 2013. L HV Sec
Freely, Jessica. *All the Colors of Love.* Tallahassee, FL: Harmony Ink, 2013. G GA Pro
Gant, Gene. *The Battle for Jericho.* Tallahassee, FL: Harmony Ink, 2013. Bi-M GA Pro
———. *Everything We Shut Our Eyes To.* Tallahassee, FL: Harmony Ink, 2013. G HV Pro
Goodman, Gabriel. *The Alliance: Surviving Southside.* Minneapolis, MN: Darby Creek, 2013.
  G/L GA/QC Pro

Harris, Michael. *Homo.* Toronto: Lorimer SideStreets, 2013. G GA Sec
Harris, S. L. *Laughter in the Wind.* Tallahassee, FL: Bella Books, 2013. L HV Pro
Hartinger, Brent. *The Elephant of Surprise.* Buddha Kitty Books, 2013. G GA Pro
Henry, Sherrie. *Last of the Summer Tomatoes.* Tallahassee, FL: Harmony Ink, 2013. G GA Pro
Herren, Greg. *Lake Thirteen.* Valley Falls, NY: Bold Strokes Books, 2013. G GA Pro
Higgins, M. G. *Bi-Normal.* Costa Mesa, CA: Saddleback, 2013. G HV Sec
———. *Falling Out of Place.* Costa Mesa, CA: Saddleback, 2013. G HV Sec
Ignatow, Amy. *The Popularity Papers: Love and Other Fiascos with Lydia Greenblatt and Julie Graham-Chang.* New York: Amulet, 2013. G GA Sec
———. *The Popularity Papers: The Awesomely Awful Melodies of Lydia Greenblatt and Julie Graham-Chang.* New York: Amulet, 2013. G GA Sec
James, Caleb. *Haffling.* Tallahassee, FL: Harmony Ink, 2013. G HV Pro
Johnson, Alaya Dawn. *The Summer Prince.* New York: Arthur A. Levine, 2013. G GA Sec
Jordan, D. *Red Lank: Orphan Maker.* Tallahassee, FL: Bella Books, 2013. L HV Pro
Kadence, Sam. *On the Right Track.* Tallahassee, FL: Harmony Ink, 2013. G GA Pro
Karre, Elizabeth. *The Fight: Surviving Southside.* Minneapolis, MN: Darby Creek, 2013. G/L GA/QC Pro
Keil, Melissa. *Life in Outer Space.* Atlanta: Peachtree, 2013. G GA Sec
Kennedy, C. *Omorphi.* Tallahassee, FL: Harmony Ink, 2013. G HV Pro
———. *Safe.* Tallahassee, FL: Harmony Ink, 2013. G GA Pro
Kerick, Mia. *Intervention.* Tallahassee, FL: Harmony Ink, 2013. G GA Pro
———. *Not Broken, Just Bent.* Tallahassee, FL: Harmony Ink, 2013. G HV Pro
King, Jeremy Jordan. *Night Creatures.* Valley Falls, NY: Bold Strokes Books, 2013. G GA Pro
Kocek, Sara. *Promise Me Something.* Park Ridge, IL: Whitman, 2013. L HV Pro
Konigsberg, Bill. *Openly Straight.* New York: Scholastic, 2013. G HV/GA Pro
Laughton, Geoff. *By the Creek.* Tallahassee, FL: Harmony Ink, 2013. G HV Pro
Lavoie, Jennifer. *Meeting Chance.* Valley Falls, NY: Bold Strokes Book, 2013. G HV Pro
———. *Tristant & Elijah.* Valley Falls, NY: Bold Strokes Books, 2013. G HV Pro
Levithan, David. *Every Day.* New York: Random House, 2013. G GA Sec
———. *Two Boys Kissing.* New York: Random House, 2013. G/FtM-Transgender HV/GA/QC Pro
Lo, Malinda. *Inheritance.* Boston: Little, Brown Books for Young Readers, 2013. Bi-F GA Pro
London, Alex. *Proxy.* New York: Philomel, 2013. G GA Pro
Lynne, Zoe. *Finding Ashlynn.* Tallahassee, FL: Harmony Ink, 2013. L GA/QC Pro
———. *That Witch!* Tallahassee, FL: Harmony Ink, 2013. L HV Pro
Malone, Jill. *Giraffe People.* Ann Arbor, MI: Bywater Books, 2013. L HV Pro
Mayfield, Jamie. *A Broken Kind of Life.* Tallahassee, FL: Harmony Ink, 2013. G HV Pro
———. *Choices.* Tallahassee, FL: Harmony Ink, 2013. G GA Pro
———. *Destiny.* Tallahassee, FL: Harmony Ink, 2013. G GA Pro
———. *Determination.* Tallahassee, FL: Harmony Ink, 2013. G GA Pro
Moskowitz, Hannah. *Marco Impossible.* New York: Roaring Brook, 2013. G GA Sec
———. *Teeth.* New York: Roaring Brook, 2013. G HV Pro
Moynihan, Lindsay. *The Waiting Tree.* Las Vegas: Skyscape/Amazon Children's, 2013. G GA Sec
Ness, Patrick. *More Than This.* Somerville, MA: Candlewick, 2013. G GA Pro
Olsen, Nora. *Swans and Klons.* Valley Falls, NY: Bold Strokes Books, 2013. L GA Pro
O'Shea, M. J. *Blood Moon.* Tallahassee, FL: Harmony Ink, 2013. G GA Pro
———. *Hunter's Moon.* Tallahassee, FL: Harmony Ink, 2013. G HV Pro
Parker, Madison. *Play Me, I'm Yours.* Tallahassee, FL: Harmony Ink, 2013. G HV Pro
Parkhurst, Johanna. *Here's to You, Zeb Pike.* Tallahassee, FL: Harmony Ink, 2013. G HV Pro
Parkinson, Will. *Pitch.* Tallahassee, FL: Harmony Ink, 2013. G GA Pro
Payne, K. E. *Another 365 Days.* Tallahassee, FL: Harmony Ink, 2013. L GA Pro
———. *Road to Her.* Tallahassee, FL: Harmony Ink, 2013. L GA Pro
Peters, Andrew J. *The Seventh Pleiade.* Valley Falls, NY: Bold Strokes Books, 2013. G HV Pro
Ramsey, Jo. *Nail Polish and Feathers.* Tallahassee, FL: Harmony Ink, 2013. G GA Pro
Redhawk, D. Jordan. *Orphan Maker.* Tallahassee, FL: Bella Books, 2013. Bi-F GA Pro

Rice, M. L. *Pride and Joy.* Valley Falls, NY: Bold Strokes, 2013. L HV Pro
Rich, Juliann. *Searching for Grace.* Valley Falls, NY: Bold Strokes Books, 2013. G HV Pro
Roman, J. *Clueless.* Tallahassee, FL: Harmony Ink, 2013. G GA Pro
Ryan, Tom. *Tag Along.* Victoria, BC: Orca, 2013. G HV Pro
Sandberg, Winter. *Private Display of Affection.* Tallahassee, FL: Harmony Ink, 2013. G HV
    Pro
Schemery, Beau. *The Last Blade.* Tallahassee, FL: Harmony Ink, 2013. G GA Pro
———. *The Unlikely Hero.* Tallahassee, FL: Harmony Ink, 2013. G HV Pro
Smith, Andrew. *Winger.* New York: Simon & Schuster, 2013. G GA Sec
Star, Neil. *The Princess Affair.* Valley Falls, NY: Bold Strokes, 2013. L GA Pro
Sutherland, Suzanne. *When We Were Good.* Toronto: Sumach, 2013. L HV Pro
Trevayne, Emma. *Coda.* Philadelphia: Running, 2013. G HV Sec
Van Rooyan, Suzanne. *The Other Me.* Tallahassee, FL: Harmony Ink, 2013. FtM-Transgender
    HV Pro
Velasquez, Gloria. *Tommy Stands Tall.* San Antonio, TX: Pinata Books/Arte Publica, 2013. G
    GA Pro
Watts, Julia. *Secret City.* Tallahassee, FL: Bella Books, 2013. L HV Pro
Wheeler, Elizabeth. *Asher's Fault.* Valley Falls, NY: Bold Strokes Books, 2013. G GA Pro

2014

Allen, Skye. *Pretty Peg.* Tallahassee, FL: Harmony Ink, 2014. L GA Pro
Anonymous. *The Book of David.* New York: Simon & Schuster, 2014. G HV Pro
Astruck, R. J. *Binary Boy.* Tallahassee, FL: Harmony Ink, 2014. G GA Pro
———. *Tabloid Lies.* Tallahassee, FL: Harmony Ink, 2014. G GA Pro
Atwood, D. E. *If We Shadows.* Tallahassee, FL: Harmony Ink, 2014. FtM-Transgender HV Pro
Bach, Ari. *Ragnarok.* Tallahassee, FL: Harmony Ink, 2014. L GA Pro
———. *Valhalla.* Tallahassee, FL: Harmony Ink, 2014. L GA Pro
Barakiya, Michael. *One Man Guy.* New York: Farrar, Straus & Giroux, 2014. G HV Pro
Batchelor, Melanie. *Remember Me.* Valley Falls, NY: Bold Strokes Books, 2014. L GA Pro
Benincasa, Sara. *Great.* New York: HarperTeen, 2014. L HV Sec
Black, Jenna. *Resistance.* New York: Tor Teen, 2014. G HV Sec
Brown, Rachel Manija, and Sherwood Smith. *Stranger.* New York: Viking, 2014. G/L GA Sec
Carter, Caela. *My Best Friend Maybe.* New York: Bloomsbury, 2014. L GA Sec
Clanton, Barbara L. *Out at Home.* Clarksonville series #5. Belton, TX: Regal Crest, 2014. L
    HV/GA Pro
Clare, Cassandra. *City of Heavenly Fire.* New York: Simon & Schuster, 2014. G GA Sec
Clare, Cassandra, Sarah Rees Brennan, and Maureen Johnson. *The Bane Chronicles.* New
    York: McElderry, 2014. G GA Pro
Clarke, Cat. *Undone.* New York: Sourcebooks/Fire, 2014. G HV Sec
deGramont, Nina. *This Boy I Love.* New York: Atheneum, 2014. G HV Sec
Demas, Corinne. *Returning to Shore.* Minneapolis, MN: Carolrhoda Lab, 2014. G GA Sec
Demcak, Andrew. *Ghost Songs.* Tallahassee, FL: Harmony Ink, 2014. G GA Pro
Eliason, Rachel. *The Best Boy Ever Made.* N.p.: Create Space, 2014. FtM-Transgender HV Pro
Ellis, Deborah. *Moon at Nine.* Toronto: Pajama, 2014. L HV Pro
Farizan, Sara. *Tell Me Again How a Crush Should Feel.* New York: Algonquin, 2014. L HV
    Pro
Federle, Tim. *Five, Six, Seven, Nate!* New York: Simon & Schuster, 2014. G HV/QC Pro
Fleet, Suki. *This Is Not a Love Story.* Tallahassee, FL: Harmony Ink, 2014. G GA Pro
———. *Wild Summer.* Tallahassee, FL: Harmony Ink, 2014. G GA Pro
Frankel, J. S. *Lindsay, Jo and the Tree of Forever.* Maryville, TN: Regal Crest, 2014. L GA Pro
———. *Lindsay versus the Marauders.* Maryville, TN: Regal Crest, 2014. L GA Pro
Fu, Kim. *For Today I Am a Boy.* Boston: HMH, 2014. MtF-Transgender GA Pro
Gant, Gene. *If You Really Love Me.* Tallahassee, FL: Harmony Ink, 2014. G HV Pro
———. *The Supernaturals.* Tallahassee, FL: Harmony Ink, 2014. G HV Pro
Gold, Rachel. *Just Girls.* Tallahassee, FL: Bella Books, 2014. MtF-Transgender GA Pro

Hale, Samantha. *Everything Changes.* Valley Falls, NY: Bold Strokes Books, 2014. L HV Pro
Hawke, Jay Jordan. *Punkawiss the Outcast.* Tallahassee, FL: Harmony Ink, 2014. G GA Pro
———. *A Scout Is Brave.* Tallahassee, FL: Harmony Ink, 2014. G HV Pro
Herren, Greg. *Dark Tide.* Valley Falls, NY: Bold Strokes Books, 2014. G GA Pro
Hesik, Annameekee. *Driving Lessons.* Valley Falls, NY: Bold Strokes Books, 2014. L HV Pro
Hoffman, Lou. *Key of Behliseth.* Tallahassee, FL: Harmony Ink, 2014. G GA Pro
Ignatow, Amy. *The Popularity Papers: The Less-Than-Hidden Secrets and Final Revelations of Lydia Greenblatt and Julie Graham-Chang.* New York: Amulet, 2014. G GA Sec
Kadence, Sam. *Unicorns and Rainbow Pop.* Tallahassee, FL: Harmony Ink, 2014. G GA Pro
Kamata, Suzanne. *Screaming Divas.* Blue Ash, OH: Merit, 2014. L HV Sec
Kerick, Mia. *The Red Sheet.* Tallahassee, FL: Harmony Ink, 2014. G HV Pro
———. *Us Three.* Tallahassee, FL: Harmony Ink, 2014. G GA Pro
Kiely, Brendan. *The Gospel of Winter.* New York: Atheneum/McElderry, 2014. G HV Pro
LaCour, Nina. *Everything Leads to You.* New York: Dutton, 2014. L HV Pro
Laughton, Geoff. *Under the Stars.* Tallahassee, FL: Harmony Ink, 2014. G GA Pro
Lavoie, Jennifer. *Tristant & Elijah.* Valley Falls, NY: Bold Strokes Books, 2014. G HV Pro
Lee, M. C. *If You Knew Jack.* Tallahassee, FL: Harmony Ink, 2014. G GA Pro
———. *You Don't Know Jack.* Tallahassee, FL: Harmony Ink, 2014. G GA Pro
Levy, Dana Alison. *The Misadventures of the Family Fletcher.* New York: Delacorte, 2014. G GA Sec
London, Alex. *Guardian.* New York: Philomel, 2014. G HV Sec
Lynne, Zoe. *Carnival-Decatur.* Tallahassee, FL: Harmony Ink, 2014. G GA Pro
———. *Finding Ashlynn.* Tallahassee, FL: Harmony Ink, 2014. L GA Pro
———. *Freeing Stella.* Tallahassee, FL: Harmony Ink, 2014. MtF-Transgender GA Pro
———. *That Witch.* Tallahassee, FL: Harmony Ink, 2014. L HV Pro
McCormack, Devon. *Hideous.* Tallahassee, FL: Harmony Ink, 2014. G HV Pro
———. *When Ryan Came Back.* Tallahassee, FL: Harmony Ink, 2014. G HV Pro
McNally, Shari. *The Story Thief.* Tallahassee, FL: Bella Books, 2014. L HV Pro
McNamara, Brian. *Bottled Up Secret.* Valley Falls, NY: Bold Strokes, 2014. G GA Pro
Michaels, Robbie. *Caught in the Act.* Tallahassee, FL: Harmony Ink, 2014. G GA Pro
Moss, Christopher Hawthorne. *Beloved Pilgrim.* Tallahassee, FL: Harmony Ink, 2014. FtM-Transgender HV Pro
Mulhall, M. B. *Heavyweight.* Tallahassee, FL: Harmony Ink, 2014. G HV Pro
Nelson, Jandy. *I'll Give You the Sun.* New York: Dial, 2014. G GA Pro
Olsen, Nora. *Frenemy of the People.* Valley Falls, NY: Bold Strokes Books, 2014. L GA Pro
———. *Maxine Wore Black.* Johnsonville, NY: Bold Strokes Books, 2014. L/MtF-Transgender GA Pro
O'Shea, M. J. *Cold Moon.* Tallahassee, FL: Harmony Ink, 2014. G HV Pro
———. *Love Blood.* Tallahassee, FL: Harmony Ink, 2014. G HV Pro
Page, Winter. *Breaking Free.* Tallahassee, FL: Harmony Ink, 2014. MtF-Transgender HV Pro
Palund, Linda. *The Little Black Dress.* Tallahassee, FL: Harmony Ink, 2014. L GA Pro
Parkhurst, Johanna. *Every Inferno.* Tallahassee, FL: Harmony Ink, 2014. G HV Pro
Parkinson, Will. *Wet Paint.* Tallahassee, FL: Harmony Ink, 2014. G GA Pro
Payne, K. E. *Because of Her.* Johnsonville, NY: Bold Strokes Books, 2014. L GA Pro
Penn, Astor. *All the Devils Here.* Tallahassee, FL: Harmony Ink, 2014. L HV Pro
Peters, Julie Ann. *Lies My Girlfriend Told Me.* Boston: Little, Brown, 2014. L GA Pro
Polonsky, Ami. *Gracefully Grayson.* New York: Hyperion, 2014. MtF-Transgender HV/QC Pro
Quintero, Isabel. *Gabi, a Girl in Pieces.* San Antonio, TX: Cinco Puntos, 2014. G HV Sec
Ramsey, Jo. *Shoulder Pads and Flannel.* Tallahassee, FL: Harmony Ink, 2014. G GA Pro
Rice, M. L. *The Melody of Light.* Valley Falls, NY: Bold Strokes Books, 2014. L HV Pro
Rich, Julianne. *Caught in the Crossfire.* Valley Falls, NY: Bold Strokes Books, 2014. G HV Pro
———. *Searching for Grace.* Valley Falls, NY: Bold Strokes Books, 2014. G HV Pro
Ricker, Jeffrey. *The Unwanted.* Valley Falls, NY: Bold Strokes Books, 2014. G HV Pro
Rossing, Nina. *Supermassive.* Tallahassee, FL: Harmony Ink, 2014. G GA Pro

Sanders, Russell J. *Special Effect.* Tallahassee, FL: Harmony Ink, 2014. G HV Pro
Sharpe, Tess. *Far from You.* New York: Hyperion, 2014. L GA Pro
Shirley, S. Chris. *Playing by the Book.* Bronx, NY: Magnus/Riverdale Ave., 2014. G HV Pro
Smith, Andrew. *Grasshopper Jungle.* New York: Dutton, 2014. G/Bi-M GA Pro
Snow, K. Z. *Ben Raphael's All Star Virgins.* Tallahassee, FL: Harmony Ink, 2014. G HV Pro
Stetz-Waters, Karelia. *Forgive Me If I've Told You This Before.* Portland, OR: Ooligan, 2014. L HV Pro
Talley, Robin. *Lies We Tell Ourselves.* New York: Harlequin Teen, 2014. L HV Pro
Tregay, Sarah. *Fan Art.* New York: Harper/Tegen, 2014. G HV/QC Pro
Verdi, Jessica. *The Summer I Wasn't Me.* Naperville, IL: Sourcebooks, 2014. L HV Pro
Waters, Tawni. *Beauty of the Broken.* New York: Simon Pulse, 2014. L HV Pro
Westerfeld, Scott. *Afterworlds.* New York: Simon Pulse, 2014. L GA Pro
Wheeler, Elizabeth. *Asher's Shot.* Valley Falls, NY: Bold Strokes Books, 2014. G HV Pro
Williams, Julie. *Drama Queens in the House.* New York: Roaring Brook, 2014. G HV/QC Sec
Wood, Jennie. *A Boy Like Me.* San Bernardino, CA: 215 INK, 2014. FtM-Transgender HV Sec
Wooten, Neal. *The Balance.* Valley Falls, NY: Bold Strokes Books, 2014. G GA Pro

2015

Adler, Dahlia. *Under the Lights.* New York: Spencer Hill, 2015. L GA/QC Pro
Albertalli, Becky. *Simon vs. the Homo Sapiens Agenda.* Balzer + Bray/HarperCollins, 2015. G HV/QC Pro
Almond, David. *A Song for Ella Grey.* New York: Delacorte, 2015. G GA Sec
Alsenas, Linus. *Beyond Clueless.* New York: Abrams/Amulet, 2015. G GA/QC Sec
Astruck, R. J. *Loving Luke.* Tallahassee, FL: Harmony Ink, 2015. G GA Pro
Bach, Ari. *Gudsriki.* Tallahassee, FL: Harmony Ink, 2015. L GA Pro
Bach, Mette. *Femme.* Toronto: Lorimer, 2015. L HV/GA Sec
Bardugo, Leigh. *Six of Crows.* New York: Holt, 2015. G GA Sec
Barnes, David-Matthew. *Fifty Yards and Holding.* Valley Falls, NY: Bold Strokes Books, 2015. G HV Pro
Barzak, Christopher. *Wonders of the Invisible World.* New York: Knopf, 2015. G GA Pro
Black, Holly. *The Darkest Part of the Forest.* New York: Little, Brown, 2015. G GA Pro
Blaushild, A. M. *Angel Radio.* Tallahassee, FL: Harmony Ink, 2015. L HV Pro
Bow, Erin. *The Scorpion Rules.* New York: Simon & Schuster/McElderry, 2015. L GA Pro
Bray, Libba. *Lair of Dreams.* Boston: Little, Brown, 2015. G GA Sec
Brooks, Kevin. *The Bunker Diary.* Minneapolis, MN: Carolrhoda LAB, 2015. G GA Sec
Brothers, Meagan. *Weird Girl and What's His Name.* New York: Three Rooms, 2015. G GA Pro
Brugman, Alyssa. *Alex as Well.* New York: Holt, 2015. Intersex HV Pro
Burns, A. M. *Guardians.* Tallahassee, FL: Harmony Ink, 2015. G HV Pro
———. *Hunters.* Tallahassee, FL: Harmony Ink, 2015. G GA Pro
———. *Witches.* Tallahassee, FL: Harmony Ink, 2015. G HV Pro
Burton, Hallie. *For a Price.* Tallahassee, FL: Harmony Ink, 2015. G HV Pro
Chase, Dakota. *Mad about the Hatter.* Tallahassee, FL: Harmony Ink, 2015. G GA Pro
Clanton, Barbara L. *Tools of the Devil.* Clarksonville series #6. Belton, TX: Regal Crest, 2015. L HV/GA Pro
Cooper, E. E. *Vanished.* New York: Tegen/HarperCollins, 2015. L GA Pro
Croker, Verity. *May Day Mine.* Tallahassee, FL: Harmony Ink, 2015. L/Bi-F HV Pro
Davey, Douglas. *Switch.* Calgary, AB: Red Deer, 2015. Bi-M HV Pro
Dawn, Nyrae. *The History of Us.* Tallahassee, FL: Harmony Ink, 2015. G HV Pro
Demcak, Andrew. *A Little Bit Langston.* Tallahassee, FL: Harmony Ink, 2015. G HV Pro
Dinnison, Kris. *You and Me and Him.* Boston: HMH, 2015. G GA Sec
Downham, Jenny. *Unbecoming.* New York: Scholastic/David Fickling, 2015. L HV Pro
Duncan, Alexandra. *Sound.* New York: Greenwillow, 2015. L GA Sec
Early, Tom. *Aspect of Winter.* Tallahassee, FL: Harmony Ink, 2015. G HV Pro
Feinstein, John. *The Sixth Man.* New York: Knopf, 2015. G HV Sec

Fleet, Suki. *The Glass House.* Tallahassee, FL: Harmony Ink, 2015. G HV Pro
Floreen, Tim. *Willful Machines.* New York: Simon & Schuster, 2015. G HV Pro
Frankel, J. S. *Lindsay, Jo and the Well of Nevermore.* Maryville, TN: Regal Crest, 2015. L GA Pro
Gaines, Sara. *Noble Persuasion.* Tallahassee, FL: Harmony Ink, 2015. L HV Pro
Gant, Gene. *Lucky Linus.* Tallahassee, FL: Harmony Ink, 2015. G GA Pro
Garvin, Jeff. *Symptoms of Being Human.* New York: Balzer + Bray/HarperCollins, 2015. Gender fluid HV Pro
Gino, Alex. *George.* New York: Scholastic, 2015. MtF-Transgender HV/QC Pro
Glass, J. D. *Red Light.* Tallahassee, FL: Ylva, 2015. L GA Pro
Gonzalez, Rigoberto. *Mariposa U.* Maple Shade, NJ: Tincture/Lethe, 2015. G GA/QC Pro
Grace, Amanda. *No One Needs to Know.* Woodbury, MN: Flux, 2015. L HV Pro
Gregorio, I. W. *None of the Above.* New York: Balzer + Bray/HarperCollins, 2015. Intersex HV Pro
Hall, Sandy. *Signs Point to Yes.* New York: Swoon, 2015. Bi-F HV Sec
Harper, Annie, ed. *Summer Love: An LGBTQ Collection.* n.p.: Interlude, 2015. L/G/FtM-Transgender HV/GA/QC Pro
Hasak-Lowy, Todd. *Me Being Me Is as Insane as You Being You.* New York: Simon Pulse, 2015. G GA Sec
Hawke, Jay Jordan. *Onwaachige the Dreamer.* Tallahassee, FL: Harmony Ink, 2015. G GA Pro
Headford, Cheryl. *Hostage.* Tallahassee, FL: Harmony Ink, 2015. G HV Pro
Helms, Rhonda. *Promposal.* New York: Simon Pulse, 2015. G GA Pro
Hesse, Monica. *Girl in the Blue Coat.* New York: Little, Brown, 2015. G GA Sec
Higgins, M. G. *Rodeo Princess.* New York: Saddleback, 2015. L HV Pro
Hopkins, Ellen. *Traffick.* New York: Simon & Schuster/McElderry, 2015. FtM-Transgender GA Sec
Hutchinson, Shaun David. *The Five Stages of Andrew Brawley.* New York: Simon Pulse, 2015. G HV Pro
Jacobs, Evan. *Father Son Father.* New York: Gravel Road/Saddleback, 2015. MtF-Transgender GA Sec
Jaffe, Sara. *Dryland.* Portland, OR: Tin House, 2015. L HV Pro
Jenson, Cordelia. *Skyscraping.* New York: Philomel, 2015. G HV Sec
Joslin, Nikolai. *Life beyond the Temple.* Tallahassee, FL: Harmony Ink, 2015. L HV Pro
Keane, Danny. *No Big Deal.* Tallahassee, FL: Harmony Ink, 2015. G GA Pro
Kennedy, C. *Slaying Isadore's Dragons.* Tallahassee, FL: Harmony Ink, 2015. G GA Pro
Key, Anne. *Stealing Bases.* Tallahassee, FL: Harmony Ink, 2015. L HV Pro
King, Jeremy Jordan. *Dark Rites.* Valley Falls, NY: Bold Strokes Books, 2015. G HV Pro
Koehler, Christopher. *Poz.* Tallahassee, FL: Harmony Ink, 2015. G HV Pro
Konigsberg, Bill. *The Porcupine of Truth.* New York: Scholastic/Levine, 2015. L GA Sec
Lane, Amy. *Triane's Son: Fighting.* Tallahassee, FL: Harmony Ink, 2015. G/Bi-M GA Pro
———. *Triane's Son: Learning.* Tallahassee, FL: Harmony Ink, 2015. G/Bi-M GA Pro
———. *Triane's Son: Reigning.* Tallahassee, FL: Harmony Ink, 2015. G/Bi-M GA Pro
———. *Triane's Son: Rising.* Tallahassee, FL: Harmony Ink, 2015. G/Bi-M GA Pro
Laughton, Geoff. *At the Lake.* Tallahassee, FL: Harmony Ink, 2015. G GA Pro
Lavoie, Jennifer. *The First Twenty.* Valley Falls, NY: Bold Strokes, 2015. L GA Pro
Lawrence, Casey. *Out of Order.* Tallahassee FL: Harmony Ink, 2015. L/Bi-F HV Sec
Levithan, David. *Hold Me Closer.* New York: Dutton, 2015. G GA/QC Pro
Li, August. *Fox Hat and Neko.* Tallahassee, FL: Harmony Ink, 2015. G/L/Bi-F HV Pro
Lynne, Zoe. *Carnival. Chattanooga.* Tallahassee, FL: Harmony Ink, 2015. G HV Pro
Mackler, Carolyn. *Infinite In Between.* New York: HarperTeen, 2015. G HV/QC Sec
Martin, R. J. *The Body.* Tallahassee, FL: Harmony Ink, 2015. G HV Pro
McCarry, Sarah. *About a Girl.* New York: St Martin's Griffin, 2015. L/G GA Sec
McMullen, Liz, and Sheila Powell. *Finding Home.* Salinas, CA: Sapphire Books, 2015. L HV Sec
McNamara, Brian. *Breaking Up Point.* Valley Falls, NY: Bold Strokes Books, 2015. G GA Pro
Mesrobian, Carrie. *Cut Both Ways.* New York: HarperCollins, 2015. Bi-M HV Pro

Michaels, Robbie. *Caught in the Middle.* Tallahassee, FL: Harmony Ink, 2015. G GA Pro
Moskowitz, Hannah. *Not Otherwise Specified.* New York: Simon Pulse, 2015. Bi-F GA Pro
Ness, Patrick. *The Rest of Us Just Live Here.* New York: HarperCollins, 2015. G GA Sec
Nielsen, Susin. *We Are All Made of Molecules.* New York: Random/Wendy Lamb, 2015. G GA
    Sec
O'Beirne, Emily. *A Story of Now.* Tallahassee, FL: Ylva, 2015. L HV Pro
————. *The Sum of These Things.* Tallahassee, FL: Ylva, 2015. L GA Pro
O'Dell, Betsy. *Deep Water.* Salinas, CA: Sapphire Books, 2015. L HV Sec
O'Tierney, Raine. *I'll Always Miss You.* Tallahassee, FL: Harmony Ink, 2015. G/Bi-M HV Pro
Paul, Marcy Beller. *Underneath Everything.* New York: HarperCollins, 2015. L HV Sec
Peppermint, Aurora. *Beneath the Scales.* Tallahassee, FL: Harmony Ink, 2015. G HV Pro
Peters, Andrew L. *Banished Sons of Poseidon.* Valley Falls, NY: Bold Strokes Books, 2015. G
    HV Pro
Ramsey, Jo. *Blue Jeans and Sweat Shirts.* Tallahassee, FL: Harmony Ink, 2015. L HV Pro
————. *High Heels and Lipstick.* Tallahassee, FL: Harmony Ink, 2015. L/Bi-F GA Pro
————. *Work Boots and Tees.* Tallahassee, FL: Harmony Ink, 2015. G HV Pro
Reed, Emily. *Fairy Tales for Modern Queers.* Tallahassee, FL: Harmony Ink, 2015. L/G/FtM-
    Transgender/MtF-Transgender/Gender fluid HV/GA Pro/Sec
Reid, Raziel. *When Everything Feels Like the Movies.* Vancouver, BC: Arsenal Pulp, 2015. G
    GA Pro
Simpson, Ellen. *Light of the World.* Tallahassee, FL: Ylva, 2015. L GA Pro
Stein, Brynn. *Ray of Sunlight.* Tallahassee, FL: Harmony Ink, 2015. G/Bi-M HV Pro
Summer, Elizabeth. *Trust Me. I'm Trouble.* New York: Random House, 2015. Bi-F GA Sec
Talley, Robin. *What We Left Behind.* New York: Harlequin/Teen, 2015. L/FtM-Transgender/
    Gender fluid/Gender variant GA Pro/Sec
Tamaki, Mariko. *Saving Montgomery Sole.* New York: Roaring Brook, 2015. L GA Sec
Thompson, Hannah. *Living with the Fall.* Tallahassee, FL: Harmony Ink, 2015. G GA Pro
Walton, Will. *Anything Can Happen.* New York: Scholastic/PUSH, 2015. G HV/GA Pro
Watson, Cricket. *Missing May.* Salinas, CA: Sapphire Books, 2015. L HV Sec
Wheeler, Elizabeth. *Archer's Out.* Valley Falls, NY: Bold Strokes Books, 2015. G GA Pro
Wilke, Daria. *Playing a Part.* New York: Scholastic/Levine, 2015. G HV/QC Sec
Wood, Fiona. *Six Impossible Things.* Boston: Little Brown/Poppy, 2015. G GA Sec
Worth, K. D. *The Grim Life.* Tallahassee, FL: Harmony Ink, 2015. G GA Pro
Zeleny, Sylvia Aguilar. *Alex.* Minneapolis, MN: Epic/ABDO, 2015. FtM-Transgender HV Pro
————. *Leroy.* Minneapolis, MN: Epic/ABDO, 2015. G HV Pro
————. *Maria.* Minneapolis, MN: Epic/ABDO, 2015. L HV Pro
————. *Mikala.* Minneapolis, MN: Epic/ABDO, 2015. L HV Pro
————. *Tom:* Minneapolis, MN: Epic/ABDO, 2015. G GA Pro
————. *Wonnie.* Minneapolis, MN: Epic/ABDO, 2015. L GA Pro

2016

Allen, Skye. *The Songbird Thief.* Tallahassee, FL: Harmony Ink, 2016. L HV Pro
Atwood, Megan. *Raise the Stakes.* Minneapolis, MN: Darby Creek, 2016. FtM-Transgender
    GA Sec
Bailey, J. Leigh. *Do-Gooder.* Tallahassee, FL: Harmony Ink, 2016. G GA Pro
Bedford, L. B. *Carefully Everywhere Descending.* Tallahassee, FL: Harmony Ink, 2016. L HV
    Pro
Bow, Erin. *The Swan Riders.* New York: Simon & Schuster/McElderry, 2016. L GA Pro
Boyette, Samantha. *18 Months.* Valley Falls, NY: Bold Strokes Books, 2016. L GA Pro
Brewer, Zac. *The Blood between Us.* New York: HarperTeen, 2016. G GA Pro
Brown, Jaye Robin. *Georgia Peaches and Other Forbidden Fruit.* New York: HarperTeen,
    2016. L GA Pro
Burns, A. M. *Finding the Sky.* Tallahassee, FL: Harmony Ink, 2016. G HV Pro
Burns, A. M., and Caitlin Ricci. *Running with the Pack.* Tallahassee, FL: Harmony Ink, 2016.
    G/Asexual GA Pro

Carter, Celia. *Tumbling.* New York: Viking, 2016. L HV Sec
Cassidy, Yvonne. *How Many Letters in Goodbye?* Woodbury, MN: Flux, 2016. L HV Pro
Cherry, Alison. *Look Both Ways.* New York: Delacorte, 2016. L HV/QC Pro
Clark, Kristin Elizabeth. *Jess, Chunk and the Road Trip to Infinity.* New York: Farrar, Straus & Giroux, 2016. MtF-Transgender GA Pro
Cooper, Bliayne. *Blind Side of the Moon.* Tallahassee, FL: Bella Books, 2016. L HV Pro
Cordova, Zoraida. *Labyrinth Lost.* Chicago: Sourcebooks Fire, 2016. L/Bi-F GA Pro
Coulthurst, Audrey. *Of Fire and Stars.* New York: Harper/Balzer + Bray, 2016. L HV Pro
Cronn-Mills, Kirstin. *Original Fake.* New York: Putnam, 2016. G HV Pro
Dawe, Ted. *Into the River.* Hoboken, NJ: Polis Books, 2016. G GA Pro
Dawn, Nyrae. *Turn the World Upside Down.* Tallahassee, FL: Harmony Ink, 2016. G GA Pro
Desir, C., and Jolene Perry. *Love Blind.* New York: Simon Pulse, 2016. L GA Sec
Devine, Eric. *Look Past.* Philadelphia: Running, 2016. FtM-Transgender GA Pro
Downham, Jenny. *Unbecoming.* New York: Scholastic/David Fickling, 2016. L HV Pro
Duyvis, Corinne. *On the Edge of Gone.* New York: Abrams/Amulet, 2016. MtF-Transgender GA Sec
Elmendorf, Dana. *South of Sunshine.* Chicago: Albert Whitman, 2016. L HV Pro
Ember, Julia. *Unicorn Tracks.* Tallahassee, FL: Harmony Ink, 2016. L GA Pro
Evangelista, Kate. *No Holding Back.* New York: Feiwel and Friends, 2016. G HV Pro
Federle, Tim. *The Great American Whatever.* New York: Simon & Schuster, 2016. G GA/QC Pro
Floreen, Tim. *Tattoo Atlas.* New York: Simon & Schuster, 2016. G GA Pro
Francis, Eve. *Fragile.* Tallahassee, FL: Ylva, 2016. L HV Pro
Garvin, Jeff. *Symptoms of Being Human.* New York: HarperCollins/Balzer + Bray, 2016. Gender fluid HV Pro
George, Elizabeth. *The Edge of the Light.* New York: Penguin, 2016. L HV Sec
Gephart, Donna. *Lily and Dunkin.* New York: Delacorte, 2016. MtF-Transgender HV Pro
Gideon, Francis. *The Santa Hoax.* Tallahassee, FL: Harmony Ink, 2016. FtM-Transgender GA Pro
Girard, M-E. *Girl Mans Up.* New York: HarperCollins/Tegen, 2016. L GA Pro
Glass, J. D. *Punk Like Me.* Tallahassee, FL: Ylva, 2016. L HV Pro
Gold, Rachel. *My Year Zero.* Tallahassee, FL: Bella Books, 2016. L/Bi-F GA Pro
Goslee, S. J. *Whatever.* New York: Roaring Brook, 2016. G HV Pro
Grant, Joyce. *Tagged Out.* Toronto: Lorimer, 2016. G GA Sec
Green, Sally. *Half Lost.* New York: Viking, 2016. G GA Pro
Hall, Sandy. *Been Here All Along.* New York: Swoon, 2016. G HV Pro
Hartinger, Brent. *Three Truths and a Lie.* New York: Simon Pulse, 2016. G GA Pro
Harvey, Sarah N. *Spirit Level.* Victoria, BC: Orca, 2016. FtM-Transgender GA Pro
Harwell, Rebecca. *The Iron Phoenix.* Valley Falls, NY: Bold Strokes Books, 2016. L HV Pro
Hattrup, Karen. *Frannie and Tru.* New York: HarperTeen, 2016. G GA Sec
Hennessey, M. G. *The Other Boy.* New York: Harper, 2016. FtM-Transgender HV Pro
Hepperman, Christine. *Ask Me How I Got Here.* New York: HarperCollins, 2016. L GA Pro
Hesse, Monica. *Girl in the Blue Coat.* Boston: Little, Brown, 2016. G GA Sec
Hoffman, Lou. *Wraith Queen's Veil.* Tallahassee, FL: Harmony Ink, 2016. G GA Pro
Hutchinson, Shaun David. *At the Edge of the Universe.* New York: Simon Pulse, 2016. G HV Pro
———. *We Are the Ants.* New York: Simon Pulse, 2016. G GA Pro
Jay, Annabelle. *Merlin's Moon.* Tallahassee, FL: Harmony Ink, 2016. G/L/Bi-F HV Pro
———. *The Sun Dragon.* Tallahassee, FL: Harmony Ink, 2016. L/Bi-F HV Pro
Johnston, E. K. *Exit: Pursued by a Bear.* New York: Dutton, 2016. L HV Sec
Kaplan, Georgette. *Ex-Wives of Dracula.* Tallahassee, FL: Ylva, 2016. L HV Pro
Kennedy, C. *Tharros.* Tallahassee, FL: Harmony Ink, 2016. G GA Pro
Kennedy, Sean. *The Ongoing Reformation of Micah Johnson.* Tallahassee, FL: Harmony Ink, 2016. G GA Pro
Keplinger, Kody. *Run.* New York: Scholastic, 2016. L/Bi-F HV Pro
Kessler, Liz. *Read Me Like a Book.* Boston: Candlewick, 2016. L HV Pro

Kokie, E. M. *Radical.* Boston: Candlewick, 2016. L HV Pro
LaCour, Nina, and David Levithan. *You Know Me Well.* New York: St. Martin's Griffin, 2016. L/G GA Pro
Larbalestier, Justine. *My Sister Rosa.* New York: Soho Teen, 2016. L GA Sec
Lawrence, Casey. *Order in the Court.* Tallahassee, FL: Harmony Ink, 2016. L/Bi-F GA Pro
Lee, C. B. *Not Your Sidekick.* N.p.: Interlude, 2016. FtM-Transgender GA Sec
Lee, M. C. *Like I Know Jack.* Tallahassee, FL: Harmony Ink, 2016. G GA Pro
———. *The Shadow Operator.* Tallahassee, FL: Harmony Ink, 2016. G GA Pro
Linn, Laurent. *Draw the Line.* New York: Simon & Schuster/McElderry, 2016. G HV Pro
Logan, Kenneth. *True Letters from a Fictional Life.* New York: HarperTeen, 2016. G HV Pro
Lou, Rachel. *The Bridge.* Tallahassee, FL: Harmony Ink, 2016. G HV Pro
Loveless, Ryan. *Ethan.* Tallahassee, FL: Harmony Ink, 2016. G GA Pro
Lynne, Calista. *We Awaken.* Tallahassee, FL: Harmony Ink, 2016. Asexual GA Pro
Lyons, Ella. *Marian.* Tallahassee, FL: Harmony Ink, 2016. L HV Pro
Madonia, Kristen-Paige. *Invisible Fault Lines.* New York: Simon & Schuster, 2016. G HV Sec
Mason, Jane B. *Without Annette.* New York: Scholastic, 2016. L GA Pro
Mason-Black, Jennifer. *Devil and the Bluebird.* New York: Abrams/Amulet, 2016. L GA Sec
Matthews, Owen. *The Fixes.* New York: HarperTeen, 2016. G HV Pro
McCormack, Devon. *The Night Screams.* Tallahassee, FL: Harmony Ink, 2016. G HV Pro
McLemore, Anna-Marie. *When the Moon Was Ours.* New York: St. Martin's Griffin, 2016. FtM-Transgender GA Pro
Mittlefehldt, Rafi. *It Looks Like This.* Boston: Candlewick, 2016. G HV Pro
Moskowitz, Hannah, and Kat Helgeson. *Gena/Finn.* San Francisco: Chronicle, 2016. L HV Pro
Moss, Christopher Hawthorne. *A Fine Bromance.* Tallahassee, FL: Harmony Ink, 2016. FtM-Transgender GA Pro
Nijkamp, Marieke. *This Is Where It Ends.* Chicago: Sourcebooks Fire, 2016. L HV Pro
Nowlin, Laura. *This Song Is (Not) for You.* Chicago: Sourcebooks Fire, 2016. G HV Sec
O'Beirne, Emily. *Here's the Thing.* Tallahassee, FL: Ylva, 2016. L GA Pro
Ormsbee, Kathryn. *Lucky Few.* New York: Simon & Schuster, 2016. L GA Sec
O'Shea, M. J. *Insolita Luna Bundle.* Tallahassee, FL: Harmony Ink, 2016. G HV Pro
Ostrovski, Emil. *Away We Go.* New York: Greenwillow, 2016. G/Bi-M GA Pro
Parkhurst, Joanna. *Thanks a Lot, John LeClair.* Tallahassee, FL: Harmony Ink, 2016. G HV Pro
Payne, K. E. *Before.* Johnsonville, NY: Bold Strokes Books, 2016. L HV Pro
Peck, Richard. *The Best Man.* New York: Dial, 2016. G GA Sec
Ramsey, Jo. *Ball Cap and Khakis.* Tallahassee, FL: Harmony Ink, 2016. G HV Pro
———. *Where No One Knows.* Tallahassee, FL: Harmony Ink, 2016. FtM-Transgender GA Pro
Redgate, Riley. *Seven Ways We Lie.* New York: Abrams/Amulet, 2016. G HV Sec
Rich, Julianne. *Gravity.* Valley Falls, NY: Bold Strokes Books, 2016. L HV Pro
Ricci, Caitlin. *Head above Water.* Tallahassee, FL: Harmony Ink, 2016. G GA Pro
Rippon, Blithe. *Stow Away.* Tallahassee, FL: Ylva, 2016. L GA/QC Pro
Roehrig, Caleb. *Last Seen Leaving.* New York: Feiwel and Friends, 2016. G HV Pro
Rossing, Nina. *Fjord Blue.* Tallahassee, FL: Harmony Ink, 2016. G HV Pro
Russo, Meredith. *If I Was Your Girl.* New York: Flatiron Books, 2016. MtF-Transgender HV Pro
Saenz, Benjamin Alire. *The Inexplicable Logic of My Life.* New York: Clarion, 2016. G GA Sec
Sanders, Russell J. *Colors.* Tallahassee, FL: Harmony Ink, 2016. G HV Pro
Sands, Kate. *As Autumn Leaves.* Tallahassee, FL: Harmony Ink, 2016. L/Gay Spectrum GA Pro
Scott, Hayden. *Refraction.* Tallahassee, FL: Harmony Ink, 2016. G HV Pro
Self, Jeffery. *Drag Teen.* New York: PUSH/Scholastic, 2016. G GA Pro
Selzer, Adam. *Just Kill Me.* New York: Simon & Schuster, 2016. G/L/Bi-F GA Pro/Sec
Sherman, Giseal Tobien. *The Farmerettes.* Toronto: Second Story, 2016. L HV Sec
Siegert, Mia. *Jerkbait.* Provo, UT: Curious Fox, 2016. G HV Pro
Silvera, Adam. *History Is All You Left Me.* New York: Soho Teen, 2016. G GA Pro

Spangler, Brie. *Beast.* New York: Delacorte, 2016. MtF-Transgender GA Sec
Spaulding, Amy. *The New Guy (and Other Senior Year Distractions).* New York: Little, Brown, 2016. L GA Sec
St. Vel, Lola. *Girls Like Me.* Boston: HMH, 2016. G HV Sec
Starmer, Aaron. *Spontaneous.* New York: Dutton, 2016. G GA Sec
Stevenson, Robin. *Under Threat.* Victoria, BC: Orca, 2016. L GA Sec
Stiefvater, Maggie. *The Raven King.* New York: Scholastic, 2016. G GA Pro
Sussman, Elissa. *Burn.* New York: HarperCollins, 2016. G HV Sec
Talley, Robin. *As I Descended.* New York: Harper, 2016. L HV Pro
Tamaki, Mariko. *Saving Montgomery Sole.* New York: Roaring Brook, 2016. L/G GA Sec
Thomas, R. G. *The Midnight Gardener and the Well of Tears.* Tallahassee, FL: Harmony Ink, 2016. G HV Pro
Thorne, Jenn Marie. *The Inside of Out.* New York: Dial, 2016. L GA Pro
Topol, Carolyn LeVine. *Run for It All.* Tallahassee, FL: Harmony Ink, 2016. G GA Pro
Van, Andi *Magic Fell.* Tallahassee, FL: Harmony Ink, 2016. G GA Pro
Van Rooyen, Suzanne. *Obscura Burning.* Tallahassee, FL: Harmony Ink, 2016. G/Bi-M GA Pro
Wallace, Kali. *Shallow Graves.* New York: HarperCollins/Tegen, 2016. L/Bi-F HV Pro
Ward, Kaitlin. *Bleeding Earth.* Culver City, CA: Adaptive, 2016. L GA Pro
Watts, Julia, and Robin Lippincott. *Rufus + Syd.* Tallahassee, FL: Harmony Ink, 2016. G GA Pro
Whaley, John Corey. *Highly Illogical Behavior.* New York: Dial, 2016. G GA Pro
White, Kiersten. *And I Darken.* New York: Delacorte, 2016. G HV Sec
Williamson, Lisa. *The Art of Being Normal.* New York: Farrar, Straus & Giroux, 2016. FtM-Transgender/MtF-Transgender HV Pro
Wittlinger, Ellen. *Local Girl Swept Away.* Moorestown, NJ: Merit, 2016. G GA Sec
Young, Shaun, *Castor.* Tallahassee, FL: Harmony Ink, 2016. G GA Pro

YA SERIES BOOKS WITH LGBTQ+ CONTENT

Sweet Valley High (SVH)

Pascal, Francine. *Amy's True Love.* Sweet Valley High #75. New York: Scholastic, 1991. G HV Sec

Sweet Valley University (SVU)

Pascal, Francine. *No Rules.* SVU #48. New York: Random House, 1999. G HV Sec
———. *Stranded.* SVU #49. New York: Random House, 1999. G HV Sec.
———. *Summer of Love.* SVU #50. New York: Random House, 1999. G HV Sec
———. *Living Together.* SVU #51. New York: Random House, 1999. G GA Sec
———. *Fooling Around.* SVU #52. New York: Random House, 2000. G GA Sec
———. *Truth or Dare.* SVU #53. New York: Random House, 2000. G HV/GA Sec
———. *Rush Week.* SVU #54. New York: Random House, 2000. G GA Sec
———. *The First Time* SVU #55. New York: Random House, 2000. G GA Sec
———. *Dropping Out.* SVU #56. New York: Random House, 2000. G GA Sec
———. *Who Knew?* SVU #57. New York: Random House, 2000. G GA Sec
———. *The Dreaded Ex.* SVU #58. New York: Random House, 2000. G GA Sec
———. *Elizabeth in Love.* SVU #59. New York: Random House, 2000. G GA Sec

Sweet Valley Senior Year (SVSY)

Pascal, Francine. *Three Girls and the Guy.* SVSY #16. New York: Random House, 2000. G HV Sec
———. *Backstabber.* SVSY #17. New York: Random House, 2000. G HV/GA Sec
———. *As If I Care.* SVSY #18. New York: Random House, 2000. G HV/GA Sec
———. *It's My Life.* SVSY #19. New York: Random House, 2000. G HV/GA Sec
———. *Nothing Is Forever.* SVSY #20. New York: Random House, 2000. G HV/GA Sec
———. *The It Guy.* SVSY #21. New York: Random House, 2000. G HV/GA Sec
———. *So Not Me.* SVSY #22. New York: Random House, 2000. G HV/GA Sec
———. *Falling Apart.* SVSY #23. New York: Random House, 2000. G HV/GA Sec
———. *Never Let Go.* SVSY #24. New York: Random House, 2000. G HV/GA Sec
———. *Straight Up.* SVSY #25. New York: Random House, 2000. G HV/GA Sec
———. *Too Late.* SVSY #26. New York: Random House, 2001. G HV/GA Sec
———. *Playing Dirty.* SVSY #27. New York: Random House, 2001. G HV/GA Sec
———. *Meant to Be.* SVSY #28. New York: Random House, 2001. G HV/GA Sec
———. *Where We Belong.* SVSY #29. New York: Random House, 2001. G HV/GA Sec
———. *Close to You.* SVSY #30. New York: Random House, 2001. G HV/GA Sec
———. *Stay or Go.* SVSY #31. New York: Random House, 2001. G HV/GA Sec
———. *Road Trip.* SVSY #32. New York: Random House, 2001. G HV/GA Sec
———. *Me, Me, Me.* SVSY #33. New York: Random House, 2001. G HV/GA Sec
———. *Troublemaker.* SVSY #34. New York: Random House, 2001. G HV/GA Sec
———. *Control Freak.* SVSY #35. New York: Random House, 2001. G HV/GA Sec
———. *Tearing Me Apart.* SVSY #36. New York: Random House, 2001. G HV/GA Sec
———. *Be Mine.* SVSY #37. New York: Random House, 2002. G GA Sec
———. *Get a Clue.* SVSY #38. New York: Random House, 2002. G GA Sec
———. *Best of Enemies.* SVSY #39. New York: Random House, 2002. G GA Sec
———. *Never Give Up.* SVSY #40. New York: Random House, 2002. G GA Sec
———. *Best of Enemies.* SVSY #41. New York: Random House, 2002. G GA Sec
———. *Touch and Go.* SVSY #42. New York: Random House, 2002. G GA Sec
———. *It Takes Two.* SVSY #43. New York: Random House, 2002. G GA Sec
———. *Cruise Control.* SVSY #44. New York: Random House, 2002. G GA Sec
———. *Tia in the Middle.* SVSY #45. New York: Random House, 2002. G GA Sec
———. *Prom Night.* SVSY #46. New York: Random House, 2002. G GA Sec
———. *Senior Cut Day.* SVSY #47. New York: Random House, 2002. G GA Sec
———. *Sweet 18.* SVSY #48. New York: Random House, 2003. G GA Sec

Pretty Little Liars (PLL)

Shepard, Sara. *Pretty Little Liars.* PLL #1. New York: Harper Tempest, 2006. L HV/GA Pro
———. *Flawless.* PLL #2. New York: Harper Tempest, 2007. L HV/GA Pro
———. *Perfect.* PLL #3. New York: Harper Tempest, 2007. L HV/GA Pro
———. *Unbelievable.* PLL #4. New York: Harper Tempest, 2008. L HV/GA Pro
———. *Wicked.* PLL #5. New York: Harper Tempest, 2009. L HV/GA Pro
———. *Killer.* PLL #6. New York: Harper Tempest, 2009. L HV/GA Pro
———. *Heartless.* PLL #7. New York: Harper Tempest, 2010. L HV/GA Pro
———. *Wanted.* PLL #8. New York: Harper Tempest, 2010. L HV/GA Pro
———. *Twisted.* PLL #9. New York: Harper Tempest, 2011. L HV/GA Pro
———. *Ruthless.* PLL #10. New York: Harper Tempest, 2011. L HV/GA Pro
———. *Stunning.* PLL #11. New York: Harper Tempest, 2012. L HV/GA Pro
———. *Burning.* PLL #12. New York: Harper Tempest, 2012. L HV/GA Pro
———. *Crushed.* PLL #13. New York: Harper Tempest, 2013. L HV/GA Pro
———. *Deadly.* PLL #14. New York: Harper Tempest, 2013. L HV/GA Pro
———. *Toxic.* PLL #15. New York: Harper Tempest, 2014. L HV/GA Pro
———. *Vicious.* PLL #16. New York: Harper Tempest, 2014. L HV/GA Pro

YA BOOKS WITH BISEXUAL CHARACTERS (FULL CODING NOTED IN CHRONOLOGICAL BIBLIOGRAPHY ABOVE)

1997

Kerr, M. E. *"Hello," I Lied.* New York: Harper, 1997. Bi-M

2001

Ryan, Sara. *Empress of the World.* New York: Viking, 2001. Bi-F

2003

Freymann-Weyr, Garret. *My Heartbeat.* Boston: Houghton Mifflin, 2003. Bi-M
Hartinger, Brent. *The Geography Club.* New York: HarperCollins, 2003. Bi-F

2004

De Oliveira, Eddie. *Lucky.* New York: Scholastic PUSH, 2004. Bi-M
Johnson, Maureen. *The Bermudez Triangle.* [Retitled *On the Count of Three* in 2013.] New York: Razorbill, 2004. Bi-F

2010

Cohn, Rachel. *Very La Freak.* New York: Random, 2010. Bi-F

2011

Sanchez, Alex. *Boyfriends with Girlfriends.* New York: Simon & Schuster, 2011. Bi-M/Bi-F

2012

Peters, Julie Anne. *It's Our Prom, So Deal with It.* Boston: Little, Brown, 2012. Bi-M

2013

Lo, Malinda. *Inheritance.* Boston: Little, Brown, 2013. Bi-F

2014

Smith, Andrew. *Grasshopper Jungle.* New York: Dutton, 2014. Bi-M

2015

Davey, Douglas. *Switch.* Calgary, AB: Red Deer, 2015. Bi-M
Hall, Sandy. *Signs Point to Yes.* New York: Swoon, 2015. Bi-F
Mesrobian, Carrie. *Cut Both Ways.* New York: HarperCollins, 2015. Bi-M
Moskowitz, Hannah. *Not Otherwise Specified.* New York: Simon & Schuster Pulse, 2015. Bi-F
Summers, Elizabeth. *Trust Me. I'm Trouble.* New York: Delacorte, 2015. Bi-F

2016

Gold, Rachel. *My Year Zero.* Tallahassee, FL: Bella Books, 2016. Bi-F
Hall, Sandy. *Been Here All Along.* New York: Swoon, 2016. Bi-M
Keplinger, Kody. *Run.* New York: Scholastic, 2016. Bi-F
Lindstrom, Eric. *A Tragic Kind of Wonderful.* Boston: Little, Brown Poppy, 2016. Bi-F
Selzer, Adam. *Just Kill Me.* New York: Simon & Schuster, 2016. Bi-F/Bi-M
Wallace, Kali. *Shallow Graves.* New York: HarperCollins/Tegen, 2016. Bi-F

YA BOOKS WITH TRANSGENDER CONTENT (FULL CODING NOTED IN CHRONOLOGICAL BIBLIOGRAPHY ABOVE)

1996

Block, Francesca Lia. *Girl Goddess #9.* New York: HarperCollins/Joanna Cotler, 1996. [short stories] "Dragons in Manhattan." FtM-Transgender

2001

Cart, Michael, ed. *Love and Sex: Ten Stories of Truth.* New York: Simon & Schuster, 2001. [short stories] "The Welcome," by Emma Donoghue. MtF-Transgender

2004

Peters, Julie Anne. *Luna.* Boston: Little, Brown, 2004. MtF-Transgender

2007

Wittlinger, Ellen. *Parrotfish.* New York: Simon & Schuster, 2007. FtM-Transgender

2009

Cart, Michael, ed. *How Beautiful the Ordinary.* New York: HarperCollins 2009. "Trev," by Jacqueline Woodson. FtM-Transgender; "My Virtual World," by Francesca Lia Block. FtM-Transgender; "The Missing Person," by Jennifer Finney Boylan. MtF-Transgender
Katcher, Brian. *Almost Perfect.* New York: Delacorte, 2009. MtF-Transgender
Rapp, Adam. *Punkzilla.* Boston: Candlewick, 2009. FtM-Transgender

2010

Edwards, Hazel, and Ryan Kennedy. *F2M: The Boy Within.* Collingwood, Victoria, Australia: Ford Street, 2010. FtM-Transgender
Hyde, Catherine Ryan. *Jumpstart the World.* New York: Knopf, 2010. FtM-Transgender

2011

Beam, Cris. *I Am J.* Boston: Little, Brown, 2011. FtM-Transgender
Bray, Libba. *Beauty Queens.* New York: Scholastic, 2011. MtF-Transgender

2012

Cronn-Mills, Kirstin. *Beautiful Music for Ugly Children.* Woodbury, MN: Flux, 2012. FtM-Transgender
Davis, Tanita S. *Happy Families.* New York: Random, 2012. MtF-Transgender
Gold, Rachel. *Being Emily.* Tallahassee, FL: Bella Books, 2012. MtF-Transgender

2013

Clark, Kirsten Elizabeth. *FreakBOY.* New York: Farrar, Straus & Giroux, 2013. MtF-Transgender/Gender fluid
Levithan, David. *Two Boys Kissing.* New York: Knopf, 2013. FtM-Transgender

2014

Eliason, Rachel. *The Best Boy Ever Made.* N.p.: Create Space, 2014. FtM-Transgender
Fu, Kim. *Today I Am a Boy.* Boston: Houghton Mifflin Harcourt, 2014. MtF-Transgender
Gold, Rachel. *Just Girls.* Tallahassee, FL: Bella Books, 2014. MtF-Transgender
Polonsky, Ami. *Gracefully Grayson.* New York: Hyperion, 2014. MtF-Transgender
Wood, Jennie. *A Boy Like Me.* N.p.: 215 INK, 2014. FtM-Transgender

2015

Gino, Alex. *George.* New York: Scholastic, 2015. MtF-Transgender
Hopkins, Ellen. *Traffick.* New York: Simon & Schuster/McElderry, 2015. FtM-Transgender
Jacobs, Evan. *Father Son Father.* Costa Mesa, CA: Saddleback, 2015. MtF-Transgender
Talley, Robin. *What We Left Behind.* New York: Harlequin Teen, 2015. FtM-Transgender

2016

Atwood, Megan. *Raise the Stakes.* Minneapolis, MN: Darby Creek, 2016. FtM-Transgender
Clark, Kristen Elizabeth. *Jess, Chunk, and the Road Trip to Infinity.* New York: Farrar, Straus & Giroux, 2016. MtF-Transgender
Devine, Eric. *Look Past.* Philadelphia: Running, 2016. FtM-Transgender
Duyvis, Corinne. *On the Edge of Gone.* New York: Abrams/Amulet, 2016. MtF-Transgender
Gephart, Donna. *Lily & Dunkin.* New York: Delacorte, 2016. MtF-Transgender
Harvey, Sarah N. *Split Level.* Victoria, BC: Orca, 2016. FtM-Transgender
Hennessey, M. G. *The Other Boy.* New York: HarperCollins, 2016. FtM-Transgender
Lee, C. B. *Not Your Sidekick.* N.p.: Interlude, 2016. FtM-Transgender
McLemore, Ann-Marie. *When the Moon Was Ours.* New York: St. Martin's, 2016. FtM-Transgender
Russo, Meredith. *If I Was Your Girl.* New York: Flatiron, 2016. MtF-Transgender
Spangler, Brie. *Beast.* New York: Delacorte, 2016. MtF-Transgender
Williamson, Lisa. *The Art of Being Normal.* New York: Farrar, Straus & Giroux, 2016. MtF-Transgender/FtM-Transgender

YA BOOKS WITH INTERSEX CONTENT (FULL CODING NOTED IN CHRONOLOGICAL BIBLIOGRAPHY ABOVE)

2014

Birdsall, Bridget. *Double Exposure.* New York: Sky Pony, 2014.

2015

Brugman, Alyssa. *Alex as Well.* New York: Holt, 2015.
Gregorio, I. W. *None of the Above.* New York: HarperCollins/Balzer + Bray, 2015.

COMICS AND GRAPHIC NOVELS WITH LGBTQ CONTENT

Comics

As anyone who works with them knows, comics pose a bibliographic challenge, since some or most of the constituent information needed is fugitive, especially dates of publication. In providing this bibliography of titles referenced in the following text we have, therefore, often resorted to citing collections rather than individual titles. We have not included publications featuring characters we have mentioned only in passing.

Barela, Tim. *Leonard & Larry.* Minneapolis, MN: Palliard, 1983.
Bechdel, Alison. *The Essential Dykes to Watch Out For.* Boston: HMH, 2008.
Braddock, Paige. *Jane's World Collection Vol. 1.* Sebastopol, CA: Girl Twirl Comics, 2006.
Cruse, Howard. *The Complete Wendel.* New York: Universe, 2011.
The Essential Rawhide Kid Vol. 1. New York: Marvel, 2011.
Flutter: Hell Can Wait. Philadelphia: 215 Ink, 2013.
Gay Comix #1–14. Princeton, WI: Kitchen Sink Enterprises, 1980–91.
Midnighter and Apollo #1. New York: DC, 2016.
Northstar #1: Fast and Loose. New York: Marvel, 1994.
Parent, Dan. *Archie's Pal Kevin Keller.* New York: Archie Comic, 2012.
The Runaways. New York: Marvel, 2003.
Stevenson, Noelle, and Shannon Watters. *Lumberjanes. Vol 1.* Los Angeles: Boom! Box, 2015.
Teen Titans Vol. 1: A Kid's Game. New York: DC, 2004.
The Young Avengers. New York: Marvel, 2005.

Graphic Novels

Bechdel, Alison. *Fun Home. A Family Tragicomic.* Boston: Houghton Mifflin, 2006.
Cruse, Howard. *Stuck Rubber Baby.* New York: DC/Paradox, 1995.
Denson, Abby. *Tough Love: High School Confidential.* San Francisco: Manic D, 2006.
Hagio, Moto. *The Heart of Thomas.* Seattle, WA: Fantagraphics, 2012.
Hubert. *Adrian and the Tree of Secrets.* Vancouver, BC: Arsenal Pulp, 2014.
Merey, Ilike. *a + e 4EVER.* Maple Shade, NJ: Lethe, 2011.
Roads, Cristy C. *Spit and Passion.* New York: Feminist, 2012.
Rucka, Greg, and Michael Lark. *Half a Life.* New York: DC, 2003.
Schrag, Ariel. *Awkward, Definition, Potential,* and *Likewise.* New York: Simon & Schuster, 2008–2009.
Stevenson, Noelle. *Nimona.* New York: HarperTeen, 2015.
Takio, Shimura. *Wandering Son.* Seattle, WA: Fantagraphics, 2013.
Tamaki, Mariko, and Jillian Tamaki. *Skim.* Berkeley, CA: Groundwood Books. House of Anansi, 2008.
Telgemeier, Raina. *Drama.* New York: Scholastic, 2012.
Williams III, J. H., and W. Haden Blackman. *Batwoman Vol.1. Hydrology.* New York: DC, 2013.
Winick, Judd. *Pedro and Me: Friendship, Loss, and What I Learned.* New York: Holt, 2000.

YA NONFICTION WITH LGBTQ+ CONTENT

LGBTQ+ Information: Self-Help/Advice Books for Teens

Alyson, Sasha, ed. *Young, Gay, and Proud.* Boston: Alyson Books, 1980.

Bass, Ellen, and Kate Kaufman. *Free Your Mind: The Book for Gay, Lesbian, and Bisexual Youth—and Their Allies.* New York: HarperCollins, 1996.

Belge, Kathy, and Marke Bieschke. *Queer: The Ultimate LGBT Guide for Teens.* San Francisco: Zest Books, 2011.

Chandler, Kurt. *Passages of Pride: Lesbian and Gay Youth Come of Age.* New York: Times Books, 1995.

Dawson, Juno. *This Book Is Gay.* Naperville, IL: Sourcebooks, 2015.

Due, Linnea. *Joining the Tribe: Growing Up Gay and Lesbian in the '90s.* New York: Anchor, 1995.

Ford, Michael Thomas. *The World Out There: Becoming Part of the Lesbian and Gay Community.* New York: New Press, 1996.

Hanckel, Frances, and John Cunningham. *A Way of Love, a Way of Life: A Young Person's Guide to What It Means to be Gay.* New York: Lothrop, Lee & Shepard, 1979.

Huegel, Kelly. *GLBTQ: The Survival Guide for Gay, Lesbian, Bisexual, Transgender, and Questioning Teens.* Minneapolis, MN: Free Spirit, 2011.

————. *GLBTQ: The Survival Guide for Queer and Questioning Teens.* Minneapolis, MN: Free Spirit, 2003.

Nagle, Jean. *Are You LGBTQ? Got Issues?* series. New York: Enslow, 2016.

Pollack, Rachel, and Cheryl Schwartz. *The Journey Out: A Guide for and about Lesbian, Gay and Bisexual Teens.* New York: Viking, 1995.

Rich, Jason. *Growing Up Gay in America: Informative and Practical Advice for Teen Guys Questioning Their Sexuality and Growing Up Gay.* New York: Franklin Street Books, 2002.

LGBTQ+ Teen Lives: Full-Length Autobiographies

Andraka, Jack, with Matthew Lysiak. *Breakthrough: How One Teen Innovator Is Changing the World.* New York: HarperCollins, 2015.

Andrews, Arin. *Some Assembly Required: The Not-So-Secret Life of a Transgender Teen.* New York: Simon & Schuster, 2014.

Cooper, Alex, with Joanna Brooks. *Saving Alex: When I Was Fifteen I Told My Mormon Parents I Was Gay, and That's When My Nightmare Began.* New York: HarperOne, 2016.

Fricke, Aaron. *Reflections of a Rock Lobster: A Story about Growing Up Gay.* Boston: Alyson Books, 1981.

Hartzler, Aaron. *Rapture Practice: My One-Way Ticket to Salvation: A True Story.* Boston: Little, Brown, 2013.

Hernandez, Daniel, with Susan Goldman Rubin. *They Call Me a Hero: A Memoir of My Youth.* New York: Simon & Schuster, 2013.

Herthel, Jessica, and Jazz Jennings. *I Am Jazz.* Illustrated by Shelagh McNicholas. New York: Dial Books, 2014.

Hill, Katie Rain. *Rethinking Normal: A Memoir in Transition.* New York: Simon & Schuster, 2014.

Jennings, Jazz. *Being Jazz: My Life as a Transgender Teen.* New York: Crown Books, 2016.

Patterson, Romaine, with Patrick Hinds. *The Whole World Was Watching: Living in the Light of Matthew Shepard.* New York: Advocate Books, 2005.

Rubin, Laurie. *Do You Dream in Color? Insights from a Girl without Sight.* New York: Seven Stories, 2012.

Wahls, Zach, with Bruce Littlefield. *My Two Moms: Lessons of Love, Strength, and What Makes a Family.* New York: Gotham Books, 2012.

LGBTQ+ Lives: Memoir Collections

Adair, Nancy, and Casey Adair. *Word Is Out: Stories of Some of Our Lives.* Photo illus. New York: Delacorte/New Glide, 1978.

Bechdel, Alison. *Fun Home: A Family Tragicomedy.* Boston: Houghton Mifflin, 2006.

Boykin, Keith, ed. *For Colored Boys Who Have Considered Suicide When the Rainbow Is Still Not Enough: Coming of Age, Coming Out, and Coming Home.* New York: Magnus Books, 2012.

Brimner, Larry Dane. *Being Different: Lambda Youths Speak Out.* New York: Franklin Watts, 1995.

Chandler, Kurt. *Passages of Pride: True Stories of Lesbian and Gay Teenagers.* Los Angeles: Alyson/Times Books, 1995.

Ford, Michael Thomas. *Outspoken: Role Models from the Gay and Lesbian Community.* New York: BeechTree Books, 1998.

———. *The Voices of AIDS.* New York: HarperCollins, 1995.

Golio, Laurel, and Diana Scholl. *We Are the Youth.* Photo illus. New York: Space-Made, 2014.

Gray, Mary L. *In Your Face: Stories from the Lives of Queer Youth.* New York: Haworth, 1999.

Hear Me Out: True Stories of Teens Educating and Confronting Homophobia. A Project of Planned Parenthood of Toronto. Toronto: Second Story, 2004.

Heron, Ann. *One Teenager in Ten: Writings by Gay and Lesbian Youth.* Boston: Alyson, 1983.

———. *Two Teenagers in Twenty: Writings by Gay and Lesbian Youth.* Boston: Alyson, 1995.

Kaeser, Gigi, and Peggy Gillespie, eds. *Love Makes a Family: Portraits of Lesbian, Gay, Bisexual, and Transgender Parents and Their Families.* Photo illus. Amherst: University of Massachusetts Press, 1999.

Kuklin, Susan. *Beyond Magenta: Transgender Teens Speak Out.* Photo illus. Cambridge, MA: Candlewick, 2014.

Labonte, Richard, and Lawrence Schimel, eds. *First Person Queer: Who We Are (So Far).* Vancouver, BC: Arsenal Pulp, 2007.

Levithan, David, and Billy Merrell, eds. *The Full Spectrum: A New Generation of Writing about Gay, Lesbian, Bisexual, Transgender, Questioning, and Other Identities.* New York: Knopf, 2006. Expanded edition New York: Ember, 2016.

Lowrey, Sassafras. *Kicked Out.* Ypsilanti, MI: Homofactus, 2010.

Luczak, Raymond, ed. *QDA: A Queer Disability Anthology.* Minneapolis, MN: Squares & Rebels, 2015.

Mastoon, Adam. *The Shared Heart: Portraits and Stories Celebrating Lesbian, Gay and Bisexual Young People.* Photo illus. New York: Harper, 1997.

Moon, Sarah, and James Lecesne, eds. *The Letter Q: Queer Writers' Notes to Their Younger Selves.* New York: Arthur A. Levine, 2014.

Rowley, Sarah E., and Robyn Ochs, eds. *Getting Bi: Voices of Bisexuals around the World.* 2nd ed. Boston: Bisexual Resource Center, 2009.

Savage, Dan, and Terry Miller, eds. *It Gets Better: Coming Out, Overcoming Bullying, and Creating a Life Worth Living.* New York: Dutton, 2011.www.itgetsbetter.org.

Savin-Williams, Ritch C. *Becoming Who I Am: Young Men on Being Gay.* Cambridge, MA: Harvard University Press, 2016.

Schultz, Jackson Wright. *Trans/portraits: Voices from Transgender Communities.* Hanover, NH: Dartmouth College Press, 2015.

Smith, Rachelle Lee. *Speaking Out: Queer Youth in Focus.* Photo illus. Oakland, CA: PM Press, 2015.

Sonnie, Amy, ed. *Revolutionary Voices: A Multicultural Queer Youth Anthology.* Boston: Alyson Books, 2000.

Sutton, Roger. *Hearing Us Out: Voices from the Gay and Lesbian Community.* Photo illus. Boston: Little, Brown, 1994.

Vitagliano, Paul. *Born This Way: Real Stories of Growing Up Gay.* Photo illus. Philadelphia: Quirk Books, 2012.

LGBTQ+ People: Individual Biographies

Aretha, David. *No Compromise: The Story of Harvey Milk.* Civil Rights Leaders series. Greensboro, NC: Morgan Reynolds, 2009.

Delalande, Arnaud. *The Case of Alan Turing: The Extraordinary and Tragic Story of the Legendary Codebreaker.* Illus. by Eric Liberge. Vancouver, BC: Arsenal Pulp, 2016.

Escoffier, Jeffrey. *John Maynard Keynes.* Lives of Notable Gay Men and Lesbians. New York: Chelsea House, 1994.

Greenberg, Jan, and Sandra Jordan. *Andy Warhol: Prince of Pop.* New York: Delacorte, 2004.

Grinapol, Corinne. *Harvey Milk: Pioneering Gay Politician.* Remarkable LGBTQ Lives. New York: Rosen, 2015.

Houts, Amy. *Rachel Maddow: Primetime Political Commentator.* Remarkable LGBTQ Lives. New York: Rosen, 2015.

Kenan, Randall. *James Baldwin.* Lives of Notable Gay Men and Lesbians. New York: Chelsea House, 1994.

Martin, W. K. *Marlene Dietrich.* Lives of Notable Gay Men and Lesbians. New York: Chelsea House, 1995.

Martinac, Paula. *k. d. lang.* Lives of Notable Gay Men and Lesbians. New York: Chelsea House, 1997.

Miller, Calvin Craig. *No Easy Answers: Bayard Rustin and the Civil Rights Movement.* Civil Rights Leaders series. Greensboro, NC: Morgan Reynolds, 2005.

Mungo, Raymond. *Liberace.* Lives of Notable Gay Men and Lesbians. New York: Chelsea House, 1995.

Nunokawa, Jeff. *Oscar Wilde.* Lives of Notable Gay Men and Lesbians. New York: Chelsea House, 1994.

O'Brien, Sharon. *Willa Cather.* Lives of Notable Gay Men and Lesbians. New York: Chelsea House, 1994.

O'Shaughnessy, Tam E. *Sally Ride: A Photobiography of America's Pioneering Woman in Space.* New York: Roaring Brook/Macmillan, 2015.

Ottaviani, Jim. *The Imitation Game: Alan Turing Decoded.* Illus. by Leland Purvis. New York: Abrams, 2016.

Rosset, Lisa. *James Baldwin.* Black Americans of Achievement. New York: Chelsea House, 1989.

Snyder, Jane McIntosh. *Sappho.* Lives of Notable Gay Men and Lesbians. New York: Chelsea House, 1994.

Staley, Erin. *Laverne Cox.* Transgender Pioneers. New York: Rosen, 2016.

Wolfe, Daniel. *T. E. Lawrence.* Lives of Notable Gay Men and Lesbians. New York: Chelsea House, 1995.

Zwerman, Gilda. *Martina Navratilova.* Lives of Notable Gay Men and Lesbians. New York: Chelsea House, 1995.

LGBTQ+ People: Collective Biographies

Aldrich, Robert. *Gay Lives.* New York: Thames & Hudson, 2012.

Archambeau, Kathleen. *Pride & Joy: LGBTQ Artists, Icons and Everyday Heroes.* Coral Gables, FL: Mango, 2017.

McHugh, Erin. *The L Life: Extraordinary Lesbians Making a Difference.* New York: Abrams, 2011.

Penne, Barbra. *Transgender Role Models and Pioneers.* New York: Rosen, 2017.

Prager, Sarah. *Queer, There, and Everywhere: 23 People Who Changed the World.* New York: HarperCollins, 2017.

Russell, Paul Elliott. *The Gay 100: A Ranking of the Most Influential Gay Men and Lesbians, Past and Present.* New York: Carol, 1995.

Stern, Keith. *Queers in History: The Comprehensive Encyclopedia of Historical Gays, Lesbians, Bisexuals, and Transgenders.* Dallas, TX: BenBella, 2009.

Tyrkus, Michael J. *Gay and Lesbian Biography.* Detroit: St. James, 1997.

LGBTQ+ History: Stonewall

Bausum, Ann. *Stonewall: Breaking Out in the Fight for Gay Rights*. New York: Viking, 2015.
Carter, David. *Stonewall: The Riots That Sparked the Gay Revolution*. New York: St. Martin's, 2010.
Duberman, Martin. *Stonewall*. New York: Dutton, 1993.
Hillstrom, Laurie Collier. *The Stonewall Riots*. Defining Moments. Detroit: Omnigraphics, 2016.
Kuhn, Betsy. *The Stonewall Riots and the Gay Rights Movement, 1969*. Minneapolis, MN: Twenty-First Century Books, 2011.
Poehlmann, Tristan. *The Stonewall Riots: The Fight for LGBT Rights*. Minneapolis, MN: Abdo, 2016.
Stevenson, Robin. *Pride: Celebrating Diversity & Community*. Victoria, BC: Orca, 2016.
Wajdowicz, Jurek. *Pride & Joy: Taking the Streets of New York City*. New York: New Press, 2016.

LGBTQ+ History: Marriage Equality

Ball, Carlos A. *From the Closet to the Courtroom: Five LGBT Rights Lawsuits That Have Changed Our Nation*. Boston: Beacon, 2010.
Cathcart, Kevin, and Leslie J. Gabel-Brett. *Love Unites Us: Winning the Freedom to Marry in America*. New York: New Press, 2016.
Cenziper, Debbie, and Jim Obergefell. *Love Wins: The Lovers and Lawyers Who Fought the Landmark Case for Marriage Equality*. New York: William Morrow, 2016.
Frank, Nathaniel. *Awakening: How Gays and Lesbians Brought Marriage Equality to America*. Cambridge, MA: Belknap Press of Harvard University Press, 2017.
Kaplan, Roberta A. *Then Comes Marriage: United States v. Windsor and the Defeat of DOMA*. New York: Norton, 2015.
Solomon, Marc. *Winning Marriage: The Inside Story of How Same-Sex Couples Took On the Politicians and Pundits—and Won*. Lebanon, NY: ForeEdge, 2015.

LGBTQ+ History: The Big Picture

Alsenas, Linas. *Gay America: Struggle for Equality*. New York: Abrams, 2008.
Bronski, Michael. *Queer History of the United States*. Boston: Beacon, 2011.
Brooks, Adrian, ed. *The Right Side of History: 100 Years of Revolutionary LGBTQI Activism and Radical Agitation for Equal Rights*. New York: Cleis, 2015.
Bullough, Vern L. *Homosexuality: A History from Ancient Greece to Gay Liberation*. New York: New American Library, 1979.
Downs, Jim. *Stand by Me: The Forgotten History of Gay Liberation*. New York: Basic Books, 2016.
Eaklor, Vicki L. *Queer America: A People's GLBT History of the 20th Century*. New York: New Press, 2008.
McGarry, Molly. *Becoming Visible: An Illustrated History of Lesbian and Gay Life in Twentieth-Century America*. New York: Penguin Studio, 1998.
Miller, Neil. *Out of the Past: Gay and Lesbian History from 1869 to the Present*. New York: Vintage, 1995.
Parkinson, R. B. *A Little Gay History: Desire and Diversity across the World*. New York: Columbia University Press, 2013.
Pohlen, Jerome. *Gay and Lesbian History for Kids: The Century-Long Struggle for LGBT Rights; With 21 Activities*. Chicago: Chicago Review Press, 2016-.
Setterington, Ken. *Branded by the Pink Triangle*. Toronto: Second Story, 2013.
Stryker, Susan. *Transgender History*. Berkeley, CA: Seal, 2008.

LGBTQ+ Issues: Social, Political, Cultural, Mental/Physical Health, Other

Andryszewski, Tricia. *Same-Sex Marriage: Granting Equal Rights or Damaging the Status of Marriage?* Minneapolis, MN: Twenty-First Century Books, 2014.
Apelqvist, Eva. *LGBTQ Families: The Ultimate Teen Guide*. Lanham, MD: Scarecrow, 2013.
Barker, Meg-John, and Julia Scheele. *Queer: A Graphic History*. London: Icon/Publishers Group West, 2016.
Bartlett, John G., and Ann K. Finkbeiner. *The Guide to Living with HIV Infection*. 6th ed. Baltimore: Johns Hopkins Press, 2006.
Biegel, Stuart. *The Right to Be Out: Sexual Orientation and Gender Identity in America's Public Schools*. Minneapolis: University of Minnesota Press, 2010.
Bornstein, Kate. *My New Gender Workbook—A Step-by-Step Guide to Achieving World Peace through Gender Anarchy and Sex Positivity*. New York: Routledge, 2013.
Bronski, Michael, Ann Pellegrini, and Michael Amico. *"You Can Tell Just by Looking" and 20 Other Myths about LGBT Life and People*. Boston: Beacon, 2013.
Chilman-Blair, Kim, and John Taddeo. *Medikidz Explain HIV*. New York: Rosen, 2010.
Clausen, Jan. *Beyond Gay or Straight: Understanding Sexual Orientation*. Issues in Lesbian and Gay Life. New York: Chelsea House, 1997.
Cronn-Mills, Kristin.*LGBTQ+ Athletes Claim the Field: Striving for Equality*. Minneapolis, MN: Twenty-First Century Books, 2017.
Decker, Julie Sondra. *The Invisible Orientation: An Introduction to Asexuality*. New York: Carrel Books, 2014.
Eisner, Shiri. *Bi: Notes for a Bisexual Revolution*. Berkeley, CA: Seal, 2013.
Erickson-Schroth, Laura. *"You're in the Wrong Bathroom!" and 20 Other Myths and Misconceptions about Transgender and Gender Nonconforming People*. Boston: Beacon, 2017.
Friedman, Laura. *Gay Marriage: Opposing Viewpoints*. Detroit: Greenhaven, 2010.
Furgang, Kathy. *HIV/AIDS*. New York: Rosen, 2015.
Gay, Kathlyn. *Bigotry and Intolerance: The Ultimate Teen Guide*. Lanham, MD: Scarecrow, 2013.
Hyde, Sue. *Come Out and Win: Organizing Yourself, Your Community, and Your World*. Boston: Beacon, 2007.
Marcus, Eric. *What If? Questions about What It Means to Be Gay and Lesbian*. New York: Simon & Schuster, 2013.
Mardell, Ashley. *The ABC's of LGBT+* Coral Gables, FL: Mango Media, 2016.
Moon, Sarah. *The Letter Q: Queer Writers' Notes to Their Younger Selves*. New York: Scholastic, 2012.
Newton, David E. *LGBT Youth Issues Today: A Reference Handbook*. Santa Barbara, CA: ABC-CLIO, 2014.
Nourse, Alan E. *AIDS*. New York: Franklin Watts, 1986.
Savage, Dan, and Terry Miller. *It Gets Better*. New York: Plume, 2012.
Skelton, J. Wallace. *Transphobia: Deal with It and Be a Gender Transcender*. Toronto: Lorimer, 2016.
Solomon, Steven. *Homophobia: Deal with It and Turn Prejudice into Pride*. Toronto: Lorimer, 2013.
Sonenklar, Carol. *AIDS*. Toronto: Lorimer, 2011.
Testa, Rylan Jay, Deborah Coolhard, and Jayme Peta. *The Gender Quest Workbook: A Guide for Teens & Young Adults Exploring Gender Identity*. Oakland, CA: Instant Help/New Harbinger, 2015.

Appendix B

Bar Graphs Representing LGBTQ+ Portrayal, Narrative Role, and Growth in Young Adult Fiction

Appendix B

**YOUNG ADULT FICTION WITH LGBTQ+ CONTENT, 1969-1999:
PRIMARY / SECONDARY**

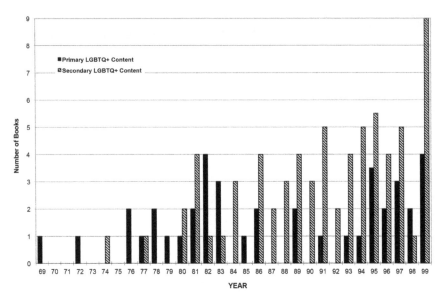

**YOUNG ADULT FICTION WITH LGBTQ+ CONTENT, 2000-2016:
PRIMARY / SECONDARY**

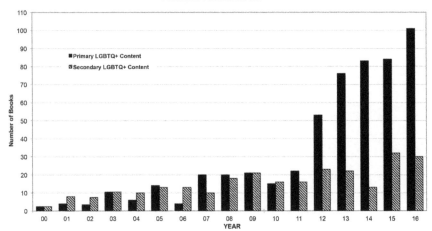

YOUNG ADULT FICTION WITH LGBTQ+ CONTENT, 1969-1999:
MALE / FEMALE

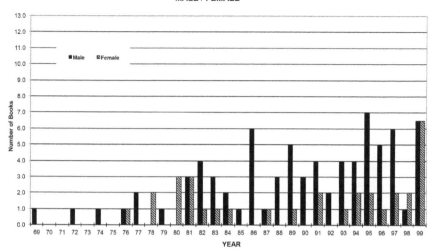

YOUNG ADULT FICTION WITH LGBTQ+ CONTENT, 2000-2016:
MALE / FEMALE

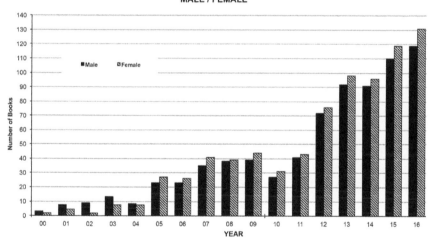

Appendix C

Book Awards for LGBTQ+ Young Adult Books

That the phrase "LGBTQ+ literature" is not an oxymoron is evidenced by two major awards that are annually presented for excellence in the field: the Stonewall Award and the Lambda Literary Award. The older of the two is the Stonewall Award, presented annually by the American Library Association's Gay, Lesbian, Bisexual, Transgender Round Table. Though presented since 1971, in 2010 a separate award was established for books for youth.

STONEWALL AWARD FOR CHILDREN'S AND YOUNG ADULT LITERATURE

2010 Award Winner

The Vast Fields of Ordinary, by Nick Burd. Penguin, 2009.

2010 Honor Books

Daddy, Papa, and Me, by Lesléa Newman. Tricycle Press, 2009.
Gay America: Struggle for Equality, by Linas Alsenas. Amulet/Abrams, 2008.
Mommy, Mama, and Me, by Lesléa Newman. Tricycle Press, 2009.
Sprout, by Dale Peck. Bloomsbury, 2009.
10,000 Dresses, by Marcus Ewert. Seven Stories, 2008.

2011 Award Winner

Almost Perfect, by Brian Katcher. Delacorte, 2010.

2011 Honor Books

The Boy in the Dress, by David Walliams, illus. by Quentin Blake. Razorbill/Penguin, 2008.
Freaks and Revelations, by Davida Wills Hurwin. Little, Brown, 2009.
Love Drugged, by James Klise. Flux, 2010.
Will Grayson, Will Grayson, by John Green and David Levithan. Dutton/Penguin, 2010.

MIKE MORGAN AND LARRY ROMANS CHILDREN'S AND YOUNG ADULT LITERATURE AWARD (SAME AWARD, NEW SPONSOR)

2012 Award Winner

Putting Makeup on the Fat Boy, by Bil Wright. Simon & Schuster, 2011.

2012 Honor Books

a + e 4ever, drawn and written by Ilike Merey. Lethe, 2011.
Money Boy, by Paul Yee. Groundwood Books, 2011.
Pink, by Lili Wilkinson. HarperTeen, 2011.
With or Without You, by Brian Farrey. Simon Pulse, 2011.

2013 Award Winner

Aristotle and Dante Discover the Secrets of the Universe, by Benjamin Alire Saenz. Simon & Schuster, 2012.

2013 Honor Books

Drama, written and illus. by Raina Telgemeier. Graphix, 2012.
Gone, Gone, Gone, by Hannah Moskowitz. Simon Pulse, 2012.
October Mourning: A Song for Matthew Shepard, by Leslea Newman. Candlewick, 2012.
Sparks: The Epic, Completely True Blue, (Almost) Holy Quest of Debbie, by S. J. Adams. Flux, 2011.

2014 Award Winner

Beautiful Music for Ugly Children, by Kirstin Cronn-Mills. Flux, 2012.

2014 Honor Books

Better Nate Than Ever, by Tim Federle. Simon & Schuster Books for Young Readers, 2013.
Branded by the Pink Triangle, by Ken Setterington. Second Story, 2013.
Two Boys Kissing, by David Levithan. Knopf, 2013.

2015 Award Winner

This Day in June, by Gayle E. Pitman. Magination, 2014.

2015 Honor Books

Beyond Magenta: Transgender Teens Speak Out, by Susan Kuklin. Candlewick, 2014.
I'll Give You the Sun, by Jandy Nelson. Dial Books, 2014.
Morris Micklewhite and the Tangerine Dress, by Christine Baldacchio, illus. by Isabelle Ma-
lenfant. Groundwood, 2014.

A separate award in each category was introduced in 2016.

2016 Award Winner—Young Adult

The Porcupine of Truth, by Bill Konigsberg. Scholastic/Levine, 2015.

2016 Award Winner—Children

George, by Alex Gino. Scholastic, 2015.

2016 Honor Books—Children and Young Adult

Sex Is a Funny Word: A Book about Bodies, Feelings, and YOU, by Cory Silverberg and Fiona
Smyth. Triangle Square Books for Young Readers, 2015.
Wonders of the Invisible World, by Christopher Barzak. Knopf, 2015.

2017 Award Winner—Young Adult

If I Was Your Girl, by Meredith Russo. Flatiron Books, 2016.

2017 Award Winner—Children

Magnus Chase and the Gods of Asgard: The Hammer of Thor, by Rick Riordan. Disney-
Hyperion, 2016.

2017 Honor Books—Children and Young Adult

Pride: Celebrating Diversity & Community, by Robin Stevenson. Orca Books, 2016.
Unbecoming, by Jenny Downham. David Fickling Books/Scholastic, 2016.
When the Moon Was Ours, by Anna-Marie McLemore. Thomas Dunne Books, St. Martin's
Griffin, 2016.

LAMBDA LITERARY AWARD FOR CHILDREN'S AND YOUNG ADULT LITERATURE

This award is presented annually by Lambda Literary to identify and cele-
brate the best lesbian, gay, bisexual, and transgender books of the year and to
affirm that LGBTQ+ stories are part of the literature of the world. The first
awards were presented in 1989 for books published in 1988. The 2nd Lambda Literary Award roster included an award for children's and young adult
literature, which was presented to *Losing Uncle Tim* by Mary Kate Jordan

(Whitman, 1989). The 3rd (1991) Lambda Awards did not include an award for children's and young adult literature, but the category was restored for the 4th (1992) Lambda Awards, and it has been presented annually every year from that day to this. The winners are:

1990 (2nd Annual) Award: *Losing Uncle Tim*, by Mary Kate Jordan. Whitman, 1989.

1991: No award category for children and young adult books

1992 (4th Annual) Award: *The Duke Who Outlawed Jelly Beans*, by Johnny Valentine. Alyson Wonderland, 1991.

1993 (5th): *When Heroes Die*, by Penny Raife Durant. Atheneum, 1992.

1994 (6th): *The Cat Came Back*, by Hilary Mullins. Naiad, 1993.

1995 (7th): *Am I Blue?*, ed. Marion Dane Bauer. Harper, 1994.

1996 (8th): *From the Notebooks of Melanin Sun*, by Jacqueline Woodson. Scholastic, 1995.

1997 (9th): *Good Moon Rising*, by Nancy Garden. Farrar, Straus & Giroux, 1996.

1998 (10th): *The House You Pass on the Way*, by Jacqueline Woodson. Scholastic, 1997.

1999 (11th): *Telling Tales out of School*, by Kevin Jennings (an adult book). Alyson, 1998.

2000 (12th): *Hard Love*, by Ellen Wittlinger. Simon & Schuster, 1999.

2001 (13th): *Out of the Ordinary*, ed. Noelle Howey and Ellen Samuels. St. Martin's, 2000.

2002 (14th): *Finding H.F.*, by Julia Watts. Alyson, 2001.

2003 (15th): *Letters in the Attic*, by Bonnie Shimko. Academy Chicago Press, 2002.

2004 (16th): *Boy Meets Boy*, by David Levithan. Knopf, 2003.

2005 (17th): *So Hard to Say*, by Alex Sanchez. Simon & Schuster, 2004.

2006 (18th): *Swimming in the Monsoon Sea*, by Shyam Salvadurai. Tundra, 2005.

2007 (19th): *The Full Spectrum*, ed. David Levithan and Billy Merrell. Random House, 2006.

2008 (20th): *Hero*, by Robin Perry. Hyperion, 2007.

2009 (21st): *Out of the Pocket*, by Bill Konigsberg. Scholastic/Levine, 2008.

2010 (22nd): *Sprout*, by Dale Peck. Bloomsbury, 2009.

2011 (23rd): *Wildthorn*, by Jane Eaglund. Houghton Mifflin, 2010.

2012 (24th): *Putting Makeup on the Fat Boy*, by Bil Wright. Simon & Schuster, 2011.

2013 (25th): *Aristotle and Dante Discover the Secrets of the Universe*, by Benjamin Alire Saenz. Simon & Schuster, 2012.

2014 (26th): *If You Could Be Mine*, by Sara Farizan. Algonquin, 2013.

2015 (27th): *Five, Six, Seven, Nate!* by Tim Federle. Simon & Schuster, 2014.

2016 (28th): *George*, by Alex Gino. Scholastic, 2015.

2017 (29th): *Girl Mans Up*, by M-E Girard. Harper Teen, 2016.

OTHER AWARDS

It is a measure of how far LGBTQ+ books have come from being simple problem novels to gratifyingly complex words of literature that they have received recognition from the Young Adult Library Services Association (YALSA).

Michael L. Printz Award

The Michael L. Printz Award, first awarded in 2000, is presented annually to the best young adult book of the year; several books with LGBTQ+ content have been named Printz Award winners or Printz honor books:

2000 honor book: *Hard Love*, by Ellen Wittlinger. Simon & Schuster, 1999.

2002 honor book: *True Believer*, by Virginia Euwer Wolff. Atheneum, 2001.

2003 award winner: *Postcards from No Man's Land*, by Aidan Chambers. Dutton, 2002.

2003 honor book: *My Heartbeat*, by Garret Freymann-Weyr. Houghton Mifflin, 2002.

2010 award winner: *Going Bovine*, by Libba Bray. Delacorte, 2009.

2013 award winner: *I'll Give You the Sun*, by Jandy Nelson. Dial, 2014.

2013 honor book: *Aristotle and Dante Discover the Secrets of the Universe*, by Benjamin Alire Saenz. Simon & Schuster, 2012.

William C. Morris Award for Excellence in First Fiction

YALSA's William C. Morris Award for Excellence in First Fiction was established in 2009 to honor a book written for young adults by a first-time, previously unpublished author. Several LGBTQ+ books have been included among the winners.

2009 honor book: *Absolute Brightness*, by James Lecesne. HarperCollins, 2008.

2010 honor book: *Ash*, by Malinda Lo. Little, Brown, 2009.

2013 honor book: *The Miseducation of Cameron Post*, by emily m. danforth. HarperCollins, 2012.

2015 award winner: *Simon vs. the Homo Sapiens Agenda*, by Becky Albertalli. HarperCollins/Balzer + Bray, 2014.

2017 honor book: *Girl Mans Up*, by M-E Girard. HarperTeen, 2016.

Margaret Alexander Edwards Award

YALSA's Margaret Alexander Edwards Award, established in 1988, honors an author, as well as a specific body of his or her work, "for significant and lasting contribution to young adult literature." Authors cited for books with LGBTQ+ content:

2003 Award

Nancy Garden, for *Annie on My Mind* (1982).

2006 Award

Francesca Lia Block, for her Dangerous Angels series: *Weetzie Bat* (1989), *Witch Baby* (1991), *Cherokee Bat and the Goat Guys* (1992), *Missing Angel Juan* (1993), and *Baby Bebop* (1996).

2016 Award

David Levithan, for *Boy Meets Boy* (2003), *The Realm of Possibility* (2004), *Nick and Norah's Infinite Playlist*, written with Rachel Cohn (2006), *Wide Awake* (2006), *How They Met, and Other Stories* (2008), and *Love Is the Higher Law* (2009).

Rainbow Book List

The Rainbow Book List is created annually by members of the Gay, Lesbian, Bisexual and Transgender round Table (GLBTRT) of the American Library Association. Each year's committee selects books published during the previous year that best reflect LGBTQ+ experiences and lives for young people (birth to age 18). The list of 30–60 titles includes picture books, middle-grade and young adult fiction and nonfiction, and graphic novels. Ten titles are starred as books of "exceptional queer representation and literary merit." Lists can be found at http://glbtrt.ala.org/rainbowbooks/.

* * *

Young adult books with LGBTQ+ content will doubtless receive future awards as the literature continues to mature.

Appendix D

Model for LGBTQ+ Portrayals/Inclusion in
Young Adult Fiction

When we first attempted a longitudinal analysis of young adult novels with LGBTQ+ content as a body of literature, we were hampered by their relatively small numbers and recent vintage. Fortunately, a much longer tradition of publication and analysis was available in the study of children's books that include other minority-status characters, most notably African American characters. Thus, in seeking models that can be used to analyze LGBTQ+ content in young adult novels, one logical place to turn is to the critical literature focused on African American content in texts for young readers.

African American characters have appeared in children's books for well over a century, but most of the early (pre–civil rights movement) portrayals were stock characters: the superhumanly strong laborer, the broadly smiling entertainer, the long-suffering but faithful servant/slave, the stern but nurturing mammy, and other predictable figures. These stereotypical—and invariably secondary—characters appeared most frequently in mass-market series books and were seen solely in relation to the central white characters. Black characters might be instrumental to the plot development, but the stories were not *their* stories. There were, however, a small number of books of children's literature—often by African American authors—that featured nonstereotypical African American characters. Beginning in the late 1960s with the blossoming of the civil rights movement and the increase of federal aid to education (including funding for school library books), the number of books with African American characters (both as protagonists and as secondary characters) gradually began to grow. The much-noted "all-white world of children's literature" was slowly (*very* slowly) becoming integrated in the decades that followed.[1]

Rudine Sims [Bishop]'s *Shadow & Substance: Afro-American Experience in Contemporary Children's Fiction* (NCTE, 1982) is one of the foundational studies of children's and young adult literature with African American characters.[2] In this study of books with African American characters published from 1965 to 1979, Sims Bishop proposed a three-part chronological model to describe fictional portrayals of African American characters. The first and earliest category, "social conscience" books, presented race as the problem and desegregation as the solution. The second category, "melting pot" books, depicted racial diversity as present but generally unacknowledged and integration a given. The third type of books were "culturally conscious" books in which African Americans are portrayed in a culturally authentic manner. This deceptively simple three-part model has proved surprisingly durable over time, and its analysis of patterns of minority group inclusion in children's literature stands up as a relevant framework for analyses of other groups' patterns of inclusion.

The plots of "social conscience" books with African American characters focused on relationships between blacks and whites (17–32). Often they involved struggles around the integration of schools or neighborhoods. There was usually an initial discomfort between strangers that was exacerbated by racial stereotypes and prejudice and remedied by education and "getting to know you" efforts. Once the mutual reeducation occurred, racial prejudice could be—and was—overcome and mutual trust established, and multicultural friendship could flourish to the mutual benefit of all groups. The "social conscience" approach in YA literature with LGBTQ+ content is most evident in "coming-out" stories, in which a character who has been assumed to be heterosexual "comes out" as gay/lesbian. The initial responses to this news are often uncomfortable, rejecting, or even overtly hostile, but by the end of most of these stories, the characters have adjusted, however uneasily, to this new information and the relationship is resumed in what we have called books of "homosexual visibility."

"Melting pot" books, Sims Bishop's second category, recognize the universality of the human experience to such an extent that they "ignore all differences *except* physical ones: skin color and other racially related physical features" (33). In "melting pot" fiction, differences may be noted in passing, but are then ignored as the characters assume a homogeneity that is seen as the key to cooperation, which means that gay/lesbian characters must appear to be no different from the heterosexual norm *except* for the fact of their sexual orientation. As Erick, the narrator of *Night Kites*, glibly responds when his older brother Pete comes out to him, "It's just another way of being" (91). A "melting pot" story with LGBTQ+ characters would be one in which a character's same-sex orientation is simply a given. As in portraying an African American character as someone who "just happens" to be dark-skinned or have other characteristically black physical features, an LGBTQ+ character in such a "melting pot" story would be portrayed as someone who "just happens to be gay," a category we call "gay assimilation."

However, given that any noticeable indication of gay/lesbian identity may be viewed as "flaunting it," the closet appears to be mandatory for peaceful coexistence. Indeed, in the early years of this literature it was hard to imagine a young adult novel labeled "contemporary realism" in which sexual orientation *could* realistically go unnoticed in the face of adolescents' hyperawareness of sexuality of all stripes and persuasions. The revelation of a character's LGBTQ+ identity was almost inevitably a notable event in the story, however matter-of-factly or neutrally this fact was presented.

In truth, the only milieu in which a character's LGBTQ+ identity could be noted in passing would probably be the LGBTQ+ community itself. Which brings us to "culturally conscious" stories, Sims Bishop's third and final category for fiction with African American characters. Sims Bishop describes "culturally conscious" books as those that

> seek to reflect, with varying degrees of success, the social and cultural traditions associated with growing up Black in the United States. In contrast to the social conscience books, they are not primarily addressed to non-Blacks, nor are they focused on desegregating neighborhoods or schools. They differ from the melting pot books in that they recognize, sometimes even celebrate, the distinctiveness of the experience of growing up simultaneously Black and American. Their primary intent is to speak to Afro-American children about themselves and their lives, though as has been pointed out, they are by no means closed to other children. (103)

Sims Bishop called for "culturally conscious" fiction representing the lives and experiences of African Americans as told from within that community. Culturally conscious fiction assumes that this culture and these people may very well be different from the mainstream culture and from people who live within the norm of white America. Until relatively recently, the overwhelming tendency in young adult literature with LGBTQ+ content has been for writers to tell the story from a mainstream heterosexual perspective. The novels told readers how LGBTQ+ people were viewed by others, but did not tell readers how LGBTQ+ people viewed themselves. Judging from recent titles, these "queer consciousness/community" stories have finally begun to be written.

NOTES

1. Nancy Larrick, "The All-White World of Children's Literature," *Saturday Review*, September 11, 1965, 63–65, 84–85.

2. Rudine Sims [Bishop], *Shadow & Substance: Afro-American Experience in Contemporary Children's Fiction* (Urbana, IL: NCTE, 1982).

Index

Harris, Michael, 144
Hartinger, Brent, 119–120, 158
Hartnett, P-P, 97
Hartzler, Aaron, 199
Harvey, Sarah N., 170, 173
Harvey Milk: Pioneering Gay Politician (Grinapol), 206
Hautzig, Deborah, 29
Head, Ann, 8
Hearing Us Out: Voices from the Gay and Lesbian Community (Sutton), 80, 202
The Heart of Thomas (Hagio), 184
Heart on My Sleeve (Wittlinger), 96, 106
Hellman, Lillian, 84
Hello, Cruel World: 101 Alternatives to Suicide for Teens (Bornstein), 179
"Hello," I Lied (Kerr), 48, 149, 158
Hennessey, M. G., 170–171, 173
hermaphrodite, 178
Hernandez, Daniel, 199
Heron, Ann, 202
heterosexual character, 70
heterosexual rape, 68
Hey, Dollface (Hautzig), 29
Hidden Voices: The Orphan Musicians of Venice (Collins), 99
Hill, Katie Rain, 200
Hillstrom, Laurie Collier, 209
Hinton, S. E., 3, 8, 74
historical fiction, 99
historical nonfiction. *See* history
history, LGBTQ+, 209–216; Big Picture in, 211–213; marriage equality in, 210–211; Stonewall in, 209–210; transgender in, 213
History Is All You Left Me (Silvera), 141–142
HIV/AIDS: LGBTQ+ fiction and appearance of, 38–40; negative side of sexuality in, 67–68; nonfiction, 216
HIV/AIDS Information for Children: A Guide to Issues and Resources (Walter and Gross), 40
Holden Caulfield, 7, 42
Hold Me Closer (Konigsberg), 140
Holland, Isabelle, 17, 18, 19–22, 31
Holly's Secret (Garden), 101
Homes, A. M., 35, 41–43
Homo (Harris), 144

homophobia, nonfiction on teens confronting, 215–216
Homophobia: Deal with It and Turn Prejudice into Pride (Solomon), 215
homosexuality: APA classification as mental illness, 24; Douglas on, 4; early adult fiction with, 5–6; first stirrings in YA literature of, 6–8; first young adult novel to deal with, 8
Homosexuality: A History (Bullough), 212
homosexual visibility, xiv; LGBTQ+ books since 2010 with, 130–138; 1970s YA novel with, 19–29; 1980s LGBTQ+ books with, 49–58; 1990s LGBTQ+ books with, 70–84; in protagonists: dealing with difficulties, 103–105; in secondary characters, 105–106; sexual abuse and, 102–103; twenty-first century LGBTQ+ books with, 99–106; in young(er) protagonists, 100–102
Hopeless Savages, 189
Hopkins, Ellen, 97, 169, 170
hormone, 165, 168, 172, 173, 175, 176
Horner, Emily, 143, 145
Hothead Paisan, 189
Houghton Mifflin Graphia (YA imprint), 93
A House Like a Lotus (L'Engle), 46–48, 60
How Beautiful the Ordinary: Twelve Stories of Identity (Cart), 97, 164–165
Howe, James, 115
Howrey, Meg, 126
How They Met, and Other Stories (Levithan), 97
Huegel, Kelly, 197
Hulse, Larry, 46
Hunter, Joyce, xiii
Huser, Glen, 100
Hyde, Catherine Ryan, 165, 166
Hyde, Sue, 215

I Am J (Beam), 165–166
If It Doesn't Kill You (Bechard), 75
If I Was Your Girl (Russo), 171, 174
I'll Get There. It Better Be Worth the Trip (Donovan), xi, 8–15, 149
I'll Give You the Sun (Nelson), 127
I'll Love You When You're More Like Me (Kerr), 39

nonfiction, 213, 216–217; male to female, 162, 174, 184, 200; progress in YA literature with growing visibility of, 146; YA literature with, 161–179

Transgender History (Stryker), 213

Transgender Role Models and Pioneers (Penne), 208

transition, 127, 161, 163, 165, 166, 167, 168, 171, 172, 173, 175, 200, 222

transman. *See* female to male transgender

Transphobia: Deal with It and Be a Gender Transcender (Skelton), 215

Trans/portraits: Voices from Transgender Communities (Schultz), 202

transsexual, xi, 162, 174

transwoman. *See* male to female transgender

Tregay, Sarah, 143

Tricks (Hopkins), 97

Trudeau, Garry, 182

True Believer (Wolff), 97, 106

Trujillo, Carla, 96

Trust Me. I'm Trouble (Summers), 159

The Truth about Alex (Snyder and Pelletier), 54

Trying Hard to Hear You (Scoppettone), 22–24, 31

Twelve Long Months (Malloy), 94

Two and the Town (Felsen), 8

Two Boys Kissing (Levithan), 144, 167, 168

Two Moms: Lessons of Love, Strength, and What Makes a Family (Wahls), 200

Two Teenagers in Twenty (Heron), 202

Two Weeks with the Queen (Gleitzman), 84, 101

Tyrkus, Michael J., 208

Unbecoming (Downham), 126, 136–138

Understanding Comics (McCloud), 96

Unlived Affections (Shannon), 41

Ure, Jean, 38, 58–59

Urrea, Luis Alberto, 96

U.S. Armed Forces, gay men in, 4

Van Buren, Abigail, 194, 218n9

Van Dijk, Lutz, 98

Velasquez, Gloria, 128

Very La Freak (Cohn), 158

Vidal, Gore, 5, 8

Vitagliano, Paul, 202

Wahls, Zach, 200

Waiting to Land: A (Mostly) Political Memoir, 1985–2008 (Duberman), 204

Wajdowicz, Jurik, 210

Walker, Kate, 75, 98

Walker, Paul Robert, 66–67, 71, 86

Wallace, Kali, 159

Wallace, Kim, 121–122

Wallace, Rich, 97

Walter, Virginia A., 40

Walton, Will, 127

Wandering Son (Takako), 184–185

Watts, Julia, 94, 122–124

A Way of Love, a Way of Life: A Young Person's Guide to What It Means to Be Gay (Hanckel and Cunningham), 33, 195–196, 198

We Are the Youth (Golio and Scholl), 179, 202

Weeping Willow (White), 68

Weetzie Bat (Block), 35, 38, 39–40, 42, 52–53, 63, 71, 74, 94, 95

The Well of Loneliness (Hall), 5

Wendel (Cruse), 182

#WeNeedDiverseBooks campaigns, 4

Wersba, Barbara, 105; *Crazy Vanilla*, 57–58, 61; *Just Be Gorgeous*, 57, 58, 61–62; *Whistle Me Home*, 57, 58, 71, 72–73

Wertham, Fredric, 182

Weston, John, 13

"What Do Young Adult Novels Say about HIV/AIDS?" (Gross), 40

Whatever (Goslee), 132–134

What Happened to Mr. Forster? (Barger), 44–45

What If? Questions about What It Means to Be Gay and Lesbian (Marcus), 215

What I Know Now (Larson), 87

What Night Brings (Trujillo), 96

What's in a Name? (Wittlinger), 97, 106

What's This about Pete? (Sullivan), 24–25, 100

What They Always Tell Us (Wilson), 94

What to Do until Utopia Arrives (ALA Gay Task Force), 14

About the Authors

Christine A. Jenkins is associate professor emerita in the School of Information Sciences at the University of Illinois at Urbana-Champaign, where she taught courses in young adult literature and resources, the history of children's literature, youth services librarianship, and literacy, reading, and readers. Her professional activities within the American Library Association have included serving on the Caldecott, Newbery, Sibert, and Margaret A. Edwards Award Committees, and chairing the Intellectual Freedom Round Table and the Library History Round Table. Jenkins coedited *Handbook of Research on Children's and Young Adult Literature* (2011), and coauthored (with Michael Cart) *The Heart Has Its Reasons: Young Adult Literature with Gay/Lesbian/Queer Content, 1969–2004* (2006) and *Top 250 LGBTQ Books for Teens* (2015). She lives in Minneapolis, Minnesota.

Michael Cart is a leading expert in the field of young adult literature, a subject he has taught at UCLA. A former president of both the Young Adult Library Services Association (YALSA) and NCTE's Assembly on Literature for Adolescents (ALAN), he is the author or editor of twenty-three books, including the gay coming-of-age novel *My Father's Scar* (1996) and his history of young adult literature *From Romance to Realism* (3rd ed., 2016). With Christine A. Jenkins, he is coauthor of *The Heart Has Its Reasons: Young Adult Literature with Gay/Lesbian/Queer Content, 1969–2004* (2006) and *Top 250 LGBTQ Books for Teens* (2015). Currently a columnist and reviewer for *Booklist* magazine, he is the recipient of the 2000 Grolier Foundation Award and the first recipient of the YALSA/Greenwood Press Distinguished Service Award. He lives in Columbus, Indiana.

Lightning Source UK Ltd.
Milton Keynes UK
UKHW010243150919

349775UK00011B/45/P